Hotel Renovation

Planning & Design

Hotel Renovation
Planning & Design

Frederic Knapp

McGRAW-HILL, INC.
New York   San Francisco   Washington, D.C.   Auckland   Bogotá
Caracas   Lisbon   London   Madrid   Mexico City   Milan
Montreal   New Delhi   San Juan   Singapore
Sydney   Tokyo   Toronto

Retail Reporting Corporation
302 Fifth Avenue
New York, NY 10001

Distributors to the trade in the United States and Canada
McGraw-Hill, Inc
1221 Avenue of the Americas
New York, NY 10020

Distributors outside the United States and Canada
Hearst Books International
1350 Avenue of the Americas
New York, NY 10019

Library of Congress Cataloging in Publication Data:
Hotel Renovation Planning & Design

Printed in Hong Kong
ISBN 0-07-035149-X

Designed: Mira Zivkovich, Inc.

C o n t e n t s

Introduction

Depending on how closely you look, hospitality renovation projects may all look the same -or so different there's no resemblance among them. Leaf through the "before" photos showing the results of previous renovations of the hotels in this book, and you'll find you can date them with ease. Current projects seem to cover the entire spectrum of style, but it's safe to say that in twenty years, they'll start to look a lot more similar to one another. So maybe all renovations in a given period are really the same. On the other hand, read the details behind the projects, and it may seem that each renovation team had to reinvent the wheel. The budget project scope, the micro-market conditions are as divergent from case to case as the existing buildings themselves. Maybe there's no common thread beyond the given of hotel and renovation.

Despite the apparently limitless variables, some important constant emerge when renovation is viewed from a greater distance. every owner or operator has to answer the same questions in renovating a property. first, how much can be spent, and when will the design and construction be performed? Will the work be done in phases, and will operations continue during construction? What choices does the market offer - and what changes does it demand? What regulatory and building code requirements apply? What will be the make-up of the renovation team, and who will really lead it? And finally, what should guests notice most once the project is complete?

Renovation projects can be divided into some broad categories, based on the answer to these questions and characteristics of the properties themselves. A hotel like the Hyatt Regency New Orleans that is doing well in a stable market does not need to be reinvented, and its renovation will be accordingly long on furniture, finishes and equipment and short on gutting of partitions. It isn't critical that such a maker-over break new ground; it just has to keep the property fresh and avoid throwing anything off balance. At the other end of the spectrum, the new owner of a previously unsuccessful property like the Houstonian or the Equinox is bound to make a bold change. Where the failed operation lacked focus, the challenge is to pinpoint a market strategy and reshape the physical plant to do it. Ideally, a major renovation will guarantee the owner a market reposition, but there is a difference between enhancing rates after an ambitious renovation and getting an entirely different clientele, as the owner of the Washington, D.C. Courtyard by Marriott did. Every renovation makes property improvements, but a reposition must radically improve design and materials while changing the basic product itself. Resurrections of long-closed hotels like the Omni-Severin, the Hotel Macdonald, and the Governor and conversions like the Broadway American and the Vintage Plaza impose no burden on the renovation team of coordinating construction with current operations, but they do impose the constriction of working with an existing building - without the benefit of an established clientele already loyal to the property. Last but not least among the types of renovations are projects which refine and evolve an ongoing operation, changing it noticeably but not radically. At the Arizona Biltmore, renovating meant carefully adjusting minor details in public spaces, adding new facilities and augmenting specific services significantly, but only fine-tuning the overall character of the property. Hilton Hawaiian Village with 2,500 rooms, from high-rise towers and a score of smaller buildings, is too huge to be transformed; a phased master plan reshaped key aspects of the property, adjusting its direction the way a helmsman steers an ocean liner.

One type of hotel worth mentioning in particular - not necessarily a classification of renovation - is the historic property. Customer loyalty, marketing cachet, local permit approvals and federal tax credits strongly influence the renovation team to retain and restore important features which make a building historic. While restoring nearly every space to its original condition is practical for a small property like the Bancroft Hotel, larger ones have to strike a compromise between restoration and renovation. Seen purely from the balance sheet, adding a tower with hundreds of new guest rooms would have been the crowning glory of the renovation of San Francisco's Sheraton Palace; in the historical perspective returning the building exactly to what it was in 1909 would have been the ultimate feat. Neither approach ultimately carried the day, but elements of each have made the renovation successful, both on the balance sheets and in the public eye.

Important commonalities exist in the renovation process, even where the properties and the projects are quite different. The owner and operator must decide a clear goal for the renovation, using their knowledge of the property and market conditions. In choosing architects, interior designers, contractors, construction managers and renovation advisers, owners and operators almost invariably opt for individuals and firms with similar experiences - and preferably personal experience. The outside members of the team must find working methods that are comfortable for the owner and operator, and the owner and operator have to give a vote of confidence to the rest of the team. With such a solid foundation, the project can get off to a good start at the beginning of the design phase; all parties should be ready to make major decisions as soon as they are needed - and be flexible in changing them whenever conditions warrant. While compatibility and cooperation are essential, leadership is also indispensable. Successful renovations come from owners and operators with a strong sense of where the property should head, architects and interior designers with a clear vision of the finished project and a construction team that knows just how to build it.

All this adds up to a successful project, but what makes a project worth looking at in a book? A daring or unusual design approach - if it's successful - can't fail to elicit interest. Ironically a design that sums up what is going on everywhere is also noteworthy, simply for being an archetype of its age. Unusual properties, distinctive buildings and out-of-the-ordinary renovation goals and noteworthy project delivery methods also make interesting studies.

Frederic Knapp

Hotel
Renovation
Planning & Design

Hotel Inter-Continental
Chicago, Illinois

Chicago boomed in the 1920s, even some of the proudest Midwesterners couldn't help envying the mystery and intrigue of the Old World, so they created buildings like the Shriners' Medinah Athletic Club. If they had seen it at the time, Evelyn Waugh or H. L. Mencken might have made light of the squeaky-clean Shriners' mystical clubhouse on Michigan Avenue. But 60 years later, irony was on the Shriners' side: a fanciful historical conceit when it was constructed, the building had become a genuine historical treasure. Long since vacated by its builders, the charmed and cursed structure caught the attention of elite European hoteliers looking for an appropriate venue in Chicago. Inter-Continental Hotels teamed up with a local developer to make the former Shriners' club into a landmark hotel.

Name	*Hotel Inter-Continental Chicago*
Location	*Chicago, Illinois*
Owner	*Inter-Continental Hotels*
Operator	*Inter-Continental Hotels*
Type of Hotel	*Luxury*
Date of Original Construction	*1929*
Number of Rooms	*887*
Bars & Restaurants	*2 restaurants / 1 bar*
Meeting Rooms (Number & Size)	*32 / 44,142 square feet*
Recreation Facilities	*Indoor pool, sauna, aerobics room, exsercise machines, massage area*
Type of Renovation	*First phase: closure for rehabilitation of public spaces, gut of guest room floors Second phase: hotel operating during renovations*
Cost	*$140 Million*
Date	*First phase: 1988 -1990 Second phase: 1993-1994*
Developer (first phase)	*M.A.T. Associates. Chicago*
Architect	*First phase: Harry Weese & Associates, Chicago Second phase: W. Steven Gross, AIA, Chicago*
Interior Designer	*Design Continuum, Atlanta, Georgia*
Consultants	*Structural Engineer: Cohen-Barreto-Marchertas*
Contractor	*First phase: Mellon-Stuart Co., Chicago Second phase: Walbridge-Aldinger*

EXOTIC WELCOME
The main lobby of the historic Medinah Athletic Club greets guests with its original Arabic "As Selamu Aleikum" portal inscription. Before the restoration, the polychromed ceiling was almost black — and the stone walls had been painted white. The walls were stripped, the ceiling restored and a custom carpet milled to match the original one.
Photograph by John Miller © Hedrich Blessing

MIGHTY PRESENCE
Although the colors and materials are.more restrained on the exterior than on the interior, the building does betray its eclectic nature to passersby, with balconies, loggias. and Assyrian-inspired projecting windows. The dome at the top of the building was regilded and the flagpole was added as part of the renovation. The smaller tower added in the 1960s is to the left, behind the historic tower. Not the only historic building left in a modern city, the hotel is listed on the National Register of Historic Places and is part of the Michigan-Wacker Historic District, noted for its concentration of early-20th-century skyscrapers which make the building look very much at home (above).
Photographs by Hedrich Blessing

ELEVATING WALLS TO A NEW HEIGHT
The Italian Renaissance design in the elevator lobby does not stop at plaster moldings — the entire wall and ceiling surface is polychromed, and frescoes fill the arches over the elevator doors. These surfaces were intact before the renovation and were cleaned and preserved (top). A historic view (below) shows the room, seen from the adjoining Court which was lit dramatically to accent its full intrigue.
Color photograph by Ira Montgomery.

COLOR REGAINED
The columns and capitals in the Court, a circulation and pre-function space on the fourth floor, had been painted white before the renovation. The paint was stripped and the capitals were regilded. The carpet was custom-milled on a floral design inspired by the original Spanish tile wainscot on the wall in the background. The wall covering in the room seen in the background (right) through the Gothic arch was custom-designed, based on historic photographs (left) of the space.
Photograph by John Miller ©
Hedrich Blessing

pressive start, history
edinah Athletic Club
vent out of business in 1934
ression, ending up as a hotel
vent through stints as a
d a Radisson, and a second
tower, 26 stories high with 500 rooms,
was added in 1961. In 1986, the property
closed, and in 1988 the restoration began.
Inter-Continental Hotels purchased the
property outright in 1989. The first
renovation project was completed in 1990,
and a second phase of work was carried
out from 1993 to 1994 without closing
the hotel.

The renovation required making order out
of a patchwork of eras and uses, while
showcasing the grandiose aspects of the
original building. The renovation team
decided to rehabilitate the public spaces
on the first eight floors of the building,
which included almost all the remaining
impressive social rooms from the
Medinah Athletic Club. Many of the
original interior finishes, hidden as
securely as Shriners' club secrets by
decades of paint, carpeting and other
alterations, were exposed and restored.
Most spaces were faithfully returned to
their original details and colors with help

from a Shriner who learned about the
project and brought in a commemorative
book printed at the opening of the club,
complete with good photographs of the
interior.

The renovation team made intentional
changes in a few rooms, such as the entry,
which had been a very masculine space
with a Celtic theme. It was opened up and
brightened considerably to welcome the
public. Except for the indoor swimming
pool on the fourteenth floor. the building
was gutted above the eighth floor to
accommodate a rational layout of new

guest rooms and systems meeting current standards. Back-of-the-house areas on the first eight floors were also gutted.

The Indiana limestone exterior of the building was cleaned and the dome, which crowns it, was gilded and fitted out with an American flag. Long-term overhauls and deferred maintenance of exterior elements proceeded through both phases of the renovation. The first round of the renovation created two hotels, the Inter-Continental in the original Medinah building and the Forum in the newer tower addition. The Forum Hotel opened in September 1989 and the Inter-Continental opened in March, 1990. Forum is a business hotel chain owned by Inter-Continental; the Chicago Forum was the firm's only location in the United States when it opened. Although operated as two

hotels, the Forum and the Inter-Continental shared management, staff, back-of-the-house areas — and clientele, as time went by. Food and beverage outlets and meeting rooms lured guests both ways between the two hotels, prompting management to fold the Forum into the Inter-Continental in November, 1993.

To consolidate the two, a new main entry lobby and registration lobby were built in

the newer (Forum) tower, the banquet rooms and guest rooms in the newer tower were renovated and a new exterior canopy was constructed at the new main entrance. The elevator cabs, public toilet rooms and back-of-the-house areas in the newer tower were also redone, and a new gift shop was constructed, allowing the existing gift shop in the historic part of the hotel to be converted into a business services center.

AERIE DINING
The Boulevard Restaurant, which overlooks the entry lobby of the historic building, gives diners not only a vantage point over comings and goings below but a close look at the historic polychromed ceiling of the lobby. Because the ceiling and column capitals are so intricate, the furniture was kept simple to keep the setting from becoming overpowering. A special dining area over the exterior entry to the lobby has a central view and a special table of inlaid wood (above).
Photographs by
Ira Montgomery.

RESTORATION DINING

The Renaissance Room was paneled in Carpathian burled elm, and lit by
Baccarat chandeliers. The paneling was thoroughly cleaned and missing
pieces restored to the chandeliers. The stack chairs are inspired by the
musical images carved in the stone posts which terminate the iron railing
along the raised seating area on the perimeter of the room (right). The
brass-finished chairs, custom-designed for the renovation, were later added
to the furniture manufacturer's standard line.

Photograph by Ira Montgomery

COME AROUND FULL CIRCLE
Document research and site investigations guided the renovation team to the original design of the ballroom. The carpet was custom designed from photographs of the original, the column capitals and ceiling were regilded after the white paint which had been applied in an earlier remodeling was removed, and the ceiling frescoes which ring the room between the columns were restored by the conservator.
Photographs by Hedrich Blessing

THE RAIN IN SPAIN
Doesn't land in the 25 meter pool built by the Shriners, but one might think it did. The Spanish-Colonial fountain, majolica tile and coffered ceiling help create the atmosphere of a hacienda — 14 floors above Michigan Avenue.
Photograph by
Ira Montgomery

MYSTERY AND MAJESTY
The Salon, a lobby lounge adjacent to the entry lobby of the historic building, echoes the eastern intrigue of the historic interiors with its Empire chairs with griffin's wing arms and loosely Persian-inspired drapes in reds and teals with gold lining.
Photograph by
Ira Montgomery

The renovation process was as complicated as the history of the building. To
minimize front-end costs and streamline
design and construction, the developer,
M.A.T. Associates, made the project fast-
track design-build. That provided a
guaranteed maximum construction cost
and a single point of responsibility for
design and construction. Design proceeded without investigations and
drawings of concealed existing elements,
and began with just schematic architectural and mechanical drawings. Then
the fun began. The original building's
structural system was significantly
different than designers had supposed.
"There were lateral (framing) elements
all over the place" requiring the designers, contractor, developer and hotel
operators to change the design every step
of the way, said architect Steve Gross,
who worked on both phases of the
renovation. "You can just imagine the
wars that arose."

The project team rolled with the
punches, even changing floor layouts to
cope with surprises when walls and
ceilings were opened, meeting constantly
on site and preparing sketches almost
daily — frequently resulting in change
orders. Even without surprises or
changes, the building would have been
complicated. Because of exterior wall
setbacks on the upper floors, there are
more than 20 different floor plans for
the guest room levels of the building.
"It's not a cookie cutter set of accommodations in any way," said Stan Allan,
chairman of Harry Weese Associates.
"The man who installed in the carpeting
wished it were".

WORSHIPFUL MASTERS, SATRAPS AND PANJANDRUMS
Suites in the renovated hotel are fit for today's rich and famous as well as the mythical royalty who inspired the public spaces in the building. Each suite has its own design and color scheme. The one at the top of the building has a two story living room, dining area, master bedroom, guest bedroom, and two bathrooms.
Photographs by Ira Montgomery.

Guest rooms feature built-in mini bar; clock radio, voice mail; telephone and hair dryer in the bathroom; and remote color television which can display messages and the guest's bill, and call the bell captain. Furniture is Empire, chosen for the guest rooms and many of the public spaces because it repeats some of the visual themes found in the eclectic period references of the historic public spaces. Rooms in the historic part of the building were small before the renovation, but the gutting of guest room floors meant that room sizes could be increased and the room count lowered.

The renovation updated the health facilities from the mystical-men's club image of the 1920s to the fitness-on-the-go and relaxation requirements of 1990s hotel guests. Facilities, originally spread over many stories, were consolidated on three levels around the original swimming pool on the fourteenth floor. The pool was restored to its 1920s exotic splendor, while the adjoining new facilities on the twelfth and thirteenth floors include a weight room with Paramount exercise equipment and free weights, an aerobics room with a suspended flooring system, and a cardiovascular room with four Lifecycles, two treadmills, and two Lifestep machines. Each changing room has a sauna and there is a massage area.

THEN AND NOW
A historic view of the ballroom (right) and a view taken after renovation (above) show the original wall covering and the one designed for the restoration from the photograph of the original. The stairway to the upper level gallery in the color photograph is new.
Color photograph by
Ira Montgomery.

NO HOTEL GENERIC
Guest room floors, completely gutted in the renovation, do not have the full eccentric eclecticism of the public spaces, but they were designed to complement the original building. Furniture in the guest rooms continues the Empire theme of public spaces, but in a looser interpretation. Carpet is an Axminster custom design. Drapes are a French toile with dark green dust ruffles and border. The furniture is a mix of woods and finishes. There are two color schemes: red and forest green.
Photograph by Ira Montgomery

Omni Severin Hotel
Indianapolis, Indiana

When Mansur Development Corporation bought the Atkinson Hotel in 1988, it had all the ingredients for a historic hotel rebirth in a city center bouncing back from urban decline - and also a lot of the hallmarks of a failed property destined for a date with a wrecking crew. Located across the street from a new "festival marketplace," one block from the Indiana Convention Center and Hoosier Dome complex, it was a venerable pre-World War II grande dame. But it had been closed by its previous owner, leaving years of deferred maintenance on top of a mish-mash of renovations which made it outmoded, not timeless.

ORIGINAL ELEGANCE
The historic hotel lobby no longer functions as the main entrance or registration area, but its restoration offers guests a space with historic prestige. Some features of the original lobby, such as the blue ceiling, red and blue upholstery and furniture style, were repeated in the new lobby.

Name	**Omni Severin Hotel**
Location	**Indianapolis, Indiana**
Owner	**Mansur Development Corp.**
Operator	**Omni Hotels, Hampton, N.H.**
Type of Hotel	**Luxury**
Date of Original Construction	**1913**
Number of Rooms	**423**
Meeting Rooms (Number & Size)	**17 / 16,000 Square feet**
Bars & Restaurants	**Severin Bar & Grill, Caffeet**
Recreation Facilities	**Health club with indoor pool and exercise facilities**
Type of Renovation	**Renovation and addition; hotel shut down during construction**
Cost	**$40 Million**
Date	**Completed January 1990**
Architect	**Ratio Architects, Inc., Indianapolis**
Interior Designer	**J.P. Courteaud, New York, N.Y.**
Consultants	**Structural engineer, addition: Gunnin Campbell, Dallas, TX Structural engineer, existing building: MTA, Indianapolis**
Contractor	**F. A. Wilhemn Construction Co., Inc.**

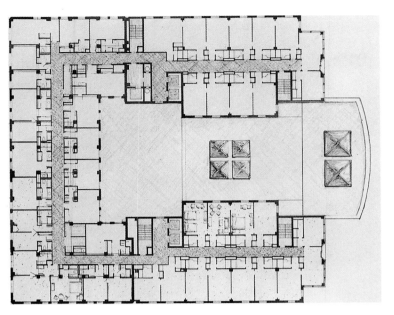

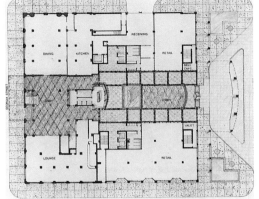

NATURAL GROWTH

On the ground floor, the lobby of the addition (plan above: green area at right with burgundy zone inside it) terminates in the new registration desk, which abuts the lobby of the original building (burgundy area at left). The motor entrance of the new lobby (far right) faces the city's rehabilitated train station. Upper floor corridors in the original hotel (C-shaped portion of building in plan at left) flow naturally into the corridors of the two wings of the addition (horizontal extensions to the right on top and bottom of drawing). Elevators and stairs are all located in new portion of the building.

NEW INTRODUCTION

The new hotel lobby, located at the center of the addition, is two stories high and has a large skylight to increase the sense of openness offered by the glass wall facing the Indianapolis Union Station festival marketplace across the street. Glass railings and the sleek fountain help reinforce the contemporary character which strongly distinguishes the addition from the historic hotel, but traditional furniture and marble which matches that in the original building serve to tie the two parts of the renovated hotel together.

Confronted by so many opportunities and problems, Mansur decided to tackle them all at once. It doubled the size of the building with an addition offering new facilities and a new look, and renovated the old part of the building to capitalize on its history. To make the most of the recently rehabilitated Union Station festival marketplace across the street from the expansion site adjacent to the original hotel, Mansur and the designer, Ratio Architects placed the main entrance and lobby of the renovated property in the addition. The addition, although carefully tailored to complement the massing, layout, design and materials of the original building, is decidedly modern, announcing strongly that the hotel is not what it used to be. Along with the new lobby, the addition contains a health club and swimming pool, retail and meeting spaces, new guest rooms, and two-level suites on its top floor.

In plan, the addition transforms the nearly rectangular original hotel into a U-shaped layout. On upper floors, the center of the U is an open courtyard, while on the ground floor it is occupied by the new lobby. Floor levels in the addition match those in the existing building, and corridors on upper floors of the addition connect to those of the original building. There were seven different guest room sizes before the renovation, with most of them small, according to Mansur President Cornelius M. Alig. The smallest rooms were combined, and rooms in the addition were sized generously, with special suite-sized rooms on the end of each wing, boasting floor-to-ceiling windows on three sides and balconies overlooking Union Station across the street. The two-story suites which top off the addition have proven popular as hospitality suites and for executive and luxury travel.

EARLY DAYS
Postcards from the 1920s show the historic Hotel Severin in its young glory.
Lobby is at lower right; photos on left and at upper right show the Old
Colony Club, an original lounge on the mezzanine overlooking the lobby

NEW EXPOSURE
The inner courtyard and south end of the addition (foreground) are clad in concrete and glass to strengthen the building's contemporary identity, while the sides of the addition (left side) are mostly brick, which blends with the old part of the building (at rear on left side). Paired window openings on the sides of the addition mimic the design of the historic building. The architects designed the concrete-framed balconies of the two-story suites at the top of the addition to avoid a visual conflict with the elaborate cornice of the original building, and chose green-tinted glass to mirror the color of patina of exposed copper elements on the old building.

COMPLEMENTARY DESIGN
The addition (at rear) takes its cues from the historic hotel (in front of drawing right) in order to blend in with it instead of overwhelming it. Floor levels are the same, roof lines match, and the brick and concrete of the addition are the counterparts of the brick and limestone of the historic hotel. The arched windows on the ground floor of the historic building had been closed for years before the renovation and were brought back to recreate the exterior. The entrance marquise was retained, but cars and taxies no longer line up as they did 50 years ago (left), because the main entrance to the hotel is now in the addition, on the opposite side of the building.

BLEND OF TASTES
The restaurant of the renovated hotel is located in the new section of the building, and while it has a contemporary tone, features such as furniture and lighting suggest the style of the original part of the property.

BRINGING BACK OLD MEMORIES
Although the Severin Ballroom in the historic part of the hotel had never been eliminated, its windows had been filled with concrete masonry. This was removed during the renovation so the windows could be restored. The original walnut and mahogany paneling had been covered with paint decades ago which could not be removed because of cost and logistical problems, but the vaulted plaster ceilings and egg-and-dart molding were restored during the renovation.

On the interior, as on the exterior, the addition was intended to look boldly new, not like an clone of the historic hotel. Although some of the furniture is traditional, much is sharply modern. Indiana-based Kimball International designed and supplied new furniture intended to complement the antiques the hotel had acquired during an earlier renovation in the 1960s. In the original hotel, important spaces such as the lobby were brought back to their historic condition. Its molded plaster detailing and monumental marble staircase were restored, and the cast iron railing of the lobby mezzanine, removed years earlier when the mezzanine was covered over, was restored and reinstalled.

The renovation included all-new mechanical, electrical, plumbing and life safety systems for the existing building. The main kitchen was remodeled, hotel offices were moved to space in the basement formerly occupied by the coffee shop, and the elevators and one stairway were removed to make room for a service area and additional guest room on each floor. Stairs and elevators serving the whole building are located in the addition.

BIGGER AND BRIGHTER
On the ends of the two guest room wings which make up the upper floors of the addition are extra-large rooms with a sitting area and a bed area. These rooms have balconies and floor-to-ceiling glass on three sides. The color schemes for guest rooms are based on rich burgundies, teals and browns.

SIXTIES LOOK
A remodel of the original hotel in the 1960s gave the building a "contemporary" look of that time, with suspended metal-grid ceilings, flush doors and wall paneling with minimal trim and moldings.

The Pfister Hotel
Milwaukee, Wisconsin

When the Pfister Hotel in Milwaukee went bankrupt and was in danger of demolition thirty years ago, local businessman Ben Marcus led a group of investors who rescued it by adding a tower with parking garage, meeting facilities and a swimming pool completed in 1966.

The 23-story tower also renovated for the first time as part of the project, still provides half the convention floor, a parking garage, recreation facilities, and a rooftop nightclub and other amenities, often missing in 19th-century hotels, but the older part of the building assures the property its image as the authentic venue for Milwaukee's establishment. Architectural features which were covered for decades have been exposed, original materials renewed and historic spaces reconstituted.

Name	**The Pfister Hotel**
Location	**Milwaukee, Wisconsin**
Owner	**The Marcus Corporation**
Operator	**Marcus Hotels and Resorts**
Type of Hotel	**Luxury**
Date of Original Construction	**1893**
Number of Rooms	**307**
Bars & Restaurants	**The English Room**
	Lobby Lounge
	Cafe at the Pfister
	Cafe Rouge
	La Playa Lounge
Meeting Rooms (Number & Size)	**8 / 24,000 square feet**
Recreation Facilities	**Swimming pool, exercise machines**
Type of Renovation	**Phased, hotel open throughout**
Cost	**Not disclosed officially**
Date	**1988 - 1993**
Architect	**Schroeder and Holt Architects, Inc., Waukesha, Wisconsin**
Interior Designer	**First phase: O'Hara & Associates, Oak Brook, Illinois**
	Second phase: Hirsch/Bedner Associates, Los Angeles, California
Consultants	**Structural Engineer: Strass-Maguire & Associates, Milwaukee, Wisconsin**
Contractor	**Tri-North Builders, Madison, Wisconsin**
	Thomas & Egenhoefer, Inc., Menomonee Falls, Wisconsin
	Hunzinger Construction Co., Brookfield, Wisconsin

ODD COUPLE

When the original hotel went bankrupt and was in danger of demolition thirty years ago, a modern addition and tower gave it the atmosphere and amenities it needed to survive in the market. Current photographs (below) literally turn the relationship around 180 degrees, showcasing the original building which has not changed much since it was new.

Photographs courtesy of The Pfister Hotel.

Guido Pfister, a German immigrant who made a fortune in the tannery in Milwaukee, envisioned the hotel and bought the land where it stands, but died before its construction. His son, Charles, and daughter, Louise, took over the project and supervised the opening in 1893. Milwaukee was a leading U.S. industrial center at the time, and the $1.5 million hotel aimed to surpass the luxury lodgings any city could offer. Outside, a monumental Romanesque Revival stone structure emphasized solidity and tradition, while inside, there was a pharmacy, separate billiards rooms and lounges for men and women, a ladies' music room, and a Turkish bath.

The hotel featured a two-story lobby with a barrel-vaulted skylighted glass ceiling, bordered by a grand open iron staircase. The ornate detailing of the capitals on the marble columns, the nearly continuous wall moldings, the upper floor railings and balustrades, and the light fixtures were typical of late-19th-century architecture, as was the industrial appearance of the glazed ceiling, creating an overall impression of a grandiose reflection of the past, made possible by an industrial boom. The skylighted glass ceiling was removed in 1926, when the hotel underwent its first renovation. Over the years, other changes occurred, obscuring original features and cutting up important spaces, such as the lobby. When Marcus rescued the bankrupt hotel, the emphasis was on competing with newer hotels by adding required facilities in the tower.

CENTENNIAL SPACE

The lobby of the original Pfister Hotel building at the turn of the century impressed Milwaukee with its opulence (facing page), and after a complete refurbishment and restoration of some of its long-concealed historic features, it helped keep the property in the limelight in 1993 (main view below, after renovation). The glass ceiling in the original lobby had been removed decades ago; instead of reconstructing it, designers added a painted sky in the vault, complete with renaissance cherubs.

Photographs courtesy of The Pfister Hotel.

When the centenary of the hotel approached, Marcus and his son Stephen, chief executive of the family hotel operation, vowed to restore the original building for the occasion. The centerpiece of the project became reclamation and refurbishment of the lobby and original features, rounded out by overhauls of restaurants. The room count was reduced from 333 to 307, and all-new systems were installed in the original building. Phased construction allowed the hotel to remain in operation during the renovation. The first phase covered guest rooms in the original building, and the second phase refurbished the remainder of the original hotel and most of the 1960s addition.

The hotel's historic lobby did not regain its skylighted glass ceiling, but a painted sky mural in the same barrel vault shape was introduced in its place. Unsympathetic changes in finishes made over the years, such as a contrasting dark and light paint scheme on molding panels and velour wallpaper applied over scagliola columns, were removed and the original materials restored. To restore the original scale of the lobby, a café-lounge which had been inserted by partitioning off one side of the space was removed, and the outside entry vestibule, not original to the building, was halved in depth.

The removal of a light-fare restaurant which had been within the historic lobby revealed a historic fireplace, mantel and ornamental chimney hood which had been shrouded by Spanish-themed paneling. When the lobby was restored to its original size, the original fireplace and surround and the imported marble flooring around the fireplace were exposed and restored. The restored space has been renamed the Lobby Lounge, and offers drinks and light meals throughout the day.

The other restaurants and bars in the hotel were not reconfigured, although all but one were updated. The English Room, the hotel's fine dining restaurant, had been altered over the decades, with the addition of discordant touches such as a bright blue acoustic tile ceiling. A major overhaul restored its original image with stained wood paneling, upholstered wall covering and a coffered ceiling with custom chandeliers. The bar, once a completely separate space, was united visually with the dining area.

HISTORIC DISCOVERY
The removal of a light-fare restaurant which had been partitioned out of space in the historic lobby revealed a historic fireplace, mantel, and ornamental chimney hood which had been shrouded by Spanish-themed paneling. The fireplace was the centerpiece of the seating area of the lobby decades ago (above) and has regained that role, with comfortable couches and back tables and lamps (bottom).
Photographs courtesy of
The Pfister Hotel.

DIRECTOR'S SUITE
*Renovated meeting rooms
include an executive
conference room which
sets a dignified, estab-
lished theme with its
traditional wallpaper and
upholstered armchairs.*
Photographs courtesy of
The Pfister Hotel.

The former Greenery coffee shop, with white booths, green and white wall covering and mirrored columns, was recast as the Café at the Pfister, with more of a bistro flavor. Natural wood gives it a warmer and richer feeling, and an archway was added to articulate better the transition between the two dining areas. The Cafe Rouge, the main restaurant in the original part of the hotel, was renovated along with the guest rooms in that building. Having suffered few changes over the years, its design stayed relatively stable during the restoration, with new finishes that elaborated the original theme. La Playa Lounge, a nightclub atop the tower which overlooks the Milwaukee skyline and Lake Michigan, had been renovated in the early 1980s; management delayed further renovation until after the main project was complete.

The renovation updated the meeting rooms, although it did not include major changes in layout. In the main space in the original building, the Imperial Ballroom the historic coffered ceiling was repainted and accented with hand-applied gold leaf and faux marble. New recessed downlights help the historic chandeliers meet contemporary lighting requirements. A new conference room was added on the second floor, and combined with an adjacent guest bedroom, it can also serve as a suite.

In the original building, guest room floor corridors and exterior walls did not change, but everything between them was gutted. Because the distance between the corridors and the exterior walls varies in different parts of each floor, the new guest rooms were laid out in three sizes: single, mini-suite (bedroom with a parlor area) and full suite (bedroom and separate parlor). The bathrooms, which had raised floors before the renovation because of constraints in installing plumbing in the 1893 construction, were rebuilt at the same floor level as the bedrooms. Although the layout of guest room floors in the tower did not change, the look was altered radically. The typical 1960s contemporary tone of the rooms and the cool gray color schemes contrasted too much with the original building. The renovation used transitional furniture including Chinese Chippendale, and Renaissance Revival, 1930s club chairs and Empire mirrors. and soft gold wall coverings to warm the rooms and relate them to the rest of the hotel. Draperies with valences and side panels and case pieces with exotic veneers help soften the rooms. The round footprint of the tower creates novel geometries in guest rooms and public spaces; floral carpeting in hallways deemphasizes the curved walls.

OLD FAVORITE
The existing red and white color scheme of the Café Rouge, which serves brunch and a luncheon buffet, was elaborated with application of contrasting colors to ceiling moldings and faux-marble paint to the columns.
Photographs courtesy of The Pfister Hotel.

HISTORY RENEWED
The Imperial Ballroom boasted a historic interior which was well preserved and did not call out for a drastic makeover. The designers made subtle moves, such as adding new drapery rich in swags, jabots, tassels and trim and restoring the ceiling.
Photographs courtesy of The Pfister Hotel.

STAYING WITH TRADITION

Guest rooms in the original part of the building (right) let the property's venerable history shine through, even though everything in them is new. Deluxe rooms feature four-poster beds, while others have pediment headboards. All have traditional furniture in mahogany, brass lamps and warm color schemes. Although the new rooms look traditional, they are far from an exact replica of the hotel's past, judging by a hotel archive view of a guest room in the 1920s. Furniture in renovated rooms in the 1960s tower (bottom) has a traditional feeling, and colors are warm and rich to strengthen the association with the original building. Generous drapes with side panels help reduce the impact of the curved exterior walls of the building.

Photographs courtesy of The Pfister Hotel.

The renovation also included installation of firesprinklers throughout the property, major upgrades in back-of-the-house areas, including kitchen and the employee cafeteria, and alterations to comply with the Americans with Disabilities Act. The mechanical, electrical, plumbing and alarm systems in the original building were replaced. The 1960s tower was renovated several floors at a time, and remained open while the original portion of the building was closed.

One part of the hotel the owner avoided changing is the art collection. Art in the hotel includes 80 original oil and water-color paintings from the collection of Charles Pfister. The hotel says this is the largest collection of 19-century art held by any hotel in the world. It is still on display, from watercolors and oil paintings in the corridors to bronze lions in the lobby.

MARBLE AND MIRRORS
Renovated bathrooms are a big change, especially in the original part of the building, which opened in 1893 with 200 private rooms—and only 61 private bathrooms. The renovated hotel has a totally new plumbing system, and a private bath in each room. This suite bath has a slick look with mirrored walls, whirlpool tub, and marble flooring and tub surround in contrasting colors. Wicker furniture complements the luxury theme while softening the feeling of the other materials.
Photographs courtesy of The Pfister Hotel.

The Wigwam Resort
Litchfield Park, Arizona

The Southwestern style would be the natural choice of any owner, operator or designer for renovating the Wigwam Resort in Litchfield Park, Ariz., but that does not mean everyone would work it the same way. Now more than 75 years old, the sprawling adobe-covered resort with three golf courses and lush gardens had already been renovated in the Southwestern style about 20 years before designer Jill Cole of Cole Martinez Curtis and Associates took it on. There were many practical and measurable criteria for the current renovation, including: improve functionality, build more *casita* guest rooms, add meeting space, and reorganize the food and beverage outlets. But primary was a less tangible goal: retain the resort's Five Diamond/Four Star rating from the Mobil and American Automobile Association guides, and keep the property firmly established as a luxury resort. Beyond obvious formulas, that means giving a property style. And for the Wigwam, the question was not which style to choose, but how to interpret the Southwestern style.

TERRITORIAL IMPERATIVE
Rustic, informal Territorial style is the real thing, not an affectation, at the Wigwam. This historic photograph shows the main lodge before golf carts —or automobiles — were the favored mode of transportation.

Name	The Wigwam Resort and Country Club
Location	Litchfield Park, Arizona
Owner	Kabuto International, San Francisco
Operator	Suncor Development Company
Type of Hotel	Luxury Resort/Conference
Date of Original Construction	Built 1919, Hotel opened 1929
Number of Rooms	331
Bars & Restaurants	Arizona Bar, Kachina Lounge, Terrace Dining Room, Arizona Kitchen
Meeting Rooms (Number & Size)	16 / 26,000 square feet
Recreation Facilities	Pool, spa, three 18-hole golf courses, nine tennis courts.
Type of Renovation	Phased, renovation construction during annual summer closing
Cost	$28 million
Date	1987-1991
Architect	Allen & Philp Architects, Inc. (main building) Scottsdale, Ariz. Shepherd, Nelson & Wheeler (tennis casitas), Phoenix, Ariz.
Interior Designer	Cole Martinez Curtis and Associates, Marina del Rey, Calif.
Contractor	Kitchell Contractors, Inc., Phoenix, Ariz.

HOME AT HEART

The Fireplace Lounge, originally the registration lobby, evokes the origins of the property as a homey private lodge for the Goodyear Tire and Rubber Company. The 1919 adobe fireplace is original; doors and windows with the Indian "god's eye" motif are custom replicas of originals.

Photograph by Toshi Yoshimi.

ALL THAT GLITTERS
Is not gold in the renovated Kachina Lounge, named for
the images of Indian dolls the hotel had in its art
collection. The centerpiece of the space, where guests
can order drinks and look out over the patio, is a new
custom-designed river rock bar topped with a shiny
hammered copper bar.
Photographs by Toshi Yoshimi.

TAKING CARE OF BUSINESS
Although the resort is primarily a vacation destination, it also offers meeting and conference facilities, which were expanded in the renovation. The Palm Room (top) offers a boardroom setting, while the Sachem Hall (left) functions as a large meeting room or ballroom. Meeting rooms all have new ceilings, new sound systems and new lighting.
Photographs by Toshi Yoshimi.

The hotel is a product of that style, and an authentic example of it. Built in 1919 as the "Organization House" for Goodyear Tire and Rubber Company operations nearby, it started out as a single lodge with adobe exterior walls, opened to the public in 1929 with 13 guest rooms and grew over the next 30 years as *casitas* (small freestanding buildings with guest rooms), a country club, and a swimming pool were added. Additional buildings were later sprinkled throughout the gardens which grew up around the original lodge. The lodge now houses public spaces, meeting rooms and back-of-the-house areas only. As the property matured, so did appreciation for Arizona's early heritage, making Southwestern or Territorial style central to the product offered to guests. When Suncor Development Company, a subsidiary of Pinnacle West Capital Corporation, bought the 463-acre resort in 1986, its latest renovation was decades old and the luxury label was in jeopardy. The new owner launched a near-total renovation, which was followed by major expansion of guest and meeting rooms.

SOMETHING NEW UNDER THE SUN
The Sun Lounge (facing page), located near the registration lobby and the path to the major lounges and food and beverage outlets, is rustic and intimate with informal seating groups in a variety of materials and colors. Elegant Indian-inspired artifacts and a reupholstered original bench on new green slate flooring with cozy-rugs, complement the original entry's ashlar slate steps (above). The new doors to the patio incorporate the God's eye motif. The lamps on the far wall are cowbell wall sconces, a design original to the hotel, almost the only element that can be found in the space before and after the renovation.
Photographs by Toshi Yoshimi.

TOTALLY WIRED
The existing vernacular "beanpot" chandeliers embody the informal and indigenous character of the Wigwam, but they did not pass muster with the electrical code. Instead of discarding them, the renovation team rewired them and had them certified for reinstallation by Underwriters' Laboratories — then replicated them for use in additional spaces.
Photograph by Toshi Yoshimi.

The renovation consisted of two phases: $8 million for refurbishing part of the public spaces during the annual summer shutdown of the property in 1987, and $20 million for redoing the rest of the property over an 11 month period ending in September 1988, followed by the expansion of the meeting rooms. By the time the project was completed, the renovation team had redesigned 175 guest rooms, built 22 new *casita* rooms around the tennis courts, and reworked the dining, entertainment and conference facilities in the main lodge. Following the renovation, three new two-story buildings with 90 deluxe guest rooms of 540 square feet each, and a new 11,000 square foot ballroom were completed in November 1991.

The previous renovation reflected "contemporary" design of the 1960s as much as it did the Territorial Style of pre-statehood Arizona which shaped the original lodge . Traditional decorative motifs were used — but abstracted into clean, crisp forms; geometric patterns showed up in carpets, but regularized in a way that suggested the Machine Age as much as the pueblo; and products like fluorescent lighting, mirrored walls and plastic laminates popped up left and right. Only an exact historic restoration would be utterly free of contemporary aesthetics, Cole admitted, and the renovation completed in 1990 is far from that. While taking into account requirements for the property's rating and guest expectations, "as much as possible, we tried to be as genuine as we could," said Cole. "Of course, we didn't put spittoons in the corners."

To tint the building in a contemporary light and make it meet current market needs without diminishing its historical essence, the designers used indigenous and traditional materials such as leathers, cottons and river rock. They found a local blacksmith to make wrought iron door hardware and selected woods similar to those found locally in 1919, which are no longer available.

Photographs guided the designers in returning spaces to their original condition or casting new elements in the spirit of the old, but some research pointed in a direction that was not so easy to follow. Although the photographs are black and white, Cole knew that the colors used in the 1920s were from Indian blankets. The traditional Indian colors, gray, black and brown, made a palette that was too dull and brown for contemporary hotel guests, so the design team reached out to the surrounding countryside for inspiration. The result is a blend of desert-jewel tones and earthy colors: lavender, turquoise, sand, green rose, terra cotta, pink, adobe and cinnamon. "The color palette is utterly artistic license," Cole said.

UPPER CRUST
The renovation added a new fine dining restaurant, the Arizona Kitchen. Its simple, spare design helps draw attention to the dramatically-lighted open kitchen; the brick floor, stucco walls and wooden ceiling add softness and a rustic feeling to the 100-seat space.
Photograph by Toshi Yoshimi.

SMALLER PORTIONS

Servings are the same size, but the main dining room, which had been one large room seating 300, was broken into three so that small numbers of diners would not feel they were eating in an abandoned warehouse. Antler-motif chandeliers and wall sconces, a stylized traditional viga and latilla ceiling, adobe walls, and stained glass windows with the God's eye motif make reference to the original hotel's traditional style. Before the renovation (left), the single dining room had large-pane windows with modern window treatment, extensive downlighting and acoustic tile on the ceiling.

Photographs by Toshi Yoshimi.

WINTER WARMTH
The new casitas surrounding the tennis courts have large living areas with fireplaces and separate bedrooms. Wood shutters with adjustable louvers in the living room add to the bright and informal feeling while emphasizing the prestige of the property.
Photographs by Toshi Yoshimi.

MORE OF A GOOD THING
To help the property eliminate its traditional annual closing during Arizona's scorching summers, the existing pool was expanded and shade structures were added (background) to supplement umbrellas. The firepit in the foreground (bottom) was added to take advantage of summer nights when the desert is pleasantly cool.
Photographs by Toshi Yoshimi.

NO PUTTING INDOORS, PLEASE

Guests don't have to be told not to practice putting in their rooms when they stay in the Fairway Casa guest rooms, which open directly onto the golf course. There are two guest room color schemes, based on the bedspread: blue (shown here), accented by terra cotta, green and cinnamon and adobe, complemented by turquoise, lavender and orange. Typical guest rooms, as well as suites, have a wet bar and eating area (top). Bathrooms have been improved from plastic laminate counters and stock tile before the renovation (bottom) to countertops and floors in a matching tile designed to replicate the soft handmade tile typical of early Southwestern building.
Photographs by Toshi Yoshimi.

There were tremendous variations amongst the guest rooms, and some bizarre features. This was good news, because it added interest and authenticity, but bad news because it created the impression that some rooms were inferior to others in the same grade. Designers tried to standardize the rooms without sterilizing them. The renovation included consistent features such as patios, minibars, separate living and sleeping areas and safes, while retaining the individuality of each room.

Although the renovated hotel looks very up-.to-date, Cole would not mind if guests think otherwise. "We wanted even the new construction to look as if it could have been built in the '20s," she said.

Arizona Biltmore
Phoenix, Arizona

The Arizona Biltmore in Phoenix seemed to have a lot going for it in 1991: a historic building with the signature of America's greatest architect, a developed 39-acre site, and a climate that has been drawing guests from thousands of miles away for a century. What change did the owners want when they began a four-year phased renovation? The best answer is "More of the same."

The $33 million renovation aimed to reinforce the luxury status of the property and add to its historic luster. In addition to renovating guest rooms and public spaces, it adds to existing amenities, including doubling the swimming pools and adding a water slide and new cabanas. A new 16,000 square foot flexible ballroom, 76 new luxury villas built for sale, and a new 18-hole putting course headed the list of additions.

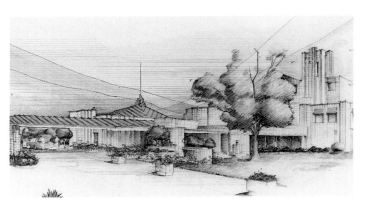

MADE IN THE SHADE
Although the renovation did not make drastic changes to the lobby, it did add a new entry and porte cochere to improve guests' first impressions. The addition keeps guests dry the few days it rains each year, and provides a respite from the Arizona sun which beats down the rest of the time.

Name	**Arizona Biltmore**
Location	**Phoenix, Arizona**
Owner	**Biltmore Hotel Properties**
Operator	**Grossmann Properties Co.**
Type of Hotel	**Resort / Luxury**
Date of Original Construction	**1929**
Number of Rooms	**498**
Bars & Restaurants	**5 restaurants / 1 bar**
Meeting Rooms (Number & Size)	**19 rooms / 39,000 square feet**
Recreation Facilities	**4 pools, 92-foot water slide, "Kids' Kabana," 2 18-hole golf courses, 18-hole putting course, lawn games, 8 tennis courts, jogging/hiking trails, fitness center and spa**
Type of Renovation	**Phased renovation, hotel open during most work**
Cost	**$33 million**
Date	**1991-1995 (Projected)**
Architect	**Vernon Swaback Associates, Scottsdale, Arizona**
Interior Designer	**Barry Design Associates, Los Angeles, California**
Contractor	**D.L.Withers Construction, Inc.**

Although the renovation included new finishes and interior design for public areas, it stressed maintaining the appearance which had made the hotel famous since Albert Chase McArthur designed it in 1929 with the collaboration of Frank Lloyd Wright. Changes in the recreation areas added new facilities, but were intended to "make it look older, not newer," according to W. Matthew Crow, president of the Arizona Biltmore.

In the historic lobby, there was more restoration than renovation. Carpeting was replaced with oak flooring with inset carpeted areas, while the Mission and Gustave Stickley-style furniture was reupholstered in a new color scheme more in keeping with the original design and desert setting. New lighting reduced glare by using a translucent glass version of the "Biltmore Block" custom-detailed exterior masonry units unique to the original hotel. The adjoining Lobby Lounge restaurant was opened to the canvas-covered Arizona Room on the exterior by replacing a bank of windows with doors.

Guest rooms retained their original number and layout. Half were redone in 1993 and the other half in 1994. The renovation did not change room and bathroom partitions, but all furniture, fixtures, finishes and soft goods were replaced. The renovated guest rooms reflect both the hotel's origins as a resort destination and its present situation in a major metropolis.

DESERT OASIS
The Arizona Biltmore has long drawn on vacationers from northern states who wanted to escape winter. The new pool and water slide (center, rear) enlarge the hotel's desert oasis, allowing guests who want to be surrounded by water to see the desert from a distance.

IMPROVING ON THE PAST
To enhance the Arizona Biltmore's luxury image, the architects studied the facades of some of its less prominent wings, which were originally lacking in ornamentation. The design shown for the Paradise Wing adds landscaping and horizontal detailing to the building to enliven it and break up the visual mass. The design was first applied to another wing of the hotel and then executed in additional locations.

POOLSIDE HIDEAWAY
Guests who want to stake out their own territory beside the property's new swimming pools can rent a tent-like canvas cabana, or go for the full luxury of a "standard" cabana built of masonry Biltmore Block (pictured here). The standard cabana includes a sitting area, wet bar, bathroom with shower and an outdoor sitting area by the pool with a canvas awning.

DESERT MIRAGE
Appearing for only about eight months, the Wrigley Lawn Pavilion was the renovation designers' answer to the demand for immediate expansion of meeting space. The fabric-roofed ballroom also served as a test market for flexible "new era" permanent ballroom which later replaced it on the same site.

PORTAL OF CHANGE
When converting an underutilized lawn into two new pools, the architects strived to integrate them into the existing site. This new entry gate structure incorporates the gate to the new pools with a shaded pool deck area, while using the architectural style and materials of the original building to fit the new into the old harmoniously.

Restraint is the last thing the renovation designers aimed to impose on guests at the pool area, where two new pools were added to the original two. The renovation also provided a water slide for those who want to do more than swim laps. The slide is hidden in a tower which looks more like a Wright folly than modern recreation equipment. The cabanas which surrounded the original Catalina pool were replaced with 25 new cabanas, ranging from canvas tents to masonry structures to two multi-room "hospitality cabanas." Another, called Kids' Kabana, is painted in primary colors and has games, a reading area and computers to keep young swimmers happily occupied after they're too waterlogged to stay in the pool.

In addition to resort amenities, the renovation added necessities sought by guests, including a new business center, with fax, cellular phones, pagers, printers, personal computers, lap tops and personal digital assistants. The phasing of construction allowed the Biltmore to provide three new kitchens without interrupting food service. A new kitchen serves meeting rooms, the main kitchen received an all-new interior, and a separate new kitchen gives the property Kosher food service. Other infrastructure changes included a new telephone system with voice mail and a new computer linked to electronic guest room locks and security apparatus. Guests can check in by mail, arriving at the property with pre-activated card keys, and check out using the televisions in their rooms.

The renovation also included construction of an unusual temporary meeting space on the location of an existing outdoor function area. Opened in September, 1993, the Wrigley Lawn Pavilion had a carpeted concrete foundation, fixed walls accented with replicas of "Biltmore Block," a state-of-the-art audio-visual system — and a tent-like fabric roof. A plain shell in which occupants supplied their own finished decor, it remained standing less than a year, but set the stage for the new permanent ballroom which replaced it on the same foundation. With subdued walls and a ceiling composed simply of a six-foot-square theatrical rigging grid with three-foot canvas curtains, all in black, the permanent ballroom lets users add whatever lighting and decoration they choose, or hire the hotel's events organizers to do so.

REFINING A CLASSIC
Oversized chairs with rattan detailing set a vacation tone in the renovated guest rooms, while Wright-inspired lamps and tables complement the architecture of the building. Balancing the historic and resort feeling, most fabrics and colors are muted desert tones, with standout Southwestern accents, leaving an overall impression of urbanity and restraint.

SLIDE WRIGHT IN
At first glance, guests new to the property might think this tower is part of the original hotel conceived by Frank Lloyd Wright, but it was actually added during the renovation. The designers executed the tower in the same style as the hotel, using the concrete "Biltmore Block" masonry at the tops and corners of the walls.

The ANA Hotel
San Francisco, California

Every city has buildings some people seem to love to hate, and hotels are just as eligible as office towers, government buildings and stores. In San Francisco, three hotels have been fixtures on the unofficial unpopularity list in recent decades, but that notoriety did not keep the ANA chain, the arm of Japan's second largest airline (Nippon Airways), from buying one of them as its first U.S. property. The ANA chain bought the former San Francisco Le Meridien, a 36-story property well-located between the Financial District and the Moscone Convention Center, and made a calculated effort to increase its architectural standing.

Name	*The ANA Hotel San Francisco*
Location	*San Francisco, California*
Owner	*ANA Hotels San Francisco, Inc.*
Operator	*ANA Enterprises, Ltd.*
Type of Hotel	*Business / Groups*
Date of Original Construction	*1983*
Number of Rooms	*673*
Bars & Restaurants	*Café Fifty Three Restaurant Lobby Bar and Lounge*
Meeting Rooms (Number & Size)	*15 / 21,000 square feet*
Recreation Facilities	*Fitness Center with exercise machines, sauna and steam room, massage*
Type of Renovation	*Reconfigure ground floor public areas, new finishes, furniture and equipment throughout. Hotel open throughout renovation.*
Cost	*$3.5 million*
Date Completed	*1993*
Architect	*The Callison Partnership, Seattle, Washington*
Interior Designer	*Barry Design Associates, Los Angeles, California*
Consultants	*Graphics: Jacquelyn Barry Structural Engineer: Structural Design Engineers, San Francisco, California Mechanical Engineer: W.L. Thompson Consulting Engineers, Atlanta, Georgia*
Contractor	*Kajima, Inc.*

REORIENTATION
The renovated spaces are articulated individually, with a more conventional and identifiable organization. The registration area focuses on a deco-inspired table accented by a three-color marble floor pattern and circular ceiling cove. The grand circulated spaces culminate with axis from the lobby to the restaurant.
Photographs by John Sutton.

Less than ten years old, the building did not have outmoded systems, decades of dinginess or giant gaps in the range of facilities demanded by the current market. Its major problem was an architectural style that detractors derided as low-budget brutalism, with a concrete exterior lacking design features other than subtle variations in color. Critics said the interior had the cold sparseness of the International Style without its strength and precision. Rather than redoing the massive exterior, ANA and its designers decided to redesign the entry and ground floor and give the interior an all new look. They chose a loose synthesis of the Art Deco and Moderne styles, thus avoiding the time warp that guests would have experienced entering an older traditional interior after approaching the relentlessly industrial facades.

The renovation made the greatest changes to the ground floor, where ANA wanted to change the original open, flowing spaces which sometimes confused guests when they tried to find their way from the entry to the registration desk. The new ground floor defines each space and organizes them around grand circulation spaces, such as a gold-domed rotunda.

A fine dining restaurant, already closed before the renovation began, was replaced with a lobby for group check-in. Offsetting the reduction in dining space, the hotel took over an adjacent alley, landscaped it and built an outdoor seating area adjacent to the restaurant and bar. Nearby, a new exterior pavilion allows the property to vie for a customary Japanese hotel market segment: weddings. The food and beverage outlets maintain a rich, masculine approach, but avoid stuffiness with bold and playful elements such as the playing-card theme which runs through from the art on the walls to the name of the restaurant, Café Fifty Three.

INTIMATE BUSINESS
The bar, inspired by the traditional "gentleman's club," but upbeat and not stuffy, features a new fireplace with marble facing surrounded by couches and cocktail seating. In addition, there is seating at the bar and a living-room-like sofa grouping.
Photographs by John Sutton.

DEFINED DINING
The renovated hotel has just one restaurant, Café Fifty Three, with a mural which continues the playing-card theme established by the Donald Salton prints in the bar (facing page, top). The restaurant is differentiated from the bar architecturally and opens onto the new rotunda (facing page, bottom). Seating areas within the restaurant are separated by bulkheads with planters to offer diners more privacy (above).
Photographs by John Sutton.

On upper floors, minor changes were made. Partitions were added in the meeting rooms, and one meeting room was converted into a richly detailed board room. A new circular stair was added from the second to the third floor to improve circulation between meeting rooms. Several guest rooms on the fourth floor were reconfigured to create the fitness center. Guest room floors have all new furniture and finishes, but no changes in partitions; in bathrooms, only the flooring, wall covering, lighting and mirrors were replaced.

Before the renovation, the interior had a range of styles in various spaces, including rattan and French provincial. The designers decided to apply a single look to the building, varying it but never crossing into other periods or styles. Because the exterior of the building is obviously so recent, authentic Art Deco or Moderne design would look out of place, so the design loosely recalls both aesthetics without being literal. Cognac-toned anegre wood paneling and moldings appear in many public spaces, and the whole hotel has custom-designed carpeting, often with patterns based on designs from books of the work of Art Deco designer Jacques Ruhlman. Light fixtures, many of which were custom-designed, echo the Deco-Moderne tone, although some are quite contemporary.

Materials, fabrics and colors were chosen to make spaces warm and sometimes clubby, but never stuffy, according to interior designer Cynthia Forchielli of Barry Design. Though jewel-tone colors often appear in carpets and fabrics, and guest room walls are rich blues, garnets, and celadon, the effect is always tailored and masculine. "It's friendly and welcoming but not fussy," said Forchielli. "This is a businessman's hotel."

CONTEMPORARY CLASSICS
Guest bedrooms feature anegre furniture and fixtures which loosely recall Streamline Moderne design. Although tapestry fabrics on lounge chairs depart from the geometric patterns found in many of the custom fabrics and carpets in the hotel, they strike a tailored tone and complement the businesslike room.
Photograph by John Sutton.

Sheraton Palace
San Francisco, California

When owner Kyo-ya Company Ltd., originally decided to renovate the Sheraton Palace Hotel in San Francisco, it had architect Skidmore, Owings & Merrill do studies for an addition rising dramatically above the back of the existing 1909 building. When the renovated hotel reopened in 1991, the tower was nowhere to be seen, but $150 million of preservation work allowed management to reposition the historic property into more lucrative business traveler and high-end social markets.

Name	*Sheraton Palace Hotel*
Location	*San Francisco, California*
Owner	*Kyo-Ya Company, Ltd.*
Operator	*ITT Sheraton Corporation*
Type of Hotel	*Luxury / Business*
Date of Original Construction	*1909*
Number of Rooms	*552*
Bars & Restaurants	*3 restaurants, each with bar*
Meeting Rooms	
Number & Size	*22 rooms / 45,000 square feet*
Recreation Facilities	*Indoor pool, exercise machines, spa*
Type of Renovation	*Complete; operations shut down*
Cost	*$150 million*
Date	*January 1989 - April 1991*
Architect	*Architect: Skidmore, Owings & Merrill, San Francisco, California Historical Architect: Page & Turnbull, San Francisco, California*
Consultants	*Food Service: Abrams & Tanaka Associates*
Contractor	*Takenaka USA*

IMPROVED RECEPTION
The registration desk, originally tucked off in a corner where the main entrance of the hotel meets the main corridor, has a new, open lobby with a much larger desk and a separate seating area. The new barrel-vaulted ceiling gives guests a preview of the Sunset Court and the swimming pool.
Photograph by Jon Miller, © Hedrich-Blessing.

OUTWARDLY UNCHANGED

Although considerable work went into repairing deterioration of the limestone wall facing and cornice at the first floor and earthquake damage to the brick walls and terra cotta window sills above, the overall appearance of the hotel's primary facades changed little in the renovation.

Photograph by Jon Miller, © Hedrich-Blessing.

INTRODUCING A NEW PAST

Although most of the building exterior was painstakingly restored to its original appearance, designers exercised their creativity on the new entry canopy. Inspired by the original marquise, which had been removed years before the renovation, it has clean lines and dramatic lighting to make it stand out from the existing building.

Photograph by Jon Miller, © Hedrich-Blessing.

Overlooked by the media in all the attention to hotel history restored, but not by the guests of the renovated hotel, were major new features housed in an addition which replaced a decades-old expansion at the back of the hotel, removed early in the renovation process. These included an indoor swimming pool and health spa, 10,000 square feet of meeting rooms, and a business center - all key parts in the strategy to attract more meetings and business travelers. "We have the best of both worlds now," said Jim Kilroy, director of marketing for the Sheraton Palace. "The charm and ambiance of a landmark historic hotel, with all the amenities travelers are looking for today."

Offering all the amenities had been a trademark for the hotel for a generation before the existing building was constructed. Two prominent Westerners, William Ralston and William Sharon, put San Francisco on the map for demanding travelers when they built the first Palace Hotel in 1875, complete with a seven-story skylighted interior carriage entrance court and five hydraulic elevators. The building was a hit with travelers, but it burned in the fire following the 1906 earthquake and was demolished. The present building, designed by Trowbridge and Livingston (designers of the St. Regis Hotel in New York), opened in 1909.

But by 1989, it was a "tired, eighty-year-old building. Dowdy." as Kilroy put it. Teaming up with San Francisco preservation architects Page & Turnbull, Skidmore decided to restore the exterior of the building and the most important public rooms, including the landmark Garden Court, a 5,000 square foot enclosed courtyard with an art glass ceiling. The cost for restoring the ceiling was $7 million, which involved removing it panel by panel, restoring it in an artisan's studio, and then reinstalling it. The off-site work proved doubly worthwhile because it meant the ceiling panels were not in the building when the Loma Prieta earthquake struck in October 1989, causing significant damage to the building.

CENTRAL SPLENDOR

The centerpiece of the hotel is the Garden Court, with its 8,000 square foot art glass ceiling and classical marble columns. San Francisco's only listed indoor landmark space, it predates the present hotel, having been a skylighted carriage entrance surrounded by balconies (above) in the previous hotel constructed on the same site in 1875, which was destroyed in the fire caused by the 1906 earthquake. Although the Garden Court (left) looked very similar after the renovation to its appearance when the hotel opened in 1909, massive effort and expense were lavished on its restoration. The ceiling glass was removed for cleaning and restoration in a stained glass specialist's studio - and thus spared from all damage in the 1989 San Francisco earthquake. The special faux-limestone plaster walls were renewed, and decorative niches were stripped of non-historic gold leaf and strengthened to resist earthquakes.

Renovation photograph by Jon Miller, © Hedrich-Blessing.

PATH OF TIME
The main corridor leads from the entrance on San Francisco's prime thoroughfare, Market Street, past the hotel's main entry lobby and the Garden Court, and on to ballrooms and the entry to second floor meeting rooms. The faux limestone walls with marble wainscot look like the ones seen in a historic photograph of the corridor (right), but many of them were actually rebuilt during the renovation (below) because of damage caused by the 1989 earthquake.
Renovation photograph by Jon Miller, © Hedrich-Blessing.

HOW TO DRAW A CROWD
Maxfield Parrish's The Pied Piper, which had hung in the hotel ever since its construction, is the centerpiece of the bar in the new Maxfield's restaurant (below). The original skylight and mosaic floor were uncovered during the renovation, and the coffered ceiling was refinished. The adjoining dining area visible through the doorway at the end of the room (opposite page) features an exhibition kitchen in a glass and dark wood enclosure. The original Pied Piper Bar (left), photographed around 1915 has the same dark wood and leather theme, but takes it a few steps further.
Renovation photographs by
Jon Miller, © Hedrich-Blessing

Page & Turnbull meticulously analyzed and replicated original materials in the Garden Court and the adjoining French Parlors and on the exterior of the building. A lengthy search led the architects to Nevada for stone to match the original where damage had occurred on the exterior over the years, while research produced a multi-pronged solution to the dilemma of how to strengthen the historic terra cotta window sills so they would not break in earthquakes.

While the renovation team was busy preserving the exterior and historic spaces in the building, it was reworking the design of guest rooms and less historic spaces and creating an all new look for the addition. The swimming pool and a new breakout room for the meeting rooms on the second floor are unmistakably modern, but they echo the Garden Court with their huge barrel-vaulted skylights. The formal ground floor corridors of the building were preserved with subtle changes to accommodate technical requirements and a palette of colors and materials which fit contemporary taste.

Skidmore designers used new materials and existing treasures such as a mosaic tile floor to create the Pied Piper Bar and Maxfield's Restaurant around the original Maxfield Parrish painting, which had been a much-loved fixture in the building for decades. Architect Hideto Horiike used an Asian-flavored design in the new Kyo-ya Restaurant, a Japanese eatery that replaced one of the ground-floor restaurants, which was not retained in the renovation.

ROOM FOR REINTERPRETATION

Guest-room walls stayed in place during the renovation - but just about everything else changed. Four-poster beds, oversized armchairs with ottomans and rich wood grain case goods set a tone of luxury, while muted wall colors and fabrics complement the restrained style used throughout the building. A guest room photographed in 1915 (above) has many of the same elements, but the lighter weight furniture and dark stained trim give a more austere bent to the room.

Renovation photograph by Jon Miller, © Hedrich-Blessing

SPECIAL ELAN
Bathrooms were gutted, but like guest rooms, their walls remained intact through the renovation, precluding a four or five fixture layout. To provide the substance of luxury within that constraint, designers crafted marble and polychrome metal vanities.
Photograph by Jon Miller, © Hedrich-Blessing

Guest-room floor layouts did not change, but all finishes and fixtures were removed and replaced. The mechanical, electrical and plumbing systems were gutted and replaced, as were kitchens and other back-of-the-house facilities. In addition to seismic improvements, the structure of the building received a major makeover in places where new support was needed for the addition with its swimming pool.

When the hotel reopened after 27 months, the original price tag and schedule for the renovation were long forgotten, largely because of damage caused by the earthquake. The history of the building was remembered by the public and the renovation was noticed by all. Operator ITT Sheraton Corp. raised its lowest room rates to $180 at the reopening and reduced its group tour bookings in favor of more business travelers and corporate meetings. The historical cachet drew back high-end San Francisco social functions which had abandoned the Sheraton Palace before the renovation; once again the property was on a par with its oldest and most famous competitors in the city. "We are the oldest hotel in the city," Kilroy said. "We feel the history of the Palace is unique. We truly are a landmark."

THE ROYAL UPDATE

Suites feature rich classical furniture and stately, muted colors to impart a sense of understated grandeur suitable for visiting royalty, but the interior design is not the original look, even if it looks timeless. A historic photograph (left) of an original suite shows more complex detailing, more furniture, and an overall appearance that looks busy to today's eye.

Renovation photograph by Jon Miller, © Hedrich-Blessing

HIGH DIVE

Perched atop the back of the hotel in place of additions from the 1930s which were demolished at the outset of the renovation, the new indoor swimming pool features a dramatic barrel-vaulted skylight. In addition to a whirlpool spa, the recreation center also includes an adjacent exercise room, sauna and locker rooms.

Photograph by Jon Miller, © Hedrich-Blessing.

SCRATCH THE SKIN
The walls and ceiling of the renovated Rose Room on the ground floor look
familiar to longtime guests, but beneath their surface are massive new steel
beams and columns supporting new meeting rooms and recreation facilities
above - including a swimming pool. The walls and ceilings are actually brand
new, because the original ballroom was leveled (after being carefully measured
and cut apart for samples) to accommodate the new structural framing.
Photograph by Jon Miller, © Hedrich-Blessing.

MEETING EXPECTATIONS
A fixture in San Francisco's social life for more than a century, the Sheraton Palace had an established reputation for balls,
dances and parties. The Gold Room retains its social connections, and to fulfill the requirements of the daytime market for
meeting rooms, the renovation provided totally new audio-visual systems and improved food service facilities.
Photograph by Jon Miller, © Hedrich-Blessing.

SIGNATURE SPACE
The Sunset Court subtly reflects the design of the historic Garden Court; its skylight strongly resembles the one over the new swimming pool, which is nearby. This new second floor breakout area is surrounded by new meeting rooms, and is connected to the ground floor by a new escalator. Fritted glass in the skylight and abstracted classical columns refer to the design of the Garden Court without imitating it.
Photograph by Jon Miller, © Hedrich-Blessing.

The Regent Beverly Wilshire
Beverly Hills, California

If it isn't easy being pretty, it's back-breaking work being beautiful. Nobody knows that better than the owners and designers who in 1987 set out to renovate the Regent Beverly Wilshire, a landmark of Los Angeles glamour which was in danger of being out-glittered by some of its neighboring rivals. The Regent chain, based in Asia, needed to make sure the property would hold its own against any in the sybaritic Los Angeles market. Sitting on Wilshire Boulevard at the foot of Rodeo Drive, the Beverly Wilshire had an unbeatable location and a regal history, thanks to the traditional design by architects Walker and Eisen, sumptuous building materials such as Carrara marble from Italy, and a clientele dominated by rulers of Hollywood, with a sprinkling of genuine royalty from abroad.

FACIAL, NOT FACELIFT
Long a presence on Wilshire Boulevard at the foot of Rodeo Drive, the hotel's original building, now known as the Wilshire Wing, was rejuvenated but not altered greatly on the exterior during the renovation. The designers reinforced the Rodeo Drive location by retaining the primary pedestrian entrance on the original facade shown here.
Photograph by Jaime Ardilles-Arce.

Name	*The Regent Beverly Wilshire*
Location	*Beverly Hills, California*
Owner	*Hotel Investment Corporation*
Operator	*Regent Hotels International*
Type of Hotel	*Luxury*
Date of Original Construction	*1928*
Number of Rooms	*300*
Bars & Restaurants	*4*
Meeting Rooms Number & Size	*9 / 25,500 square feet*
Recreation Facilities	*Pool, free weights, exercise machines, health and beauty treatments*
Type of Renovation	*Phased, hotel open during construction*
Cost	*$100 million*
Date	*1987 - 1993*
Architect	*Gruen Associates, Los Angeles, California*
Interior Designer	*Project Associates, Beverly Hills, California*
Consultants	*Decoration: Betty Garber, Westwood, California*
Contractor	*Peck/Jones, Los Angeles, California*

PAMPERED APPEARANCE
The renovation did not leave shops as raw space for tenants to finish on their own. The florist space near the Café features a trompe l'oeil ceiling mural (top).
Photograph by Jaime Ardilles-Arce.

REDEFINING THE CENTER
The renovated lobby is much larger than the original lobby and reinforces the sense of hierarchy in the ground floor design. The two story space is surrounded by hotel services and concessions and sets the tone for the interior of the building with three-color marble flooring, intricate woodwork and antique furniture.
Photograph by Jaime Ardilles-Arce.

The hotel prospered, but years of additions and remodelings made it a muddle of expensive materials rather than a palace of fine design. Regent decided to bring the blur of styles and schemes into stunning, opulent focus, and turned the challenge over to architect Kurt Franzen of Gruen Associates and interior designer Glenn Texeira of Project Associates. Major programmatic elements included a new pool and elaborate spa and a guest-room upgrade which reduced the count in the original part of the property from 248 to 148.

The designers had an ample budget and could start with a clean slate inside the building, but they had to work within the constraints of the structural layout, exterior architecture and site design of the original Italian Renaissance building, and a bland 1971 addition. That meant interior column spacings which did not align with window locations, facades which harmonized like a 1920s flapper wearing bell-bottom pants, and a fractured entry sequence which deposited guests who arrived by car at the back door of the main lobby on Rodeo Drive.

In place of the disarray in the interior design, the designers adopted a classic but not stuffy approach with the lavishness and easy-going classical elegance which is a trademark of Beverly Hills. Within this unified and even grandiose framework, the character, colors and styles of the individual spaces vary so that the hotel is dignified without being pompous or stiff. The color palette is rich but restrained, the furniture includes ornate antiques and more inviting reproductions, and acres of marble topped off with miles of moldings assure guests they are getting their money's worth at rates which start above $300.

LUXURY AND LEISURE
Located near the hotel lobby, the informal Lobby lounge offers afternoon tea, cocktails and light dining. Its interior features comfortable leather chairs, sofas covered in melon velvet and Louis XVI round tables with inset antique rouge marble. The window treatment masks the structural misalignment between the interior columns and window openings on the exterior walls (above).
Photographs by Jaime Ardilles-Arce.

ELEGANCE EVERYWHERE
Luxury doesn't end with the lobby, as guests discover as soon as they enter the adjacent women's room and men's room. Dark wood paneling graces the men's room (bottom), while large vanities in the women's room accommodate guests who want to make a grand entrance (right). Both spaces have extensive marble in contrasting colors.
Photographs by Jaime Ardilles-Arce.

REPAST PERFECT

The Dining Room was one of the boldest moves made by the renovation designers to encourage the rich and famous to frequent the Beverly Wilshire. There are numerous clear views — and lots of obstructions — from table to table in the restaurant, so that anyone famous who eats there might — or might not — be seen by anyone else in the restaurant. Management promoted the operation as a center for "power dining" and Richard Hack of the Hollywood Reporter called it "the hottest lunch spot in town."

Photographs by Jaime Ardilles-Arce.

To clear up the architectural confusion, the designers revamped the layout of the major public spaces, introducing a recognizable hierarchy to guide guests through the inevitable complexity caused ᵉ placement of the buildings on the The expanded main lobby facing leo Drive is connected to the motor ᵣance on the opposite side of the ᵈing with a clear and finely-detailed ᵤence of spaces to make the link ᵣween the two entrances easy to find. range of lounges, cafes and restaurants ᵢcourages visitors to explore the rest of ᵉ ground floor.

On the second floor, a new spa aims for the opulence one might expect from a Hong Kong luxury chain at its debut in Los Angeles. An outdoor pool, separate saunas and steam rooms for men and women, a sun deck and snack bar, a gym with free weights and exercise machines, and an array of beauty treatments and massages are intended to make guests want to spend a long time in the spa. Guests who don't want to leave at all can avail themselves of the two-bedroom cabana suite overlooking the sun deck.

TOP SHELF DETAILING

*More than 150 woods went into the wall paneling and custom-fabricated French Bar with stools and separate stand-up bar. **The Bar** features Biedermeier and Regency furnishings, with chair upholstered in cognac leather and sofas in brown embossed velvet.*

Photograph by Jaime Ardilles-Arce.

For those who would rather stay in a regular guest room, the renovated hotel provides large rooms with at least two televisions each, two-line telephones and electronic signals to summon a floor steward or keep staff from disturbing the occupants. The signature of the Regent chain is deluxe bathrooms; each marble bathroom in the Beverly Wilshire has a large soaking tub, a separate shower, a telephone, a scale, and a hair dryer. The 50 suites in the original part of the building have special furniture collections as well as additional sitting rooms or bedrooms. Rooms in the newer wing were renovated in a similar fashion; renovations proceeded on one floor at a time to allow the hotel to continue operating during construction.

Although the renovation set out to reduce the jumble and clutter of the building, it did not attempt to make the property a taut, relentless design statement. The goal was to match the worldwide standard for hotels, combining a European-inspired aesthetic, Asian levels of luxury, California informality and a Los Angeles-class of high-profile presentation. By varying the designs of the individual spaces but tying them loosely together with compatible styles and materials, the renovation offers luxury everywhere but in a relaxed way that implies that opulence is an assumption, not an assertion. This approach might be what guests would expect from an Asian-owned luxury hotel in Beverly Hills.

MEDITERRANEAN INSPIRATION
In renovating the 1971 Beverly wing, designers incorporated a new second floor pool, sun deck, and health spa. The interior of the spa strikes a contemporary note, while the pool takes its Mediterranean inspiration from Sophia Loren's pool in Italy (opposite page).
Photograph by Jaime Ardilles-Arce.

DOWN-HOME L.A. CAFE
The most informal food and beverage operation in the hotel is the Cafe, where the Main Street USA drugstore meets Southern California conspicuous consumption. The result is striped floors in marble, Manuel Canovas fabric Roman shades, and espresso drinks as well as banana splits on the menu.
Photograph by Jaime Ardilles-Arce.

WHO NEEDS A PRESIDENT?

Some hotels seem overly optimistic naming suites "presidential" but at the Beverly Wilshire, the top suite has attracted a list which makes Presidents look like anti-climaxes. Woolworth heiress Barbara Hutton lived there, and other guests included Elvis Presley, Elton John, Ringo Starr, Andrew Lloyd Webber, Stevie Nicks and enough foreign royalty to qualify the suite as an international palace. With a square footage - and daily rate - of 4,000, it has a living room, a dining room, two sitting rooms, two bedrooms, and two and a half baths. Interior themes range from formal European furniture with Oriental influences in the living room (top left, facing page), to the English estate tone of the dining room (top, this page). The library adds a touch of elegance, with its airy feeling that avoids the academic look of dark wood shelves (left, this page). The spaces in the suite are united by the grand central hall, reminiscent of a 19th-century mansion with its inlaid wood floor and Corinthian columns (bottom, facing page).

Photographs by Jaime Ardilles-Arce.

WHO NEEDS A PRESIDENT?
The bedrooms are more American and comfortable,
with a big sofa and lots of pillows in the master
bedroom (above) and comfortable chairs in the second
bedroom (bottom). The Regent chain's obsession with
bathrooms shows up in its full glory in the master
bathroom, where oversized vanity mirrors give the
illusion of even more marble than the room actually has
(right). A marble vanity with three-way mirror caters to
guests who want to set fashion firsts, whether or not
they happen to be First Lady (p. 84, top right).
Photographs by Jaime Ardilles-Arce.

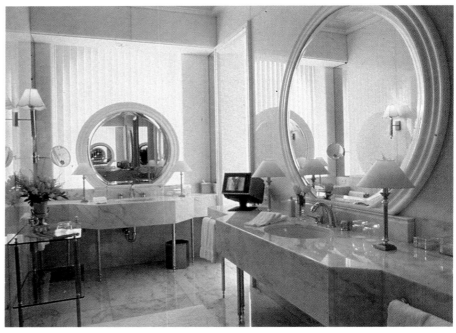

EASY-GOING OPULENCE
The Regent Beverly Wilshire offers three categories of suites and three categories of bedrooms. Suites (top right) tend toward the more formal, while guest rooms (center) show their comfortable side first; both emphasize high-grade materials and low-key detailing which avoids the overbearing look of a period reproduction interior. Suites and guest rooms are designed in four color themes: wheat, peach, rose and celery. A large one-room suite is known as the Warren Beatty suite for the famous actor who lived there for long periods (below).
Photographs by Jaime Ardilles-Arce.

The Beverly Prescott Hotel
Los Angeles, California

How do you fit a traditional-style urban boutique hotel into the city with a soul of trend-setting youthfulness and a body of suburban sprawl?

Buying old hotels in the center of the city and renovating each property with an individual flavor launched Bill Kimpton as a hotel entrepreneur in San Francisco and later in Portland and Seattle. But Kimpton interpreted his own formula slightly differently when he continued to Los Angeles, where old just means anything that's not brand new, and there is no city center. So instead of renovating an architecturally rich historic property in downtown Los Angeles like the Checkers Hotel, Kimpton bought a humdrum thirty-year-old hotel on the west side of the city.

Name	**The Beverly Prescott Hotel**
Location	**Los Angeles, California**
Owner	**B.I.L.**
Operator	**Kimpton Hotel and Restaurant Group, Inc.**
Type of Hotel	**Boutique**
Date of Original Construction	**1961**
Number of Rooms	**140**
Bars & Restaurants	**Rox Restaurant**
Meeting Rooms (Number & Size)	**2 / 5,300 square feet**
Recreation Facilities	**Outdoor pool, exercise cycles, rowing machines, step aerobics**
Type of Renovation	**Hotel shut down during construction**
Cost	**$12.5 million**
Date Completed	**April 1993**
Architect	**Three Architecture**
Interior Designer	**Hotel: Cheryl Rowley Interior Design, Beverly Hills with Patrick de Monfreid Restaurant, pool & rooftop meeting room: Ron Leiberman, Design Development Co.,Tarzana, California**
Consultants	**Mechanical Engineer: Tom Gilbertson and Associates, Moraga, California**
Contractor	**R.D. Olson Construction, Anaheim, California**

SOUTHERN CALIFORNIA

If a Southern California hotel isn't on the beach, it's sure to have a pool. The renovation added stone paving to the patio around the existing pool, and fitted it out with canvas cabanas and decorative lanterns (below). The entire exterior was painted one color (facing page) to reduce the high-rise boxiness it had before the renovation (left).

Renovation photographs by Fred Licht Photography; pre-renovation photographs by Kimpton Hotel and Restaurant Group, Inc.

Kimpton decided to market his new Beverly Prescott hotel to the younger segment of the entertainment industry concentrated nearby in Beverly Hills, Century City and West Hollywood, appealing to those on the way up, but not too far up the ladder to appreciate an informal, relaxing property with moderate prices. The next step was to make the former Beverly Hillcrest Hotel into a Kimpton hotel. Built in 1961, the twelve-story structure had a blah "contemporary" exterior of that period and an interior that ran the gamut of mediocre design from the past three decades: rust color shag carpets with red flocked wallpaper, French provincial furniture, and a recently redone beige-on-beige lobby.

Kimpton commissioned designer Cheryl Rowley to make the property into "an emotional adventure unlike any hotel in Los Angeles." She set out to give Los Angeles something new because she was "tired of seeing very beige hotel properties." The ground floor was gutted, but the exterior and partitions on the guest room floors were left almost unchanged, so Rowley had the challenge of redefining the property mostly through interior design.

She chose a bright and lively palette and an eclectic blend of finishes and furnishings to enliven the spaces and give them a strong Southern California character. A new entry loggia provided a transition between the existing porte cochere and the lobby. The "living room" with fireplace—a standard feature in Kimpton hotels—was separated from the circulation path, and touches like limestone flooring that begins in the exterior loggia and continues into the lobby create an indoor-outdoor connection that complements the bright colors to lighten the lobby and make it authentically Southern Californian.

YOU'VE ARRIVED
Before the renovation, the doors at the porte cochere led directly into the lobby. To give guests a more defined sense of arrival and entry, designer Cheryl Rowe created a covered exterior Loggia with outdoor furniture (top). Upon entering the lobby, guests find a stopping space focused on a gossamer day bed (right).
Photographs by Fred Licht Photography.

HOME SWEET HOME
Every Kimpton hotel lobby has a comfortable "living room" with a fireplace; the Beverly Prescott provides this traditional touch while maintaining its eclectic Los Angeles nuance through eclectic, whimsical lamps and objets d'art and furniture and fabrics which blend traditional and current styles.
Photographs by Fred Licht Photography

Guest rooms were divided into two themes, one geared to men and one to women. To compensate for the limited size of the bathrooms, which were not changed, Rowley added a small wall to create an entry foyer adjacent to them in each room. Guest room doors have a leather strap and a leather and chrome tag for the room number, inspired by the hardware found on luggage.

Like all Kimpton hotels, the Beverly Prescott has a restaurant with its own name, operation and personality. Ron Leiberman, hired to do the restaurants in several previous Kimpton hotel projects, was brought in to design the restaurant, rooftop meeting room, and pool. Leiberman gave the Rox Restaurant a subdued spirit, with natural materials and colors drawn from the native landscape of Southern California. Guests enter through a patio area with a bougainvillea arbor and wrought iron gates to reach the dining area with coffered ceilings and cherrywood floors.

CONTRASTING SUITES
The property's twelve suites include two geared toward business travelers, with a large round table for meetings and restrained furniture and colors (above). The deluxe suite, marketed to individual travelers, strikes a more romantic tone, with floral fabrics and chaise lounges (right).
Photographs by Fred Licht Photography

HIS AND HERS
To appeal to male and female business travelers, the hotel has two guest room schemes, the "stripe" room with a feminine touches like floral drapes (below) and the "checkerboard" room, named for its bold, graphic headboard design (facing page). Case goods are mahogany with gold accents, with some fruitwood pieces. Nightstands are hand-painted to resemble draped fabric. Although each room has full-wall sliding glass doors onto its balcony, the extensive drapery gives the renovated rooms a more intimate feeling than the original modern building had (left).

Renovation photographs by Fred Licht Photography; pre-renovation photographs by Kimpton Hotel and Restaurant Group, Inc.

GARDEN VARIETY
Guest rooms feature a granite-topped cast stone pullman in the bathroom instead of a conventional vanity. The piece is inspired by garden consoles.

Bancroft Hotel

Berkeley, California

Many renovations strive to change a hotel building to fend off an unwanted change in the business which occupies it, but at the Bancroft Hotel, the renovation made the building appear unchanged so that it could house an entirely new operation. The Bancroft, which was not designed as a hotel but became one after a $2 million restoration, still looks remarkably similar to the way it looked when it was completed in 1928. Continuity was the watchword of the renovation, both out of necessity and by design, allowing the owner to keep a tight budget and offer a product tailored to its local market niche.

Name	**Bancroft Hotel**
Location	**Berkeley, California**
Owner	**Ross Family**
Operator	**Martin Ross**
Type of Hotel	**Small / Moderate Price**
Date of Original Construction	**1928**
Number of Rooms	**22**
Bars & Restaurants	**None**
Meeting Rooms Number & Size	**1 / 4,000 square feet**
Recreation Facilities	**None**
Type of Renovation	**Conversion from sorority house**
Cost	**$2 million**
Date	**October 1992 - November 1993**
Architect	**Berger Detmer Architects, San Francisco, California**
Interior Designer	**Candra Scott & Associates, San Francisco, California**
Consultants	**Historic Preservation: Randolph Langenbach, Berkeley, California Structural Engineer: Steven Tipping & Associates, Emeryville, California**
Contractor	**Ryan Associates, San Francisco, California**

NOCTURNAL ACTIVITY
By day, few major changes made during the renovation are visible on the exterior of the building. At night, extensive new lighting draws the eye to the features of the street facade (below) and welcomes guests to the main entrance (opposite page).
Photographs by Andrew McKinney.

The former College Women's Club building is a fixture of its neighborhood, dating from the same period as the historic buildings on the University of California campus across the street. Designed by Walter T. Steilberg, a noted California architect, the building had the classic but subtly eclectic design of the golden age of San Francisco Bay Area architecture. Constructed as a university women's club, it had meeting space, a dining room, lounges and sleeping rooms. Developer Martin Ross, whose family had owned the building since the late 1970s, decided to convert the structure into a hotel after a series of other uses which followed the demise of the women's club in 1973. Hospitality offered a higher profit than the likely alternatives, and preservation of the historic aspects of the building offered not only marketable cachet in the history-conscious Bay Area, but ready development approval from city officials and a twenty percent federal tax credit for the cost of the project.

The existing building translated easily into hotel use, except the diminutive sleeping rooms - sized for single visiting scholars in the 1920s, not hotel guests in the 1990s. Reducing the number of guest rooms to allow an increase in room size did not make sense because there were only twenty-two rooms to begin with, and getting approvals for an addition to the building would be very difficult.

IMAGES OF THE EAST
Architect Walter Steilberg incorporated many Chinese influences in the original design of the building, an approach which was continued in the renovation design. The Chinese-inspired guest room furniture was custom-built based on designs originally drawn by Steilberg. The Chinese theme is not overpowering; draperies and bedspreads are damask, and the small chandeliers (not visible) from the 1920s came from a local salvage yard.
Photograph by Andrew McKinney.

UNCERTAINTY OF AGE

The old appearance of the lobby is authentic overall, but many of the individual elements changed in the renovation. The ceiling was disassembled then reinstalled one foot lower following installation of new structural elements and insulation. The furniture is antique, but acquired during the renovation. The chandeliers, original to the building, were rewired and fitted with mica during the renovation. The iron standing lamps have custom shades with Latin calligraphy, giving the room a warm light and an erudite feeling (bottom). Fabrics for the sofas and armchairs are cut-velvets, tapestries and mohair. The lobby is one end of the main meeting room, which is usually vacant when not in use (right).

Renovation photographs by Andrew McKinney.

And sixty-five years after its construction, the building needed a costly update of finishes and systems, so the renovation team did not have the luxury of reconfiguring the interior anyway. The key to making the existing rooms appealing, said architect Miles Berger, was to capitalize on charm, making guests focus on the authenticity of the historic design rather than the size of the rooms.

The visible result of the renovation is a careful retention of original features, with new elements detailed to imitate or complement the existing ones. When building on the eclectic motifs and influences in the building, interior designer Candra Scott avoided the often-revived Arts and Crafts movement and emphasized other ones to distinguish the project from the instant-old-looking buildings popping up like mushrooms in the Bay Area. Guest-room furniture was custom built on previously-unexecuted designs by Steilberg identified by the project team during its research. Steilberg, who collected Chinese antiques and researched and photographed Chinese decorative arts for decades, used Chinese materials and motifs prominently in the building. The renovation continued this theme, commissioning Chinese-style art for the guest rooms and using a Chinese design from the 1930s as the basis for the pattern of the custom Axminster carpeting.

CALIFORNIA CLASSIC
The Bancroft is a good example of the homegrown style of architecture which evolved in California in the early 20th century, mixing elements of the Mediterranean, Classical, and Arts and Crafts styles. Details like the projecting top story and the lattice spandrel panels below the windows make the basically rectangular building look like much more than a box and the variety of balconies make the small rooms seem special (above). The biggest change on the exterior since the early days has been the maturation of the trees and shrubs (facing page).
Renovation photographs by Andrew McKinney.

The basement, which originally housed a cafeteria, was renovated as leased office space. There are new rest rooms and a new coat room in the basement, and the owner hopes to add a restaurant there or possibly on the first floor. New ramps and a wheelchair lift made the basement accessible to the handicapped; additional measures brought the ground floor up to accessibility standards, but the upper two floors of sleeping rooms were not included in the accessibility program because of the lack of space for an elevator and accessible bathrooms. In addition to a new roof and a new coat of paint, exterior work included rebuilding some of the decks and balconies and renewing landscape elements.

The renovation also included much work that is not visible, from a new roof to new foundations, new electrical and plumbing supply systems, plaster and stucco. Most difficult was the seismic upgrade, which necessitated dismantling the coffered ceiling in the main meeting room to allow installation of a new structural diaphragm and steel moment frame. While the ceiling was open, new sound insulation went in, along with new lighting and a new audio system. This subtle camouflage of major changes in the building typifies the approach taken in the renovation, which offers guests the now-trendy club-like atmosphere more by keeping the old look than by adding a new look.

COZY WELCOME
The entry lobby typifies the spare but plastic interpretation of Mediterranean architecture made famous by Julia Morgan, architect of William Randolph Hearst's San Simeon castle. Walter Steilberg, architect of the Bancroft, worked in Morgan's office before starting his own practice. The biggest change made during the renovation was the addition of a custom-pattern carpet.
Renovation photographs by Andrew McKinney.

Hilton Hawaiian Village

Honolulu, Hawaii

For Hilton Hawaiian Village on Honolulu's Waikiki
Beach, with 2,500 guest rooms, 80,000 square feet of
meeting space and more than 75 retail spaces in
about two dozen buildings on 22 acres, renovation is
as routine as laundry. And at this scale, a major
renovation poses almost superhuman challenges:
how to reposition the long-time largest property in
the state, how to coordinate construction in a maze
of buildings ranging from thatched hut to 35-story
high-rise, and how to give a new look to a site where
a motley crew of structures has been accumulating
for 60 years. Enthusiastic after completing the latest
tower on the property and vigilant as they saw luxury
mega-resorts proliferate in Hawaii, co-owners Hilton
Hotel Corporation and Prudential Insurance Company of America decided in 1982 to take on the
challenge of renovating Hilton Hawaiian Village, as
part of an overall $1-billion upgrade program for
existing Hilton properties in the United States.

WATER, WATER EVERYWHERE
*The renovation left the oceanfront Rainbow Tower practically
surrounded by water. The new double "super pool" is in the
foreground, while the Hilton Lagoon is behind the tower to the
right, with the Pacific Ocean and Waikiki Beach beyond.*
Photography by Karen Suenaga for WAT&G.

Name	**Hilton Hawaiian Village**
Location	**Honolulu, Hawaii**
Owner	**Hilton Hotels Corporation**
	Prudential Insurance Company of America
Operator	**Hilton Hotels Corporation**
Type of Hotel	**Resort**
Date of Original Construction	**Pierpont Hotel built in 1920s.**
	Hotel and neighboring cottages incorporated into village in 1954; Hilton operation in 1961.
Number of Rooms	**2,542**
Bars & Restaurants (hotel operated)	**6 restaurants / 10 bars**
Meeting Rooms (Number & Size)	**11 divisible into 33 / 60,464 usable square feet; 82,359 square feet including breakout and outdoor areas**
Recreation Facilities	**Pools, exercise area, gym, spa, ocean beach, private dock with catamaran, submarines and other boats**
Type of Renovation	**Phased, hotel open throughout**
Cost	**$102 million**
Date Construction	**1986-1988**
Architect	**Wimberly Allison Tong & Goo, Honolulu, Hawaii**
Interior Designer	**Public Spaces: Hirsch Bedner & Associates**
	Guest Rooms: Hilton Design Consultants
	Landscape Architect: Woolsey, Miyabara & Associates, Inc.
	Structural Engineer: Martin & Bravo, Inc.
	Mechanical Engineer: Ferris & Hamig Hawaii, Inc.
	Electrical Engineer: Douglas V. MacMahon, Ltd.
	Lighting Design: Grenald Associates
Contractor	**Albert C. Kobayashi, Inc.**

GOOD EVENING AND WELCOME

Guests arriving after dark may not be able to see the Pacific Ocean through the new open-air entry building, but the spectacle they do see is grand. From flaming torches flanking the porte cochere (center, background), through the open-air entry lobby (center), to a lighted fountain in a "lagoon" (foreground), lighting fills in exotic animation lost when the sun sets on the palms and the surf.

Photograph by Augie Salbosa.

The renovation project was appropriately named the Hilton Hawaiian Village Master Plan. It would take four years to design and two years to construct, at a cost of $102 million. Involving demolition, new construction, renovation of existing buildings, landscaping, and site and utility work, the plan was divided into four phases so that the property could remain in operation throughout construction. Definitely a make-over and not an expansion, the project brought a net loss of 37 guest rooms and about 50,000 square feet of building—but it increased open space on the site by 20 percent and transformed standard rooms to luxury. Although the changes run the gamut, there were a few goals which unified the project:

- Add order to the overall property
- Emphasize the beachfront Hawaiian setting in site layout and landscaping
- Improve and expand public spaces and recreation facilities, linking them with food and beverage outlets
- Upgrade the guest rooms, pushing the property's market range higher
- Improve the central lobby and arrival experience

Many of the components of the project fulfilled more than one of these goals, the site layout being the best example. The site is roughly a square, with the west side formed by the ocean and a lagoon dug in the 1950s at the order of industrialist Henry Kaiser, then owner of the hotel. Two guest room towers line the south side, while a seven story garage and conference center building dominates the north side. In between, a fourth guest room tower straddles the shore between the ocean and the lagoon, the center of the site is divided between low buildings and landscaped outdoor areas, and a fourth guest room tower with a low-rise meeting room wing takes up the east end of the site. Kaiser launched the "Hawaiian Village" concept by adding authentic-looking Hawaiian- and Polynesian-style buildings to an existing hotel, but in the following decades, an army of buildings gradually choked off the open space. The variety of sizes, shapes, colors and alignments, compounded by the contrast between the towers and the lower buildings, added up to what the master plan architects, Wimberly Allison Tong and Goo, diplomatically referred to as a mishmash. Arriving guests couldn't even see that the property was on the ocean and got lost in the maze of buildings before reaching the beach.

The site design goal of maximizing openness and the connection with the beach was simple, but the constraints were powerful: the towers and parking garage were too large to demolish or move, while the low buildings between them provided essential retail and restaurant/lounge space—and the Hawaiian village theme itself. The design team had to make the most of the limited demolition which was feasible, so it decided to clear the center of the site, landscape it lavishly, and then make it the nexus of the programmatic elements of the master plan. The site now centers on an open-air one-story entry building constructed on a rise overlooking a 10,000 square foot "super pool" surrounded by stone terraces, gardens and naturalistic fountains, connecting to Waikiki Beach and the Pacific Ocean. Arriving guests can look through the building to the pool and the beach, with views of other landscaped areas on the site to either side. Three new bars and two new restaurants adjoin or overlook the new centerpiece on three sides.

The goal of unifying the property visually meant that the new entry building and other new construction could not be decked out in the thatched-roof garb used decades ago by Kaiser, because of the contrast that they would make with the high-rise buildings. The new construction is simple, somewhat ambiguously modern, with materials and detailing chosen to reinforce the Hawaiian theme, and lots of open-air spaces and heavy landscaping, indoors and out. The landscaping includes 300 kinds of plants, with area fauna ranging from penguins, flamingos, ducks and macaws to ornamental koi carp. The centerpiece of the landscape scheme is the new "super pool," actually two swimming pools surrounded by a stone sunbathing deck, lava grottoes and carp ponds.

The most striking use of the indoor-outdoor concept was in the Rainbow Tower, where the lagoon frontage of the building housed kitchen and laundry facilities before the renovation. The designers removed these back-of-the-house facilities to make room for meeting rooms

CHEESEBURGER IN PARADISE
The most popular restaurant in the renovated hotel is the Rainbow Lanai, an informal three-meal eatery surrounded by a koi pond. It features a buffet breakfast, as well as light fare such as hamburgers and cheeseburgers. The lanai (Hawaiian for porch or deck) adjoins the new "super" pool and the beach, and stretches below the balcony of the fine dining Bali-by-the-Sea restaurant (interior, rear).
Photograph by Augie Salbosa.

CLEARING AWAY CLUTTER
The existing ground level plan of Hilton Hawaiian Village before the renovation shows a handful of major structures along the edges of the site — and a swarm of smaller ones choking off much of the space in between. The ground level Master Plan shows the "super pool" and landscaping made possible by demolition of low buildings in an area strategically located at the center of the property.
Drawings by Wimberly Allison Tong & Goo (WAT&G).

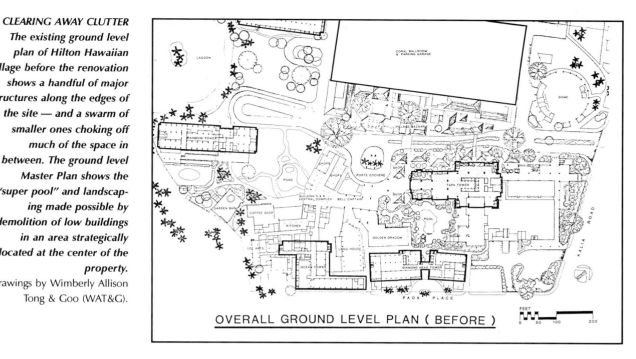

OVERALL GROUND LEVEL PLAN (BEFORE)

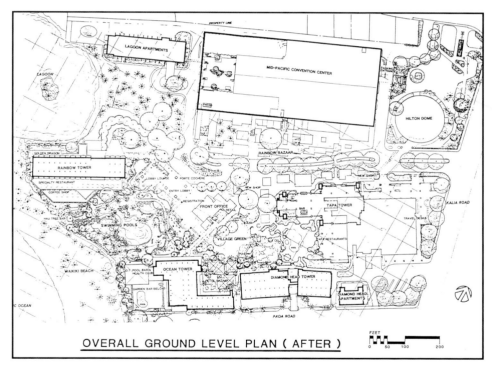

OVERALL GROUND LEVEL PLAN (AFTER)

and the hotel's Cantonese restaurant, the Golden Dragon. On the other side of the building, they extended the bottom two stories of the building to accommodate the fine dining restaurant, Bali-by-the-Sea, and the Rainbow Lanai, a new informal three-meal-a-day restaurant which quickly became the busiest at the property.

While the site design and landscaping concentrated on artfully recasting the property within its existing form, designers faced few restraints in renovating the

Ocean Tower — and stripped it to the bones. Before the renovation, the 300,000 square foot 1956 structure had 282 standard rooms. The makeover added two stories to the guest tower and replaced an adjacent apartment building with a two-story wing housing a bar, a cabaret, a discotheque and a health club with a rooftop pool. The renovation replaced a transmitter penthouse on the tower with two additional guest room floors, added two elevators, removed 14 meeting rooms, and increased the room count to 348.

Renamed Ali'i Tower (Hawaiian for "royalty") and placed in Hilton's top-of-the-market "Towers" product line the building offers guests a separate registration lobby, rooms with marble baths, mini-bars and coffee makers, and exclusive use of the health club and rooftop pool. Two other guest room towers, the 782 guest room, 1967 Rainbow Tower and the 380 guest room, 1960 Diamond Head Tower, were also renovated, with new finishes in rooms and public areas as well as infrastructure upgrades.

SWITCHING BASES

Before the renovation, the bottom floors of the Rainbow Tower had a weak visual connection with the nearby lagoon (foreground, top). The ground floor was almost windowless and housed only back-of-the-house spaces, while the restaurant on the next level looked beyond the lagoon shoreline more than at it. The renovation started by cleaning up the lagoon and planting palm trees along the shore, then extended the building toward it with spaces which draw guests into contact with the water (center, after renovation). The Golden Dragon Restaurant has a large deck for outdoor dining with red pagoda-like shade structures (bottom), while the ground-level meeting rooms below it all open onto the lagoon and a private garden.

Before photo by WAT&G; after photos by Karen Suenaga for WAT&G.

TUNNEL VISION
Sitting on top of six levels of parking garage, the convention center is a long haul from the rest of the property. The escalators which connect it to ground level were formerly hidden in metal-clad enclosures reminiscent of 1970s stadiums (bottom). The renovation replaced those structures with a new enclosure that lets meeting-goers see the light at the end of the tunnel (left). Before photo by WAT&G; after photo by Karen Suenaga for WAT&G.

The hotel's conference center, located above the parking garage, received a major workover of existing function rooms, the pre-function area, and the kitchen. Adjacent garage space was leveled and converted into a 6,000 square foot junior ballroom, the South Pacific, with new adjoining breakout space and meeting rooms. Site infrastructure work included a tie-in to central mechanical and electrical equipment in the Tapa Tower through a new utility loop.

To keep hotel operations running smoothly at 85 percent occupancy during construction, signs and barriers directed guests away from construction areas during each phase. An architectural model, signs, and newsletters kept guests informed about what was happening and why. Management gave guests chocolates and coupon books and threw weekly construction parties with entertainment. Complaints averaged twelve a day. Individual guests were not notified in advance of the renovation; groups were warned. One group insisted on management stopping construction during its one-week stay.

The physical renovation was accompanied by a revision of the rest of the property's product. To bolster its Hawaiian theme, the hotel recruited native Hawaiian artisans and crafts specialists to work in residence on site, and instituted a Hawaiian culture training program for its employees.

Management pronounced the completed renovation a success — and followed up with the predictable sequel: a major expansion. Wimberly Allison Tong and Goo received the commission to study where a new tower could be located to build the site out to the floor area ratio allowed by planning regulations for Waikiki. They recommended replacing the 1957 geodesic showroom dome with a 25-story, 400 room tower tailored for the business travel market. The hotel also

embarked on design and state approvals for building a man-made reef to turn the lagoon into a tropical snorkeling area. Hilton adopted "Return to Paradise" as its theme in marketing the Master Plan Renovation to guests, but for management and its designers, the renovation work week in paradise always seems to last seven days.

ROOFSCAPE TO LANDSCAPE

Before the renovation, the beachfront Ocean Tower was hemmed in by a clutter of low buildings which choked most of the center of the property and made guests walk a labyrinthe to find the beach. The Ocean Tower (above) had an assortment of air-conditioning gear and a television transmission station and antenna on its roof — all in plain view from the balconies of the other three towers on the property. The renovation started by demolishing the low buildings, added the "super" pool (center) and copious landscaping, and then gutted the tower and renamed it the Ali'i Tower, complete with private sundeck and pool. The renovation cleared mechanical equipment off roofs as part of an effort to improve the views from upper story hotel rooms throughout Waikiki Beach.

Before photo by WAT&G; after photo by Karen Suenaga for WAT&G.

Hotel Vintage Plaza
Portland, Oregon

Bill Kimpton became the best known innovator in San Francisco hospitality by buying small hotels in the center of that city, renovating each one with luxury touches and a relaxed, individual flavor, and offering competitive prices. When he began his expansion to Portland, Oregon, with a century-old downtown hotel, he hardly had to worry about differentiating it from his other properties. The building had been gutted and rehabbed into speculative office space almost a generation earlier, leaving the top floor ringed with sloping greenhouse windows and a modern atrium rising from the ground floor lobby to the roof.

Name	**Hotel Vintage Plaza**
Location	**Portland, Oregon**
Owner	**Portland Hotel Associates**
Operator	**Kimpton Hotel & Restaurant Group, Inc.**
Type of Hotel	**Boutique**
Date of Original Construction	**1894**
Number of Rooms	**107**
Bars & Restaurants	**Pazzo Restaurant**
Meeting Rooms (Number & Size)	**7 divisible into 9 / 4,000 square feet**
Recreation Facilities	**Exercise room with exercise cycles, step machine, rowing machine**
Type of Renovation	**Conversion from unfinished speculative office rehab of original hotel building**
Cost	**$14 million**
Date Reopened	**May, 1991**
Interior Designer	**Hotel: Nan Rosenblatt Interior Design, San Francisco, California** **Restaurant: Ron Leiberman, Design Development Co., Tarzana, California**
Consultants	**Mechanical Engineer: Tom Gilbertson and Associates, Moraga, California**
Contractor	**Baugh Construction, Portland, Oregon**

OUTWARDLY UNCHANGED
The renovation gutted the interior of the building, but kept the exterior in its historic condition—with the temporary addition of a rather noticeable announcement of the hotel's arrival.
Photograph by John Vaughn.

CORPORATE PERK
Kimpton Group requires a wood-burning fireplace in
every hotel lobby. The fireplace subtly reinforces the
wine theme through the color of its marble facing
and the floral relief over the mantel.
Photograph by John Vaughn.

Kimpton chose a wine theme to celebrate Oregon's growing stature in viticulture. A wine cellar would be installed in the lobby and each guest room would be named after an Oregon winery. All that remained was to flesh out the interior of the building to fit the Kimpton vision. Unfortunately, the one specific requirement for the lobby in Kimpton's credo of generous, but unstuffy, classical design is a wood-burning fireplace — not an atrium.

"That was our first challenge," said interior designer Nan Rosenblatt, who had already renovated several San Francisco Kimpton hotels when she took on the Portland property. Although the project called for gutting interior partitions throughout, the exterior envelope and the atrium had to stay. Her mission was to accommodate the traditional, comfortable look of a Kimpton hotel within the shell, complete with atrium and greenhouse windows.

The skylit atrium opens onto every floor of the building, and the designers decided to take advantage of its light without spending a fortune trying to remake it into a more conventional space. They painted everything in the same color, including the wall sconces and railings, and then added a mass of plants to soften the space. The atrium posed a particular challenge at the lobby, which the Kimpton approach always details with a comfortable "living room." To create warmth and intimacy, Rosenblatt created two sitting areas, one oriented to the fireplace and one to a music area where a pianist plays a baby grand. Both turn their backs on the atrium, allowing guests to enjoy the light without looking at the towering, modern space itself.

The previous renovations of the building also complicated the meeting space design. There, windows spanning between two floors presented a challenge, exposing the legs and knees of those trying to do business to the view of passersby.

SIDE ATTRACTION

Kimpton hotels stress lots of amenities in an easy-going, tried-and-true atmosphere, not sleek styling and dazzling, soaring spaces. Instead of focusing the new lobby on this existing atrium, the renovation left it in place but directed guests' attention elsewhere. Filled with plants, the atrium brings natural light to all floors of the hotel, but is not its symbolic center. Before the renovation, the atrium had several colors and contrasting railings (left). The entire space was painted out white in the renovation to make it more harmonious with the traditional flavor of the hotel.

Pre-renovation photo by Kimpton Hotel and Restaurant Group, Inc. Renovation photograph by John Vaughn.

Rosenblatt used Roman shades and draw drapes to frame the windows more conventionally while allowing their exterior appearance to remain the same.

On the guest room floors, the constraints of the building and the Kimpton quest to avoid the ordinary added up to what Rosenblatt called "three hotels in one." At the top floor, the existing greenhouse windows were left in place, and nine special "Starlight" rooms were designed to fit under them. Although the rooms are no larger than the standard ones on lower floors, the dramatic sloping glass which forms most of their exterior walls gives them the atmosphere of a penthouse or a skybox. Kimpton also created nine "townhouse" suites, each two stories high with a private stair. There is a living room and powder room on the lower level and a bedroom and bath on the upper floor. The floors containing the "Starlight" and "Townhouse" accommodations are fitted out as "concierge levels," with their own living room, wine tastings, and concierge service.

Like all Kimpton hotels, the property includes a restaurant with its own identity which is operated separately from the hotel. As it commonly does, Kimpton Group hired a different designer for the restaurant, and later hired a high-profile executive chef to launch the operation. Designer Ron Leiberman gave Pazzo Ristorante a wine cellar theme, with large wood shelves along the perimeter display-ing the wine stock, topped by ornamental glass and ceramic wine jugs and bottles. A pyramid of wood fermenting casks and hams hanging to cure add to the theme. Shallow arches in the ceiling suggest a stone structure, while earth tone colors and area rugs build on the informal flavor with a touch of the rustic.

MAKE YOURSELF AT HOME
A Kimpton trademark is "living rooms" instead of lounges and lobbies, with informal furniture intended to coax guests into using the spaces to relax. As an added incentive, the operator serves wine each afternoon in this club level lounge.
Photograph by John Vaughn.

GETTING DOWN TO BUSINESS
In addition to appealing to the boutique market, the Vintage Plaza includes seven meeting rooms to accommodate conventional hotel business. This board room is one of two in the property.
Photograph by John Vaughn.

GUTTED TWICE
Although the building was originally a hotel, it was gutted and partially rehabbed as speculative office space, but never occupied, before the renovation began.
Photograph by Kimpton Hotel and Restaurant Group, Inc.

HOUSE VINTAGE
Standard room sizes and shapes vary as dictated by the building configuration. Color themes are based on hunter green, deep plum, cerise, taupe and gold, with rope medallion patterned fabric. They include granite night stands and chests, honor bar and refrigerator, hair dryers, daily newspaper and free shoe shine.
Photograph by John Vaughn.

AERIE VARIATION
Existing greenhouse windows at the perimeter of the top floor inspired the "Starlight" rooms, with light paints and fabrics, white case goods and rattan furniture. The rooms have deluxe baths with whirlpool tubs.
Photograph by John Vaughn.

UPSTAIRS DOWNSTAIRS
The two-story "Townhouse" suites have the same case goods as the standard rooms, but the rest of their design is special. To develop the winery theme, colors are based on chardonnay grapes, cabernet grapes on a black ground and burgundy. The suites, which feature a sitting room (bottom) with stairs up to a bedroom (top), also have more accessories than the standard rooms.
Photographs by John Vaughn.

The Governor Hotel
Portland, Oregon

The lobby of the Governor Hotel features a huge mural commissioned for the renovation, picturing the early 19th century expedition of Lewis and Clark through uncharted wonders of North America. The voyage of the hotel property from its beginning 100 years after Lewis and Clark up to the 1992 renovation was similar in some ways, and almost as exotic. It started with two luxurious buildings in the early 20th century, led to decline so bad one of the buildings was used as the location for an abandoned building scene in a movie, and culminated with a one-year-long renovation creating a luxury property.

HISTORICAL FIGURES
Some of the figures in the lobby mural are larger than life-size; scenes depict sites throughout the state. The mural painter retraced the Lewis andClark route through Oregon to research sites, fauna and flora and historic clothing and tools. She also traveled to New York to study the palette used in a 1930s Works Progress Administration-style mural in Rockefeller Center.
Photograph by Langdon Clay.

Name	The Governor Hotel
Location	Portland, Oregon
Owner	The Governor Hotel Associates
Operator	Salishan Lodge
Type of Hotel	Luxury
Date of Original Construction	1909
Number of Rooms	100
Bars & Restaurants	One each
Meeting Rooms (Number & Size)	9 / 14,000 square feet
Recreation Facilities	Exercise machines, lap pool, indoor track, steam room, whirlpool
Type of Renovation	Hotel shut down during renovation
Cost	$15 million
Date	1991-1992
Architect	Stastny & Burke; Architecture, Portland, Oregon
Interior Designer	Candra Scott and Associates, San Francisco, California
Consultants	Historic Consultant: Heritage Investment Corp., Portland, Oregon; Kitchen Consultant: Allan King and Friends, Reno, Nevada; Structural Engineer: KPFF, Portland, Oregon
Contractor	P & C Construction Co., Gresham, Oregon
Masonry Restoration	Pioneer Waterproofing Company, Portland, Oregon

ALL ROADS LEAD TO OREGON

The design of the lobby is pure Oregon, but the sources cover a lot more territory. The carpet was custom made in England to match the original one found in the hotel, with the pattern enlarged and the colors changed to the palette used in the renovation. The 60-foot mural depicting the expedition of Lewis and Clark was painted on canvas in California by artist Melinda Morey. The pendant light fixtures, originally from a hotel in Los Angeles, came from a New York salvage dealer. The round table in the foreground was custom made for the project; its surface is a radial-keyed veneer designed to look like the end-grain of a log; the drawer faces are studded leather and the pulls are hand made metal birds' heads.

Photograph by Langdon Clay.

FREQUENT GUEST
The standard wall sconce for the renovation was based on an art deco original that interior designer Candra Scott obtained from a San Francisco lighting fixture company. She had the face cast for reproduction, added the mica headdress panels, and applied a faux-bronze finish.
Photograph by Langdon Clay.

FAMILIAR FACE
The Indian head relief on each side of the fireplace was inspired by the custom wall sconces made for the renovation project. The image is not original to the hotel, but its repetition unifies the interior and emphasizes the made-to-order character of the interior.
Photograph by Langdon Clay.

BAR MIX
The bar illustrates the eclectic sources of the hotel interior and the predominant color theme of the public spaces. The focal photograph behind the bar shows an American Indian dancing in front of a Chinese dragon; this cultural match continues in the hotel's signature Indian head wall sconces and the backlit Chinese ceramic grilles under the bar.
Photograph by Langdon Clay.

The Governor Hotel, originally known as the Seward Hotel, was built in 1909 following a tourist boom in Portland set off by the 1905 Lewis and Clark Exposition. Designed by William C. Knighton, a local architect who was appointed State Architect by Governor Oswald West, the gray terra cotta building is ornamented with blue and off-white relief blocks in elaborate anthropomorphic forms which appear to synthesize contemporary European and Pre-Columbian motifs. The renovated hotel is far larger than the original structure, thanks to the annexation of the adjacent historic Princeton Building, which was constructed as the Portland Elks Temple, modeled after the Renaissance architectural monument Palazzo Farnese in Rome. The original Seward-Governor building is now known as the west wing and the Princeton Building is called the east wing.

Connected on the ground floor only, the two buildings are different in function and style. The renovation project originally involved only the Governor Building, but an unfortunate delay in financing the project had the fortunate effect of adding the Princeton Building to the

KEEPING UP APPEARANCES

The renovation included dramatic lighting for the exterior of the building, along with restoration of some of the ground floor store fronts, which had been removed during the property's earlier decline. Exterior improvements also included removal of metal fire escapes, cleaning brick and terra cotta, restoring the entry canopy and installing new awnings.

Photograph by Langdon Clay.

project after design was already under way. The designers linked the buildings, but did not try to make them look or function as if they had always been united. The meeting and banquet space is concentrated in the east wing and the lobby and most of the guest rooms are in the west wing.

Although both are listed on the National Register of Historic Places, the west wing is a vernacular interpretation of the Vienna Secessionist movement while the east wing is by-the-book Renaissance. The east wing is an American social palace typical of its early 1920s era, with ceilings as high as 33 feet, an 80-foot long banquet hall with white and gold Sienna marble, marble columns and huge fireplaces. Largely intact, it posed no design quandry to the renovation team, which limited changes to restoration tasks like replacing damaged paint and plaster.

The west wing was in relatively good condition on the exterior, but the interior was outmoded, deteriorated and, because of previous retail conversions, very disjointed. The upper floors were to be gutted and the ground floor reconfigured, leaving the interior a bare armature. To flesh it out with a distinct character and personality, interior designer Candra Scott of San Francisco studied the original design of the hotel and the history and wildlife of her native Oregon. Instead of bright colors and a formal look, she chose a palette based on autumnal Oregon with rich, warm golds, persimmons and greens. Some elements of the original design, such as the signature geometric bell-motif medallion and the carpet pattern, were replicated with little or no change. Where research uncovered designs unappealing to

NEW DINING VENUE
The new restaurant occupies the former location of the lobby. The space retains its original mahogany paneling, casework and ceiling, all stripped and refinished (left). Ground floor public spaces were reconfigured extensively for retail use and natural wood detailing was painted out after the hotel's decline in the Great Depression (bottom).
Before photograph by Stastny and Burke; renovation photograph by John Hughel.

eyes of today's market — there were only rocking chairs in the original lobby — Scott added her own intentionally eclectic mix of Oregon vernacular, Craftsman, chinoiserie, Adirondack, Native American, and demolition salvage.

On the ground floor, the mahogany-paneled lobby with a wood-burning fireplace looks like as if it had been sympathetically reworked during the renovation, but it is actually a newly created space. The original lobby is now the restaurant. Guest room floors, although completely gutted and reconfigured, respect the location of the original windows (many of which were restored) and include fireplaces in many rooms, even though the original hotel did not have them. The entire west wing has all-new building systems and elevators.

The top two floors of the east wing, which were gutted and marketed unsuccessfully as speculative office space in the 1985 renovation of that building, were re-gutted and renovated as guest room floors along with the upper stories of the west wing. The remaining floors of the east wing, originally the social function rooms of the Elks Temple, were restored for use as meeting rooms. Both buildings needed a seismic upgrade, which was straightforward in the gutted west wing but required extra design effort in the east wing, where historic interiors could not easily be disturbed for structural work.

ROOM FOR CHANGE
The original guest rooms were not grandiose by today's standards — many did not have private baths. Years of economic decline added a thick layer of shabbiness to the spartan base by the time of the renovation, which started with full interior demolition (below). The color palettes in the new guest rooms are a lighter version of the lobby colors, wheat, sage, and soft browns. The casings and moldings replicate the original ones in the building.
Before photograph by Stastny & Burke; renovation photograph by Langdon Clay.

IN THE HALLWAYS OF POWER AND PRESTIGE
When it opened in the 1920s, the Elks Temple was designed to give Portland a meeting place worthy of Europe's aristocracy. The grand spaces, restored in 1985 and touched up again in 1992, are now available as hotel meeting space. Each room has a distinct style and special materials (clockwise from bottom left): the ballroom ceiling has caricatures of Elks Club personalities painted in and between the lunettes; a typical hallway leading to the meeting rooms has a two-color marble floor and a barrel-vaulted ceiling with ornate detail; another meeting room features elaborate classical columns; and the rich wood shelves, paneling and coffered ceiling remain in the former library.
Bottom left photograph by Langdon Clay, others by John Hughel.

PARTY CRASHER

Business displaces pleasure where a ballroom was converted to office space. The original Elks Temple had six floors, most of them double-height social spaces. This floor, originally a ballroom, was converted for office use in the 1980s with the insertion of a two-story office pavilion, which was retained in the 1992 hotel renovation as the hotel business center. Merry-makers need not worry: most of the other gathering spaces of the original Elks Temple were retained as meeting and banquet rooms.

Photograph by John Hughel.

The St. Regis

New York, New York

John Jacob Astor commissioned New York
architects Trowbridge and Livingston to
make his St. Regis Hotel the ultimate
statement of European opulence and
classical design. By contemporary ac-
counts, his beaux-arts property on Fifth
Avenue met that goal when it opened in
1904. An addition in 1927 made the great
hotel larger, but not necessarily grander,
and subsequent renovations only left the
marks of time, not a classical patina, on
the building. At the top of New York's
hotel market, past glory is a plus, but
perfection in the present is must.

BRIGHT NEW FACE ON A BELOVED LANDMARK
*Exterior changes were minimal, stressing repair and preservation
of the building, which is a New York City landmark. Dramatic
new exterior lighting showcases the termination of the limestone-
clad beaux-arts facade. Fixtures had to be carefully concealed on
balconies and other unobtrusive locations. The St. Regis towered
above its neighborhood when it was completed in 1904, but at
eighteen stories it is dwarfed by today's Manhattan hotels.*
Photograph by Anthony P. Albarello.

Name	*The St. Regis*
Location	*New York, New York*
Owner	*ITT Sheraton Corporation*
Operator	*ITT Sheraton Corporation*
Type of Hotel	*Luxury*
Date of Original Construction	*1904 / Wing Added 1927*
Number of Rooms	*313*
Bars & Restaurants	*Astor Court* *King Cole Bar and Lounge* *Lespinasse*
Meeting Rooms *(Number & Size)*	*20 / 15,185 square feet*
Recreation Facilities	*Exercise machines, massage room, sauna*
Type of Renovation	*Gutting and interior reconstruction* *Hotel shut down for 3 years*
Cost	*$100 million-plus*
Date	*Fall 1988 - September 1991*
Architect	*Brennan Beer Gorman Monk / Architects,* *New York*
Interior Design	*Brennan Beer Gorman Monk / Interiors,* *New York* *Graham Design, Woburn, Massachusetts* *ITT Sheraton Corp.*
Consultants	*Structural Engineer: DeSimone,* *Chaplin & Dobryn Consulting Engineers* *Mechanical Engineer: Flack & Kurtz* *Consulting Engineers* *Lighting: Theo Kondos Associates*
Contractor	*Tishman Construction Co., Inc.*

NEW YORK'S FINEST
During the renovation, inquiries about the hotel from New Yorkers centered on three features, according to project manager Gustin Tan: the lobby, the St. Regis Roof — and the barber shop. The last element, Fodera Hair Stylists, occupies a new space on the lower level.
Photograph by Anthony P. Albarello.

SEEKING A CENTER

The strengthened organization of the public spaces on the ground floor of the 1927 wing pivots around a new public space, the Astor Court, which connects the King Cole Bar, the Lespinasse restaurant, and the new entry lobby. Marble columns and gilded composite-order Roman capitals and entablature, a trompe-l'oeil painted sky on the ceiling, and a classical Maria Theresa crystal and bronze chandelier make the space grand, but the effect is not harsh, thanks to the soft, creamy tone of the painted plaster surfaces and the marble flooring. The original hotel's design is recalled in varietal furniture with strains of French 19th-century beaux-arts and Louis XVI styles.
Photograph by Anthony P. Albarello.

CLEAR ILLUSION

The new Astor Court is intended to recreate the spirit of the great art glass ceiling which the original 1904 hotel contained but lost years before the renovation. Classical columns with mythical-looking paintings in the entablature frieze and a crystal chandelier suggest the glory of yesteryear in a space which was actually created only yesterday.
Photograph by Anthony P. Albarello.

ELEGANCE AT EASE

In the Cognac Room between the reception lobby and new entry lobby, designers restored the original marble fireplace, mahogany paneling, gold leaf plaster moldings and vaulted ceiling, adding silk damask draperies to create a palatial atmosphere worthy of a robber baron. French chairs and sofa with tapestry-patterned upholstery reinforce the richness but soften the formality of the space enough to encourage late 20th-century guests to make themselves at home.

Photograph by Anthony P. Albarello.

ARTISTIC SPIRITS

"Old King Cole" painted by Maxfield Parrish in 1906 had been a resident at the St. Regis since 1935, reigning over the main restaurant and bar before the renovation. Creation of the more formal Lespinasse restaurant called for a separate space for the painting, which had originally hung in the bar at the Knickerbocker Hotel. The new King Cole Bar is located in what was a service and retail area before the renovation. The 8 foot by 29 foot mural dominates the bar. Visible through glass doors to Astor Court, it serves as the visual terminus of the new spatial axis of the ground floor. Cherrywood paneling and fabric and carpet colors reinforce the warm hues in the painting, while Tuscan pilasters next to the mural mirror those inside it. Simplified but exaggerated molding profiles strengthen the masculine flavor of the space and stand out in the intimate penumbra which contrasts with the strong lighting on the painting.

Photograph by Anthony P. Albarello.

WELCOME CHANGE
Where the florist shop existed before the renovation, a new entrance from 55th Street with marble flooring, a French console and elaborate torchieres gives the ground floor an opulent sense of spaciousness. The floral fabrics and plush upholstery in the adjacent sitting area soften the formality enough to make mortal guests linger.
Photographs by Anthony P. Albarello.

ITT Sheraton, which had operated the hotel since 1966 and became owner in 1988, vowed to regain Astor's vision when it retained Brennan Beer Gorman / Architects and Brennan Beer Gorman Monk / Interiors of New York as renovation designers in 1988. The key, according to Gustin Tan, project manager for interior architecture, was to embody "the good, old tradition, so it would never go out of fashion," avoiding like the plague any touches which would prompt guests in 1998 to see a "1980s look" in the property.

Interestingly, if Astor were alive today, he would barely recognize the interior of the hotel, despite the praise of guests and critics who think it has been carefully restored to its original condition. Except

for parts of the first two floors, the whole building was gutted and reconfigured. Guest rooms grew in size and shrank in number from 557 to 313, circulation and building systems improved and a host of odd construction configurations and design statements which had accumulated over the years disappeared.

Old friends who swear the building hasn't changed can be forgiven: the renovation did restore some of the most significant spaces without changing them much. The lobby and second floor meeting rooms in the original part of the building were restored, and the ambience of the famous St. Regis Roof ballroom and the barber shop, two other features dear to New

Yorkers, were carefully preserved, while the rest of the building was recreated in its original spirit, if not in its exact image.

The renovation replaced three ground floor retail slots with a new entry and sitting area, tying these and adjacent reconfigured bar and restaurant spaces into a unified order with a new double-height court. The new space, Astor Court, was intended to evoke the original hotel's famous Palm Court. The original court's stained-glass ceiling had a Belle Époque air of Paris, while the new one suggests a more 17th-century France, with classical marble columns, gilded capitals, and a trompe-l'oeil painted sky on the ceiling.

ATTENTION TO DETAILS
Restoration of the lobby included preservation of the details like the ornate revolving door (left) which gave the hotel its original beaux-arts appeal when it opened in 1904. The brass letter box and mail chute (above) have outlived the four-cent stamp, and will undoubtedly survive longer than the 32-cent version after their restoration.
Photographs by Anthony P. Albarello.

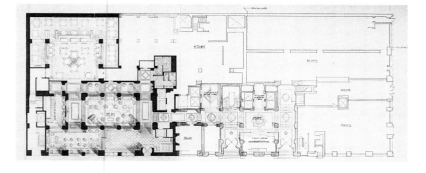

SUBTLE CHANGES
Slight rearrangements in the lobby, such as moving the concierge desk, required major effort. The architect traveled three times to Italy to match the existing floor marble in areas exposed for the first time because of changes.
Photographs by Anthony P. Albarello.

QUIET EXTRAVAGANCE
ITT Sheraton decided to
position the new fine
dining restaurant,
Lespinasse, boldly at the
high end of New York
restaurant market. In an
age where catering to
conspicuous consumption
can be a risky business,
the designers stressed
precision and elegance,
but not decadence, in
creating an 18th-century
French dining room. The
same creamy hues used in
the adjacent Astor Court
add softness to the spare
and exacting classical
detailing which was
incorporated to insure
the character of the room
against eventual rear-
rangement and replace-
ment of furniture fabrics
and artwork. Gold leaf
and mirror panels accent
the space without
overwhelming it.
Photographs by
Anthony P. Albarello.

New meeting rooms on the second floor of the 1927 wing are grouped around a double-height pre-function area created by removing a mezzanine slab. The corridors on guest room floors were moved to allow five-fixture bathrooms to be located uniformly on the hallway side of the rooms, with each element in the rooms laid out with classical balance and order to make the design look "as inevitable as possible," according to Tan.

In addition to all-new back-of-the-house areas, the project incorporated new circulation features even where the original design did not change. Two new elevators take guests from the lobby directly to the St. Regis Roof ballroom,

keeping them out of the four guest room floor elevators, which handled all upper floors before the renovation. Handicapped accessibility was achieved through installation of wheelchair lifts between areas on different levels within a single floor, because ramps were not compatible with the style of the building. The new large express elevators to the ballroom stop on guest room floors when activated by a key for the handicapped.

ADDED CACHET

The Fontainbleau Suite in the 1927 wing is a completely new room, created by demolition of a mezzanine above the second floor level to allow a double-height ceiling. Plaster moldings, gold leaf and chandeliers and sconces (detail, right) similar to the ones in the original 1904 ballrooms made the new meeting rooms so successful after the reopening that unfinished space in the basement was later reconfigured to create two more new suites, the Maisonette and the Iridium.

Photographs by Anthony P. Albarello.

BREAKFAST AT TIFFANY'S
The renovated hotel features three unique specialty suites, one designed by Christian Dior, and another by John Loring, design director of Tiffany & Co. The dining room of the suite Loring designed is inspired by London clubs of the era of the construction of the St. Regis. The hotel's other suites proved so popular after the reopening that alterations have been undertaken to convert regular corner guest rooms on each floor into suites.
Photograph by Anthony P. Albarello.

HEIGHT OF ELEGANCE
The St. Regis Roof ballroom, located at the top of the building and near the top of New York Society's food chain, was subtly reworked as part of the renovation. The cloud-painted ceiling replaces an earlier solid-color canopy; the French curves of the cove around the ceiling hide ventilation and other utilitarian gear. While restraint was the watchword in decorating lower public spaces, extravagance was the order of the day in the ballroom, with lavish draperies, applied decoration, painted vaults, and crystal chandeliers.
Photograph by
Anthony P. Albarello.

weren't even hotel luxuries when the century began but have become necessities as it comes to an end: a business center and a fitness center. Both are located on the new "lower level" in what used to be the basement, which has been upgraded with new circulation spaces, the barber shop, and two meeting rooms. The business center has office machines, a reception area and a private office for guests. The nearby fitness center includes a good-sized room with exercise machines, a massage room, a sauna and changing rooms.

SLIGHT CHANGE OF VENUE
The Versailles Ballroom (abowe) and the Louis XVI Suite (left) were not gutted during the renovation. The popular reception spaces on the second floor of the original 1904 section of the building did receive new mechanical, audio-visual and life-safety systems along with a complete refurbishment of their finishes.
Photographs by Anthony P. Albarello.

CLASSICAL COMPOSITION
Guest rooms have tie-back draperies, Louis XV and Louis XVI furniture, crystal chandeliers, and painstaking coordination of architecture, fixtures and furniture. If the basic elements of 18th century millwork are interpreted with strength and simplicity, "then a room will at least have 'good bones' and shouldn't need gilded spaghetti to make it look elegant," according to designer Jinnie Kim of Graham Design. Room features are coordinated so that guests don't enter on the sidewall of a room or look up from their beds at the edge of a sofa. Color schemes are based on palettes of muted blue or green, silver and blue, or ruby red.
Photographs by Anthony P. Albarello.

MARBLE, MARBLE EVERYWHERE
All bathrooms have five fixtures, including two sinks in a marble countertop, a tub with marble surround, a toilet room, and a separate shower stall. When ITT Sheraton opted for the bathroom upgrade during the design process, architects had to go back to their drawing boards and gut all guest room floors and move corridors to accommodate the change.
Photographs by Anthony P. Albarello.

The Broadway American Hotel

New York, New York

When the years have blurred the appeal of an old building into grime-covered blandness, a limited-budget renovation design might reconfigure the most outmoded rooms or floors to current standards, replace the most damaged systems and building fabric, and then refinish everything in a fresh but not too daring style. New York architect Manuel Castedo took a very different tack in renovating a twelve-story hotel on Manhattan's West Side. He inserted eye-catching new walls and ceilings to reconfigure major public spaces, leaving cut-outs to expose remnants of the original building and its plaster detailing. The new elements are figural, rectilinear and graphic, an intentional contrast with the old. And eschewing the conventional approach of treating the whole building uniformly, the renovation team left guest-room floor layouts intact, allowing a higher budget for public spaces and items which see a lot of wear.

FINER THINGS
The decision to retain guest room floor layouts allowed the renovation designers to devote more money to areas guests see most, such as these service counters in the outer lobby.
Photograph by Ashod Kassabian.

Name	*The Broadway American Hotel*
Location	*New York, New York*
Owner	*Benjamin Franklin Associates*
Operator	*Benjamin Franklin Associates*
Type of Hotel	*European-style Economy*
Date of Original Construction	*1919*
Number of Rooms	*400*
Bars & Restaurants	*None*
Meeting Rooms (Number & Size)	*None*
Recreation Facilities	*None*
Type of Renovation	*Phased, hotel open during construction*
Cost	*$10 million*
Date	*1990-1992*
Architect	*M. Castedo Architect, New York*
Interior Designer	*M. Castedo Architect, New York*
Consultants	*Mechanical, Electrical and Plumbing Engineers: Peter Franzese and John Taylor, New York*
Construction Manager	*TFC Associates, New York*

The building, originally constructed as a luxury apartment house, had been converted to a single room occupancy hotel many years before the renovation, leaving only scattered traces of its grand beginnings. There were ten different guest room configurations, some without private baths. The team decided not to pitch the property at the standard hotel market, but to gear it instead to foreign travelers willing to trade the amenities of mainstream digs for something with an offbeat flavor—and low rates. That created crucial room within the construction budget, which was already tight because of exterior work, new high-speed elevators, and replacement of plumbing and electrical systems.

The ground floor was reconfigured completely, with new interiors which belie the budget limitations. Floors in the entry area are honed granite, woodwork is American cherry, and original artwork was commissioned from a New York artist for the project. The interior design bears out the hotel's name by emphasizing its American character to give foreign guests something they don't get in other countries—or at other hotels.

OUTWARD SIGNS
Changes to the brick and limestone exterior of the building were relatively limited. New store fronts and awnings spruced up ground floor commercial space (above). At the hotel entrance, a simple canopy was added to the existing black granite entry. Despite this restrained design, even passersby get a hint of the new interior when they see the star-spangled wood podium and backlit glass wall behind it (left).
Photographs by Ashod Kassabian.

On the guest room floors, the renovation team put its efforts and budget into making rooms attractive and durable. All guest room furniture was custom designed, with emphasis on daring and enduring construction. Bathroom walls are tiled and the ceiling and fixtures are heavy-duty; bedspreads are custom made by an elevator protection pad manufacturer, and wall paint is crisp-looking Zolatone multicolor splatter, which also happens to hide dirt and wear better than a solid color.

Castedo said his design goal was to promote New York and the Broadway American in a playful manner. It's impossible to predict guests' senses of humor or their reaction to the entire city, but it seems a fair bet that they will remember this hotel as different from the rest.

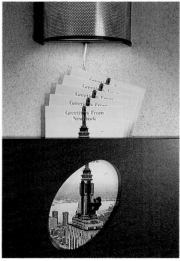

BEDTIME COMPANION
Renovated guest rooms have soft uplighting and blue and gray color schemes to soothe guests after experiencing the stimulating lobby and city outside. Those seeking excitement need look only as far as the cutouts in the custom headboards. Greeting them from this vantage point is none other than King Kong. Postcards of his visit to the Empire State Building are displayed for guests' use, aimed at promoting the hotel and New York in a lighthearted way.
Photograph by Ashod Kassabian.

LAYERS OF EXPOSURE
Although the renovation reconfigured ground floor spaces, it did not eliminate all traces of the original design. Large figural openings in the new ceiling reveal the original ceiling and double as indirect lighting sources. (view from opposite ends of lobby, below left and right). The back-lit glass wall grid brightens the space the way windows onto a courtyard would; guests who take a closer look at the small glass hemispheres in the wall panels find they are windows which reveal photographs of New York landmarks like the Empire State Building (top, left). The colors and pattern of the painting at one end of the lobby reappear in the carpet layout.
Photographs by Ashod Kassabian.

Essex House
New York, New York

"Everything You Remember. And More," was the promise Japan Air Lines subsidiary Nikko Hotels International gave New Yorkers when it bought the Essex House from Marriott in 1985 and launched a major renovation. The new owners hired interior designer Pierre Yves Rochon of Paris and architects Brennan Beer Gorman of New York, instructing them to recreate the spirit of the original 1931 hotel rather than replicate it to the letter. Once a landmark of 1930s design and a major venue of the New York entertainment world, the Essex House had lost its focus over the years, becoming an architectural muddle and a slightly dimmed star in the constellation of New York hotels.

ART DECO IMAGE
The original design of the Essex House was an Art Deco composition visually characteristic of New York between World War I and II. The renovation capitalized on the image of the original exterior of the building as a towering advertisement of the hotel's prestige in New York's history. The exterior received a cleaning, the details were regilded, a new entrance marquise compatible with the rest of the exterior was installed, and dramatic lighting increased the effect at night. The building has a prime location at the foot of Central Park, and is a familiar monument on the skyline
Photographs: (facing page, top) by Peter Vitale, above by Maury Englander.

Name	**Essex House Hotel Nikko New York**
Location	**New York, New York**
Owner	**Nikko Hotels International**
Operator	**Nikko Hotels (USA)**
Type of Hotel	**Luxury**
Date of Original Construction	**1931**
Number of Rooms & Suites	**595**
Bars & Restaurants	**1 bar / 2 restaurants**
Meeting Rooms (Number & Size)	**8 / 11,211 square feet**
Recreation Facilities	**Exercise machines, freeweights, steam room, footbath room, sauna, "therapy" showers, locker rooms, health and beauty treatment rooms**
Type of Renovation	**Hotel closed, complete interior renovation**
Cost	**$175 million**
Date	**January 1990 - October 1991**
Architect	**Brennan Beer Gorman, New York**
Interior Designer	**Pierre Yves Rochon, Paris**
Construction Manager	**Tishman Construction, New York**

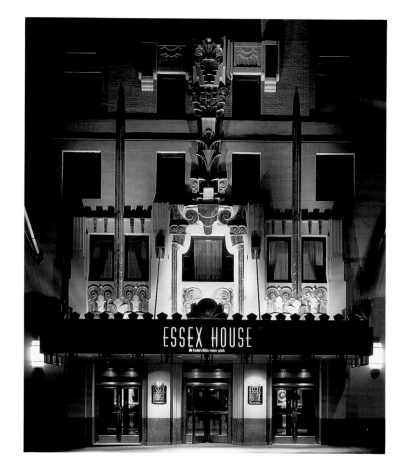

DON'T ASK ITS AGE *The new lobby looks like a restoration of the "original" Art Deco space, although in fact only the hand-crafted bronze elevator doors are original. Square black marble columns with Deco fluting (right rear corner), etched glass and metal consoles and grilles look like restorations of original elements from the 1930s, while furniture, lamps, objets d'art and a pair of Gatsby-style paintings cover a wider, more ambiguous, range suggesting an Art Deco space which has been carefully seasoned to maturity over the decades.* Photograph by Peter Vitale.

NO HO-HUM HOTEL RESTAURANT
Les Celebrités, the 55-seat fine dining restaurant created in the renovation, is not a reworking of an original operation, it is a total original in itself.
Photograph by Peter Vitale.

ROUND TRIP
Before the renovation, the lobby of the Essex House had an English club look, adjoined by a nautical-theme bar and restaurant. The renovation changed the image of the lobby and eliminated the adjoining bar, but the English club look survived in the new Journeys bar, which adjoins the back of the three-meal restaurant. Hunting prints hang on the dark wood walls, large leather chairs and couches seem to be waiting for eccentric gentry to sit and read the London Times, and the fireplace boasts a real wood fire in this very warm, but not-too-cozy space.
Photograph by Peter Vitale.

The renovation team redesigned ground floor spaces to bring back the rich, but not decadent, look the hotel had in the 1930s, and reconfigured them to make them more functional and generous. The existing lobby bar was replaced by a seating area, which made room for new windows, opening the view to Central Park across the street. The registration desk was moved, a new concierge desk was added, and a special lobby for the 148 condominium apartments in the hotel replaced the existing business center.

The lobby renovation interprets the hotel's signature Art Deco theme with enough ambiguity to create the impression of an original space which has evolved over time. The main corridor connecting the lobby with the secondary hotel entrance further softens the Art Deco theme, striking a more classical tone with dark-stained casework and paneling. A similar corridor bisects the main one at right angles, connecting the bar and the ballroom and adding a sense of classical organization as well as convenient circulation.

Tucked almost invisibly off this corridor lies the boldest design and marketing venture of the renovation, the Les Celebrités fine dining restaurant. Some other restaurants in the Nikko chain have the same name, but it's safe to say no restaurant in the world has the same interior. Its Lalique centerpieces, Frette linen, Bernardaud china, Christophle silver, Schott Zwiesel crystal, and Italian marble columns may not be strictly unique, and perhaps the rich red walls in the reception salon, dramatic lighting throughout and bold, luxurious fabrics

FRENCH GARDEN
At the front of the Cafe Botanica, the renovation designers had no trouble creating the garden atmosphere they had in mind for the main restaurant: Central Park was across the street, so they increased fenestration and complemented the verdant view with rattan and wicker furniture, floral pattern fabrics, and a palette of green, terra cotta and beige. At the rear of the restaurant, the windows on Central Park are too far away to make much of an impression, so designers created a private French garden with large plants, a stone fountain and a painted "sky" ceiling, enclosed in metalwork custom-fabricated in France.
Photograph by Peter Vitale.

have parallels elsewhere, but this space is definitely one of a kind thanks to its piéce de resistance: celebrity art. Not paintings of celebrities or collected by them — paintings by celebrities. Although the restaurant seats only 55, it attracted plenty of attention from critics, who weighed its merits pronounced it a success in food and design, making reservations almost as hard to get as invitations to celebrity parties.

Cafe Botanica, the property's larger, three-meal-day restaurant, occupies the same space the main restaurant had before the renovation. It has a garden theme with light colors, flower-patterned carpeting, fabrics and table settings, and an airy, open layout. The renovation included the addition of windows to make the space seem like an extension of Central Park across the street and a small palm court at the rear, with a partially-glazed metalwork enclosure, a replica of an original the designers found in a small town in France. Faster than the TGV through the channel tunnel, hotel guests can go from the French palm court to a very proper British setting just by walking through the door to the Journeys Bar. Another example of the non-literal interpretation of the "original" Essex House, this bar picks up the theme of the Bombay Bicycle Club bar in the original hotel. Bits of the original plaster ceiling remained and were replicated during the renovation, but the rest of the design is new.

The renovated ballroom takes guests back to France again, with sparkling new Renaissance pilasters, gilding, white walls with panel molding, frescoes and hand-crafted French chandeliers, all inspired by Versailles and introduced during the renovation. The original two-tier Colon-nade Room, famous decades ago as a venue for the Big Band Sound, had been made one level by the 1960s; and was later

ELEGANT PAUSING PLACE
The elevator lobbies on guest room floors have murals copied from a painting at The Metro-politan Museum of Art. Custom-pattern carpeting throughout the building was imported from France and Italy.
Photograph by Peter Vitale.

SUITE SUCCESS

The living room of a renovated suite makes its impact with generous wall and ceiling moldings, plenty of traditional furniture and strong, confident carpet and fabric colors and patterns (bottom). Pre-renovation rooms made an impact with lurid carpet colors, hyperactive fabric designs and a smorgasbord of furniture reminiscent of discount stores (top and center).
Photograph (bottom) by Peter Vitale.

redone in generic modern style with gray and maroon tones.

The new business center on the second floor features three private offices as well as the standard machines and services. The renovation also included new heating and air-conditioning systems, new elevators and all new kitchens.

On the guest-room floors, the renovation reduced the room count from 711 to 595 while increasing the number of suites and replaced the chain-hotel-style interiors with 12 different designs and 120 room configurations. Within that variety, there are unifying constants: furniture is Louis XVI in all rooms on the Central Park side of the building and Chippendale on the other side. In all permutations, understated art balances rich wall colors and striking custom fabrics. The goal for guest room renovations was to make guests feel as if they were staying at a friend's house. This "friend" has no financial problems, judging by the custom carpets and marble bathrooms, the VCR, three two-line speaker telephones with data port, electronically-locked safe, individual climate control and mini-bar in each room and the robes, scales, hand-held hair dryers and television speakers in each bathroom. Considering the historic reputation and clientele of the Essex House, such opulence isn't too much of a surprise — in fact, it might simply be described as "Everything You Remember. And More."

VIEW WITH A ROOM
The north side of the hotel looks out on Central Park, giving guests a view which can't be beat in New York. Before the renovation, the thick-pile carpeting in saturated colors, plaid wall-covering and medley of furniture and fabrics may have distracted guests who thought they would enjoy the park view (above). Although the renovated guest rooms have strong colors and fabrics and rich Louis XVI furniture, the unity of design and substantial, traditional materials give them a more understated quality
Photograph (facing page) by Peter Vitale.

The Equinox
Manchester, Vermont

No matter how beautiful it is or how significant the events and guests it has seen, even a historic hotel has to fit into the current market, or "it's history," as the expression goes. At the Equinox, one renovation gave new life to the historic building, but the business floundered until a second makeover looked to the marketplace, and repositioned the property as a destination resort.

LONG LINE OF HISTORY
The Equinox began as the Marsh Tavern; the building grew with the business as successive owners added and acquired adjacent structures. The building has had 17 major architectural changes and additions over the years, and exhibits six different styles of architecture. The renovation did not include substantial changes to the rambling front elevation of the hotel which faces the village green.

Name	**The Equinox**
Location	**Manchester, Vermont**
Owner	**Equinox Resort Associates**
Operator	**The Gleneagles Group**
Type of Hotel	**Resort**
Date of Original Construction	**1769**
Number of Rooms	**136, plus 27 in investor-owned townhouses**
Bars & Restaurants	**2 restaurants / 1 bar**
Meeting Rooms Number & Size	**8 rooms / 14,000 square feet**
Recreation Facilities	**18-hole golf course, indoor and outdoor pool, 3 clay tennis courts, spa with health and beauty treatments, free-weights and exercise machines, exercise classes, sauna and steam room**
Type of Renovation	**Phased market reposition, partial hotel shut down**
Cost	**$13 million**
Date	**1991 - 1993; reopened 1992**
Master Renovation Designer	**Tag Galleon**
Architect and Interior Designer	**Ahearn & Shoffner, Boston, Massachusetts**
Contractor	**Albany**

The Equinox began in 1769 as the Marsh Tavern; a few years later it was a meeting place for the Vermont Green Mountain Boys during the American Revolution. In the 19th century, it attracted Mary Todd Lincoln as a summer guest as it grew into a grand, rambling monument of New England architecture set between a village green and two mountain ranges.

By the 1980s, the Equinox was past its prime as a business and nearing the point of no return as a building, prompting a group of concerned Vermonters to jump in and save the hotel with a renovation. Physically preserved, the property still did not find a niche in the hospitality market. In the early 1990s, a group of investors led by operators of the Gleneagles Hotel and Golf Course in Scotland took over and renovated the Equinox again, focusing it as a luxury destination resort.

Their strategy started with an ambitious rebuilding of the property's golf course, upgraded its other recreation facilities, made over the main hotel building, and built a group of upscale shops at the hotel's doorstep. The finished product enabled the operators to market the property as a modern resort with a historic background.

The renovation began with a $3.5 million rebuilding of the 18-hole golf course originally designed by Walter Travis in 1927. Rees Jones rebuilt and upgraded the course, following the original routing and retaining its desirable features. The clubhouse and a fitness center built for the 1985 renovation underwent minor renovations. Rounding out the resort product, the operators coordinated guests'

access to nearby fishing, hunting, riding, hiking, skiing, and canoeing.

Renovating the main hotel building presented a challenge: using a Vermont flavor to differentiate the property from similar resorts elsewhere without turning it into a generic Vermont inn. The solution was to temper the New England look with the substantial feeling of a 150 room resort hotel. Traditional, sober furniture, colors and materials bear out the monumental size and design of the building, while eclectic furniture, including many antiques, look as if they had accumulated over 200 years. Rich, varied fabrics, some of them eccentric, and hints of the local fishing and hunting pursuits create a sense of place. "We wanted it to feel like a really nice sweater," said renovation master designer, Tag Galleon.

OUTDOOR ATTRACTION
The centerpiece of the market reposition was the rebuilding of the golf course on its original routing while moving greens back and recontouring them, rebuilding bunkers, and raising several fairways to improve drainage. The golf course redesign also included a new irrigation system and modern grasses to replace the existing turf.

BOLD REVISION
The Colonnade restaurant interior strikes a bolder and grander note after the renovation (below). The painted stenciling on the ceiling is based on a historic technique and pattern, and gives the room a more detailed appearance than it had before the renovation with its airy solid blue ceiling (right). The draperies, the chandeliers, the red walls, and the green and gold carpet installed in the renovation add to the rich, formal tone of the renovated space.

YOU'VE ARRIVED

The new lobby lets guests know they're at a substantial hotel as soon as they enter the two-story space (below). The furniture is eclectic, but slightly grand and decidedly not rustic or rickety. The rich yellow and white paint scheme sets the tone for the simple, stately Federalist period suggested in the guest room interiors. The previous renovation in the 1980s used velvet and fringe upholstery to create a more Victorian design in the lobby to complement the later style found on the exterior, but the spatial effect was severely limited by the low ceiling in the room (two photographs, left).

The most conspicuous architectural change was moving the lobby, previously located awkwardly at one end of the building, with a ceiling less than eight feet high. To provide an entry with a sense of arrival and convenient circulation, the designers removed existing guest rooms at the center of the structure, creating a new two-story lobby which looks out on the property's courtyard. That freed up the old lobby space for expansion of the Marsh Tavern, the oldest portion of the business.

The rest of the public spaces were all renovated within their existing configurations. Back-of-the-house, the only major change was addition of a small kitchen. Guest-room configurations stayed the same, but bathrooms were gutted and replaced. The existing case goods received new finishes, while the soft goods, architectural finishes and detailing were all replaced.

The renovation took advantage of the need for shopping in a destination resort. The hotel owned buildings on the other side of the village green, and renovated and reconfigured them all for lease as commercial space, later acquiring and renovating additional buildings as business grew. The operators market the renovated property as a year-round resort with a variety of sports and relaxations; a newsletter highlights the activities and special events offered each season and runs features on the businesses around the hotel and their merchandise and services.

NEW FEDERALISM
Guest rooms were revised in a simple, calm design with a touch of the Federal style (above), de-emphasizing the slightly rustic flavor of the existing rooms (right). A fluted picture rail molding was added, a new tweedy carpet replaced the existing one, and case goods were refinished in a bleached natural maple tone.

WHERE IT ALL BEGAN
The hostelry was born as the Marsh Tavern in 1769, and the same space still serves the same function under the same name within the much-evolved Equinox. The renovation which brought the property back from the brink of demolition in the mid-1980s used black and red checkered wall covering to create a homespun, Revolution-period feeling (below). The renovated tavern has a dark green and tan wall covering, a heavy tapestry-like fabric for upholstered furniture, and an assortment of sofas, wingback chairs, and Windsor captain's chairs to provide a more comfortable and substantial environment than the previous collection of all open-wood furniture (right).

Washington Courtyard
Washington, D.C.

One look at the Quality Hotel in Washington, D.C. would probably be enough to make anyone guess why its owner, the Wyoming Hotel Corporation, decided to renovate the property in 1992. With mirrors on the walls and ceiling, the lobby was awash in wavy reflections which looked like the set from a low-budget sci-fi movie about an aquarium gone awry. Guests who ventured further reached a dining room which looked like a tract house interpretation of a medieval dungeon. Not surprisingly, the owner decided that replacing the mostly package-tour clientele with business travelers would require replacing the look of the building as well.

New Name
A year after the renovation, the property switched from a Quality Inn franchise to Courtyard by Marriott. The green awnings, lighted at night to help identify the affiliation, were among the relatively few alterations required by Marriott for the relabeling.

Name	**Washington D.C.Courtyard by Marriott**
Location	**Washington, D.C.**
Owner	**The Wyoming Hotel Corporation**
Operator	**Courtyard by Marriott**
Type of Hotel	**Business / Three Star**
Date of Original Construction	**1968**
Number of Rooms	**148**
Bars & Restaurants	**Bailey's Bar, Claret's Restaurant**
Meeting Rooms (Number & Size)	**2 / 315 square feet each**
Recreation Facilities	**Swimming pool**
Type of Renovation	**Hotel shut down during renovation, fast-track design-build**
Cost	**$5.5 Million**
Date	**March - September 1992**
Architect	**Brennan Beer Gorman / Architects**
Interior Designer	**Brennan Beer Gorman Monk / Interiors**
Consultants	**Structural Engineer: Cagley & Assoc. Mechanical Engineer: JVP Engineers, P.C. Electrical Engineer: Cobb & del Castillo, Ltd.**
Construction Manager	**Coakley & Williams Construction Co., Inc.**

CORRIDORS OF POWER
The renovated lobby (top) and front desk (left) replace the modern minimalist look of the pre-renovation hotel with a dignified traditional appearance. Patterned carpets, tapestry window treatments, and stained casework are topped off by Waterford chandeliers.
Photographs by Dan Cunningham.

MIRROR, MIRROR ON THE WALL
. . .and on the ceiling, too. Before the renovation, the small lobby and front desk featured mirrored walls and ceilings. Though possibly intended to create the illusion of a larger space, in this photograph they make it seem that the hotel was under water.

MIXED METAPHOR
Before the renovation, the ground floor featured the medieval look as well as the space age. Next to the many-mirrored lobby was a dungeon-like restaurant, complete with a crude imitation open-beam ceiling and other mix-and-match combinations of contemporary and "antique" elements.

After a seven-and-one-half month fast-track renovation carried out under a design-build arrangement with construction manager Coakley & Williams, the property had a completely different atmosphere, a controlled, understated traditional theme. Within a year, the transformation was completed by a switch to the Courtyard by Marriott label.

By focusing the makeover on the most prominent parts of the building, Wyoming, Coakley & Williams and designers at the Washington offices of Brennan Beer Gorman/Architects — Brennan Beer Gorman Monk/Interiors (BBG) effected a major change of image on a limited budget and schedule. Exterior work was concentrated on the ground floor, and changes to interior partitions were limited almost completely to the first floor. Remaining portions of the building received new finishes, but little more. The renovation also included modification of the mechanical system, installation of firesprinklers and life-safety improvements.

Located on the corner of Connecticut Avenue, a commercial thoroughfare, and LeRoy Place, a side street with historic townhouses, the bland building was at odds with its surroundings. It was impossible to blend the massing of the nine-story hotel with the nearby three-

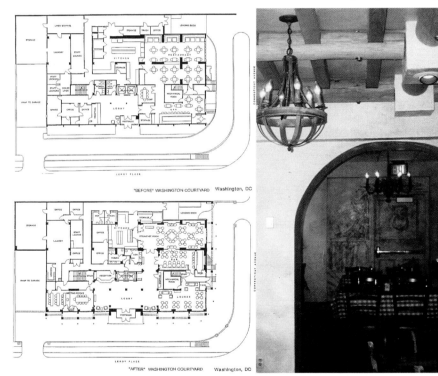

"BEFORE" WASHINGTON COURTYARD   Washington, DC

"AFTER" WASHINGTON COURTYARD   Washington, DC

story townhouses, and the budget did not allow for extensive redesign of the exterior, which Mark Boekenheide, partner-in-charge for BBG described as "a big hulking commercial structure." To alleviate the effect of the size of the building, it was painted a lighter color, and application of synthetic stucco arches at the parapet introduced visual order and a smaller scale.

Most of the exterior budget went into the ground floor, where pedestrians see the

building close-up and get their strongest impression. A large retaining wall at the sidewalk level received a coat of stucco, detailed to imitate cast stone, while a stairway at the street corner was moved to allow more room on the sidewalk. Additional landscaping, lighting, lighted signs, new windows at public areas, and replacement of the store front at the entry rounded out the effort to give the building more identity and pedestrian charm — and win the approval of a neighborhood group and the District's historic review board.

SMART AND BRIGHT
While the lobby and restaurant strike a formal, elite note, Bailey's Bar relaxes a bit with bright but easy-going fabrics, a bold color scheme, and ample downlighting instead of chandeliers.
Photograph by Dan Cunningham.

TOUCH OF CRYSTAL
Claret's Restaurant is smaller than the dining room that existed before the renovation, but it can claim Waterford chandeliers and beveled mirrors.
Photograph by Dan Cunningham.

Interior changes on the ground floor were driven not only by the owner's need for a new look, but by business differences between the package tour and business travel markets. The large restaurant and kitchen shrank to accommodate a more generous lobby and the introduction of meeting rooms. Guests can see the single biggest design change before they enter the ground floor: twelve new windows. "It was like a tomb" with just one window in the lobby before the renovation, Boekenheide said, so the designers tore out an exterior wall and replaced it with glazing "to get some life into the lobby."

Although the renovated first floor spaces share a sense of traditional dignity and warm, rich colors and materials, they vary from the sedate and slightly clubby lobby to the somewhat richer restaurant and the bright and energetic bar. The hotel's Irish ownership explains the lobby and restaurant Waterford chandeliers, which it provided directly to the job. They stand out as the most opulent element in the property, compatible with the style of the rooms, but contrasting with the suspended-grid acoustic system used in the ceilings.

On guest-room floors, crown moldings, striped wall coverings, and increased lighting from new ceiling and wall fixtures provide a general upgrade for circulation areas. Narrow side tables and mirrors in each corridor and half-inch wood moldings applied to the flush guest-room doors help break up the length and monotony that simple, unadorned hallways can have. The budget limit is more evident in the amount of work done on the

POINT OF INTEREST
Guest-floor hallways have shallow side tables on the midpoint of the wall to break up the monotony of a faceless passage. Wall sconces help accent the table, while surface fixtures on the ceilings keep the entire corridor relatively bright.
Photograph by Dan Cunningham.

LUXURY WITH LIMITS
Bathrooms in the standard guest rooms are compact, leaving too little room for installation of vanities. To make the most of the space, the renovation design provides pedestal sinks with glass shelves above, large mirrors, and 12-inch-square marble tiling on the walls and floors. Marriott usually requires vanities in bathrooms in the Courtyard series, but accepted the space-conscious design for the Washington property.
Photograph by Dan Cunningham.

CAREFULLY MEASURED
Standard rooms carry out the traditional look of the public spaces, but on a more limited budget for materials and details. The television armoire, like other wood case goods, adds a substance to the very simple room — and also saves space by eliminating the need for a dresser.
Photograph by Dan Cunningham.

A CUT ABOVE
The large rooms at the end of each floor of the hotel have one king bed, a writing desk, easy chair with ottoman, and wood base and crown moldings, plus a larger bathroom than the standard rooms.
Photograph by
Dan Cunningham.

INSIDE THE BELTWAY
Although they may not get White House invitations, at least VIPs visiting Washington don't have to compete with the President for this fancy hotel room. The Presidential Suite has a living-dining room in addition to the bedroom and bathroom. It follows the theme of other guest rooms in the hotel, but with chandeliers, oriental rugs and higher-grade fabrics. Movers and shakers can relax in an armchair while keeping an eye on the capital scene.
Photographs by
Dan Cunningham.

SUMPTUOUS BATHING
The bathroom in the presidential suite features a whirlpool bath tub and separate shower, marble vanity and built-in hair dryer. Marble on the floors and walls matches that found in other bathrooms in the hotel.
Photograph by Dan Cunningham.

guest rooms, which have less detail but maintain the traditional theme of the ground floor with wood headboards and case goods. Television armoires with dresser drawers conserve space in the rooms. They are arrayed in nine different ways on each floor, none with an excess of space. The rooms at the ends of each floor are enlarged and have wood base and crown moldings, a king-size bed, better finish materials, a writing desk, mini-bar and marble-tiled baths with vanities. Completed in time for the 1993 inauguration, the presidential suite has a living-dining room, all-marble bathroom and bedroom with king-size bed, and a second bedroom with two queen beds and its own bathroom.

Like the design, the renovation process was judiciously calculated to make the most of the owner's investment. Coakley & Williams gave Wyoming a single point of responsibility for design and construction and a fixed price at the outset of the project, and acted as construction manager. BBG had performed a pre-purchase survey for Wyoming and had worked with Coakley & Williams previously, so the design-build team could hit the ground running.

It certainly had to do that, with only seven-and-one-half months for design and construction, and a schedule which called for awarding subcontracts at the 75 percent stage of design for most work.

Wyoming decided to shut the hotel down for construction and steer regular guests to a nearby property it owned, avoiding a longer renovation which might drive some of them away permanently. The renovation was not tailored to the Courtyard by Marriott brand change, but only limited changes, such as landscaping, resurfacing the deck and removing an existing wood bar at the swimming pool; painting the parking garage and adding the chain's signature green awnings, were required when the switch was made a year after the renovation.

Hyatt Regency New Orleans
New Orleans, Louisiana

When the Hyatt Regency New Orleans opened in the mid-1970s, it gave the Crescent City a dose of slick, splashy architecture. Guests arriving at the motor entrance passed through a wall of glass doors into a lobby with a strong spare interior and up a two-story escalator to a 27-story atrium. The tables were turned when the property got its first major renovation in the early 1990s. The designers introduced New Orleans tradition to the perennially new-looking hotel, replacing giant mobiles and mass-produced materials with traditional chandeliers and marble.

STILL LOOKING NEW
The exterior appearance of the hotel did not change during the renovation, despite introduction of a more traditional look on the interior. The 32-story hotel is part of a complex which includes an office building, a convention center, and the Louisiana Superdome.
Photograph by Ken Glaser.

Name	*Hyatt Regency New Orleans*
Location	*New Orleans, Louisiana*
Owner	*Prudential Realty Corporation*
Operator	*Hyatt Hotels Corporations*
Type of Hotel	*Convention*
Date of Original Construction	*1979*
Number of Rooms	*1,384*
Bars & Restaurants	*5*
Meeting Rooms Number & Size	*35 rooms / 90,000 square feet*
Recreation Facilities	*Rooftop swimming pool, health club with exercise machines, weights*
Type of Renovation	*Phased renovation, hotel closed only 2 days*
Cost	*$16 million*
Date	*1992 - 1995*
Architect and Interior Designer	*Public Spaces, Meeting Rooms: Newmark Diercks Design Inc., Greenwood Village, Colorado Regency Club: Gayle Bird Interiors, Ltd., New Orleans, Louisiana Guest Rooms: Rosemont Purchasing, Chicago, Illinois*
Consultants	*Technical Architectural Services: John Hardy Group*
Contractor	*Case & Associates, Houston, Texas*

BEGINNING AND END

The scope of the renovation did not allow replacement of the existing brown brick walls the full height of the registration lobby, so the designers had to find a location to end the new interior and let the old one continue. They topped off the new registration, bellman, and concierge desks with illuminated etched glass canopies, framing the new composition, and upstaging the existing wall, which continues behind it. The new canopies incorporate to make a subtle reference to traditional New Orleans design without contrasting too much with the contemporary styling of the hotel. The remodeling also provided a new finish to the same height on the structural columns, replacing the existing brown brick with mahogany and marble. The new materials are detailed to stress the verticality of the column and de-emphasize its width.

Photograph by Karl Francetic.

In the lobby, the sleek, open look and consistent, limited range of materials used in the original design were scrutinized by the designers during the renovation. They reduced the amount of brown brick, the original wall and floor finish material, and increased the amount of architectural detail. The designers removed the doors at the center of the store-front construction motor entrance, moved the wall outward, and installed new brass doors to create a stronger sense of arrival and spatial sequence. The redefinition continues inside the lobby, where the new marble flooring is articulated with a band of contrasting colors along the axis from the entry to the main lobby. Materials, detailing, and furniture in the lobby flesh out the more formal, traditional overtone of the renovated interior, recalling classical motifs subtly to avoid clashing with the contemporary overall style of the building.

Subtle changes were made to the Hyatt's signature - an atrium large enough to house a small skyscraper. The existing tent-like canopies which defined the restaurant and cocktail lounge on the atrium floor gave way to mahogany baldacchino-style structures with a New Orleans character in their detailing and wrought iron railings. In the hotel's Regency Club on the concierge level, a more pronounced transformation of style took place. A spare, modern design was replaced with traditional sofas, armchairs, draperies, and lighting. Substance to accompany the style included a new business center for guests on the upgrade floor, with work areas, office machines, and a video phone.

The meeting space in the hotel is divided in two areas and also underwent a facelift during the renovation. The renovation added a business center and a hotel-operated flower shop to the smaller of the two facilities. At the rooftop pool deck, two existing suites were converted into hospitality suites catering to business and meeting guests. Each has a mini-kitchen, a service bar, a table for conference or dining use, and a seating area. Additional guest room space at the pool deck was converted into a new health club, with stair and cycling exercise machines, weight-lifting machines, and free weights. The renovation also included an overhaul of the restaurant and bars of the hotel.

WELCOME TO THE CLUB
The Regency Club Lounge on the hotel's concierge floor traded in its existing sharp, contemporary design for a traditional look. Comfortable classic furniture, tall floor lamps and conservative art impart a steady, slightly understated air to the room. The suites on the concierge level, which were Chinese modern style before the renovation, also switched to a more traditional look, with wrought iron details and crystal chandeliers.
Photograph by Ken Glaser.

MEET THE NEW MEETING SPACE

The renovation revamped the finishes in each of the meeting rooms. This included: the 25,000 square foot French Market Exhibition Hall (top), the smaller conference center rooms, and the concourse and meeting rooms in the separate Regency Conference Center (bottom), located in an adjoining building connected to the hotel (center).

Photographs by Ken Glaser.

NEW FROM THE GROUND UP
The 27-story atrium was too large to renovate completely, so the design concentrated on the part guests see (close-up): the restaurant and lounge on the atrium floor level. Existing fabric canopies were removed to allow construction of elaborate gazebo-like wood structures which enclose the food and beverage areas. The wrought iron railings and cupolas give the new works a French Quarter trademark, while the simplified classical order of the columns blurs their traditional design enough so that they do not clash with relentless contemporary styling of the building.
Bottom photograph by Karl Francetic; photograph (right) by Ken Glaser.

NEW OLD LOOK

The renovation added traditional motifs, expensive materials and intricate detailing to the lobby to alleviate the free-form, omnivalent quality of its original design. French- and Spanish-inspired chairs, settees and tables are grouped around Tai Ping rugs in formal seating clusters to break up the space and order it in an understandable way. The renovation removed huge mobiles in the two-story spaces at each end of the lobby (top), replacing them with 12-foot high chandeliers (bottom). In the lower area in between, the original flat ceilings (center left) were modified with new vaults which feature wrought iron and crystal chandeliers (center right).

Top and center left photographs by Newmark Diercks; center right photograph by Ken Glaser; bottom photograph by Karl Francetic.

La Quinta Inns
Reimaging Program for all Properties in Chain

In most chains, headquarters keeps an eye on renovations, but is not responsible for the design concept and does not check the details to assure a uniform look. Not so at La Quinta Inns, where headquarters created a single renovation design and then executed it at more than 220 properties in less than a year. The unusual renovation process, tellingly named a "reimaging program," reflects the profile and business strategy of the budget motel chains - to produce a uniform look, and do it in a hurry.

LOBBY LOGO
The reimaging project added towers (facing page) to many properties and reworked those already in place. The chain's new logo (above) is a prominent feature on the towers, which serve to tell freeway drivers where and what La Quinta motels are. At properties where drivers would not be able to see a tower from the interstate, or where the building or sign were already very visible, no tower was added.
Photographs by La Quinta Inns, Inc.

Name	**La Quinta Inns**
Location	**More than 220 motels in 29 states**
	Headquarters: San Antonio, Texas
Owner	**La Quinta Inns, Inc.**
Operator	**La Quinta Inns, Inc.**
Type of Hotel	**Economy-priced motel**
Date of Original Construction	**First motel: 1968**
Number of Rooms	**Approximately 26,000**
Bars & Restaurants	**None in typical property**
Recreation Facilities	**Outdoor pool in typical property**
Type of Renovation	**Properties open during renovation**
Cost	**$55 million**
Date	**May 1993 - June 1994**
Architect and Interior Designer	**Design Concept: Fugleberg Koch Architects, Winter Park, Florida**
Consultants	**Marketing and Design: SBG Partners, San Francisco, California**
	Advertising Agency: GSD&M, Austin, Texas

GUIDING PRINCIPLE

To simplify the task of designing a renovation for more than 220 motels, the designers made a "kit of parts." The "kit" identified the redesigned elements, such as the landscaping, porte cochere repaving, the new tower, and exterior architectural trim and railings shown in this rendering of the master design concept (top).
Rendering by Fugleberg Koch Architects.

GREEN EVOLUTION

In a move to make the properties appear more welcoming and residential, and to differentiate them from institutional-looking competitors, the renovation team added trees, shrubs and other landscaping (bottom) to soften the main elevations of the buildings (left). The arches over the top-floor windows and at roof level in the center of the building were part of the "kit of parts." The arches also display prominently the new company logo.
Photographs by La Quinta Inns, Inc.

Redesigning franchise properties can be as easy as herding cats, but La Quinta had a formidable advantage in executing a total makeover: almost all properties are company-owned. The firm was determined to take advantage of that fact to produce a uniform product appealing to its existing customers and inviting to new guests, and to execute the transformation practically overnight to maximize its impact. The low-price, limited-service chain, also sought to differentiate itself from competitors and increase revenues.

A prime motivation for the reimaging was the considerable variation among individual properties in the chain, which made it impossible for designers to produce one set of working drawings suitable for all buildings. Instead, La Quinta began with the big picture, putting together a team consisting of management and outside firms for architecture and interior design, advertising and corporate image. The team first chose the overall goals for the reimaging

and then attacked the details to produce what Trish Rhem, director of interiors for Fugleberg Koch, called a "kit of parts." Those design elements were then used by the individual teams La Quinta later put together to renovate each property. Many "parts" from the "kit" were used on practically every motel in the chain, but any time a particular design element was not appropriate for a specific property, it was not used there.

RED CARPET ARRIVAL
In addition to new planting, the reimaging changed the landscape treatment of hard surfaces. Existing asphalt paving was removed at the porte cochere and replaced with patterned concrete reminiscent of stone paving. The color of the new paving complements the roofing, which did not change.
Photographs by La Quinta Inns, Inc.

Although the reimaging did not reposition the chain in the market, it did move in a different position on the map for the source of the exterior style of the motels. The original motels had a "Mexican primitive" style (La Quinta means "country house" in Spanish); and the reimaging moved north of the border, so to speak, settling upon the "Santa Fe look" of the Southwestern United States instead. The existing earth-tone paint on the masonry walls and long beam and rafter extension were deemed heavy and unappealing, so the building exteriors were repainted in white to give a bright, crisp feeling, with green trim and matching bronze-patina railings and medallions. The beam and rafter extensions were shortened, and new arches and other architectural detailing were added to give a sense of richness and a residential quality. The design also included extensive changes to landscaping to increase "curb appeal" and lure first-time guests. Landscaping and building detail were added mostly on the front of the motels; where other sides of the building also acted as the entry to properties, they also received the exterior upgrades.

Gary Mead, the president and chief executive officer who had recently taken over the firm, ordered photographs of the signs of all the properties in the chain — and discovered that they were different sizes, shapes, and colors. Even the words on the signs varied — but they were all dull. He decided to redo the signs, the company logo, and even the name. The company streamlined its name from La Quinta Motor Inns, dropping "Motor" as outdated. The designers made a logo for the new name, brightening it with a Southwestern-blue background and yellow and purple sunburst. The number and placement of signs installed at each property during the renovations depended on sight lines from nearby roads and freeways.

The blues and purples carry over from the sign to the building exterior and then into the interiors. The quarry tile floors, brown and orange plastic laminates, and dark brown-stained woodwork were targeted as dull, institutional and uninviting like the exteriors. The designers added lighter flooring and furniture and additional architectural details, such as columns, faux stone and wall fountains to create warm, inviting, bright interiors. The renovations expanded each lobby to accommodate a new buffet for the free continental breakfast the chain had introduced just before reimaging began.

La Quinta launched a retraining program for employees to go along with the reimaging, augmented by new uniforms, a new advertising campaign, and a new slogan, "You're not staying at a hotel. You're staying with us."

When the reimaging program was complete, a guest survey showed that not only the exteriors and the lobbies, but also the guest rooms were rated higher than they had been before the makeover. That was quite a compliment, since the project did not include any changes to the guest rooms. This vote of confidence was not mistaken, just premature. La Quinta began planning and designing a program to upgrade the guest rooms late in 1994.

NEW COLORS, NEW SPACES
Lobbies received the most extensive redesign of any portion of the properties (opposite page, bottom). Existing fluorescent lighting was removed and replaced with incandescent fixtures, existing soffits were removed to make the lobbies feel more spacious, new registrations desks with lower counter heights were installed to make guests feel less separated from hotel staff, and new architectural columns helped define circulation areas and added detail (opposite page, right). While the existing lobbies feature a lot of dark browns (opposite page, left), the new palette consists of pale background colors with accents of greens, blues and orange. Those colors carry over from the new exterior treatment, as do the plants added in the reimaging. Faux-stone accents added to make lobbies more ornate and appealing include stone wall fountains (left).
Photographs by la Quinta Inns, Inc.

The Ritz-Carlton Kansas City

Kansas City, Missouri

Would you expect to find an understated Boston-Brahman hotel interior in a Moorish-theme shopping center in the middle of the Great Plains? If the property had the Ritz-Carlton name, you probably would, and if you checked into the Ritz-Carlton Kansas City in the Country Club Plaza shopping complex that's exactly what you would find. This combination is what was in store when the Ritz-Carlton Hotel Company teamed up with shopping center developer and previous hotel owner J.C. Nichols Company to transform the existing Alameda Plaza Hotel into a Ritz-Carlton.

Name	*The Ritz-Carlton Kansas City*
Location	*Kansas City, Missouri*
Owner	*Ritz-Carlton Hotel Company*
Operator	*Ritz-Carlton Hotel Company*
Type of Hotel	*Luxury*
Date of Original Construction	*1972*
Number of Rooms	*374, including 28 suites and 15 with handicapped accessibility*
Bars & Restaurants	*4*
Meeting Rooms Number & Size	*11, plus 6 conference suites / 22,500 square feet*
Recreation Facilities	*Outdoor pool, fitness center with exercise equipment and aerobics area, sauna and steam room for men and women*
Type of Renovation	*All finishes, limited layout changes. Hotel open throughout renovation.*
Cost	*$30 million - $40 million*
Date	*May 1898 - February 1990*
Architect	*Milton Pate Associates, Atlanta, Georgia Linscott, Haylett, Wimmer & Wheat, Kansas City, Missouri*
Interior Designer	*Hirsch/Bedner & Associates, Atlanta, Georgia*
Consultants	*Sasaki Associates, San Francisco, California (landscape architects)*
Contractor	*J. E. Dunn*

AGES APART
The airy, Mediterranean-contemporary informality of the Alameda Plaza lobby with rugged clay flooring and romantic furniture and accessories (facing page) gave way to the much more formal and precise mood of the paneled Ritz-Carlton lobby with its emphasis on 19th century-style English furniture (below).

The hotel, a curved twelve-story tower with a six-story wing housing public spaces, had opened as a luxury property in 1972 to broaden the scope of the upscale shopping center. By the late 1980s, the hotel was poised for a larger role, and the renovation had to transform it into part of the Ritz-Carlton chain — without requiring a shutdown. With neighbors like Gucci and Saks Fifth Avenue in the 55-acre shopping complex, there was no problem with the location. There was only one obstacle separating the existing hotel from its new siblings in the Ritz-Carlton chain: image. The existing hotel extended the Moorish look to the interior, but when Ritz-Carlton became the innkeeper, it was time for Ali Baba to check out.

While the Moorish theme survives on the exterior to make the hotel compatible with the surrounding retail complex, the interior has become by-the-book Ritz-Carlton. The chain's hotels are not clones, but the common palette of rich wood casework and paneling, tapestries, draperies, and oil paintings is the basis for the interior of each property to remind guests of the ambiance of the original Ritz-Carlton in Boston or the grand antecedent, the Ritz in Paris.

The designers left intact the floor-to-ceiling windows typical of post World War II construction, and more appropriate for the airy feeling of the Kansas City location than smaller, but more traditional glazing might have been. They removed the Moorish arches and ceilings, clay-tile floors, plaster walls and rough-timber detailing that had been used to make the Alameda Plaza complement the retail complex outside, and built an interior enclave of wood paneling, restrained carpeting, 18th and 19th century art and antiques in public spaces, and Drexel Heritage reproduction furniture in guest rooms.

AIRY TO ELEGANT
The former Pam Pam West was a diner which served up informal food from an open kitchen at counters and banquettes. The spaces, lighting, styles and materials were loosely modeled on the building's overall theme to complement lighter dining (left). When Ritz-Carlton designers remade the space, the kitchen was relegated to back-of-the-house and the eatery was redefined with more formal spaces, sconces and chandeliers, reproduction antique furniture and detailed wall moldings (below). The Cafe continues to serve simpler fare; light colors, open spaces and lack of wood wall paneling distinguish it from the fine dining Rooftop Restaurant.

NIGHT MOVES, RIGHT MOVES
The former Rooftop Lounge struck a tone of Old World intrigue, with fanciful arches and low lighting (left). Remodeled as The Bar, the space looks like the haunts of England's old boy network, with hunting prints, reproduction side tables, a fireplace and full-paneled walls (below).

The guest rooms and public spaces required relatively few changes in layout, and the back-of-the-house needed no significant reconfiguration. The biggest change in layout was the expansion of the two-story main ballroom by eliminating a meeting room which had intruded into its upper-level. New movable partitions allow the 12,000 square foot ballroom to be divided into four smaller spaces. The change added eleven percent to the meeting space available in the building. Creation of the chain's signature Ritz-

Carlton Club on the top two guest room floors required adding a private connecting stair and eliminating three guest rooms to make space for the club lounge. Two or three existing rooms were combined to create each new suite in the renovated building.

Guest rooms were completely renovated with individual refrigerators with honor bars, safes, computer modem connections, and Italian marble bathrooms with telephones and hair dryers. The new

business center offers amenities including fax, teleconferencing, copying, and secretarial service.

The existing outdoor pool was augmented with a new indoor fitness center with exercise equipment, an aerobics area, and sauna and steam room for men and women. Existing poolside landscaping at the Garden Terrace was refined and trees, shrubs, and flowers were added at the motor entrance to establish the property's new character before guests see the interior.

GREENER PASTURES Although the striking and unmistakable exterior of the structure retained its original appearance during the remodeling (below), landscaping was added at the motor entrance to the site of more than three acres to make the property more appealing from the point where guests first see it (left).

ROOFTOP FACELIFT

Diners at the property's top eatery look out over Kansas City, but the interior before the renovation might have suggested Marrakech or Damascus with its white and brown color theme, Mediterranean materials and Thousand-and-One-Nights ceiling (right). The renovated Rooftop Restaurant strikes a simpler tone with rich carpeting throughout, extensive wall paneling, and art and armchairs which suggest an understated club atmosphere (below).

FROM HAREM TO HARROD'S
The Mediterranean theme continued into the guest rooms before the renovation, with bright white walls, dark-wood-and-wrought-iron accessories and ornately carved headboards (left). Renovated rooms have muted wall colors and furniture intended to evoke London, not the Near East (below).

PUSHING THE ENVELOPE
The renovation extended the original ballroom and eliminated a meeting room which had intruded on the upper level of the two-story space, creating a low-ceilinged zone at one end of the room. The new ballroom has a uniform two-story ceiling throughout; the space can be subdivided into four "Salons" with sound-insulated moveable partitions.

The Houstonian Hotel

Houston, Texas

Never a run-of-the-mill operation, the Houstonian Campus chalked up quite a few distinctions by the time Redstone Properties acquired it in 1992. Its latest distinction - bankruptcy attracted the turnaround management firm and engendered a makeover to redefine and redirect the unusual but unsuccessful property.

RANCH WITH A PEDIGREE

The new lobby of the hotel illustrates the market strategy of the renovation. The Houstonian derived significant room sales from meetings in the 1980s, and when meetings slackened, the hotel operation went into the red. The renovation disengaged the two market segments, aiming at filling guest rooms with upscale frequent individual travelers. A large restaurant which had catered to meetings before the renovation was removed and replaced with this "great room" which recalls an urbane but earthy Texas hunting lodge or ranch.

Photograph by Richard Payne.

Name	*The Houstonian Hotel*
Location	*Houston, Texas*
Owner	*Redstone Hotels, Inc., Houston, Texas*
Operator	*Redstone Hotels, Inc.*
Type of Hotel	*Luxury*
Date of Original Construction	*1980*
Number of Rooms	*292*
Bars & Restaurants	*4; one in hotel, three in other buildings in complex*
Meeting Rooms Number & Size	*34 rooms / 33,000 square feet*
Recreation Facilities	*Private fitness club with 25-meter pool, gymnasium, jogging track, exercise equipment, racquetball, handball, squash and tennis courts, rock-climbing wall. Separate spa with exercise, beauty and weight-loss facilities.*
Type of Renovation	*Phased renovation; hotel open throughout renovation*
Cost	*Hotel: $14 million Fitness Club: $2.5 million*
Date	*June 1993 - April 1994*
Architect	*Public Spaces: Good Fulton & Farrell, Dallas*
Interior Designer	*Guest Rooms: Daiker Howard, Dallas Fitness Club: HOK Houston Manor House and Public Spaces: Vivian/Nichols Associates Inc., Dallas*
Consultants	*Mechanical, Electrical and Plumbing Engineers: B. L. & P. Engineers, Dallas Structural Engineers: The Sadler Group, Fort Worth*
Contractor	*Guest Rooms and Public Spaces: Case & Associates, Houston Fitness Club, Roofing: Constructors & Associates, Houston*

The Houstonian was constructed as a multifaceted campus at the end of the 1970s, with the Houstonian Hotel, a medical fitness center, a conference center, and an office building on its 18 acres, previously occupied by several large houses. Each piece was supposed to fit with the others, making a profitable network. Things didn't work out that way, and even though it boasted the President as a legal resident, the operation foundered.

When the new owner Redstone began the renovation in early 1993, it set out to reinforce the athletic club, the conference facility and a separate women's health spa in the complex to capitalize on their strength. Redstone calculated that the hotel's 300 rooms constituted just ten percent of the overall hotel capacity in the retail hub around the nearby Galleria mall. By upgrading, the new owners aimed to attract the frequent individual travelers at the top of that market to make the hotel operation profitable, too.

The hotel-conference center, fitness club, and health spa are in separate buildings, so Redstone selected individual designers for each one, providing an overall design statement and coordinating their work. The project began with the guest rooms, then the fitness club, then the spa, the conference center and finally, the public spaces of the hotel.

KITCHEN VIEW
The Cafe provides diners with a novel view of the kitchen, without the bother of noises, smells or even a window to wash. The trompe-l'oeil mural of a European kitchen scene, executed by a Dallas artist, also complements the color scheme of the restaurant. Imposing banquettes are balanced by country farm and wicker chairs.
Photograph by Richard Payne.

*INFORMAL PRESTIGE
The Bar, a stylized interpretation of the Ruhlmann period, balances an affluent atmosphere with more informal touches. Chessboard tabletops suggest a brainy, leisurely crowd, while the nude painting reminds us that this is a men's bar in Texas. Hardwood floors, burled wainscoting and silk upholstery are tip-offs that it is oil men, not cowboys, who come here for drinks.*
Photograph by Richard Payne.

CLASSIC MEETS CONTEMPORARY
The Presidential Suite mixes traditional and current design themes. Armchairs are a modified contemporary version of the Martha Washington chair, with bold red cotton moirè fabric. The sleek glass top of the table reveals traditional console supports, while timeless elements such as the chandelier and the antique reproduction sideboard balance the modern windows.
Photograph by Richard Payne.

Completed in 1980, the four-story main hotel building is most notable as the legal residence George Bush maintained in Houston during his employment at a more famous address in Washington, D.C. The unobtrusive modern exterior did not change in the renovation because Redstone wanted to emphasize the lush existing landscaping on the campus, not the buildings. The renovated public rooms are designed to look like an elegant but informal country lodge of a Texas millionaire, set fortuitously ten minutes from the center of Houston. The original generic contemporary lobby and registration areas were gutted and reconfigured so that guests enter the registration area and proceed to the main lobby, which is modeled after the "great room" of a wilderness lodge. Wood flooring with area rugs, plush sofas, and iron light fixtures help create the lodge atmosphere, focusing on a two-sided fireplace of Texas proportions. A monumental metal stair to the mezzanine level was added in the registration area.

Guest rooms received new custom-patterned drapes and bedspreads and traditional Kimball armoires, desks, and tables. Bathrooms were redone with marble floors and vanities. Each room has a two-line speaker phone with data port, a telephone in the bathroom, a mini bar, and a choice of 35 movies on the television in addition to the usual cable fare. Guest rooms retain their original layout, except that seven new suites were created by combining individual rooms. All the existing suites, except the one occupied by the Bushes, were divided back into separate rooms. The top floor was upgraded as a new concierge level with a 2,000 square foot concierge lounge and a business center. Its guest rooms have upgraded finishes and higher ceilings.

QUIET LUXURY
Guest rooms have traditional furniture; custom fabrics; soft, simple colors; and understated moldings. The simple window treatment takes advantage of the floor-to-ceiling windows of the contemporary building, providing a close-up view of the thick canopy of trees outdoors.
Photograph by Richard Payne.

FAME, FORTUNE AND FITNESS

The 125,000 square foot Fitness Center at the Houstonian isn't your average gym, and with initiation fees that run into the four figures, it attracts Houston's movers and shakers, not the average Joe. The renovation started with such workaday elements as a new roof, and then got into the serious work of making the center reflect the lifestyle — both economic and athletic — of the members. Before the renovation, the exercise room was a sea of weights and machines, with a warehouse atmosphere created partly by its unfinished ceiling (below). To make the workout flow clear and effective, the renovation (left and opposite page bottom) divided the space into separate zones for cardiovascular, free weight and stretching and toning work, using different flooring and ceiling materials instead of building walls to separate the zones and define circulation areas (hatched paths in drawing at top of opposite page). The ceilings were painted a tough-looking black and light fixtures were relocated to relate to the design below them. Users enter the workout area at the cardiovascular area (photograph at intersection of path in; right hand side of drawing), where the energy level is high, and can go to the stretching and toning area (top of drawing) when they want to cool down away from the stimulus of others' workouts. Next to the cardiovascular area (center of right hand zone of the drawing), exercise machines and the free weight area flank the circulation path, and at the bottom is a boxing ring (foreground in bottom photograph, opposite page; bottom zone oriented on the diagonal in the drawing). The windows at the perimeter of the workout room were left unobstructed to give members a good view of the greenery outside the building. The renovation also redid the locker rooms (top and bottom rooms immediately to the left of the workout room in the drawing).

Photographs and drawing provided courtesy of HOK Houston.

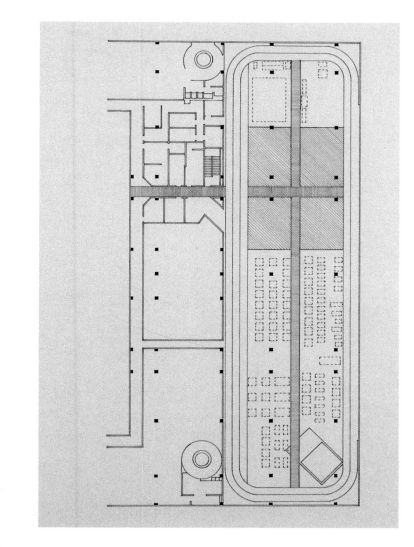

Over the years, the original medical fitness center evolved into a high-end recreation business and the most profitable part of the Houstonian Campus, with initiation fees of $4,500 to $12,500 and 3,200 names on its membership roster. The 125,000 square foot club, also available to hotel guests, has a 25-meter pool, a full-court gymnasium, a banked indoor running track with pacing lights, an exercise room, racquetball, handball, squash and tennis courts, a rock-climbing wall, men's and women's sauna and massage rooms, and facilities for medical evaluations. A $2.5 million updating gave the athletic facility new locker rooms, new exercise equipment and conversion of one racquetball court into a computer-simulation golf clinic.

The separate Phoenix Spa is located in a 1930s mansion which is now part of the campus. It offers a beauty and health regimen for women who want to lose weight, exercise or get treatments. Clients can come for day use or stay in one of the five guest rooms in the self-contained facility, which also has its own dining room and special menu. The 1994 renovation of the spa gave it new finishes throughout, with no major changes of fixtures, equipment or room layout. The Manor House restaurant occupies a Georgian-style house built on the campus before the hotel. It received new fixtures and finishes and a marble bar.

The renovation of the conference center building and hotel meeting rooms includes new leather armchairs for 20 in the executive boardroom, which has a private patio and balcony. No changes in room layouts were made, but new audio-visual systems were installed.

Sheraton Harbor Island Hotel
San Diego, California

Running hard to stay ahead of a hot nearby rival is a predicament familiar to many hotel owners and operators; ITT Sheraton and Harbor Cal San Diego found themselves in an odd twist on this familiar tale: they owned the hotel which was giving them unwelcome competition. To remedy the problem, they folded the Sheraton Grand on Harbor Island into the larger Sheraton Harbor Island operation just three hundred yards away, and did so with a fast-tracked design-build renovation that reads like the hotel version of Japanese "just in time" manufacturing techniques.

Name	**Sheraton Harbor Island Hotel**
Location	**San Diego, California**
Owner	**Harbor Cal San Diego**
Operator	**ITT Sheraton Corporation**
Type of Hotel	**Convention / Resort**
Date of Original Construction	**East tower: 1972; west tower: 1969**
Number of Rooms	**1,048**
Bars & Restaurants	**Harbor's Edge, Waterworks, Bakery, Quinn's Bar, Lobby Lounge**
Meeting Rooms (Number & Size)	**42 / 73,000 square feet**
Recreation Facilities	**Sand volleyball courts, marina with sailboats and jet ski rentals, two pools, tennis, children'srecreation center, spa and fitness center with exercise and weight equipment, body andbeauty treatments**
Type of Renovation	**Phased renovation, no total shutdown**
Cost	**$32 million**
Date	**1994 - 1995**
Architect	**Wimberly Allison Tong & Goo, Newport Beach, California**
Interior Designer	**Wilson & Associates**
Consultants	**Food Service: Thomas Ricca Associates, Engelwood, Colorado Lighting: Bouyea & Associates, Dallas, Texas Landscape Design: Peridian Inc., Irvine, California**
Contractor	**Charles Pankow Builders, Ltd.**

FLORAL EFFUSION

Landscaping changes included additional palm trees and grass, plus a variety of flower areas and ornamental plants and grasses (above). A number of new fountains enliven the landscape, each with a specific character tailored to its location. At the stair to the east tower swimming pool area, a whale sculpture on axis with the main building entrance reinforces the ocean theme of the marina setting. The one-story restaurant in the background was extended during the renovation; before the remodeling, a smaller restaurant overlooked a recreation area of hard surfaces and sand (facing page).

The $32 million project required only six months for design work and four months for the major portion of construction, with phases overlapped constantly. Followed up by another four-month construction phase for the second half of the property a year later, the renovation corrected a mixed metaphor of marketing which had been an impediment ever since 1979, when Sheraton took over what were originally designed as two separate hotels at San Diego's Harbor Island marina. The smaller Sheraton Grand boasted large upscale rooms, but guests were not always keen to pay higher rates than those charged by the larger Sheraton Harbor Island only a stone's throw away. The solution was to combine the two, repositioning them at the upper end of the convention market which provides about 70 percent of their market.

The project began with the commission to the Newport Beach, California, office of architects Wimberly Allison Tong & Goo. WATG prepared a design concept in two months for the repositioning of the larger east tower (formerly the Harbor Island), including a gut of the public spaces, new pools and landscaping, new food and beverage outlets, additional meeting rooms, and a make-over of the health club. Then contractor Charles Pankow came on board, putting pricing packages together as WATG spent the next four months on the construction documents. Before the documents were complete, the project went in for a building permit and the approval of the San Diego Port Authority, which owns the site. Construction was under way by the time the finishing touches had been made on the design. The east tower reopened in the spring of 1994.

Changes at the east tower are apparent to guests before they reach the building. New landscaping and a new porte cochere introduce a realigned entry and a new lobby with a view of the marina, something guests did not get before the renovation. The four food and beverage outlets in the east tower before the renovation were replaced by three, dominated by a new three-meal restaurant with massive windows overlooking the marina.

BILLOWING SAILS

The new Waterworks poolside bar and restaurant took a novel approach to the nautical theme in replacing an existing stucco-and-tile-roof food and beverage outlet. Its wave-form roof is framed with round pipe stock and covered in canvas to make a visual link with the sailboats tied up in the slips at the marina.

MAKING A GRAND ENTRANCE
The new east tower lobby continues the exotic resort theme of the exterior landscaping. A trellis-like wood grid spans the room, revealing a ceiling painted with a trompe-l'oeil sky. The lobby offers clear sight lines through the hotel and out to the marina; arriving guests had to negotiate a series of turns to catch a glimpse of the marina before the renovation.

NEW APPROACH
Before the renovation, guests arriving at the main east tower got out of their cars under a long, narrow canopy and passed through doors which led directly to the elevator core (above, left). The arrangement was direct and efficient for those already familiar with the hotel, but the renovation designers decided to provide a more formal and welcoming arrival sequence for the benefit of newcomers. A large porte cochere makes the arrival point look more substantial, and the entry doors lead to the new lobby which overlooks the marina (above, right).

Renovated accessible guest rooms brought the property into compliance with the Americans with Disabilities Act. On the exterior, L-shaped swimming pools gave way to serpentine ones with seahorse sculptures at their perimeter. The renovation increased the number and variety of landscaping features, stressing free and curvilinear forms to foster a resort image. The health club was gutted and redesigned, with treatment rooms added to its exercise and relaxation facilities. A year after construction shut down the east tower for its four-month metamorphosis, construction crews arrived at the west

tower (formerly the Sheraton Grand on Harbor Island) for a similar period, rebuilding the lobby and meeting spaces, putting new finishes in the restaurant, renovating all 350 guest rooms and updating the heating and air-conditioning system. Because the towers are separate and only one was closed at a time, the renovation never required a complete shutdown of the property. But because Sheraton already had advance bookings for meetings by the time the renovation project received the corporate go-ahead, even a partial shutdown meant farming out solid business to other properties.

To limit the loss - and to avoid turning away future bookings - the owner and operator fast-tracked design and construction. Southern California's economic downturn worked to their advantage, providing an ample supply of construction contractors willing to complete the job in short order. The fast-paced strategy proved that "If you can't beat 'em, join 'em" even applies when two competitors have the same parent.

RESORT AMBIANCE
The renovation replaced two L-shaped swimming pools with new free-form ones which complement the organic curvilinear forms of the new landscaping elements. The seahorse sculpture is a fountain which shoots water into the pool.

LIGHTEN UP

The exterior massing of the buildings did not change overall, but the renovation sought to give them a softer, lighter quality by repainting in a peach tone and replacing some of the rectilinear shapes on the roof line with arcs (below). The new curved hood at the top of the elevator tower also provided a spot for the Sheraton crest, something lacking on the marina side of the building before the renovation (right).

Hotel Macdonald
Edmonton, Alberta

How many times has a renovation team been commissioned to restore the grandeur of a historic property, with the Catch-22 that most of the property is a bland recent expansion, an eyesore but a necessity on the balance sheet? And how often do the designers wish they could just tear down the addition and give the owners and operators what they literally asked for: the famous hotel, restored to its historic grandeur. It took eight years, two owners, and a fluctuating local economy, but when the renovation of the Hotel Macdonald in Edmonton was complete, the final outcome matched the first impulse of the team.

TOWN AND COUNTRY
While the office buildings of Edmonton practically come to its front door step, the Macdonald has plenty of breathing room on the other side, where the green valley of the North Saskatchewan River opens a wide vista.
Photograph by Mary Nichols.

Name	**Hotel Macdonald**
Location	**Edmonton, Alberta**
Owner	**Canadian Pacific Hotels and Resorts**
Operator	**Canadian Pacific Hotels and Resorts**
Type of Hotel	**Luxury**
Date of Original Construction	**1915**
Number of Rooms	**198**
Bars & Restaurants	**Harvest Room / Library Bar**
Meeting Rooms	
Number & Size	**8 / 13,400 square feet**
Recreation Facilities	**Health club, including indoor pool, sauna, steam room, squash, exercise machines, game room**
Type of Renovation	**Hotel closed during construction; guest-room floors reconfigured**
Cost	**$28 million (Canadian)**
Date	**1988 - 1991**
Architect	**IBI Group, Edmonton, Alberta**
Interior Designer	**Heather Jones & Associates, Toronto, Ontario**
Consultants	**Structural Engineer: Read Jones Christoffersen Mechanical Engineer: Hemisphere Engineering, Inc.**
Contractor	**Stuart Olson Construction**

ENTER A DIFFERENT AGE

As soon as guests reach the lobby, they can see that historic inspiration was not just an exterior treatment that stopped at the front door. The renovation extended the original wall paneling in the lobby (below) higher to give the room a more calm and serene quality. The oak pilasters and entablature were added to make the arched opening to the Confederation Lounge more formal and visually articulate. The adjacent registration area (left) features faux-finish plaster detailing around wall openings which imitates the limestone on the exterior of the building. It did not exist in the lobby before the renovation, but appears in a historic ballroom photograph.

Photograph by Mary Nichols

Completed by the Grand Trunk Railway in 1915, the Hotel Macdonald put Edmonton on the map of the golden age of Canadian railroad hotel building. Reminiscent of a Renaissance chateau, with an Indiana limestone exterior and large, formal public rooms with Edwardian interiors, it was one of a group of properties the railroads constructed to fill passenger trains by luring affluent guests to cross Canada. Forty years later, as elite travelers with steamer trunks and nannies disappeared from sleeping cars and mass middle-class travel took over, the owners remade the Macdonald to fit the current hotel profile. They added a modern 15-story tower, dwarfing the original building, which they transformed on the interior. The up-to-date design did not succeed in the long run, and the property closed in 1983 after a gradual decline.

Then-owner Canadian National Hotels studied what to do with the property, and in 1985, the City of Edmonton designated the building and its Confederation Lounge, lobby, Wedgwood Room and Empire Ballroom as a Municipal Heritage Resource, putting on the pressure to preserve it. CN joined with a local real estate company on an ambitious renovation, demolishing the addition in 1986, but it floundered in a slow economy. CN sold its hotel chain to rival Canadian Pacific Hotels in 1988, and the renovation got back on track the following year. The final outcome returned the hotel, which is perched on a bluff at the edge of downtown Edmonton overlooking the North Saskatchewan River, to the prominent place in the hospitality market it had occupied when it opened.

Demolition of the tower addition on the city side of the hotel made room for a new formal garden which acts as an urban forecourt and shows off the traditional exterior amidst Edmonton's modern high-rise buildings. On the river side, the renovation added gardens and exposed the basement floor where new meeting space and a health club were added. On the interior, the most important public spaces were restored to their original design. Major ground-floor rooms such as the Confederation Lounge, the Empire Ballroom, and the Wedgwood Room were restored to their historic appearance. Other rooms were modified or redesigned in a manner compatible with the original building; rooms on the mezzanine overlooking the lobby were reworked as meeting rooms.

Although the renovation demolished the tower and barely added any space to the original building, it actually increased guest room space by two floors. The area under the steeply sloping roof which had previously been used for staff bedrooms, storage, a printing shop and air-handling equipment became new suites, four of them two stories high. Windows which follow the roof plane provide light to the new rooms without requiring construction of dormers. The existing guest room floors needed a complete reworking — some guest rooms had no bathrooms before the renovation. The renovation added bathrooms, increased the size of guest rooms and the room count in the original building from 196 to 198.

HISTORIC PATTERN
The Wedgwood Room, named after the fine china because of its intricate detailing, is located in the octagonal tower at one end of the building. Over the years, it was home to the Edmonton Press Club - and to visiting U.S. soldiers during World War II. The plaster fresco on the domed ceiling was restored by hand during the renovation.
Photograph by Mary Nichols.

ROOTS OF THE NATION

In the Confederation Lounge, the restoration work included an embossed ceiling with ornamental plasterwork designed by Canadian artist Arthur Hasley and a 9-by-18 foot Frederick Challener painting of the Fathers of Confederation, copied after an original which was lost in a fire in Ottawa. One of three rooms where historical accuracy was tantamount, it was almost indistinguishable after the renovation (below) from its condition in a historic photograph (right). The window treatment of whimsical heavy lace and brocades is new; it was chosen to allow a lot of light in and leaven the sober atmosphere of the room.

Historic photograph provided courtesy of the Alberta Provincial Museum Archive.
Renovation photograph by Mary Nichols.

IT DISAPPEARED OVERNIGHT
The addition constructed in the 1950s
towered over the hotel, bearing its name
like a sign of the times to the public
(above). Time was unkind to the addition,
which is nowhere to be seen in a similar
view taken after the renovation (right).
Photograph by Mary Nichols.

SERVICE AND AMBIANCE
The Harvest Room restaurant occupies a desirable ground floor location with a view of the private hotel gardens and the river valley below. The only thing not close at hand before the renovation was the kitchen, but that problem was solved by moving the kitchen to a main floor space next to the restaurant.
Photograph by Mary Nichols.

TALKING, DRINKING AND EATING ALLOWED
The Library Bar has bookshelves, wood paneling, and a refined atmosphere, but guests don't need to fear angering the librarian if they want to have a cocktail and a conversation.
Photograph by Mary Nichols.

GREENER PASTURES
Landscaping at the back of the hotel created a series of private gardens overlooking the North Saskatchewan River (left) which are heavily used for events during the summer. Focal points include a new gazebo (bottom, left) and fountain (bottom, right).
Photograph by Mary Nichols.

The renovation included the new mechanical and electrical systems, accessibility improvements, fire alarm and fire sprinklers usually associated with a major building overhaul, and a few less common infrastructure upgrades, including new exit stairs and vertical and horizontal fire separations. The elevators, which had been removed when the addition was constructed, were rebuilt in their original location, with new penthouses to allow them to reach the new suites in the former attic.

Exterior work was fitted closely to the interior renovations on both sides of the building. A new ballroom gallery and pre-function room were tied to the new park in front of the building where the tower addition previously stood.

All these changes add up to a bold restoration of the building, offering guests a chance to experience a hotel from another age without having to give up modern amenities. But why would an owner give up the tower addition, with more than 250 guest rooms and additional meeting rooms?

The answer: for a major market reposition. When it closed in 1983, the Macdonald had sunk to lower regions of the hotel market, but when it returned, it was the most prestigious - and most expensive - hotel in town. At the Macdonald, the literal interpretation of restoring a grand historic hotel started with the building and carried through to the product, as well.

WATER IN THE BASEMENT
Many renovations try to keep it out, but at the Macdonald a major accomplishment was adding a swimming pool and spa to the basement as part of the new health club.
Photograph by Mary Nichols.

RESTORED TO THE THRONE
The Empire Ballroom (above) remained relatively unchanged through the early 1950s (below), but later its original design was usurped when a rathskeller-style interior with a low ceiling was inserted in the space. During the renovation the half-timber ceiling of the impostor was removed, exposing the original one, which was restored and painted to match its original design (top, opposite page). The renovation augmented the ballroom with a new pre-function room and gallery (left) connecting to the rest of the hotel. Its construction enabled the renovation team to convert the existing corridor to the ballroom into kitchen space, thus improving service access to food and beverage operations.
Renovation photograph by Mary Nichols.

LADIES AND GENTLEMEN
*The Jasper Room, a meeting room on the mezzanine level, is
located in the former Gentlemen's Writing Room, which was
set aside for men in the original hotel. The nearby Ladies'
Drawing Room was provided for women to await their male
escorts before entering lobby, which they were not permitted
to do alone. The Drawing Room has become a meeting space,
and yes, ladies are now permitted
to appear unescorted in the lobby.*
Photograph by Mary Nichols.

THE DETAILS OF HISTORY
*The original door hardware displays
the initials of the Grand Trunk
Railway, the line which built the
hotel. The renovation refinished and
retained the hardware.*
Photograph by Mary Nichols.

LIGHT, BRIGHT, AND RELAXING
Guest rooms and suites have a residential quality, with light color schemes; prints
of fishing flies and equestrian scenes reflect themes from the area. Furniture
influences are mostly turn-of-the-century.
Photograph by Mary Nichols.

ON THE STREETS OF TIME
A historic view of the end of the building from 100th Street shows the hotel almost identical to its condition after the renovation.
Photograph provided courtesy of the Alberta Provincial Museum Archive.

NOT A HUMBLE GARRET

The renovation created eight new suites in former attic space on the eighth and ninth floors, but they are unlikely to be occupied by bohemians traveling on a limited budget. Four of the suites cover two stories, with private stairs connecting the living and sleeping areas. The sloped walls and complex geometry created by the roof are used to enliven the space or accent important elements such as the soaking tub in the bathroom (center). The 2,500 square foot, two-floor Royal Suite (top) has two bedrooms, three baths, and a living room large enough to entertain 50 people. Oversize furniture matches the scale of its living room; the seating can be moved from the center of the room to the walls for large receptions. A large single guest room on the suite floor (bottom) has a seating area, beds with fancy duvets and a warm
color scheme to combat the effect of short days during Edmonton's long winters.
Photograph by Mary Nichols.

The Chateau Frontenac
Quebec City, Quebec

The Chateau Frontenac might strike guests as a rambling, artful monument symbolizing everything that characterizes the city of Quebec which surrounds it. Those who notice that the property has been remodeled and expanded would discover that the recent project likewise seems to encompass all the elements of hotel renovation from A to Z. The phased updating includes reworking public spaces, adding new facilities to keep up with changes in the hospitality industry, replacing worn finishes and fixtures, conserving the cherished historical image of the property and, at the same time, carefully crafting new imagery.

FITNESS AND FUNCTION
At the tip of the roof above the fitness center in the addition is a large cooling tower exhaust grille, detailed to match the seams in the copper roofing around it. The architects placed a light inside the grille to illuminate the escaping vapor stream at night, adding a high-tech modern wrinkle to the imposing castle-like form of the building.
Photograph by Denis Farley.

Name	The Chateau Frontenac
Location	Quebec City, Quebec
Owner	CP Hotels and Resorts
Operator	CP Hotels and Resorts
Type of Hotel	Luxury
Date of Original Construction	1893
Number of Rooms	610
Bars & Restaurants	Le Champlain, Caf de la Terrasse, Bar Saint-Laurent, Vranda Saint-Laurent, Bistro
Meeting Rooms (Number & Size)	20 / 22,000 square feet
Recreation Facilities	Indoor swimming pool; fitness center
Type of Renovation	Phased renovation and addition; hotel open throughout
Cost	$57,000,000 (Canadian)
Date of Renovation	1987 - 1993
Architects	Renovation of existing hotel: Dorval & Fortin and St. Gelais, Tremblay & Belanger, Quebec Design of new wing: Le Groupe Arcop, Montreal
Interior Designer	Alexandra Champalimaud et Associs, Montreal
Consultants	Mechanical, Electrical & Structural Engineers: Solivar Groupe-Conseil, Quebec Mechanical and Electrical Engineers: Liboiron Roy Caron et Associs, Montreal Landscape Architect: Sandra Donaldson, Montreal
Contractor	Renovations: Beauvais et Varret Inc., Les Constructions Bland et Lapointe Inc., Construction B S L Inc., Beauvais & Marquis Inc., J.E. Verreault & Fils Lte, Quebec New Wing: J. E. Verreault et Fils Lte, Quebec

SETTING THE CITYSCAPE
Set on the Cape Diamond promontory overlooking the Quebec City, the
Chateau Frontenac gives visitors the feeling of staying in a European castle as
they look out over the rooftops below.

The fortress-like hotel, built by the Canadian Pacific Railroad in 1893, underwent its last major renovation in 1973, when CP embarked on a program to counter the "stuffy" image for which some critics had reproached the property. That project retained the overall image and most of the details of the historic building, while inserting some more "up-to-date" features and designs. As the 100th birthday of the property approached, CP Hotels and Resorts launched a multi-faceted project, this time stressing faithfulness to history in the existing portion of the building and steering design innovations into an addition and back-of-the-house facilities.

The hotel was built by William Van Horne, president of Canadian Pacific, with the design by influential U.S. architect Bruce Price. The original building, called the Riverview Wing, had 170 rooms and three suites. Its success led to construction of the Citadel Wing in 1899, followed by the Mont-Carmel Wing in 1908, and later the Saint Louis Wing and finally the Central Tower.

In 1987 and 1988, guest rooms in the Mont Carmel and Riverview wings and the lower floors of the Central Tower were renovated. From 1989 to 1993, the guest rooms in the St. Louis Wing and on the upper floors of the Central Tower underwent renovation, along with food and beverage outlets, the retail spaces and the exterior area at the entry. The alterations converted some storage and staff sleeping rooms on the top floor into additional guest rooms, while combining small existing guest rooms to create one or two larger rooms out of two or three existing rooms. In addition to finishes and furniture-fixtures-and-equipment overhaul, the renovation included life safety and building systems upgrades and rationalization of back-of-the-house areas, including a reconfiguration which made the main kitchen more compact to allow better access and circulation for meeting rooms.

When the CP and its architects began designing a new health club for the hotel, they knew they would have to deal very carefully with the strict historic preservation review by the city of Quebec, but they were in for a surprise: city officials urged them to make the addition larger than they had originally planned. The renovation team willingly followed the city's suggestion, erecting the new Claude Pratte Wing over the existing parking garage which adjoined the hotel.

As a result, the four-story wing, completed in 1993, has not only a fitness center and outdoor terrace, but 66 new guest rooms.

The addition posed a number of challenges, but the renovation team saw them as opportunities to weave the new construction into the warp and woof of the historic building. Guest-room configurations had to change from floor to floor where floor plates shrink under the steep roof which takes up half the height of the

addition. Although the exterior materials of the addition are almost identical to those of the existing hotel, their brand new appearance contrasts with the weathered look of the historic building. The difference is easy to see today, but in 50 years it won't be, said architect Bruce Allen of Le Groupe Arcop. That might seem like a long time, but in the perspective of the Chateau Frontenac, it is just another link in a very long chain.

THE SPICE OF LIFE

Variety is the watchword in guest-room layouts in the new Claude Pratte Wing. Some rooms have regular windows; some have dormers. On the floor above the health club, rooms are long and deep, each with a sitting area and a sleeping area. Higher up, the exterior walls are much closer to the corridors, so rooms are narrow and wide. All the rooms in the new wing are large, and corner rooms have the added advantage of good views over the rooftops of Quebec; some incorporate circular turret spaces (above).
Photographs by Denis Farley.

Elévation rue Mont-Carmel

Hôtels et Villégiatures ◼◀ Canadien Pacifique

Le Château Frontenac

agrandissement de l'aile Mont-Carmel

JUST ADD 50 YEARS

The designers decided to match the exterior materials and design elements of the existing historic portions of the hotel in the addition; in a few decades weathering will blur the distinction between new and old. The roof of the addition (center of photograph left, left side of elevation drawing above) is the same design as the historic roofs and picks up the main ridge line of the existing Mont Carmel Wing, which it adjoins. The new roofing is copper; time will give it the same green patina seen on the copper of the main tower (left side of photograph).

Photograph by Denis Farley; drawing by Le Groupe Arcop.

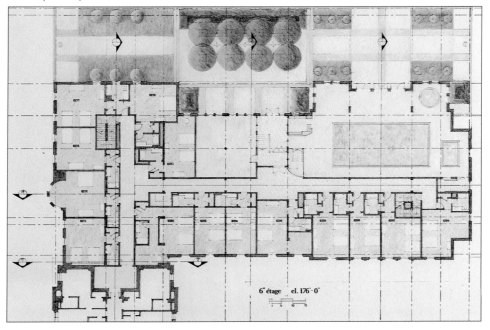

6ᵉ étage   el. 176'-0"

NOOKS AND CRANNIES

The brick and limestone exterior of the addition match the materials of the older portions of the building as closely as using current building materials can. The limestone banding on the walls extends the design of the existing building — as do the floor levels on the interior. The stone facing on the lower portion of the parking garage below the addition already existed, but the brick and stone design above it was added during the renovation to disguise ventilation openings as windows. Most of the details in the addition are based on ones from the original building, but others like the crenellations of the parapet around the new roof terrace (left) were created anew for the addition.

Photographs by Denis Farley.

THE SPA THAT CAME IN FROM THE COLD
Wintertime visitors who don't like the cold have a swimming pool, a wading pool and a whirlpool spa to console them in the new health club (above). A work-out room, massage rooms and a steam room are available to those who get waterlogged, and during good weather, the outdoor terrace next to the pool gives the health club an open-air feeling (left).
Photographs by Brigitte Ostiguy.

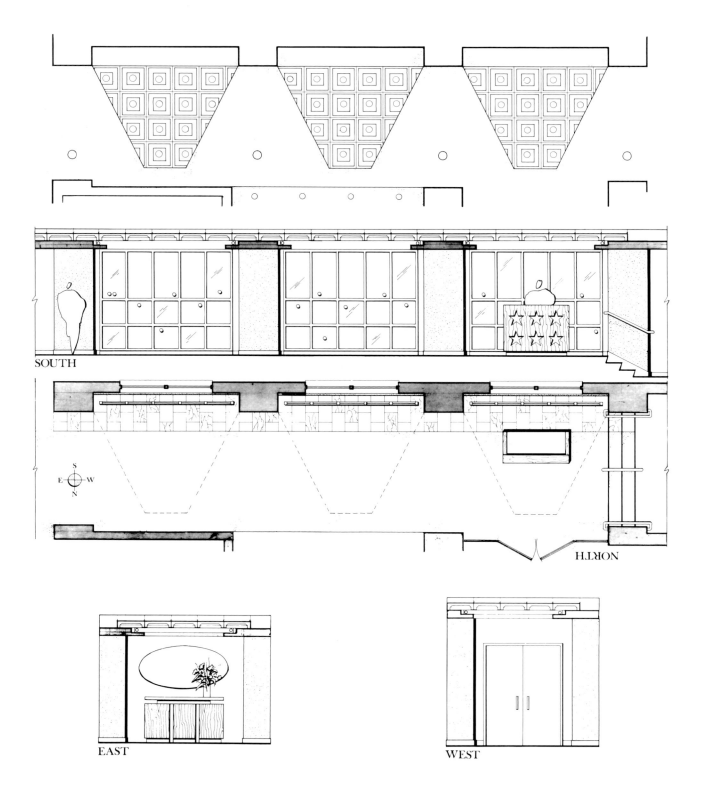

SOUTH

NORTH

EAST

WEST

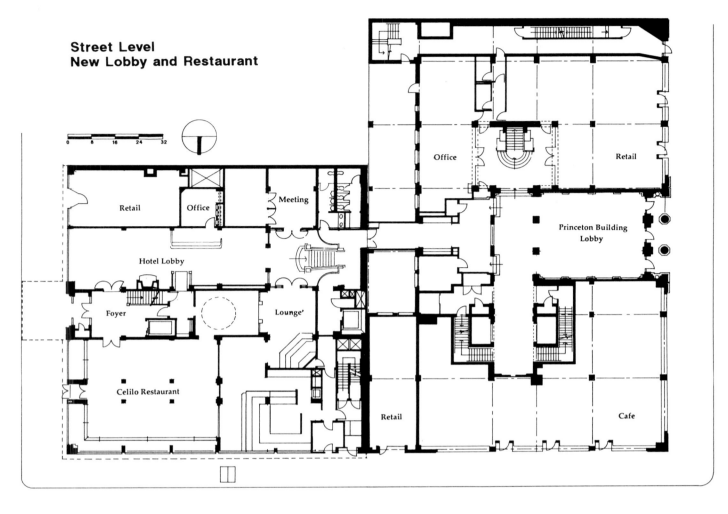

**Street Level
New Lobby and Restaurant**

**Second Through Fifth Floors
Partial Plan**

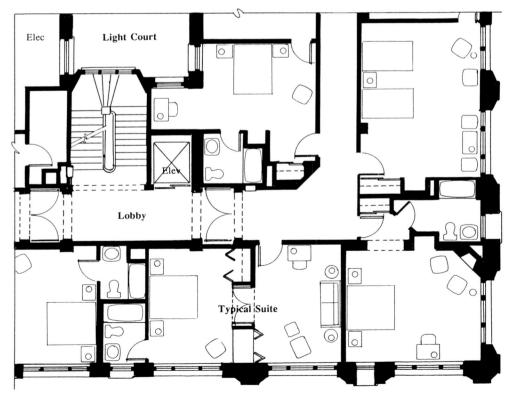

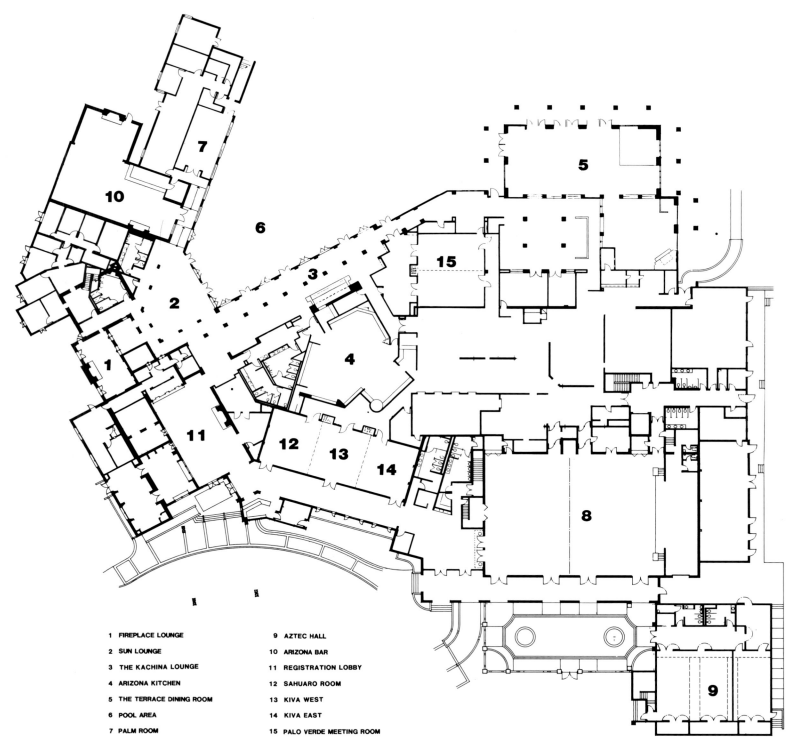

1 FIREPLACE LOUNGE

2 SUN LOUNGE

3 THE KACHINA LOUNGE

4 ARIZONA KITCHEN

5 THE TERRACE DINING ROOM

6 POOL AREA

7 PALM ROOM

8 SACHEM HALL

9 AZTEC HALL

10 ARIZONA BAR

11 REGISTRATION LOBBY

12 SAHUARO ROOM

13 KIVA WEST

14 KIVA EAST

15 PALO VERDE MEETING ROOM

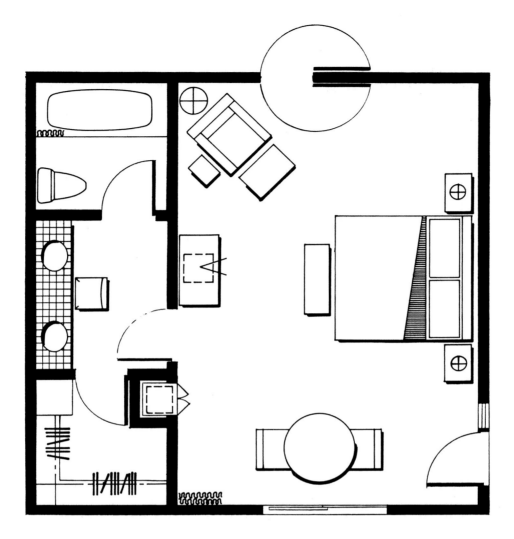

GUESTROOMS

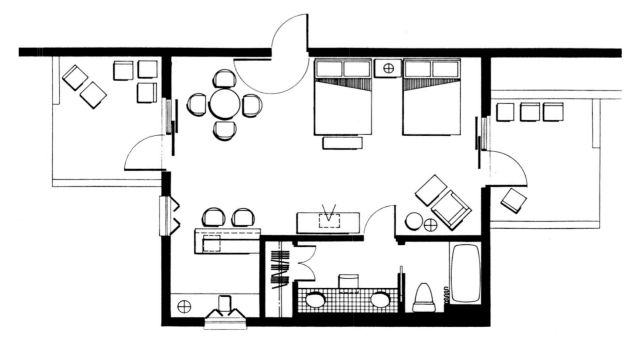

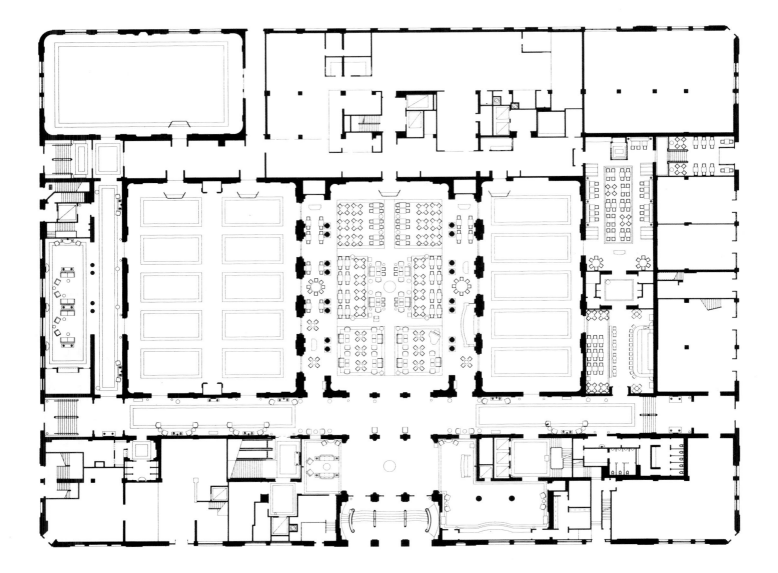

Ground Floor Plan

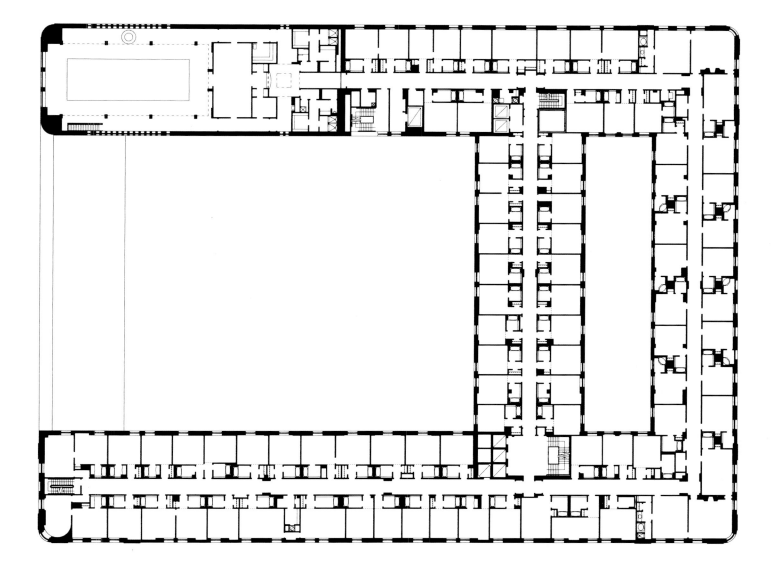

Fourth Floor Plan

Jennifer Bartlett: Early Plate Work

Jennifer Bartlett: Early Plate Work

Brenda Richardson

With an Introduction by
Allison N. Kemmerer

Addison Gallery of American Art
Phillips Academy
Andover, Massachusetts

Distributed by
Yale University Press
New Haven and London

Jennifer Bartlett: Early Plate Work

Organized by the Addison Gallery of American Art

Phillips Academy, Andover, Massachusetts

Generous support for this exhibition and publication was provided by the Locks Foundation,

Evelyn H. and Robert W. Doran (PA 1951), and the Sidney R. Knafel Fund.

Exhibition dates:

September 12–December 10, 2006

Published by the Addison Gallery of American Art

Phillips Academy, Andover, Massachusetts

Addison Gallery of American Art

Phillips Academy

180 Main Street

Andover, Massachusetts 01810

www.addisongallery.org

Distributed by:

Yale University Press

302 Temple Street, P.O. Box 209040

New Haven, Connecticut 06520-9040

www.yalebooks.com

ISBN-13: 978-0-300-11771-4

ISBN-10: 0-300-11771-X

Library of Congress Cataloging-in-Publication Data

Richardson, Brenda.

Jennifer Bartlett : early plate work/Brenda Richardson. – 1st ed.

p. cm.

Published on the occasion of an exhibition held at the Addison Gallery of American Art,

Sept. 12–Dec. 10, 2006.

ISBN 0-300-11771-X

1. Bartlett, Jennifer, 1941—Exhibitions.

I. Bartlett, Jennifer, 1941- II. Addison Gallery of American Art. III. Title.

ND237.B275A4 2006

759.13—dc22

2006015741

Frontispiece: Jennifer Bartlett at work in Benita Olinger Potter's garden shed, Southampton, New York, 1975

Editor: Joseph N. Newland, Q.E.D.

Designer: Takaaki Matsumoto, Matsumoto Incorporated, New York

Printed and bound by Toppan Printing Co., Tokyo, Japan

Contents

Lenders to the Exhibition

Allen Memorial Art Museum, Oberlin College, Oberlin, Ohio

The Baltimore Museum of Art, Maryland

University of California, Berkeley Art Museum

Paula Cooper Gallery, New York

Penny Cooper and Rena Rosenwasser

James F. Duffy, Jr.

Maxine and Stuart Frankel Foundation for Art

Herbert F. Johnson Museum of Art, Cornell University, Ithaca, New York

Sally and Wynn Kramarsky

Mr. and Mrs. William Lamont, Jr.

Locks Gallery, Philadelphia

Museum of Contemporary Art San Diego, California

The Museum of Modern Art, New York

Neuberger Museum of Art, Purchase College, State University of New York

The Parrish Art Museum, Southampton, New York

Private collection

Gilbert and Lila Silverman, Detroit, Michigan

Estate of Jack Tworkov

Tate, London, United Kingdom

Walker Art Center, Minneapolis, Minnesota

Acknowledgments

It is with great pride that the Addison Gallery of American Art presents *Jennifer Bartlett: Early Plate Work*. This landmark exhibition and publication mark the first museum study devoted solely to the early plate paintings. We are certain that this project will inspire renewed attention to this important and formative body of work as well as reveal its significance to Jennifer Bartlett's career and to the history of contemporary art.

The realization of this exhibition is due to the resolve and commitment of Allison N. Kemmerer, Curator of Photography and of Art after 1950. Allison has worked with exceptional dedication to forge the most meaningful exhibition possible. Sharing Allison's conviction about the importance of Jennifer Bartlett's work, Brenda Richardson crafted an exquisite and perceptive essay that greatly enriches the endeavor. We are honored to have had the privilege of working with such a respected scholar.

This project could only have come to fruition through the immeasurable help and generosity of many individuals. We are extremely grateful to Sueyun Locks of Locks Gallery, who has been zealous in her devotion to the project from its earliest stages. We are indebted to the staff at the Bartlett studio, particularly Nancy Brody, Joan LiPuma, Ricky Manne, and David Nelson, who promptly attended to myriad details and requests with grace and good humor.

The Addison is deeply indebted to the Locks Foundation, Evelyn H. and Robert W. Doran (PA 1951), and the Sidney R. Knafel Fund, whose generous support was instrumental in realizing the exhibition and publication.

Joseph N. Newland revealed his incomparable editorial mastery in his sensitive and graceful editing of the manuscript. Designer Takaaki Matsumoto, assisted by Hisami Aoki and Amy Wilkins, has captured the spirit of Bartlett's work both in its seriousness and its exuberance, with a sophisticated and elegant design. We are pleased to be working with Yale University Press, who will be distributing this publication.

The Gallery appreciates the generosity and support of all those whose loan of works was crucial in assembling the exhibition and who are listed elsewhere. In addition, we wish to thank the following people for their numerous efforts to provide us with expertise, information, and images for the book: Albright-Knox Art Gallery, Buffalo, New York; Artists Rights Society (ARS); Richard and Ann Artschwager; Amanda Parmer and Paula Cooper, Paula Cooper Gallery, New York; Frank R. DiDaniele, Jr.; Virginia Dwan Collection/Dwan Gallery Archives, New York; Sabine Sarwa, Hauser & Wirth, London; Mr. and Mrs. Alan P. Hoblitzell, Jr.; Kate Hoblitzell; the Judd Foundation, Marfa, Texas; Ellsworth Kelly; John Kemmerer; Werner H. Kramarsky; Shelley Lee, Estate of Roy Lichtenstein, The Roy Lichtenstein Foundation, New York; Philip Mott, Doug Schaller, and Renee Shortell, Locks Gallery, Philadelphia; Sara A. Weldon, Louis K. Meisel Gallery, New York; Therese M. James, Museum of Contemporary Art San Diego; Jon Mason, PaceWildenstein, New York; Holly Frisbee, Philadelphia Museum of Art; Irwin and Marcia Schloss; Richard Schloss; Susanna Singer; Silke Sommer; Xan Price, Sonnabend Gallery, New York; Visual Artists and Galleries Association, Inc. (VAGA); Lauren Jaeger, Mary Zlot and Associates, San Francisco; Britte Le Va and Joe Zucker.

The staff of the Addison has displayed its usual exemplary skill in organizing projects and transforming them into masterful presentations of art and word. Special thanks is due to Emily K. Shubert, Charles H. Sawyer Curatorial Fellow for 2003–2005 and Jaime DeSimone, the Addison's present curatorial fellow, who were an essential part of the project from the beginning, assisting the curator with absolutely every level of organization. Associate Registrar James Sousa and Louann Boyd of Boyd Associates managed the loans for the exhibition with skillful efficiency. Chief Preparator Leslie Maloney and her crew led by Brian Coleman and Austin Sharpe demonstrated their usual creativity—and in this case incredible patience—in installing over one thousand 12 x 12 inch steel plates.

Most important, we offer our utmost gratitude to Jennifer Bartlett. Her generous spirit and enduring commitment to this project made her a pleasure to work with and ensured the extraordinary quality of both the exhibition and catalogue.

Brian T. Allen
The Mary Stripp and R. Crosby Kemper Director

Connecting the Dots
Allison N. Kemmerer

Increasingly streaming and webbed, the twenty-first-century world is one that threatens to grow clotted with the rampant, automatic, and effortless multiplication and simultaneity made possible by cellular technology, video on demand, MP3s, Wi-Fi, fiber optics, Webcasts, electronic scanning, and e-mail. Despite, or perhaps because of, this electronic and digital tangle, people still have a fundamental, primal need for linear narrative, to clearly see how someone got from point A to point B, to understand how bewildering arrays of dots are—or can be—connected.

This narrative, linear urge is particularly problematic when considering the art of Jennifer Bartlett, in which links or connections between various bodies of work are not always easily evident. Ambitious in scope and seemingly infinite in variety, Bartlett's work is filled with challenging paradoxes and apparent contradictions. Her fluid movement between abstraction and figuration, her blending of the analytical and intuitive, the conceptual and the sensuous, and her investigation of multiple artistic styles, points of view, and materials make her work resistant to easy definition or categorization. The embrace of chance and willingness to explore the many paths and ideas generated during the actual process of working has led her in many directions. Frequently unsettled and disoriented by the resulting variety and seeming discontinuity of Bartlett's corpus, many a critic has mistakenly interpreted each recently created body of work as a "fresh start" or a "new direction." Others have searched for a maddeningly elusive—and perhaps mythical—singular voice by praising the artist for at last "finding her own particular style," in the works that especially appeal to them. Still others commend the multiple voices in her work, thinking of them as part of a conversational whole.

The truth is that Bartlett found her distinctive voice in 1968, and it has guided her ever since. That was the year she began painting on one-foot-square steel plates coated with white enamel and overlaid with a light gray, quarter-inch grid. A logical outgrowth of the drawings she had been making on graph paper, it is a format Bartlett worked in exclusively for the next eight years. Although her art has undergone many transformations since the 1970s, the vision that emerged in these early paintings has remained steady throughout the artist's career. Acting as a blueprint of sorts, these early plate works contain the fundamental building blocks that underlie and give rise to all that follows.

Typical of Bartlett's process, the early plate paintings grew out of a self-assigned task. Once she settled on using the square steel plates for her paintings, she committed herself to "working on the plates for five years, no matter what was coming out on them." Much like a connect-the-dots game in which basic parameters are provided but the end result remains a mystery until the puzzle is solved, Bartlett had no idea what this assignment would produce or where it would take her. Using rules and systems of her own devising to determine the placement of her hand-painted dots within the square grids on appliance-white industrial steel, Bartlett created an extraordinary group of works made all the more remarkable by the range of expression achieved within such a tightly constrained methodology and limited and opposing materials.

The variety and depth of this body of work is the result of Bartlett's determination to examine a situation from every angle, of being guided, as Brenda Richardson so eloquently describes in her essay here, by "what if" propositions. In these early paintings, Bartlett takes the basic components of plate, grid, and dot and shows us the unbelievably varied things one can do with them. From austere and mathematically precise to atmospheric and romantic, from rigorously structured and patterned to more freehand and painterly, from abstract to figurative, these paintings are a testament to the nearly endless possibilities born of an intense investigation of rigidly limited means.

The diverse styles and themes expressed in the individual plate paintings mature and coalesce in Bartlett's epic *Rhapsody* of 1975–76. Extending and elaborating on the investigations embodied in the earlier plate paintings, the 987-plate *Rhapsody*, as the artist herself has said, serves as an encyclopedia of possibilities—of all the things a painting might be. A summation of Bartlett's concerns at the time, *Rhapsody* also informs all of the work that follows. Even as the artist has continued to explore new terrain, each resulting work is grounded in the fundamentals first explored in these early plate works—the grid as infrastructure, seriality, organizing systems, opposition, and dots—as these basic components continually take new forms and arrangements, guided by a deft hand and inquisitive mind.

When viewed as a whole, Jennifer Bartlett's oeuvre can seem like an expanding universe of scattered, seemingly random dots with little or no common bond to draw them together out of the chaos of creation and into a harmonized, internally consistent sphere. Yet the deeper one's gaze penetrates into the process and methodology underpinning her creative ferment, the easier it is to recognize how those dots are connected, how those works exist within a streaming, glittering web of Bartlett's rigorous and rhapsodic creation.

What If?

Brenda Richardson

The trajectory of Jennifer Bartlett's early plate work is art world legend, culminating in the 987-plate *Rhapsody*, 1975–76 [pl. 35], premiered at New York's Paula Cooper Gallery in May 1976 and enthusiastically welcomed by John Russell in *The New York Times* as "the most ambitious single work of art" he had seen in New York City. It was *Rhapsody* that brought to an unpredictably triumphant close the first significant chapter of Bartlett's artistic life. This glorious, epic work—dazzling and profound as it is—has cast a long shadow over the radical plate work that preceded it.[1]

It was late spring 1967. Jennifer Bartlett had just moved into a loft at 131 Greene Street in Lower Manhattan. She was twenty-six years old, and married (since 1964) to Ed Bartlett, a Yale medical student she had met when they were both undergraduates in northern California, she at Mills College from 1959 to 1963. After completing her M.F.A. at Yale's esteemed School of Art and Architecture in 1965, Bartlett had triangulated marriage, employment (teaching art at the University of Connecticut in Storrs, about two hours from New Haven), and painting. The last, for her, entailed frequent visits to museums and galleries in New York City to look at art. Two years of this unsatisfactory routine were enough. Bartlett moved to Manhattan, where the Greene Street studio became her anchor. For a time she sustained both job and marriage on a commuting basis (she and Bartlett divorced in 1972).[2]

In the late sixties, artists who took over raw space in the primarily industrial area of SoHo lived and worked quasi-legally—something between squatters and urban campers—under New York City's A.I.R. (Artist in Residence) accommodation. The SoHo artists of those years exemplified lives of single-minded mission on the one hand and uncommon deprivation on the other. Bartlett took to the new bohemia like a duck to water. Née Losch, she was raised upper middle class (her father was an engineer, her mother a commercial artist) in Long Beach, California, the eldest of four children (two girls, two boys). Bartlett was precocious, contrary, and artistic from the start. In SoHo she found herself in the right place at the right time.

In the evolution of the history of contemporary art, the preceding year had been galvanic. It was in 1966 that the baton was passed from the Pop artists to the Minimalists, who saw their work validated in a number of unusually influential New York exhibitions. The Jewish Museum came first, with *Primary Structures* (April 27–June 12) [fig. 1], the exhibition generally credited with affirming Minimalism as a prevailing style. Then a few months later the Guggenheim Museum presented its *Systemic Painting* (September 21–November 27), curated by Lawrence Alloway. That autumn also saw two important guest-curated exhibitions of radical new art in Manhattan galleries. At the Fishbach Gallery was *Eccentric Abstraction* (September 20–October 8), curated by critic Lucy Lippard, who selected work by nine sculptors, including Louise Bourgeois, Eva Hesse, Bruce Nauman, and Keith Sonnier. At the same time, the Dwan Gallery presented *10* (October 4–29), a group show curated by Robert Smithson and featuring the new geometrically reductive painting and sculpture [fig. 2].[3] Bartlett saw all four shows.

Jennifer Bartlett is, in many ways, a renegade. She recalls that even in her years as an art student at Mills and Yale she essentially liked almost everything she saw. She loves art, and she loves the artist's impulse toward idiosyncratic self-expression. Unlike most serious artists, Bartlett never compartmentalized her tastes: she likes both painting and sculpture, she gravitates equally toward abstraction and representation. She has never been attracted exclusively, or necessarily, to work that aligns with her own. And "her own," in any case, ranges widely.

In 1967, when she settled in New York City, and clearly under the influence of the various reductive forms she was seeing in Manhattan museums and galleries,

Figure 1. Installation view of *Primary Structures*, The Jewish Museum, New York, April 27 to June 12, 1966. Left: Donald Judd (1928–1994), *Untitled*, 1966, and *Untitled*, 1966; center: Robert Morris (born 1931), *Untitled (2 L beams)*; and right (above): Robert Grosvenor (born 1937), *Transoxiana*, 1965

Full figure and plate captions begin on page 117.

Bartlett experimented with minimalist forms herself. For one work, she cut out squares of raw canvas, then drew a grid in blue pencil on each square; she sewed them together in weblike fashion (trying to keep the pencil grids aligned), added grommets, and hung the piece on the wall. For another, she stretched a canvas nine by twenty feet and painted it with a grid of rectangular blocks, leaving a reveal to separate the blocks. (By virtue of a measurement error, the artist was left with a truncated row of blocks at the bottom of the canvas. Making the kind of decision that would characterize her future work as well, she ended up painting in the "border" row as if it were the same as the others. As Bartlett says, she's consistently "adaptable to circumstances.") She then mixed as many colors as she could manage—she thinks it was something like 250—and painted each block in a different color, with colors arranged by chance. She now thinks of these works as the "false starts" that mark an artist's transition from student to professional. Just the same, the works that she describes are clear predecessors to the plate work to come.

At the time, Bartlett was also constructing assemblages of small everyday items that she scouted and purchased at the hardware store, manipulated (melted, painted in a uniform color, smashed, whatever), and then arranged in sculptural groupings, often scattered or otherwise randomly arrayed. She gradually began to focus more closely on the kind of art she needed to make for herself and migrated with new commitment toward the systems-based art that had only recently claimed public attention.

Bartlett was one of many in her generation of artists whose encounter with Minimalism was transformative. These artists, most in their mid-twenties and best described as emergent, intuitively grasped that Abstract Expressionism would never be old-fashioned but it *was* now historical. And they also knew that in Minimalism they found kindred spirit, if not form. The best of this generation began to build on the Minimalist sensibility by riffing on its fundamental tenets with elaborated, sometimes quirky, forms of expression, very often rooted in representational imagery.

Several of the young artists experimenting with hybrid forms were among Bartlett's closest friends in the early SoHo years. She sustained nearly familial relationships with, in particular, Elizabeth Murray and Barry Le Va. Bartlett and Murray first met in 1962 when both were students at Mills College, and they have been friends ever since. Bartlett and Le Va both attended Woodrow Wilson High School in Long Beach, where they met around 1956 (their parents were friends as well). Bartlett was also close at the time with Jonathan Borofsky (a Yale acquaintance), costume and theater designer Bob Israel, and painter John Torreano. And living in lofts at 101 Prince Street, just around the corner from Bartlett, were Chuck Close and Joe Zucker, two artists whose work in those years evolved in seeming tandem with Bartlett's own.

Close had studied art at Yale, completing his M.F.A. in 1964, thus overlapping Bartlett's time there (in their New Haven years Bartlett and Close often paired up to travel into Manhattan to look at art together). By the fall of 1967 Close had taken a studio on Greene Street a few blocks south of Bartlett's, and then in 1970 moved to the Prince Street building. Zucker had studied art at the School of The Art Institute of Chicago, completing his M.F.A. in 1966. He moved to New York and his Prince Street studio in the fall of 1968.

In those years Close was not painting the portraits constructed of gridded dots and circles with which he is most closely identified today. He was painting very large-scale, photographically faithful portraits of friends and acquaintances. He used a traditional system of gridded squares as a device for enlarging the image from its photo source to the scale required for his oversize hand-painted canvases. Close did his first dot drawings in the summer of 1973, airbrushing dots in each square of the grid [fig. 3].[4]

Figure 2. Installation view of *10*, Dwan Gallery, New York, October 4–29, 1966. Works, clockwise from center foreground, by Carl Andre, Jo Baer, Donald Judd, Sol LeWitt, Robert Smithson, and Robert Morris

Figure 3. Chuck Close (born 1940),

Susan/Pastel, 1977

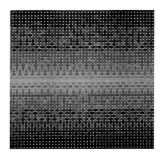

Figure 4. Joe Zucker (born 1941), *Joe's*

Painting #125, 1965

Figure 5. Joe Zucker (born 1941), *The 100-Foot*

Wall (detail), 1968–69

Zucker and Bartlett, for their part, shared a strikingly skewed artistic bent and a similarly perverse sense of humor. Zucker was deeply engaged with the pressing issues of the day—the Vietnam war, sexism, racism. He and a number of other artists in that circle (though not Bartlett) were convinced that the political issues about which they cared the most could be expressed through their art, albeit subversively and in essentially abstract form. As Zucker recently articulated that late sixties commitment:

> Some of us believed that meaning could be embedded in imagery without paint depicting it. Artists like Richter and Polke were trying much the same thing in Germany at the time. I had some quixotic notion that we could say things—get at real-life issues, maybe—that weren't traditionally addressed in art. Jennifer [Bartlett] wanted to make art that had no gender, but she didn't otherwise share feelings about putting politics into art. In formal terms, though, both of us were peculiarly reductive in our approach, and both of us came at our art from a conceptual basis. We also share a pointedly literary orientation to our work.[5]

Bartlett affirms her ambition to make gender-free art, which in her case would seem to be less a political goal than a matter of personal strategy in an art world manifestly biased toward white males. From today's perspective, she states unequivocally that she believes "the art of an era defines its era," but emphasizes that she's never been interested in addressing sociopolitical issues in her own art. Bartlett summarizes her artistic intentions relative to subject matter as "pictorial and perverse."

By 1965, when Zucker was still in graduate school in Chicago, he was painting weave patterns [fig. 4] that share distinctly common ground with Bartlett's early plate work.[6] Like the plate pieces, Zucker's weave paintings were composed of obsessively small strokes in repetitive patterns. Organized serially, the paintings progressed in incremental permutations. There were thirteen paintings in the series (titled *125, 125A, 125B,* through *125L*). With each canvas, the magnification of the weave became larger. Then in 1968, new to New York and his large loft studio, Zucker embarked on a self-imposed painting "assignment." He set out to make a painting a day for one hundred days, with each segment measuring eight feet high and one foot wide. Each day's painting had to be executed in a different style and/or in different materials. The work was titled *The 100-Foot Wall,* 1968–69 [fig. 5], though Zucker himself referred to it as his "Sears catalogue," since it represented an inventory of materials and ideas he could call on at will.

> The result is a virtual lexicon of styles: drawings of weave patterns are interspersed among silkscreened photographic blowups from *The Primary Structures of Fabric,* an assemblage of a magnifying glass hanging over a piece of fabric, acidly colored paintings of expressionistic characters, a bisected *Charioteer* and mixed media constructions of tacky materials found in profusion on the streets of Lower Manhattan.[7]

In fact, the *Wall* was never finished. After about a year—the artist had not managed a painting a day—Zucker simply saw no point in continuing. He came to realize that the process was essentially pedantic and, unexpectedly, every bit as restrictive as any other way of working. "In other words," he says now, "having *no* style was just as constricting as having *any* style." When he stopped, there were thirty-some panels to the piece and it ran about fifty-five feet in length (several panels measure more than a foot in width).

Figure 6. Joe Zucker (born 1941),
Rose Lake (detail), 1969

Figure 7. Richard Artschwager (born 1923),
Untitled (All Over Pattern), 1965

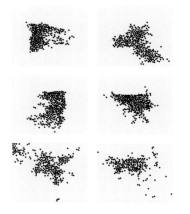

Figure 8. Barry Le Va (born 1941), *Bearings Rolled*
(Six Specific Instants: No Particular Order), 1966–67

Bartlett's own lexicon of painting styles, *Rhapsody,* painted six years after Zucker's, was similarly organized in one-foot-wide vertical rows (with one-inch intervals between plates); it is just under eight feet high (seven twelve-inch plates plus one-inch intervals between them). *Rhapsody*'s 987 plates are organized—with episodic, and thus startling, departures from its otherwise metronomic grid—in 142 vertical rows (plus lateral intervals) totaling just over 153 running feet.[8] An echo of *The 100-Foot Wall* is present in *Rhapsody* insofar as the rich dialogue between any two congenial artists necessarily resonates in their art. But the paintings themselves are utterly different. Zucker's *100-Foot Wall* was an exercise (it's revealing that the artist titled it "wall" rather than "painting") and an assemblage of parts. Bartlett's *Rhapsody* is a painting, integrated in its complexities, carefully planned, and highly refined in its execution. Still, Bartlett was a part of the *Wall*'s moment, and something of that predetermined program of implementing a grand-scale artwork—not to mention curiosity about the history of painting and painters—is evident in *Rhapsody.* A more concise lesson in the fundamentals of art-making is seen in Bartlett's stately *Drawing and Painting,* 1974 [pl. 32], a seventy-eight-plate work that offers demonstration, step by step, of the progression from line to plane.

In *The 100-Foot Wall* Zucker used many art mediums, including one he invented: cotton balls soaked in acrylic paint. After he abandoned his hundred-foot plan, he embarked on a series of paintings composed in his new medium, the first of which, in 1969, was *Rose Lake* [fig. 6]. The cotton-ball paintings were a natural extension of his earlier basket-weave paintings—both spoke to the very substance of canvas. Disparaged by some for his unlikely and somehow way-too-humble art medium, Zucker says that he drew encouragement from the supportive response of artist Richard Artschwager, who admired the new work. Artschwager, a generation older than Bartlett and Zucker, expressed in his own work a serious commitment to the methods and materials of fabrication. He made abstract sculpture that mimicked furniture; and he painted on Celotex, a textured industrial material with a speckled, dotlike matrix. Artschwager, who had done his own basket-weave paintings in 1965 [fig. 7], praised Zucker's cotton-ball paintings for the ingenuity of a medium that "used the fabric of the canvas itself and at the same time served as a module to establish scale."[9]

It was at about this same time (1968–69) that Bartlett determined her own "module to establish scale," namely, the dot. Zucker remembers that Bartlett would call and ask what he was doing. "I'm rolling," he would reply (meaning shaping cotton balls and then rolling them in paint). "I'm dotting," she would counter. The very demands of the process, for both Bartlett and Zucker, advanced the work's authority. "I had a Zen-like attitude about making those particles," Zucker reports. "The character of the process determined the character of what I ended up with. *How* we made things gave validity to what they *looked* like." This personal attention to the means of fabrication, to process, to duration (even to endurance), represented a departure from the dominant modes of both Pop art and Minimalism, whose protagonists relied significantly on commissioned fabrication.

Indeed, the embrace of process as integral to the quality of the "product" coincided with the evolution of "process art," promulgated by several prominent figures who claimed the process of making or doing as the artwork itself. Bartlett's friend Barry Le Va was notable among this group [fig. 8], but Bartlett also particularly admired the process work of Vito Acconci, Robert Morris, and Dennis Oppenheim. Of all the artist-friends in Bartlett's several overlapping circles, she says she felt most competitive in those years with sculptor Joel Shapiro, whose wall and floor pieces in the late sixties fell within the parameters of process art. It was in the spring of 1969 that curators Marcia Tucker and James Monte organized their profoundly influential exhibition *Anti-Illusion: Procedures/Materials* at New York's Whitney Museum of American Art. All about process, the show included work by twenty-two artists, including Bartlett's friends Le Va and Shapiro.

By the late sixties, Lower Manhattan (including Little Italy) had become a village of artists with shared ambitions and overlapping sensibilities. Lynda Benglis, Jake Berthot, Mel Bochner, Jackie Ferrara, Nancy Graves, Eva Hesse, Robert Mangold, Brice Marden, Ree Morton, Robert Moskowitz, Judy Pfaff, Dorothea Rockburne, Alan Saret, Richard Serra, Robert Smithson, and Pat Steir—and countless others— were all around at the time. Like Bartlett, they were strikingly ambitious to secure a place for their art in an arena beyond their studios.

If Lower Manhattan was a village of working artists, it was equally a village of socializing artists. If you weren't there at the time, it is difficult from the perspective of today's highly evolved, well-financed, globally networked art world to imagine what it was like to be a part of that village in the late sixties and early seventies. The atmosphere was intense and high-energy. For the most part, artists had no money. Exhibition space was scant, art periodicals were few, dealers showing the most advanced art were scarce, collectors were virtually unknown. Artists looked to each other for support both moral and practical. Active networking, much of which took place in favored "art bars" or in each other's lofts, was the usual way to spend an evening. Work was work all day, and play was work all night. Talking or, more often, arguing about art (and each other) kept everyone going. Many of these artists were intellectuals, sophisticated and well read in contemporary criticism and philosophy (Wittgenstein, above all); cliques bonded through shared art affinities, and relations could be fiercely competitive.

Bartlett's art and social life intersected several overlapping circles. At Yale she had met Irish artist Michael Craig-Martin and his wife, painter Jan Hashey, and the Craig-Martins and the Bartletts became good friends. Bartlett traveled to London to visit Hashey and Craig-Martin, where she was introduced into the lively world of contemporary English art, music, and literature. It was in this context that she met collectors Charles and Doris Saatchi, artists David Hockney, Howard Hodgkin, and Richard Smith, and many others. For years after, she traveled regularly to England and maintained close ties there, including, in particular, those with Mark Lancaster and Max Gordon, both of whom she had met on that first visit. Through Lancaster, Bartlett met Jasper Johns and became part of a circle that included Julian Lethbridge, with whom she became romantically involved. Composer John Cage was an intimate part of the Johns circle, as were other performing artists. Through Paula Cooper, Bartlett met composer Philip Glass; she already knew Steve Reich, with whom she had studied music appreciation at Mills College. Vanguard dancers and musician/composers, and even writers and poets, were more likely to perform or recite in artists' lofts or art galleries than in traditional performing arts venues. There was a natural and very lively interaction among artists of similarly radical sensibilities that was never constrained by the medium in which they worked.

All of this very much appealed to Bartlett, who never wants to be constrained, whether by medium or anything else. She describes herself as a "multi-tasker," meaning that she wants to do a lot of different things at the same time. She wants to evade being channeled by critical convention into a consistent medium or style. Bartlett admiringly names Sol LeWitt's work as a model of what she neologically calls "fragmented" or "fractured" art. All she means is that LeWitt works, creatively and successfully, in virtually every medium and in every conceivable forum, and that's what she wants for herself as well.

Figure 9. Eadweard J. Muybridge (1830–1904), *Plate 44. Walking Taking Off Hat*, 1885, from *Animal Locomotion*, 1887, *Volume 7, Males & Females Draped & Misc. Subjects*

One of Bartlett's most intimate networks was the one centered on Paula Cooper and her gallery. Although Bartlett wasn't officially represented by Paula Cooper until 1974, she knew Cooper as a friend well before that. Joel Shapiro showed with Cooper (Shapiro was then married to Amy Snider, whose sister was painter Jenny Snider; Shapiro later married painter Ellen Phelan, whom Bartlett had known since they overlapped as artists-in-residence in Detroit several years before). Eventually, Cooper represented Elizabeth Murray and Jonathan Borofsky, as well as Shapiro and Bartlett. It was an incestuous world of artists linked through school (notably Yale) or as gallery mates or, not infrequently, in matters of romance.

Paula Cooper also showed the work of Sol LeWitt, one of the most influential of the "High Minimalist" generation. Artists of the younger cohort looked to LeWitt as an advanced artist of rare intellect, integrity, and innovation, as both a consummate professional and a radical thinker. LeWitt was known as a nurturer of fellow artists and a mentor to many (Bartlett among them). Thus nothing was as consequential to the authentication of this evolving late sixties art as publication of LeWitt's "Paragraphs on Conceptual Art" in the June 1967 issue of *Artforum*. It was a manifesto for the new systemic art, work that relied on thinking rather than feeling. LeWitt identified the new movement as "Conceptual art," choosing "conceptual" specifically to contrast the new art forms with conventional artworks designed to be viewed perceptually.

LeWitt prioritized the mind over the eye. The artist and the art were to be judged by the quality of the idea that generated the work. It certainly mattered what the artwork looked like. But the form of the work was to grow directly out of a concrete concept rather than from some inchoate feeling expressed abstractly by the maker. "Paragraphs on Conceptual Art" was both definition and clarion call. For the new generation of which Bartlett was a part, LeWitt's words provided resounding affirmation as well as crystalline direction. In a recent interview in *Bomb* (2005), Bartlett described LeWitt's "Paragraphs" as "one of the great mid-century poems" and joked that "on a good day I could follow 15 of his 32 rules."[10]

LeWitt's art, of course, was even more influential than his manifesto. He demonstrated that sculpture could be painted, sculpture could hang on the wall, sculpture could be implied, sculpture could be as much interval as volume. But in 1964 LeWitt had also created two versions of *Muybridge*, a sculpture constructed in painted wood, photographs, and flashing lights. They were homage to Eadweard Muybridge, whose photographic motion studies of the 1880s [fig. 9] revolutionized received ideas about animal and human locomotion while proving by means of serial imagery that film could capture movement and thus depict elapsed time. LeWitt was surely drawn to Muybridge's work for its filmlike animation in sequencing slightly variant images. But LeWitt also understood the significance of Muybridge to his own "search for a more objective method of organization."[11] LeWitt's multi-faceted grasp of the implications of Muybridge's locomotion studies was central not only to his "Paragraphs on Conceptual Art" but also, over time, engendered lively interest in Muybridge's work among a wide circle of engaged artists, notably including Bartlett.

Many artists at the time were devising serial imagery derived from permutations of geometric forms. In the mid-sixties, Frank Stella was already among the most influential of painters. Since the late fifties he had been painting series of essentially objectified canvases in regulated variations of verticals, horizontals, and diagonals [fig. 10]. Most of his series were named for their geometric configurations (Concentric Squares, Mitered Mazes, Notched V, Running V, Irregular Polygon) and his work was often identified in those early years as "geometric abstraction." But by 1966 the foundation of Stella's work was better understood as integral to the Conceptual art movement

Figure 10. Frank Stella (born 1936), *Fez*, 1964

Figure 11. Robert Ryman (born 1930), *Winsor 34*, 1966

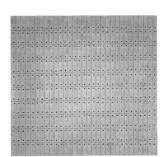

Figure 12. Eva Hesse (1936–1970), *Untitled*, 1967

Figure 13. Agnes Martin (1912–2004), *Untitled*, 1962

and his paintings were included in the Guggenheim's *Systemic Painting* show.

In the same years, artists Robert Ryman and Eva Hesse were advancing the cause of systems-based art with highly original work founded on principles of serial construction and/or methods of objective organization. Ryman, already in the early sixties one of the most compelling and respected artists of his generation, did all-white paintings with myriad integral strokes [fig. 11]. By the late sixties Ryman had introduced a compound format of multiple sheets of paper painted in white and then glued or stapled to the wall in serial formation, sometimes gridded, sometimes linear. A bit later Ryman also made paintings composed of multiple units (including some on a metal ground) in serial permutations. At about the same time, Hesse was creating uniquely passionate sculptures and drawings that featured slightly irregular alignments of oddly organic geometries [fig. 12].

Agnes Martin painted many of her most evocative grids in the early and mid-sixties [fig. 13]. Jo Baer was recognized by the mid-sixties for her strikingly reductive edge-painted canvases, often painted in serial form as diptychs or triptychs. Already in 1962 Baer had exhibited her Graph Paintings, work that many viewers find almost withholding in the rigor of their geometric configurations painted on graph paper. Notable in the early sixties run-up to Bartlett's work, too, would be the dot-scattered paintings of Larry Poons, whose work was embraced under the rubric of Color Field painting. Yayoi Kusama was also active in New York in the early sixties, another model for Bartlett's notion of an ideally "fractured" body of work. She did performance, installation, painting, sculpture, collage [fig. 14], furniture. And, ironically (given the range of her work), Kusama may be the only artist to be as completely identified with dots as Bartlett herself.

Serial construction, systems-based organization, and number or counting schemes were explored by many of the most interesting young artists. Bartlett's friend Jon Borofsky did a counting piece in 1969, *Counting from 1 to Infinity*, composed of stacked sheets of paper. One of the most advanced in this group was Mel Bochner (whose work was much admired by Bartlett), who used his own cut-and-recomposed drawings and photographs to create "magic square" works and who rendered set theory in visually compelling form. Bochner also conceptualized floor installations of counting pieces composed of pebbles and rocks, and measurement works that delineated the dimensions of interior spaces and architectural elements. Like Ryman, Bochner created installation works in which serial permutations were aligned in gridded format [fig. 15]. More or less in this same camp were artists as diverse as Hanne Darboven and Lawrence Weiner [fig. 16], among many others who were using the repetition of numbers and words and nonverbal marks to create expansive serial works.

Of special interest in relation to Bartlett's plate work is the art of Carl Andre. In the late 1950s (at the same time as Stella's "Black Paintings," 1958–59), Andre was creating wood-block sculptures of strict geometric form, as well as geometrically ordered drawings, some composed on the typewriter [fig. 17]. His revolutionary floor sculptures composed of twelve-inch-square metal plates, first made in 1967, were publicly premiered that year in a solo show at Dwan Gallery New York. These multi-unit grids of "tiles" have enormous impact both visually and physically (underfoot). Bartlett doesn't recall having focused on the particular composition of Andre's floor sculptures, but acknowledges that she very well may have made a subliminal connection. Of course, it's also true that the foot-square unit, the most basic of measuring divisions, was not at all uncommon in the geometric art of the day. And sculptors like LeWitt and Judd had by this time replaced wood with metal (for its smooth surface) as their material of choice, including (for Judd) perforated steel with a dot matrix of its own in its industrial pattern of tiny holes [fig. 18].

Figure 14. Yayoi Kusama (born 1929),
Accumulation of Nets (No. 7), 1962

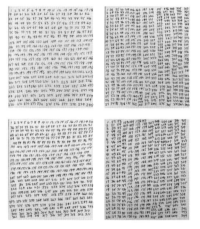

Figure 15. Mel Bochner (born 1940), 24 Reading
Alternatives (detail), 1971

Figure 16. Lawrence Weiner (born 1942),
Untitled, 1965

In October 1968 Sol LeWitt did his first wall drawing, arguably the most revolutionary of all modernist artworks. He created a work by drawing in pencil directly on a painted wall surface for an exhibition at the Paula Cooper Gallery in New York [fig. 19]. It was dramatic introduction of an "art without borders." Neither space nor time could delimit the LeWitt wall drawing: it owned the room and its light and its air; it existed forever (even after it was painted over); it could be executed by others without loss of authenticity. At that moment, it was clear that art could be anything the artist imagined it to be.

That same year, 1968, Bartlett settled on her plan to use metal as a painting support. She says she loved the look of New York City's enameled steel subway signs bolted to their tiled walls, and she apparently decided to make art of a similarly solid yet jaunty (and somehow purposeful?) character. In the *Bomb* interview, Bartlett was more specific about her choice of metal support, revealing a shrewd and pragmatic understanding of her own practices as an artist:

> I'd noticed New York subway signs. They looked like hard paper.
> I needed hard paper that could be cleaned and reworked. I wanted a
> unit that could go around corners on the wall, stack for shipping. If
> you made a painting and wanted it to be longer, you could add plates.
> If you didn't like the middle you could remove it, clean it, replace it
> or not. There had to be space between the units to visually correct
> plate and measuring distortions.[12]

She debated for weeks about the dimensions of her new "canvas," not least because at the time the United States was deliberating whether to convert to the metric system and Bartlett wanted her constructions to conform to standard measurements. She knew she would be using multiple units in modular arrangements (though at the outset she surely never envisioned growing her works in multiples of a hundred!). Hence, her decision about size was equally about weight and what she—and a sheetrock wall—could handle.

In the end, Bartlett settled on one-foot-square, 16-gauge, cold-rolled steel plates, with one side coated in appliance-white baked enamel. (Over time, distinct color variations have emerged in the enamel ground of the plates. The plates, even within the same piece, can range from their characteristic appliance-white to a white of faintly greenish-gray or blue cast. It is not clear whether these variations are due to the medium's aging—"inherent vice" in the jargon of the museum profession—or simply derive from using plates drawn from different production runs.) Each plate is hole-punched at its four corners for the purpose of nailing it to a wall. There are no records, but the artist guesses that initially she would have ordered something like a hundred plates from industrial supplier Gersen Feiner in New Jersey, the same source she still uses.

Bartlett included in her first order a batch of larger rectangular plates, measuring eighteen by twenty-four inches and without corner holes. She had an idea that she could use these plates as floor supports for a more structured presentation of the scatter-piece assemblages she had worked on the year before. She also wanted to incorporate words in those pieces. Bartlett had in mind the punning language works of Belgian artist Marcel Broodthaers (who was in turn indebted to the precedent "naming" work of his fellow Belgian, Surrealist René Magritte). In one of these works, for example, she took a hank of blue-painted rope and set it on a plate on the floor. Using commercial press-type, she then imprinted either ROPE or BLUE on

Figure 17. Carl Andre (born 1935), *Untitled*, 1960

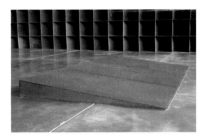

Figure 18. Donald Judd (1928–1994), *Untitled*, 1965

Figure 19. Sol LeWitt (born 1928), *Wall Drawing #1, Drawing Series II 18 (A & B)*, October 1968

the plate. For whatever reason, the floor pieces never made it past the studio stage and they were stored away. The artist moved directly on to wall-hung plates.

Bartlett painted on a few of the new white plates, working freehand, but she fairly quickly decided that she needed a more defined template. Because at the time Bartlett (like nearly everyone) was drawing on graph paper, she naturally opted for a ruled-line grid, which she had silkscreened in gray epoxy on each plate. (Jo Watanabe, recommended to Bartlett by LeWitt, screened the earliest plates.) The white-enameled steel plates were imprinted with a classic graph-paper grid. Each twelve-inch-square plate is rule-divided into one-inch segments (twelve across and twelve down, for a total of one hundred forty-four per plate); and each one-inch square is further divided, by slightly thinner gray lines, into quarter-inch segments (sixteen squares of four across and four down). Accordingly, each plate has 48 ruled squares in each quarter-inch row (vertical or horizontal); 192 squares in each of the inch bands (vertical or horizontal); and a total of 2,304 quarter-inch squares per plate.

The decision-making that led the artist to her small gridded square plates is utterly congruent with her temperament. Bartlett is more than exceptionally bright; her intellectual grasp is prodigious. Equally dominant in her character is her obsessive reliance on work to fill nearly every hour of every day. It is rare to find Bartlett *not* working: she is always writing, drawing, painting, constructing, talking, thinking, or planning. When she's at work in her Long Island studio, she considers it *leisure* to take an hour's hard swim in the ocean. Since 1985, when her daughter Alice was born, she has concurrently dedicated herself to full-time parenting. (Bartlett and her second husband, French actor Mathieu Carrière, met in 1980, married in 1983, and separated by 1992. An acrimonious, protracted divorce and custody suit unsettled the artist's life and work for eight years subsequent to the separation.)

After four decades of making art, the body of work that Bartlett has created is noteworthy in quantity and scope alike. She has also written a great deal, mostly fiction and what might loosely be described as vernacular prose poetry. Her transparently autobiographical *History of the Universe: A Novel*, a much condensed version of a thousand-odd pages Bartlett began writing in the late sixties, was published in 1985.[13] The novel is rather like a print version of *Rhapsody*—not surprising since Bartlett was working on both immense narrative works at the same time. Words accrete like dots on a plate and form lines; lines run on, then stop; characters weave in and out and reappear under different names; countless lists thread through the pages by way of building description.

Productive (and compulsive) as she is, Bartlett asserts that she's not mechanically adept and not especially good with numbers or even particularly logical. She describes her mathematical abilities as limited to counting, and she shrewdly selects her studio assistants in part for their complementary skills. (LeWitt's "Paragraphs" states tersely: "Conceptual art doesn't really have much to do with mathematics, philosophy, or any other mental discipline. The mathematics used by most artists is simple arithmetic or simple number systems.") Despite her agile mind, Bartlett insists she struggles to come up with ideas about what to make (i.e., subject matter—as opposed to content, or imagery, both of which come readily to the artist once she begins to work). With this droll and implacable self-assessment and with a desire to work virtually without respite—and with implicit deference to LeWitt's "rules" of Conceptual art—Bartlett devised a program within which she could invent infinite variations.

She decided in 1968 that the twelve-inch plate would serve as the module for each work, with a one-inch space separating one plate from another in multi-plate works. She would generate patterns or imagery by dotting color spots within the quarter-inch squares of the superimposed grid. She defined her palette by limiting it to the twenty-five colors (and their mixes) of Testor's enamel, readily available from crafts suppliers. And she committed herself to generate each work from specific instructions that would form a conceptual template. She deliberated potential templates by posing "what if" propositions, for example, in *House Piece* [pl. 9], 1970:

> I subjected this house scene to various scenarios. What would happen if one element of the landscape left the painting in sequence, until the plate was blank? Now I realize I should have done it both ways, starting and ending with a blank plate. Adding and subtracting. I zoomed in on the house, through the open door, looking through a window with the landscape behind it that you couldn't see because the house was in front of it. What would happen if I rotated the house, the four quadrants of the image? What if?[14]

Bartlett seems to have arrived at her idea to dot-paint by way of Georges Seurat. In the *Bomb* interview, she told Elizabeth Murray that en route by train from California to Yale in 1963, she stopped off in Chicago to look at art. She went to The Art Institute of Chicago, where she saw Seurat's monumental pointillist masterpiece, *A Sunday on La Grande Jatte—1884*, 1884–86. Long a fan of van Gogh's work (which had first dazzled her as a high school teen when in the summer of 1957 she saw a major van Gogh exhibition at the Municipal Art Gallery in Los Angeles), she must have immediately recognized the leap from the Dutchman's passionate impastoed daubs to the Frenchman's obsessive color dots. It took a few years, but the impact of Seurat's approach would come to define her work. As she would subsequently pronounce, wryly, "When in doubt, dot."[15] And Bartlett proceeded to dot her own way into art history.

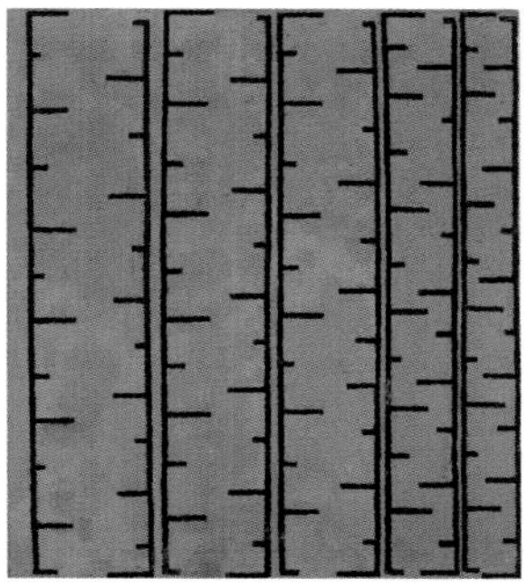

Figure 20. Elizabeth Murray (born 1940), *Shrinking Lines to the Right*, 1974

dot[1] (dot) n. **1.a.** A tiny round mark made by or as if by a pointed instrument; a spot. **b.** Such a mark used in orthography, as above an *i*. **2.** A tiny amount. **3.** In Morse and similar codes, the short sound or signal used in combination with the dash and silent intervals to represent letters, numbers, or punctuation. **4.** *Mathematics.* **a.** A decimal point. **b.** A symbol of multiplication. **5.** *Music.* A mark after a note indicating an increase in time value by half. —**dot** v. **dot·ted, dot·ting, dots.** —*tr.* **1.** To mark with a dot. **2.** To form or make with dots. **3.** To cover with or as if with dots: *"Campfires, like red, peculiar blossoms, dotted the night"* (Stephen Crane). —*intr.* To make a dot. —*idiom.* **on** (or **at**) **the dot.** Exactly at the appointed time; punctual or punctually: *arrived at nine o'clock on the dot.* [Middle English **dot*, from Old English *dott*, head of a boil.] —**dot'ter** n.

dot[2] (dŏt, dō) *n.* A woman's marriage portion; a dowry. [French, from Latin *dōs, dōt-*, dowry. See **dō-** in Appendix.] —**dō'tal** (dot'l) *adj.*

dot·age (dō'tij) n. A deterioration of mental faculties; senility. [Middle English, from *doten*, to dote.]

dot·ard (dō'tard) n. A person who is in his or her dotage. [Middle English, from *doten*, to dote.]

dote (dōt) *intr.v.* **dot·ed, dot·ing, dotes.** To show excessive love or

23

fondness: *parents who dote on their only child.* See Synonyms at **like**[1]. [Middle English doten.] —**dot'er** n.

—*The American Heritage Dictionary of the English Language* (3d. edition)

Over the span of less than a decade, between late 1968 and 1977, Jennifer Bartlett painted something on the order of 125 works on 12-inch-square metal plates, ranging from 1-, 2-, or 3-plate works right up through the 987-plate *Rhapsody*. The early plate work is typically identified as ending with *Rhapsody* and the several large multi-plate place-name works of 1977 (*131 Greene Street/Patmos* is composed of 126 plates, for instance; *Day and Night 27 Howard Street* has 96 plates; and *17 White Street* is an 81-plate work).

The artist never stopped making plate pieces, though after 1977 Bartlett often combined plate-ground paintings with other mediums, notably including oil on canvas and, later, wood and concrete constructions, and even plate glass. She has incorporated her plates in several prominent commissioned installations, and she episodically creates stand-alone pieces composed exclusively of plates even as, side by side, one finds works in other mediums as well (most often oil on canvas or pastel on paper). She has frequently used what is to her the intimately familiar plate medium to experiment. In 1998 she did a group of paintings, some on canvas, some on plates, with a spatter technique. And in 2000 she did a series in which she painted freehand on modular arrangements of metal plates. In 2003 Bartlett embarked on yet another distinctive body of plate work. Using larger plates, she routinely crossed over the ruled boundaries of the silkscreened squares; the grid is still primary armature but it's not impregnable to paint. In this more recent plate work the artist also paints dots that vary in size, sometimes enlarged to the point at which they become motif rather than technique. Bartlett adopted language and communication as her subject for these plate pieces (in other words, human foibles and connections, or the lack thereof). And while she does not quite liberate herself from the rule of dots in these paintings, she has introduced a mutated, elusive, dancing dot that can be as much brush stroke as brush point. Equally dramatic is the transformation of her subject matter from images to words. She has always been both painter and writer. Now she is dotting her own words into paint (giving new definition to the dot and dash of Morse code!) [fig. 21].

The first of the new works were single-panel pieces delineating short exchanges of dialogue—sometimes impudent, often banal, occasionally heartbreaking—with respective voices differentiated by color. There are limp or smart-alecky jokes. (For those who might segue to the joke paintings of Bartlett's younger contemporary Richard Prince, think instead of the young Bartlett herself, notorious for her funny, smart-ass, energetic, sharp-tongued, excess-loving, girl-about-SoHo ways in the early seventies). True to form for Bartlett, the word pieces have grown to multi-plate works, some now wall-size with complex narratives. In contrast with the earliest plate pieces, the current work is explicit and unboundaried; it overflows with words and tales, and is animated by both vivid imagination and frank autobiography. Even at that, however, Bartlett doesn't make it easy for the viewer to read her painted stories. A technique of dripped and broken dots provides sufficient camouflage to assure the reader's undivided attention.

Squaring: 2; 4; 16; 256; 65,536, 1973–74 [pl. 26]. Starting at upper left corner, dot plates in accordance with successive squaring from the number two (2 x 2 = 4, 4 x 4 = 16, 16 x 16 = 256, 256 x 256 = 65,536). **Plate 1:** Place two dots in upper left two spaces. **Plate 2:** Place four dots in upper

Figure 21. Jennifer Bartlett (born 1941), *Would You Like a Coke?*, 2003

Figure 22. Jasper Johns (born 1930), *Map*, 1961

Figure 23. Roy Lichtenstein (1923–1997),

Frightened Girl, 1964

left four spaces. **Plate 3:** Place sixteen dots from upper left corner.

Plate 4: Place 256 dots, continuously, in the top five and a third rows.

Plates 5–33: Place 65,536 dots continuously until finished (28½ plates).

Among the first of Bartlett's early-period plate pieces, probably dating from late 1968 but possibly 1969, is the two-plate pictorial *Earth from Moon/Mars* [pl. 1], imaging the planets side by side (blue-and-white Earth on the left, and a glowing golden Mars on the right). Precise dating of the very earliest plate pieces—before they had been exhibited—can be challenging since Bartlett's studio records were haphazard at the time. The first U.S. space probe to send thousands of pictures from the lunar surface was Surveyor I in 1966; the first manned circumlunar flight was that of Apollo 8 at the end of December 1968; and the first manned lunar landing was, famously, that of Apollo 11 on July 20, 1969. Either of the latter two could have inspired Bartlett's artwork featuring a view of Earth from the Moon, a perspective that before those Apollo flights would have seemed as alien, even fanciful, as that of the planet Mars itself. Bartlett painted *Earth from Moon/Mars* freehand and absent the silkscreened grid she soon added to her plates. Whenever she feels the need, Bartlett employs image projection of photographic sources, sometimes just to provide a rough outline, sometimes for more precise guidelines. But the realistic pictorialism of the *Earth/Mars* piece is rare in the artist's early work. One doesn't see it again until *Rhapsody*, where pictorial (or "rendered") imagery crops up in vertical rows 33–40 and again in rows 82–86.

Similarly anomalous is *Series XIV (Map)* of 1971–72 [pl. 14]. It too is a pictorial work, albeit dot-accreted rather than rendered freehand. And because the subject is a printed map, the image is, by definition, graphic. This United States map is the paradigm of every American child's schoolroom experience. (The artist thinks she turned to an at-hand standard atlas for the map she used in this work.) Bartlett volunteers, however, that she also had Jasper Johns's iconic 1961 *Map* painting [fig. 22] in mind as she set out to paint both an homage and an inversion of sorts. Her laboriously hand-painted dots slyly mimic the underlying dot pattern of every mechanical reproduction (and also point to Roy Lichtenstein's classic dot-pattern cartoon works [fig. 23] as well as to the vintage cartoons and comic books that inspired the Pop artist). In her *Map* Bartlett thus literally painted the mass-produced schoolroom graphic, inclusive of the paradigm's subvisible photoreproductive dots. (In 2003 Bartlett returned to "map making." Often taking liberties with geographical and cartographic facts, she did freehand—that is, not dotted—paintings of maps of Africa.)

Johns's lush, colorful *Map* would seem downright expressionist by comparison were it not for the subversively expressionist quality of Bartlett's own dot paintings. At a glance, these early plate works may look mechanically robotic in execution. But close viewing reveals an astonishing range of dot applications, some intentional, some simply a product of the dotting technique. No two dots look alike. No dot is perfectly round. Some dots come closer to the elliptical, some to the rectangular, some are little more than a blip. In color, even a black dot can appear a myriad of tonalities, from solid shiny black to striated matte elephant gray. The artist applied more than one dot per brushload of paint; the progression of points on the plate's grid can, in some cases, be tracked visually from denser to thinner.

Akin to the wall drawings of Sol LeWitt, each and every one of Bartlett's plates of this period was painted in accord with specific directions. Unlike LeWitt, however, Bartlett did not inscribe each work's program as its title or otherwise share the scheme with the work's viewers. But in most cases the program is not so arcane as to be terribly challenging to figure out. In other cases, a marathon of looking may not untangle the artist's dotting scheme. Anyone who assumes the programs are consistently transparent need only consider the narrative [author's version] of *Edge Lift*, 1974 [pl. 29], as but one example:

> *Edge Lift*, 1974 [nine-point painting]. Start by painting dots in all nine-point positions on all nine plates. **Plate 1:** Add dots in all boundary spaces except in space 1/14 immediately north of Point 1. **Plate 2:** Place dots in all boundary spaces except in space 4/1 to the immediate left of Point 2. **Plate 3:** Place dots in each space on the diagonals northwest and southwest between Point 3 and the left-hand boundary. Leave blank the boundary edge of the resulting triangle (spaces 11/1 through 23/1). Dot all remaining boundary spaces. **Plate 4:** Place dots in each space on the diagonals northwest and southwest between Point 4 and the left-hand boundary. Leave blank the boundary edge of the resulting triangle (spaces 10/1 through 24/1). Dot all remaining boundary spaces. **Plate 5:** Place dots in each space on the diagonals northwest and northeast between Point 5 and the upper boundary. Leave blank the boundary edge of the resulting triangle (spaces 1/5 through 1/43). Dot all remaining boundary spaces. **Plate 6:** Place dots in each space on the diagonals northeast and southeast between Point 6 and the right-hand boundary. Leave blank the boundary edge of the resulting triangle (spaces 5/48 through 40/48). Dot all remaining boundary spaces. **Plate 7:** Place dots in each space on the diagonals northeast and southeast between Point 7 and the right-hand boundary. Leave blank the boundary edge of the resulting triangle (spaces 12/48 through 35/48). Dot all remaining boundary spaces. **Plate 8:** Place dots in each space on the diagonals northwest and southwest between Point 8 and the left-hand boundary. Leave blank the boundary edge of the resulting triangle (spaces 34/1 through 40/1). Dot all remaining boundary spaces. **Plate 9:** Dot all boundary spaces.

As with LeWitt's wall drawings, certain of Bartlett's early plate works could, in principle, be executed by others if given the authorization and the right materials. The surprise and delight of these programs lie less in their dot schemes than in the unexpectedly diverse and rhythmic patterns that emerge from regulated mark-making. And, often, no one was more surprised by the visual outcome than Bartlett herself. The artist recounts how stunned she was when, plate after plate, row after row, a parabola shape repeatedly formed as she followed her dot scheme in *Series VIII (Parabolas)*, 1971 [pl. 13]. She never anticipated that would happen and, with each new plate, she expected the parabola repeat to vanish but, to her amazement, it never did.[16]

Unlike LeWitt, however, who after the early years seldom acted as his own draftsperson, instead setting out detailed drawing instructions for others to execute, Bartlett has always done all of her own "drawing." That fact alone may have embedded a vague notion of, say, LeWitt the Conceptualist, in counterpoint to Bartlett the Craftswoman. But there is no question that Bartlett is fundamentally a conceptualist, and has been from the outset. She wasn't born with a natural painterly "touch." In fact, Bartlett famously declared that she launched the series of two hundred drawings that ultimately became *In the Garden*, 1980–81, because she "had decided to learn to draw."[17] She doesn't start an artwork by making a random mark on plate or canvas. She doesn't feel the urge to "make a painting," as such. She is a thinker; she plots a course for herself, an assignment, a specific task that can be described in words. And then she executes that defined task in her particular medium of choice at the moment.

Despite received opinion, however, it's not true that Bartlett doesn't *like* to paint. Quite the contrary. She revels in paint. (The only part of painting she doesn't like, Bartlett says, is the middle stage of making the work. At that point, she explains, it seems as if the painting has no relationship to the idea that started it and at the same time there is as yet no clear image of where it's going to end.) The fact is, that if Bartlett didn't like to paint, she would never spend so much time doing it. She has plenty of stories to tell, and she's a writer. But she continues, primarily, to spend most of her time creating narrative paintings—scores of paintings, series of paintings, cycles of paintings, sometimes a seemingly never-ending stream of paintings. It is perhaps instructive to suggest that Bartlett paints less from eye to hand and more from brain to gut. One is not initially impressed by the eloquence of her line or the arabesque of her brushwork, but rather by the visceral honesty and startling imagery of her painted stories. The paint on her plates and canvases often implies an assertively physical artist. Whether dot-accreted or rendered freehand, Bartlett's paintings are unashamedly expressive. Her colors are descriptive and evocative of the subject's mood; her brush-work is active and intense.

Never an abstract artist, Bartlett came as close to geometric abstraction as she ever would in these very early plate pieces, in which she dotted the tiny squares on the steel-ground grid in accordance with specific instructions to herself. Among the simplest of these instructions are the counting assignments. Adopting a template of nine twelve-inch plates, for instance, Bartlett might count from one to nine (*1 Dot, 2 Dots*, 1973 [pl. 25]). Beginning in the upper left corner of the first graphed plate, and working left to right and top to bottom (as in Western writing and reading), apply one dot, leave a blank space, apply another dot, leave a blank space, et cetera, until one runs out of spaces. On the second plate, apply two dots, leave a blank, two more dots, blank, dot dot, blank, dot dot, blank, and so forth. On the third plate: dot dot dot, blank, dot dot dot, blank. . . . The program continues through nine plates and is utterly legible to the viewer. Similarly, in *5/6*, 1972, alternate five blank squares with six dots, continu-ously over the nine plates, until you've used up all the spaces. Bartlett rarely had a preconceived idea of what composition might emerge from any given dot program. Although she kept notebooks with sketched diagrams and numerical notations, the sketches seldom appear to have a literal correlation to an extant plate work. Very occa-sionally, she did full-color renderings, more for her own pleasure in making drawings than as a schematic to project or implement a work. In practice, if the dotted results of a single plate or an entire work did not please her, she wiped the plate(s) clean to be used in subsequent work.

Dotting hundreds, thousands, even multiple thousands, of points of paint into specified, precisely counted, quarter-inch squares day after day has to be unimaginably tedious, muscle-straining, mind-bending work. But Bartlett painted every dot by hand, personally. For all her reliance on skilled studio assistants over the years, she has never asked her assistants to execute dots, no matter how precise the language of the particu-lar work's instructions. The only exception in Bartlett's entire body of work was for the 1971–72 *Series XIV (Map)*. As she ran out of time to finish the physically demand-ing piece (which she was determined to include in a forthcoming exhibition—her commercial gallery premiere, at the Reese Palley Gallery), she called on Elizabeth Murray to help finish the dotting.

In light of what sometimes seems the oddly circumscribed nature of Bartlett's art historical reputation, it's difficult to avoid thinking that some viewers see Bartlett's plate pieces as "women's work," as a craft variant somehow descended through the line of female pottery decorators and print colorers in England and America who came to prominence in the early twentieth century [fig. 24]. Their work was known, especially, for its discreetly but elegantly rendered floral and landscape imagery, directed to the domestic market. These "lady painters" in some metaphorical sense were seen as "drawing within the lines" (as good little girls mostly do, while unruly little boys scrawl willy-nilly all over the page)—just as Bartlett "dots within the lines" quite literally. The seductive charm of Bartlett's pointillism—one dot after another laboriously laid down on the tip of a delicate brush by a remarkably steady hand and obsessive will—can mask the sparkling imagination, conceptual originality, and programmatic rigor that consistently inform the artist's plate pieces.

In any case, in those years (the early seventies) in the New York art world, it was still a boy's club. Even as Bartlett was typically seen as a spitfire, seasoned observers may have glimpsed a more somber, or at least conflicted, soul. Bartlett was as self-deprecating as she was generous; as acerbic as she was insightful; and as competitive (even compulsively so) as she was committed. Bartlett could run warm or chill; she could exude bitter or sweet. Her uncommon facility with words could be turned as easily to toxic effect as to anodyne. On one point, however, she was never less than perfectly clear: in the art world, at least, the girls had to fight their way into the boy's club. There was, after all, sound logic driving Bartlett's ambition to make art that had no gender. It was a moment when younger generations of exceptional female artists were asserting themselves in unprecedented numbers—Jackie Ferrara, Nancy Graves, Eva Hesse (whose death in 1970, at age thirty-four, marked such a stunning loss), Ree Morton, Elizabeth Murray, Judy Pfaff, Dorothea Rockburne, Susan Rothenberg, Pat Steir, Jackie Winsor. Yet women did not achieve the recognition or financial success, much less the stardom, of their male peers. It was precisely this contradiction that inspired the founding in 1985 of the Guerrilla Girls, whose bold graphics and public interventions documented the sexism and racism that tainted virtually every aspect of the contemporary art world.

Bartlett was dogged, however, in her determination to succeed as an artist. In 1970 artist Alan Saret invited Bartlett to exhibit her new plate works in his SoHo studio at 119 Spring Street.[18] It was a large space where Saret lived and worked from 1969 until early 1971 (at the time he was working on sculpture that required a lot of room). Since exhibition venues were so scarce, especially for emergent artists, Saret offered his street-level ground floor to acquaintances who could make use of it, including performing artists (Saret recalls that dancers Laura Dean and Joan Jonas both performed there). Attendance was generated by word of mouth, and Saret estimates that maybe fifty to a hundred people might see any given show.

The Saret room was sizable, approximately forty by sixty feet. By 1970 (judging by present documentation of the body of work) Bartlett may have had thirty or forty plate pieces ready to be exhibited or, she thinks, perhaps even more. Many of those 1969–70 works were small (one-, two- or three-plate pieces). Several of the works that were most likely on view in the Saret show were color exercises, like *Plates Divided by Six Colors*, 1970, with stacked blocks of color; or *CN 2040*, 1970, with carefully counted-off lines of color. The group probably included the seductively instructive *2,304 Colors*, 1970 [pl. 6], in which Bartlett used every one of the available Testor colors and their multiple overlapping combinations. Other pieces from these first two years included studies of lines—*Lines* and *Lines (Set B)* [pl. 7], both 1970—in which the generated patterns closely resemble the stitches of bargello needlepoint.

Others of these earliest works were limited to the color black and were strict geometric programs. *Intersection*, 1970 [fig. 25], for instance, is a small-scale work (it is

Figure 24. Wallace Nutting's colorists at their workstations, Massachusetts, c. 1915

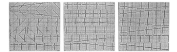

Figure 25. Jennifer Bartlett (born 1941),

Intersection, 1970

Figure 26. Installation view of *Jennifer Bartlett,*

Reese Palley Gallery, New York, 1972

only three plates wide), but it's a signature Bartlett and a classic of ascetic rigor. Using only black dots in seven-dot segments, the artist methodically counts off the possible intersections of horizontal, vertical, and diagonal orientations. The resulting patterns are unexpectedly choreographic, as if a stick-figure dancer had kicked her way across the floor only to collapse in exhaustion. *Intersection*'s scripted jig-jog scheme, however, equally reads as some bizarre chromosomal printout. Or, for that matter, simply as abstract art. In any reading of *Intersection* (and in this regard, the same applies to *Big Intersection* of 1972 [pl. 17]), one is struck by Bartlett's nimble ability to evoke strikingly dynamic and layered effects from the most ascetically reductive geometries. Bartlett reiterates that subtle authority over and over again in these early abstract plate pieces, never more confidently than in 1972 pieces like *3 Diagonals* and *Four Right Angles* [pl. 16], works in which a few lines in unexpected alignments somehow convey energy simultaneously kinetic and contained.

These same plate pieces still look entirely fresh and, even now, so bold that it's hard to believe it has been nearly four decades since they were first shown. As low-key as her plate work premiere may have been, Bartlett's next exhibition got quite a buzz going. In January 1972 the artist installed hundreds of plates in New York's large and then-prominent Reese Palley Gallery on Prince Street in SoHo [fig. 26].[19] For the Palley show, Bartlett blanketed the gallery walls with plate works dating from 1969 to 1972, including pieces that had been shown at Saret's. She purposefully mixed abstract and representational works, declining to segregate by type of imagery.

One of the most provocative Palley juxtapositions, as it turned out, was the very large 1970 *House Piece* [pl. 9] next to *Big Intersection*, 1972 [pl. 17]. *House Piece* is a sixty-one-plate work with numerous irregularly spaced intervals; it can easily hold a wall thirty feet long, or more. Like most of these first plate pieces, *House Piece* was painted in a palette limited to black plus red, yellow, and blue (in a few of these early works Bartlett used green and violet in addition to the primaries). *House Piece* is notable for its introduction of pictographic elements that would inhabit Bartlett's work forever: house, windows, path, clouds, mountain, horizon, flying birds, a pond with ducks. All were rendered in dots, of course, and the combination of primary colors and simple geometric forms signaled a childlike charm and simplicity, belying the schematic planning and disciplined execution that the work actually required.[20]

Big Intersection is a fifty-two-plate work that is as ascetic and perverse as *House Piece* is cozy and pictorial. At the scale of *Big Intersection*, its relatively few dotted lines seem nearly scrawled in character, its Xs and Ls and wan triangles limp rather than dance through their permutations toward resolution at the far right. It's unusually rigorous in its geometric configurations and very demanding of the viewer's attention.

> Some people would like the intersection piece, and hate the house piece. I was curious about that. I became increasingly interested in setting up a circumstance where each system I had used—the house, a different set of suppositions than the intersection piece—became a "what if" situation. In 1971 Richard Artschwager, whose work I admire, came to the studio and said, If I'd invented these plates I'd really try different sizes, and different-sized grids. I thought, I see what you mean.[21]

For Bartlett, the purposeful conjunction of *House Piece* and *Big Intersection* in the Palley exhibition was the manifesto of a multi-faceted artist determined not to limit her options. Bartlett staked her claim from the outset to both representation and abstraction: she would work in either genre, often mixing them in the same piece, and in her hands the genres did not seem to be the polar opposites that then-current art world convention dictated. This became a first principle of her circle of contemporaries (notably including Close, Murray, and Zucker) as they forged new possibilities for vanguard art.

Bartlett's surprise at observers' love-hate response to the *House Piece/Intersection* dichotomy led her to a seemingly perverse decision, given her embrace of both. For her exhibition at the Paula Cooper Gallery in 1974, the artist created an installation composed exclusively of pieces with black and/or red dots, all of which were abstract in composition. In the contest with representation, "The house piece had lost," Bartlett quips.[22] And it was clear from the complexity and commanding presence of the 1973–74 work that Bartlett had hit her stride. The Cooper show included the notable "nine-point" pieces [fig. 27], which reflect extraordinary invention and systemic logic alike.

> Nine-Point Paintings [author's narrative]: A series of nine-plate works painted between 1972 and 1974. All have a palette limited to red and black. Each of the nine-point paintings was begun with an identical predetermined placement of nine points on each plate. The positions of the set points were determined by a random drawing of slips numbered 1 through 48. One slip was drawn to set the horizontal-row position and one slip was drawn to set the vertical-row position for each of nine points. (Drawn slips were returned to the pool, which accounts for repetition of row-number positions.) All nine points are dotted in either red or black on all nine plates of each work in the series.
>
> The original nine set points are documented visually in the plate piece *Nine Points*, 1972 [pl. 23]. The points, all of which are red (making *Nine Points* the only plate work of the period to be exclusively red on white) are positioned as follows, with the horizontal row cited first and the vertical row second: Point 1 @ 02/14. Point 2 @ 04/02. Point 3 @ 17/08. Point 4 @ 17/09. Point 5 @ 21/24. Point 6 @ 22/30. Point 7 @ 23/36. Point 8 @ 37/05. Point 9 @ 48/41.

Figure 27. Installation view showing Jennifer Bartlett's *Nine Points*, 1973–74, and other Nine-Point pieces, Paula Cooper Gallery, New York, March 1974

Bartlett's nine-point concept reveals her affinity not just for objective systems of organization, but for chance methods of composition. In this, she pays implicit homage to John Cage, whose commitment to aleatoric methods in making musical decisions impressed her so deeply.

But Cage was not alone in this approach. Among visual artists of Cage's generation, Ellsworth Kelly is notable for creating works whose compositions were determined by chance. Kelly began experimenting with such techniques after meeting Jean Arp in France about 1950. Arp, along with others in his Surrealist circle, had used *"les lois du hasard"* to create artworks as early as 1915. Kelly invented "rules." For *Seine* of 1951 [fig. 28] he turned to a traditional design exercise: "take a rectangle of a certain size and make something visually interesting using fifty percent black and fifty percent white." But for *Study for "Seine": Chance Diagram of Light Reflected on Water* (also 1951, and also limited to black on white), Kelly invented a system very close in conception to the one Bartlett used for her *Nine Points*. Both artists limited themselves to a single color on a white ground; both used a grid as the skeletal framework; both relied on a combination of simple counting and randomly assigned positions on the grid to generate composition. Kelly's system of grid positions assigned by numerical placement depended on random drawings from a box, too:

A grid of little rectangles was laid out on paper [an elongated horizontal], forty-one units high by eighty-two long. . . . Forty-one numbered slips of paper were put into a box and mixed up. Then . . . , a number was drawn and its corresponding space filled in, and the number put back into the box. For the next row two numbers were drawn, filled in, and returned; the next, three, and so on. When the center was reached and all forty-one rectangles were blackened, the operation was reversed.[23]

Over time, Bartlett would continue to introduce chance and randomness to her art practice. In addition, she accepts the occasional counting or alignment mistake in dotting her plates as chance and she ordinarily incorporates those missteps as part of the work (rather than wiping the plate clean in order to correct the error).

Bartlett also showed series works in the 1974 show, like the utterly delightful, brain-twisting Black 6" Squares series and the wildly imaginative "positive-negative" group [pls. 30 and 31], in which various black-and-white options became graphic representations of presence and absence, volume and void, being and nothingness. Interestingly, the gallery's printed list of works included brief "keys" written by Bartlett to describe the generative scheme of each piece, e.g., "*Chicken Tracks* [pl. 20]. Plate 1: horizontal, vertical, diagonal extension of one unit from nine points." Lawrence Alloway, reviewing the exhibition for *Artforum* (and having acknowledged Bartlett to be a writer as well as painter), commented on the descriptive keys: "Thus the visual display is augmented by the commentary, but the verbal account does not amount to much. There is a kind of pedagogic obviousness about the described system which is a far cry from the complex interplay of signifiers in [the work]."[24]

In May 1975 Bartlett began the work that she would finish nearly a year later and that art writer Roberta Smith memorably described as "the story of the mind in action."[25] In a dramatic but obviously necessary shift of approach, Bartlett planned the overall layout of *Rhapsody* in advance. She made notes; she thought through sequences and conjunctions; she did sketches and diagrams (all of which were working drawings, not renderings). In the plate work that preceded it, the artist had assumed an essentially ad hoc approach in which she followed her own instructions in order to discover what might emerge. With *Rhapsody* Bartlett planned to relate the history of modern art in close to a thousand separate plates for an artwork that would cover more than twelve hundred square feet of wall space. Ad hoc was not an option. Each "what if" had to be calculated for its interaction with all the other "what ifs." There had to be overarching governing rules and designated elements if the whole was to convey coherence as a painting. Bartlett knew what she wanted:

> *Rhapsody* came out of the dialogue between *[Big] Intersection* and *House*. I began thinking about pieces not having edges: how do you know when a painting ends? I thought, what if it doesn't end? What if a painting is like a conversation between the elements in the painting? I was thinking of a painting that wouldn't have edges, that would start and stop, change tenses and gears at will. It needed to be big and fill the space in which it was shown.[26]

Although in the process of making, Bartlett occasionally broke her own rules, the system she established specified the following parameters:

Figure 28. Ellsworth Kelly (born 1923), *Seine*, 1951

Colors: twenty-five
Lines: horizontal, vertical, diagonal, curved
Shapes: square, triangle, circle
Sizes: large, medium, small
Images: mountain, house, tree, ocean
Techniques: dotted, freehand, ruled, and measured.

Each motif (i.e., each color, each line, each shape, each size, each image, each technique) had a "usual" sequence or order, and each had to be combined at least once with each of the others. Despite all the planning and all the rules, however, the work evolved and changed along the way. In other words, *Rhapsody* as it exists could never be recreated from the planning sketches and diagrams and rules. Furthermore, Bartlett never saw the finished work in its entirety until it was installed at Paula Cooper's. The artist's studio was not nearly large enough to contain the whole of *Rhapsody*; Bartlett filled her walls three times over before the work reached completion. The artist could not have foreseen the final outcome. *Rhapsody* is transfixing in its amplitude, eye-popping in its joyful color and images, and mesmerizing in its rich texture of interwoven stories. Smith articulates the work's intellectual dimensions:

> *Rhapsody* tells . . . the story of the mind in action, making up a story as it goes along and discovering the world in the process. The mind in *Rhapsody* is Bartlett's, but it could actually be anyone's. It is a mind working very hard to make art, to grow, and to show how thought makes itself visually manifest in increasingly complex, resonating ways. Thus *Rhapsody* is also the story of a mind learning to think: naming, ordering, acting on habit and impulse, and making progress both ways. And all this is done so directly and legibly that any other mind can easily enter in—to look, read, and listen—adding more thoughts to those already there.[27]

Rhapsody, along with the few large place-name pieces dating from 1977, brought to a close the first phase of Bartlett's plate work. *Rhapsody*—and perhaps just as meaningfully, the acclaim showered on Bartlett because of *Rhapsody*—meant that nothing would ever be the same for the artist. There is "before *Rhapsody*" and there is "after *Rhapsody*."

One obviously notable aspect of *Rhapsody* relates to scale. Even as Bartlett's dot was one kind of device to establish it, her twelve-inch plate was another. She had used multiple plates to create large works before. But *Rhapsody* proved that small increments could be building blocks to monumental scale. The eminently flexible (and refreshingly practical) additive approach that Bartlett introduced to such effect in conceiving *Rhapsody* as an installation piece would ultimately find echoes in contemporary art around the world. For Bartlett's part, by 1978 she had already moved on to more baroque expressions that pretty much left the grid and its constraints behind.

But there's something else, too, in Bartlett's regimented dots and her grid and its constraints that factors meaningfully into the nature of the art that she forged in that pivotal SoHo decade from 1968 through 1977. In the 1990s she began to piece together flashbacks of fragmented imagery of disturbing scenes, which coalesced over time into detailed memories of childhood physical and sexual abuse that she suffered for four to five years beginning when she was age seven. Sinister threats programmed her to silence and it was a silence she maintained, even to herself, for four decades.

Bartlett is the first to acknowledge the skepticism that can greet allegations of abuse based on recovered memory.

> You have to think of the memories not as an onion that you can peel away at, but as having a hunchback that you don't know about. Something like a silent friend or partner who's beside you all the time and who you're completely unaware of.
>
> When people are in the position of having seen and participated in terrible things, the desire on everyone else's part is that these people forget as quickly as possible. I remember hearing in school, well, why did the Jews hang around and let the Germans do that to them? And I find that one of the most horrifying thoughts possible, because what kind of person could ever imagine that another group of people would build ovens to bake them in, and gas them? You cannot imagine it, it is not within one's power to imagine that.
>
> And I think the most distressing thing about being a person who was unfortunate enough to have been in a situation where there was torture, where there was abuse, where there were unimaginably disgusting and frightful acts, is that everybody wants you not to remember. Everybody wants you to go back to normal life, to look on the bright side of things, to put the past in the past and let sleeping dogs lie, and that's an impossible task, because these things did happen in ordinary life and in the real world. And in daylight and at nighttime. And they were organized and carried out by real people.[28]

In her art, clues to the darkness of Bartlett's past surfaced in her *24 Hours: Elegy* series of 1992–93 and another series of works that she called the Earth group, of 1993–95, and then in a 2000–2002 series she calls "the monster paintings." These paintings, mostly in bright, merry colors, are built up in large-scale dots that, to a greater or lesser degree, sometimes camouflage the imagery. Each painting features one or more stylized human figures (rounded, almost balloonlike cartoon shapes) who peer from a window, stand at a balcony, fall under a car's wheels, undergo surgery, look in a mirror, hide. What's so sad about these pictures is that we're never sure if "the monster" is a bogeyman or the artist herself. There are two paintings titled *Monster Drawing* in both of which the balloon figure is applying dots to flat surfaces that look distinctly like Bartlett paintings. Tragically, it is not unusual for those who are abused to assume blame and cast themselves as "monstrous."

But in that formative early decade beginning in the late sixties, long before she remembered any monsters, the art Bartlett made was preternaturally controlled. Each element was precisely defined and boundaried. Each tiny dot was confined in a ruled box that protected it from contact by its neighbors. Each steel square was precisely spaced in separation from all other steel squares. In her installations, Bartlett had inviolable measurement rules that applied to the display of works: two feet between series, one foot between sets within a series, and of course a one-inch perimeter interval between individual plates. In her art Bartlett faithfully sustained precision, isolation, fences, boundaries, protected geometries, regulated intervals, measure. And, of course, she chose "hard paper"—invulnerable steel—for an art support. For a long time, Bartlett lived without the most basic protections and regularities. And memory, unfortunately, is not subject to measurement. But what was grievously breached in life, she reconstructed in art.

Bartlett's long repressed and then (unprompted) recovered memories are not only part of who she is—and unknowingly had been for more than forty years—but are also, necessarily, an integral part of the art she makes. Every work of art, no matter how abstract, is an embodiment of aspects of its maker's character, style, spirit, interests, beliefs. Each artwork is idiosyncratic, a reflection of one person's history, intellect, and emotion. Certainly trauma of the magnitude Bartlett remembers embeds defining character in her art, as in her life.

And what if? What if the recovered memories are flawed? It's too late to matter. Bartlett is the woman, and the artist, who inhabits her reality. What she remembers is bonded to her brain and body. For outsiders to seek documentary confirmation of any part of her recounting becomes superfluous—even demeaning—in the face of that conviction. For herself, Bartlett secured a certain degree of independent confirmation and then came to personal terms with seeking no more. She decided it's not how she wanted to spend her time.

And what if she were a different person, without nightmares and scourging memories? Then she would have given us a very different body of art. We might never have seen works as transparent and graceful and authoritative as, say, *Four Right Angles*, 1972 [pl. 16], or as audacious as *One-Foot Line*, 1974 [pl. 30], or as celestial as *Count*, 1972 [pl. 15]. What if *Rhapsody* had never been? Jennifer Bartlett attributes the generative vitality of her plate work to her revelation about the permutations potential in "what if." Indeed, What if?. . . Bartlett responded with a body of work memorable in its cerebration, balance, and daring. The artist has described her childhood as "dark and mysterious." In conversation Bartlett calls her growing-up years "the dark time." Despite (or because of?) those times, she countered with a decade of painted metal plates suffused with light and air, singing with pictorial enchantment and perverse geometries.

NOTES

1. The definitive work on Bartlett's *Rhapsody* is Roberta Smith (with Notes by the Artist), *Jennifer Bartlett: Rhapsody* (New York: Harry N. Abrams, 1985). Smith eloquently parses the history and meaning of *Rhapsody*, row by row. Between Smith's meticulous and insightful readings of the work and Bartlett's own documentary plate-by-plate detailing, this exceptional book is mandatory grounding in Bartlett's art. It also includes extraordinarily beautiful color illustrations of the painting, both in large segments and small details.

2. For biographical background I am indebted to Calvin Tomkins's "Profiles [Jennifer Bartlett]: Getting Everything In," *The New Yorker*, April 15, 1985, pp. 50–68, also printed under the title "Drawing and Painting" in Marge Goldwater et al., *Jennifer Bartlett* (New York: Abbeville Press, 1985), pp. 9–37.

    I am additionally indebted, of course, to Jennifer Bartlett, who was generous in giving me time with her at her New York studio and who offered complete access to her archives and files. Her office (efficiently staffed by Joan LiPuma and Ricky Manne) provided me with annotated photographs and documentation on the early plate works, material that proved essential to my writing.

    Bartlett herself was at all times candid and forthcoming. She shared information about the work and about the history of the period under discussion, as well as intimate personal history. As for the text itself (which she read for purposes of fact checking and clarification), Bartlett was quick to correct and supplement content but otherwise refrained from editorial comment. I am extremely grateful to the artist for her warm cooperation and support; and I am proud to be associated with her in the context of this unusually significant body of work.

    Throughout the text, quotations or paraphrased citations attributed to Bartlett derive from New York studio meetings or telephone conversations that took place between July and November 2005.

3. For excellent comprehensive studies of the history of Minimalism, see James Meyer, *Minimalism: Themes and Movements* (London: Phaidon Press, 2000); and James Meyer, *Minimalism: Art and Polemics in the Sixties* (New Haven and London: Yale University Press, 2001).

4. Robert Storr, *Chuck Close* (New York: The Museum of Modern Art, 1998), p. 206. Storr's book is a valuable resource for study of Close's history and work.

5. Joe Zucker, telephone conversations with the author, October 18 and October 28, 2005. Throughout the text all comments from Zucker derive from these conversations. I want to thank Joe for his generosity in speaking with me at such length and with such thoughtful recollections. Although in 1976 I organized for The Baltimore Museum of Art an exhibition (with a small catalogue) of Joe's cotton ball paintings, our paths have crossed infrequently since then, which is my loss. For further information on Zucker's earlier work, refer to Krane's 1982 catalogue (see n. 6). A more recent article provides both background and sharp insight on Zucker's work to the present: Carroll Dunham, "Joe Zucker's Fiber Optics," *Artforum* 39 (April 2004), pp. 117–21. See also, Stephen Westfall, "Zucker's Color Constructions," *Art in America* 92 (May 2004), pp. 130–33.

6. See Susan Krane, *Surfacing Images: The Paintings of Joe Zucker 1969–82* (Buffalo, N.Y.: Albright-Knox Art Gallery, 1982), p. 8: "These were cool, illusionistic renderings of strips of color, with carefully modeled edges and shadows, that seemed to pass over and under one another and hover in a shallow pictorial space. Many of the large unified images were, in fact, derived from the book, *The Primary Structures of Fabric.* . . . These weave paintings were most often conceived and plotted in strict series. In one group, for example, Zucker systematically varied the width of the painted strips of weft and woof so that the overall grid became progressively larger throughout the series and, concurrently, the range of color became progressively narrower."

    For the record, it is precisely "common ground" that Zucker's weave paintings share with Bartlett's early plate work, rather than a direct link. Bartlett would never have seen the weave paintings; Zucker left them stored in Chicago when he moved to New York.

7. Krane, p. 9. In the summer of 1992 *The 100-Foot Wall* was exhibited at The Parrish Art Museum (Southampton, New York). In conjunction with the exhibition, the Parrish published a brochure, *Joe Zucker: 100-Foot-Long Piece* (note variant title), featuring a full-color reproduction of the work and a text by Terry R. Myers.

8. *Rhapsody* is composed of 987 plates. Texts often cite the work as having 988 plates. Perhaps because *Rhapsody* is an attenuated rectangle with a right-angle perimeter, observers assume it must have an even-number count of plates. But the drunken line looping down seven plates in rows 67–69 breaks the gridded regularity of *Rhapsody*, thus accounting for the odd-number total. Another "irregularity" of *Rhapsody* are the clusters of nestled plates (i.e., absent the one-inch interval that otherwise applies) in rows 43–45, 49–52, and 59–62.

9. Artschwager's response and comments as reported to the author by Zucker (see n. 5).

10. Jennifer Bartlett, interviewed by Elizabeth Murray, "Jennifer Bartlett by Elizabeth Murray," *Bomb* 93 (Fall 2005), p. 57. This issue of *Bomb* appeared at a propitious moment for my purposes and I have relied on it for citations throughout the text. Also see http://www.bombsite.com/jenniferbartlett/jenniferbartlett3.html.

11. Sol LeWitt, quoted in Alicia Legg, *Sol LeWitt* (New York: The Museum of Modern Art, 1978), p. 77.

12. Bartlett, *Bomb* interview, p. 56.

13. Jennifer Bartlett, *History of the Universe: A Novel* (New York: Moyer Bell/Nimbus Books, 1985).

14. Bartlett, *Bomb* interview, p. 58.

15. Bartlett, quoted in Deborah Eisenberg, *Air: 24 Hours/Jennifer Bartlett* (New York: Harry N. Abrams, 1994), p. 125. This book is an invaluable document on Bartlett's work and, more generally, on the art of painting itself. The 24 Hours series is recorded in depth and in detail; Bartlett is eloquent in revealing how she paints, what she paints, and why she paints; and Eisenberg is not only an acute and savvy listener but is fearless in expressing how much she *doesn't* know in order to advance her own understanding on the reader's behalf.

16. In the *Bomb* interview, p. 58, Bartlett briefly talked about this piece and inadvertently calls it *Ellipse*. But it is definitely the *Parabolas* piece she is describing.

17. Tomkins, "Getting Everything In," p. 66.

18. Alan Saret, telephone conversation with the author, October 20, 2005. I am grateful to Saret for his forbearance in sharing memories of now distant times. He was generous in responding to my questions, despite the fact that we are not acquainted and my call came out of the blue.

19. Reese Palley styled himself "merchant to the rich," generating substantial profits from sales of Boehm porcelain birds and other high-end objets d'art. His base of retail operations was Atlantic City. Unlikely outsider that he was, Palley nevertheless decided to compete in the world of contemporary art and opened his first gallery in San Francisco in 1969. With Bay Area art historian Carol Lindsley as curator, the Palley Gallery presented a series of exhibitions of artists from both East and West Coasts. With the critical success of the San Francisco gallery, Palley opened a second gallery, in New York, in March 1970. In a typically contrarious move, Palley opted to set up in the pioneering SoHo neighborhood (only Paula Cooper preceded Palley in operating out of SoHo). James Harithas was Palley's first-season New York gallery director, followed by Dave Hickey for its second season, after which Lindsley served as curator, concurrently, of the New York and San Francisco galleries. Palley closed both galleries in 1972.

    Palley's two spaces offered enviable bicoastal opportunities for East and West Coast artists alike (several of whom had shows in both galleries). Over the three years of Palley's entrepreneurial experiment with contemporary art, the two galleries programmed solo or group exhibitions featuring—besides Bartlett—Billy Al Bengston, Bruce Conner, Howard Fried, Terry Fox, Nancy Graves, Stephen Kaltenbach, Paul Kos, Lee Krasner, Barry Le Va, Lee Lozano, Brice Marden, Tom Marioni, Bruce Nauman, Yoko Ono, Dennis Oppenheim, Peter Plagens, Ken Price, Ed Ruscha, John Torreano, Joe Zucker, and many others.

20. Artist Joel Shapiro also worked with an abstract "childlike" house form, creating beautiful small sculptures in both metal and painted wood, some designed to sit on the floor. Shapiro's earliest work using a house motif dates from 1973.

21. Bartlett, *Bomb* interview, p. 58.

22. Bartlett, *Bomb* interview, p. 59.

23. E. C. Goossen, *Ellsworth Kelly* (New York: The Museum of Modern Art, 1973), p. 30 [text caption]. Goossen writes in detail of Kelly's introduction to Arp and the senior artist's use of chance, as well as articulating Kelly's interest in chance as reflected in nature and its impact on his work over time (see pp. 28ff.). In November 2005 telephone conversations with the author, however, Kelly cautioned that the Goossen text is flawed by numerous errors of fact and interpretation.

24. Lawrence Alloway, "Reviews: Jennifer Bartlett," *Artforum* 9 (May 1974), p. 64.

25. Smith coined this perfect phrase for the title of her text in *Jennifer Bartlett: Rhapsody* (see n. 1). Although a great deal has been published about *Rhapsody*, I here rely on Smith's book and acknowledge my indebtedness to her precedent work. Additionally, I had the advantage of "living with" *Rhapsody* daily for nearly two months when we brought it to The Baltimore Museum of Art, where I was then curator, for exhibition in the fall of 1978.

26. Bartlett, *Bomb* interview, p. 59.

27. Smith, pp. 12–13.

28. *Air*, pp. 122–23.

Plates

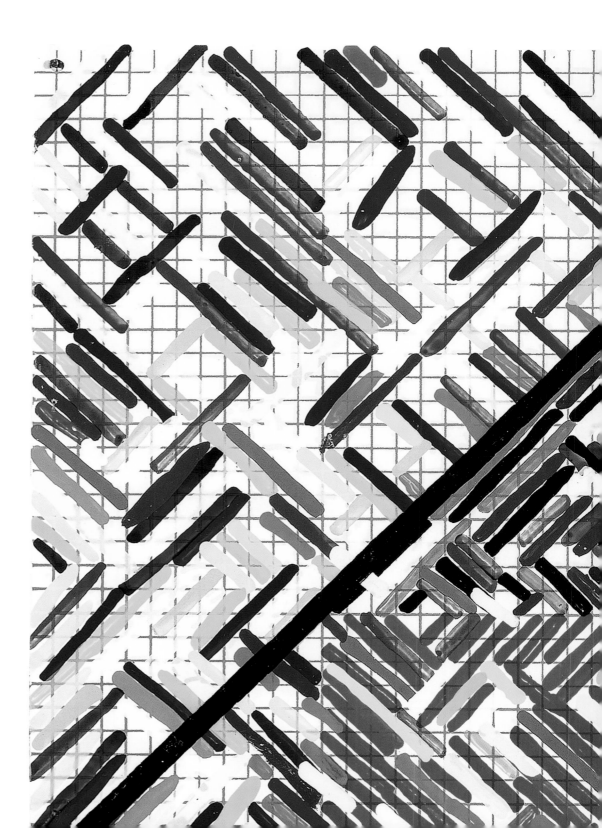

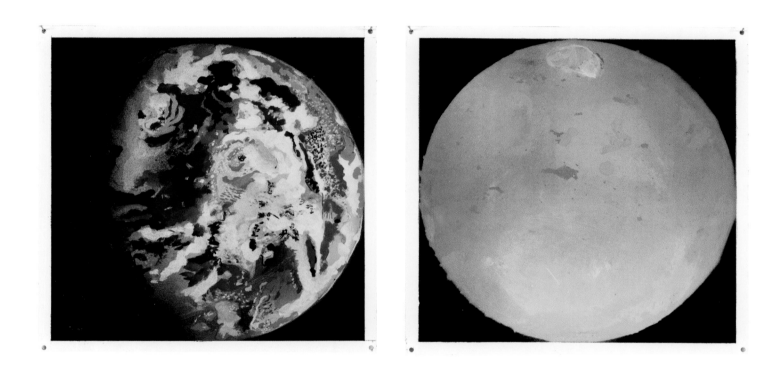

1. **Earth from Moon/Mars**, 1968–69
Enamel over grid silkscreened onto baked enamel on steel plates
12 x 25 inches (30.5 x 63.5 cm)

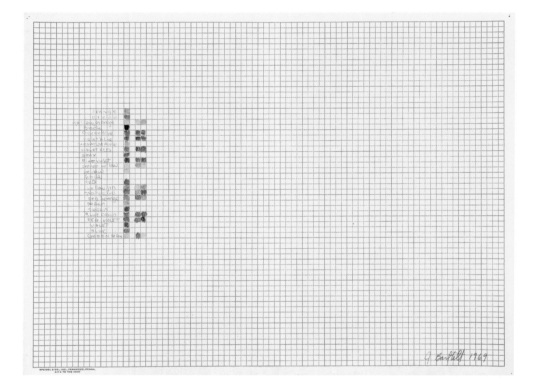

2. **Untitled (Color titles with mixing)**, 1969
Crayon and pencil on graph paper
17 x 22 inches (43.2 x 55.9 cm)

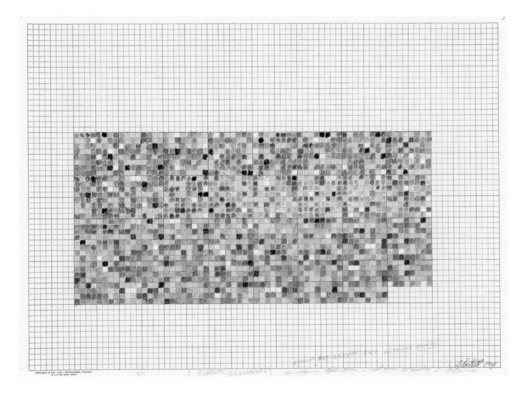

3. **Untitled (Random sequence)**, 1969
Crayon and pencil on graph paper
17 x 22 inches (43.2 x 55.9 cm)

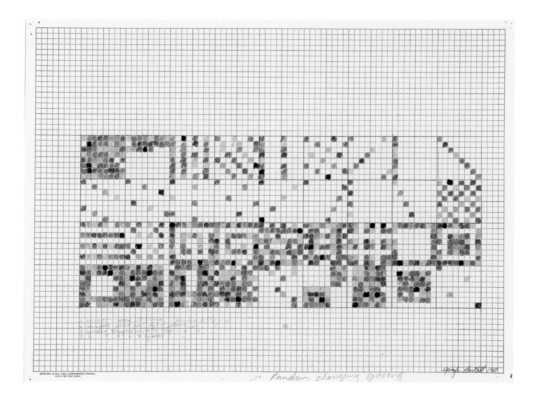

4. **Untitled (Random changing spacing)**, 1969
Crayon and pencil on graph paper
17 x 22 inches (43.2 x 55.9 cm)

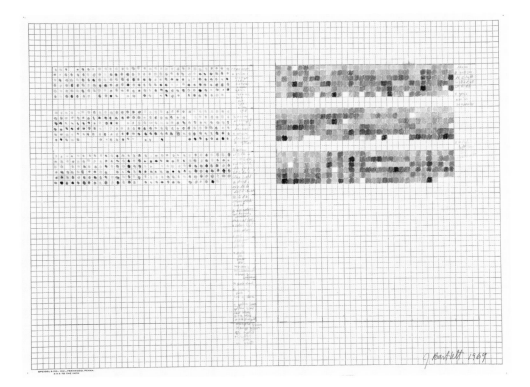

5. **Untitled (Color titles with samples)**, 1969
Crayon and pencil on graph paper
17 x 22 inches (43.2 x 55.9 cm)

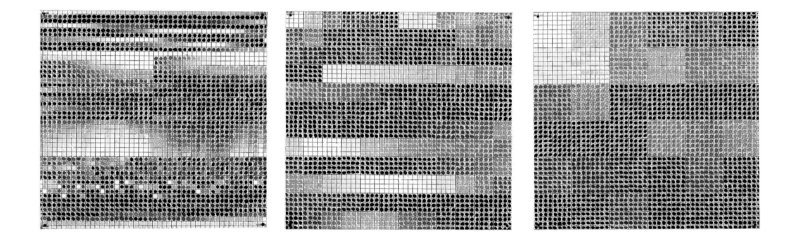

6. **2,304 Colors**, 1970
Enamel over grid silkscreened onto baked enamel on steel plates
12 x 38 inches (30.5 x 96.5 cm)

7. **Lines (Set B)**, 1970
Enamel over grid silkscreened onto baked enamel on steel plates
77 x 12 inches (195.6 x 30.5 cm)

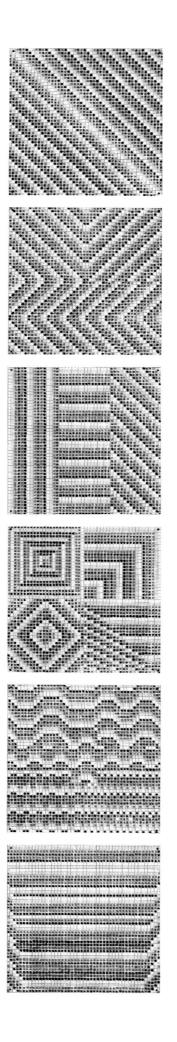

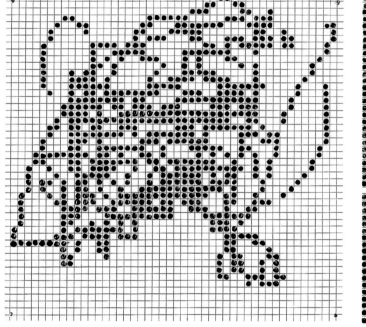

8. **Beethoven's 13th**, c. 1970
Enamel over grid silkscreened onto baked enamel on steel plates
12 x 25 inches (30.5 x 63.5 cm)

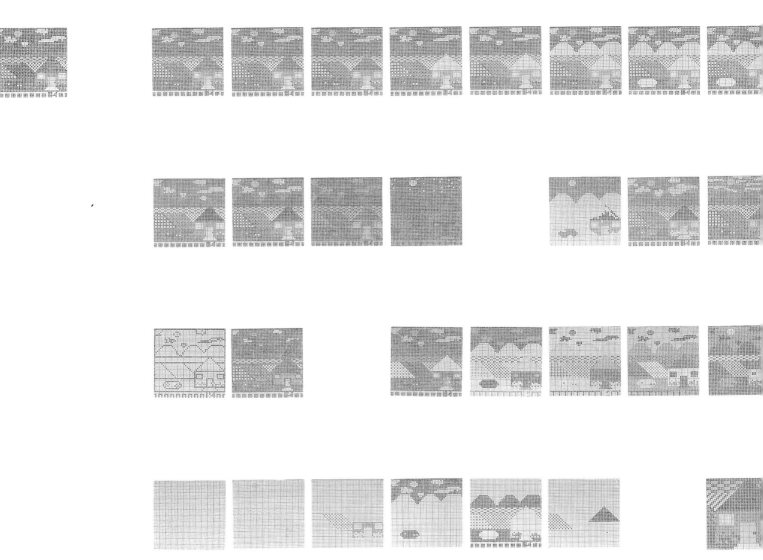

9. **House Piece**, 1970
Enamel over grid silkscreened onto baked enamel on steel plates
90 x 259 inches (228.6 x 657.9 cm)

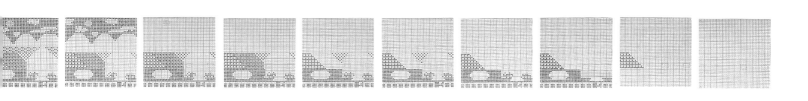

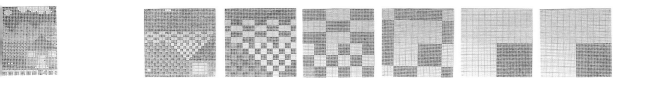

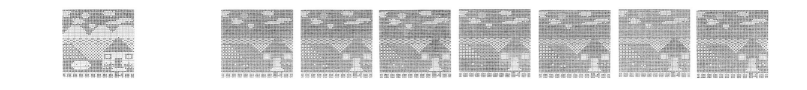

10. **Equivalents**, 1970
Enamel over grid silkscreened onto baked enamel on steel plates
116 x 25 inches (294.6 x 63.5 cm)

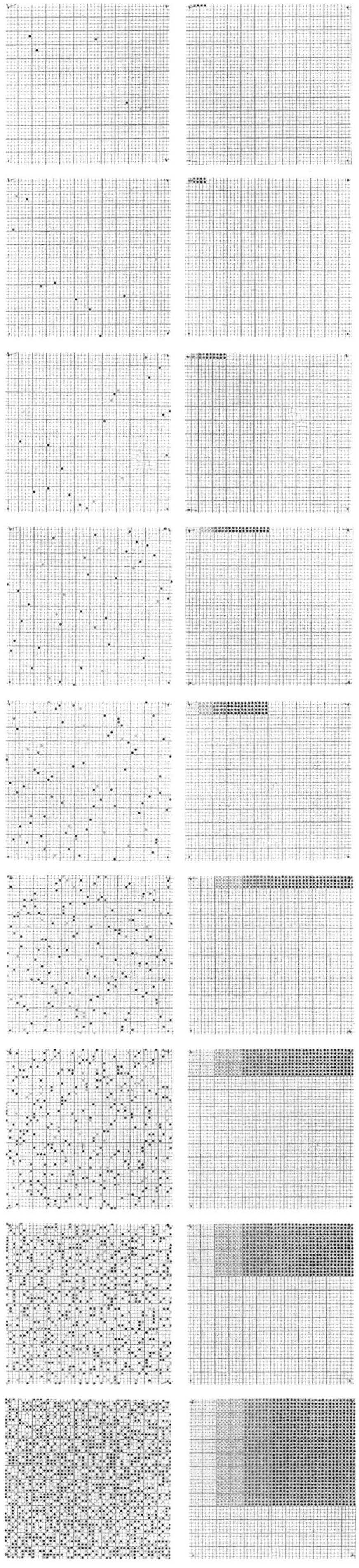

11. **Binary Combinations**, 1971
Enamel over grid silkscreened onto baked enamel on steel plates
64 x 88 inches (162.6 x 223.5 cm)

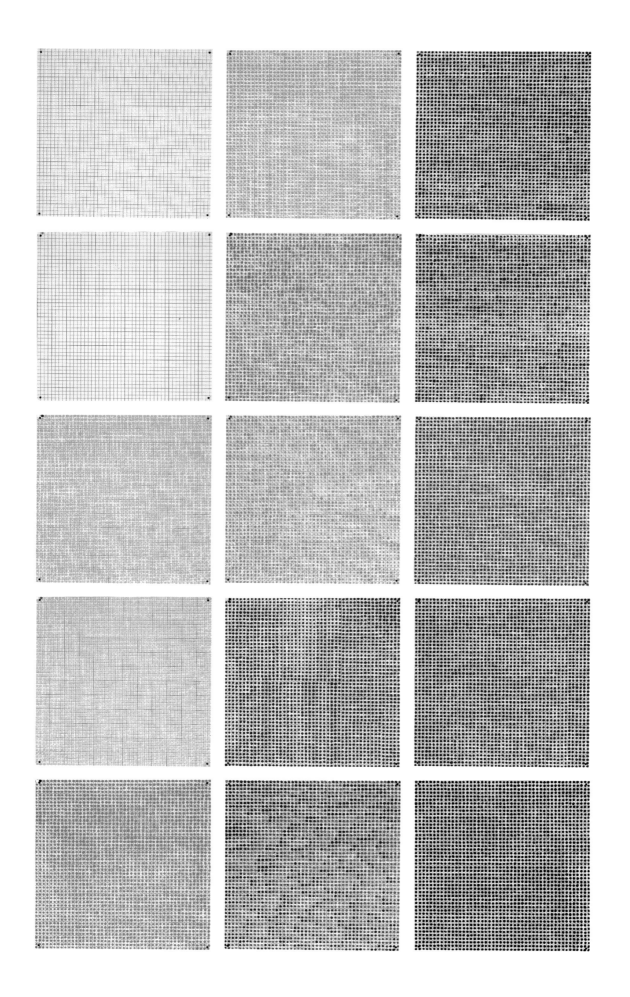

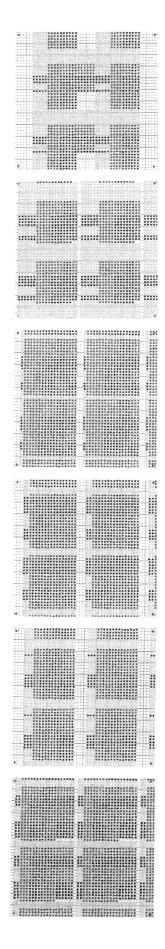
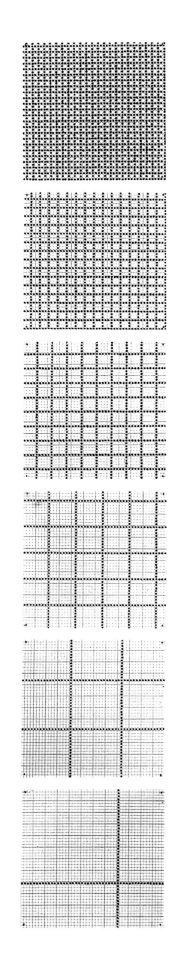

12. **Series XVIII (Grids)**, 1971
Enamel over grid silkscreened onto baked enamel on steel plates
71 x 122 inches (180.3 x 309.9 cm)

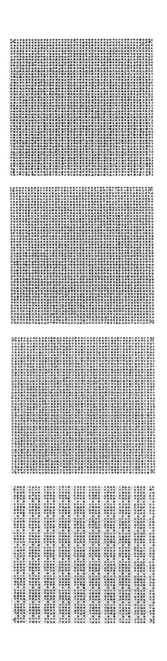

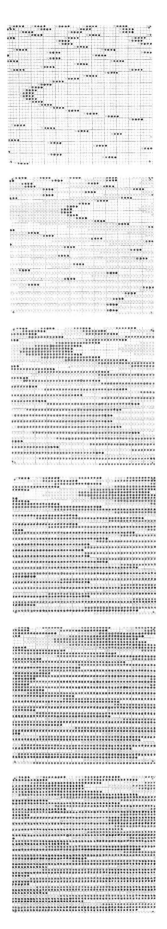
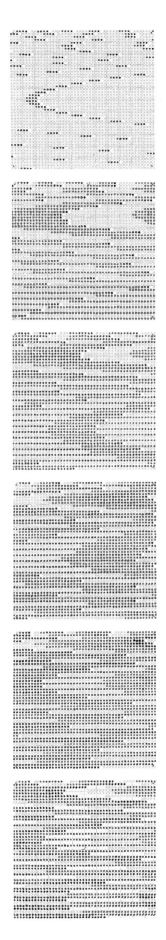
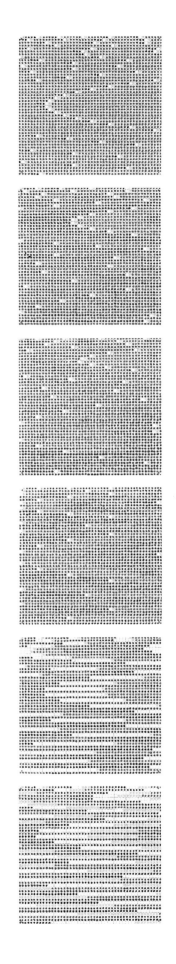

13. **Series VIII (Parabolas)**, 1971
Enamel over grid silkscreened onto baked enamel on steel plates
77 x 132 inches (195.6 x 335.3 cm)

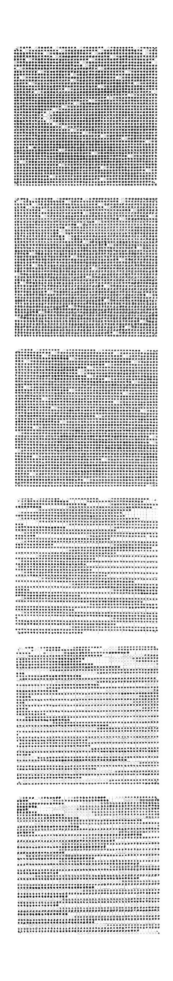
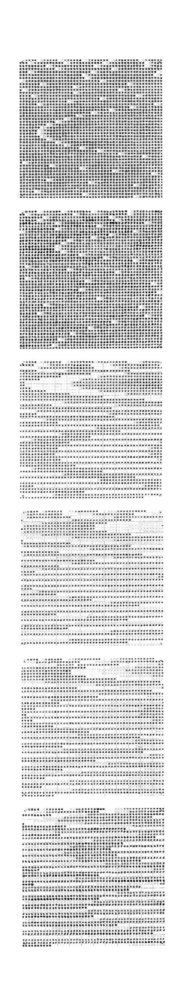
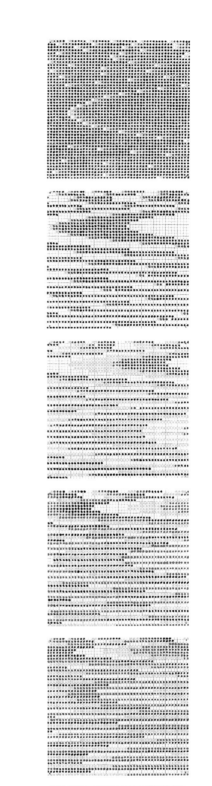
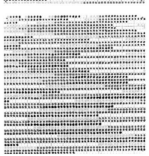

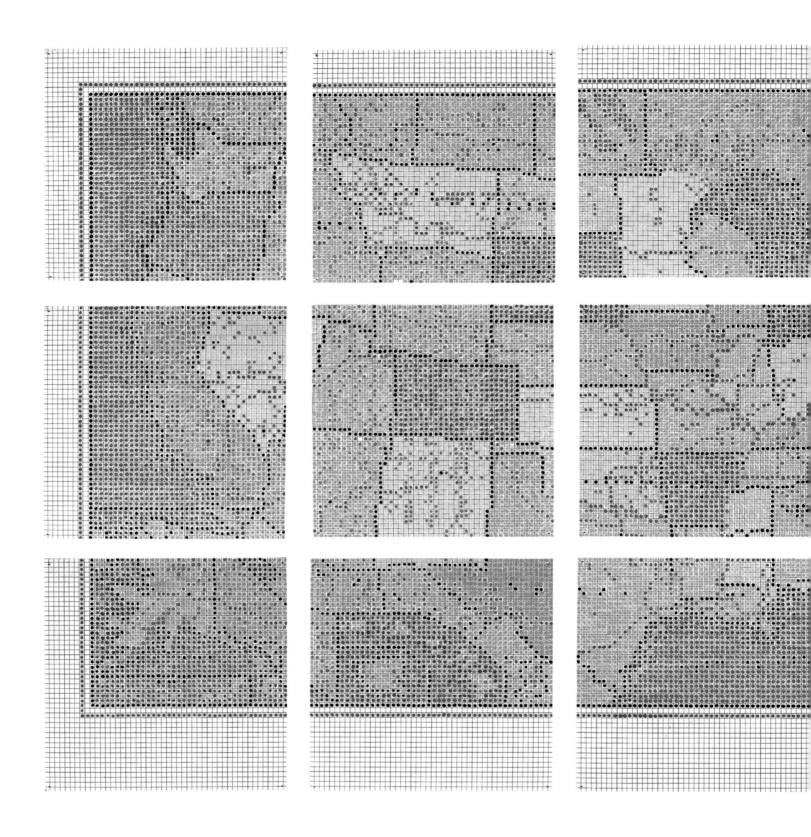

14. **Series XIV (Map)**, 1971–72
Enamel over grid silkscreened onto baked enamel on steel plates
38 x 64 inches (96.5 x 162.6 cm)

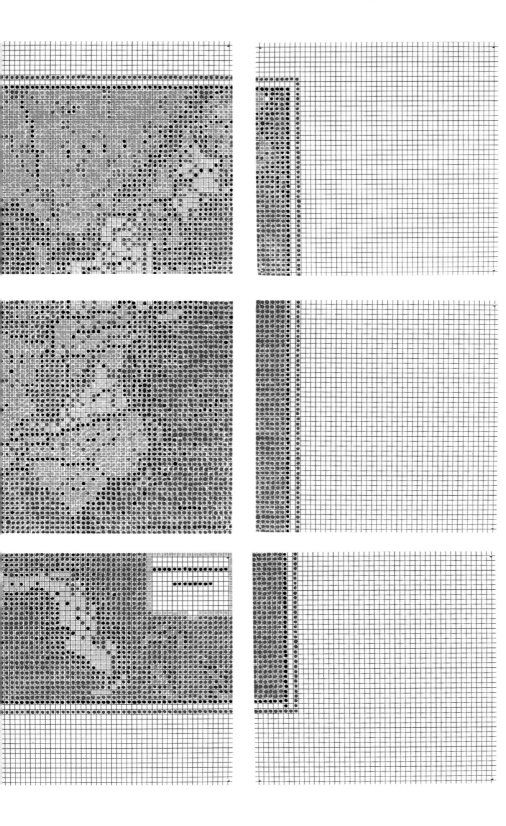

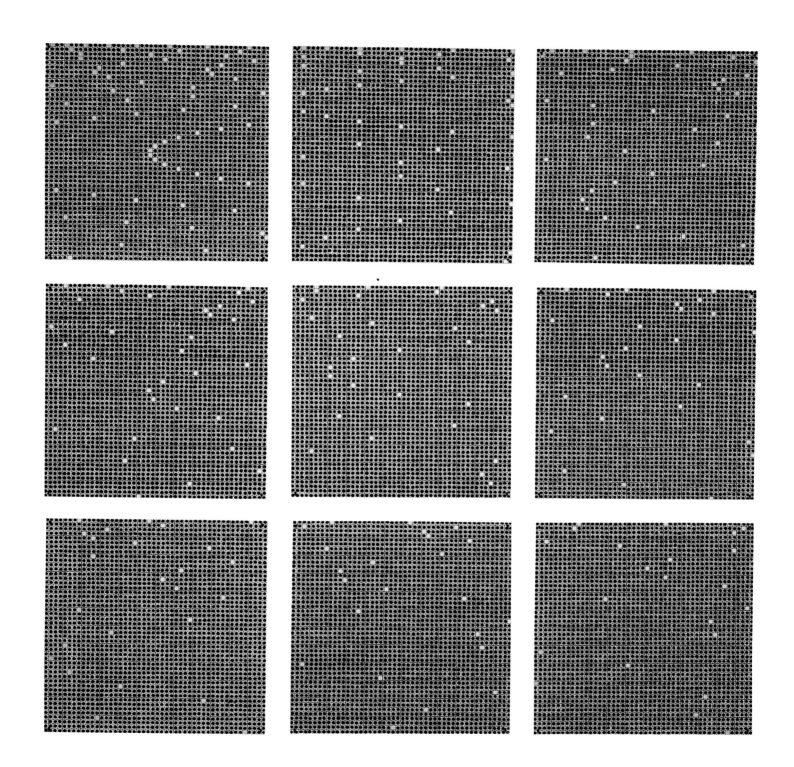

15. **Count**, 1972
Enamel over grid silkscreened onto baked enamel on steel plates
38 x 38 inches (96.5 x 96.5 cm)

16. **Four Right Angles**, 1972
Enamel over grid silkscreened onto baked enamel on steel plates
103 x 64 inches (261.6 x 162.6 cm)

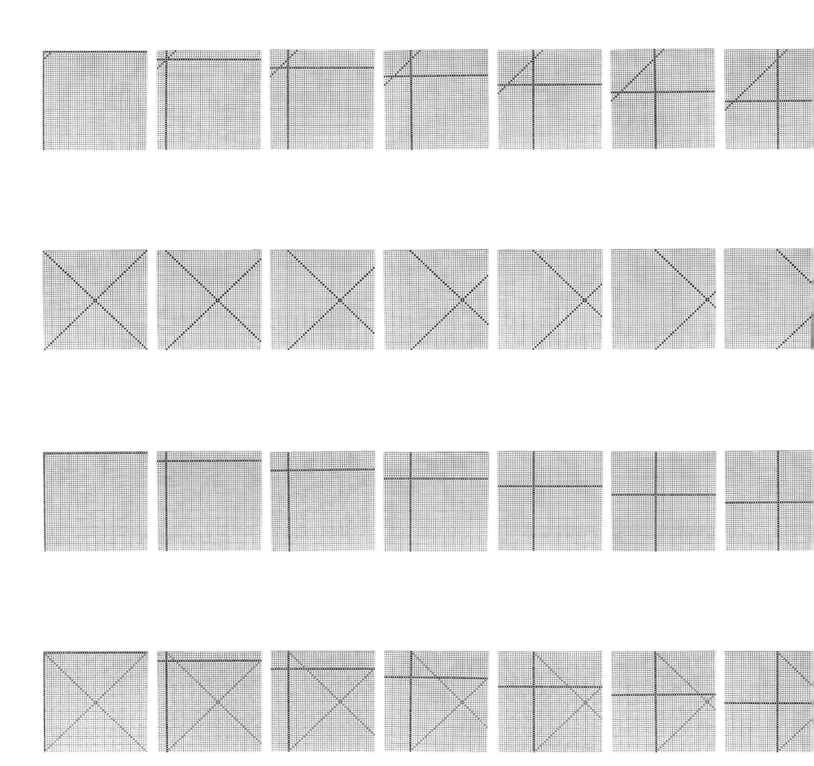

17. **Big Intersection**, 1972
Enamel over grid silkscreened onto baked enamel on steel plates
84 x 168 inches (213.4 x 426.7 cm)

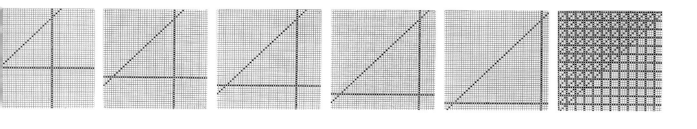

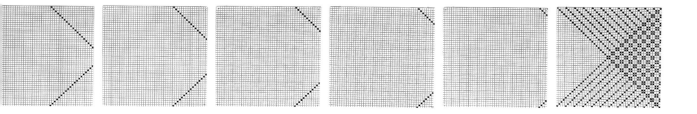

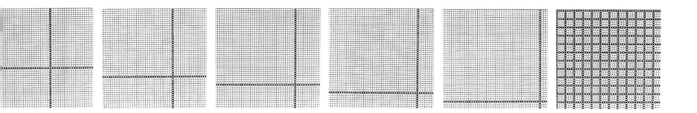

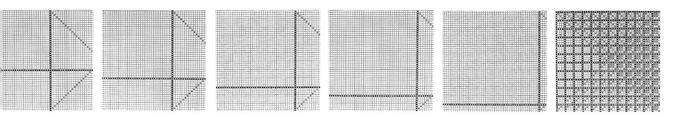

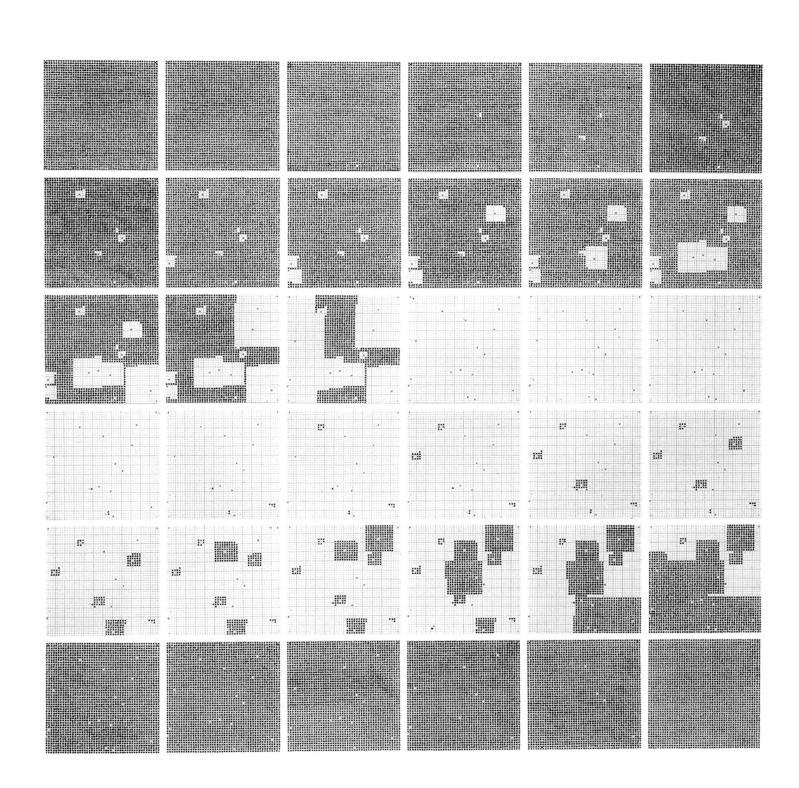

18. **Surface Substitution on 36 Plates**, 1972
Enamel over grid silkscreened onto baked enamel on steel plates
77 x 77 inches (195.6 x 195.6 cm)

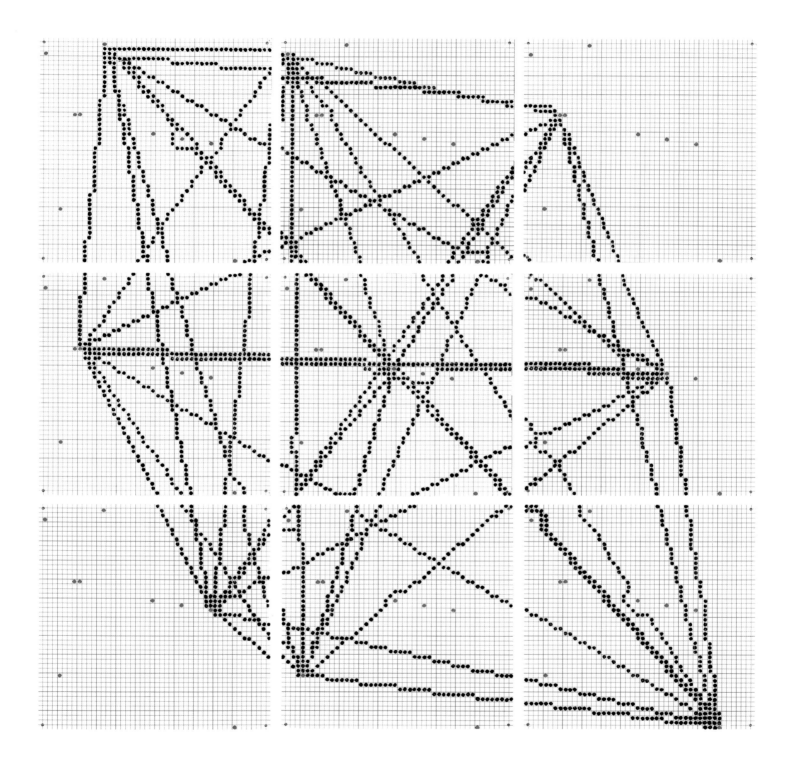

19. **2001**, 1973
Enamel over grid silkscreened onto baked enamel on steel plates
38 x 38 inches (96.5 x 96.5 cm)

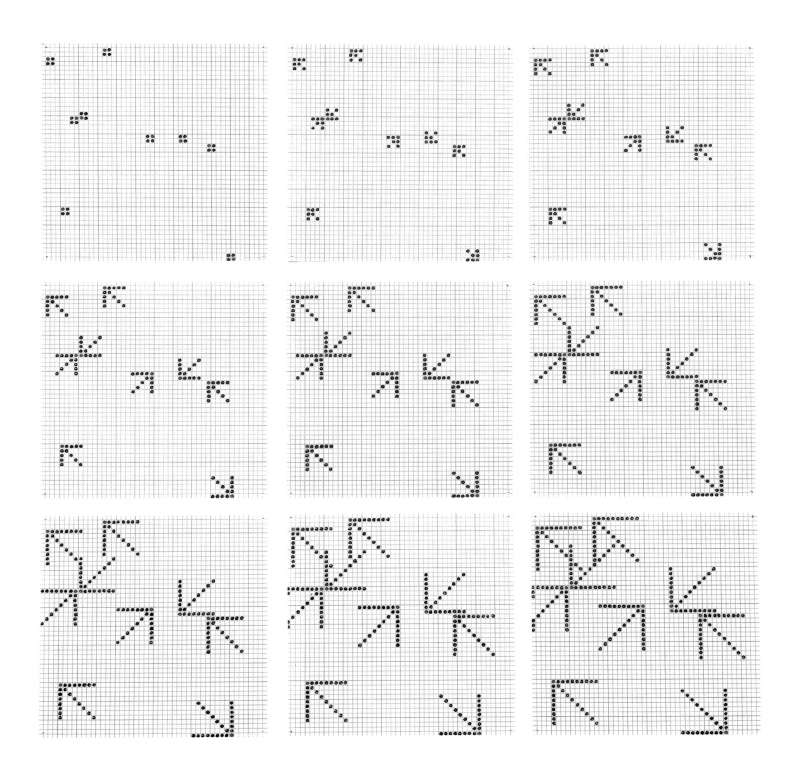

20. **Chicken Tracks**, 1973
Enamel over grid silkscreened onto baked enamel on steel plates
38 x 38 inches (96.5 x 96.5 cm)

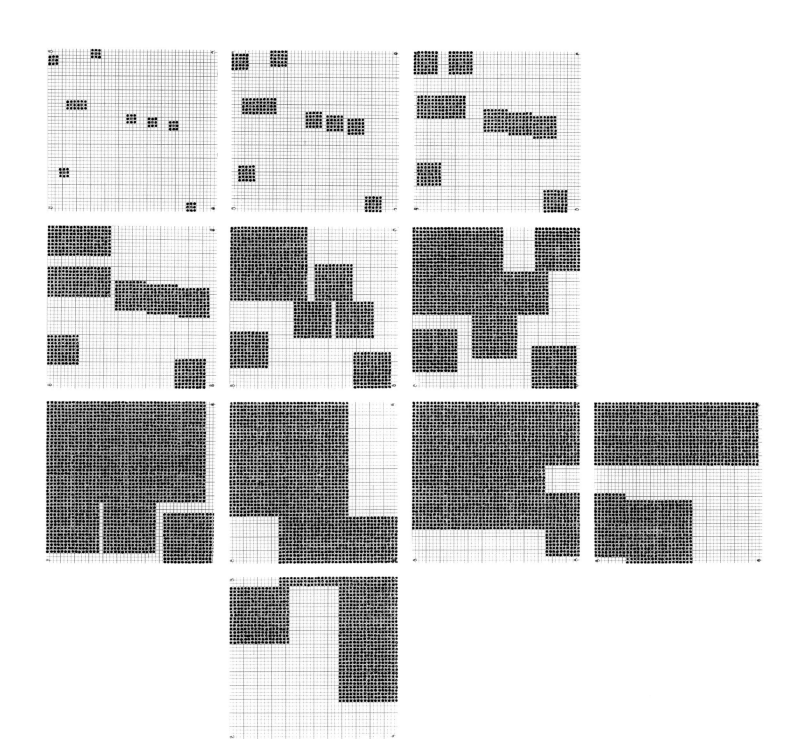

21. **Enclosure Drift**, 1973
Enamel over grid silkscreened onto baked enamel on steel plates
51 x 51 inches (129.5 x 129.5 cm)

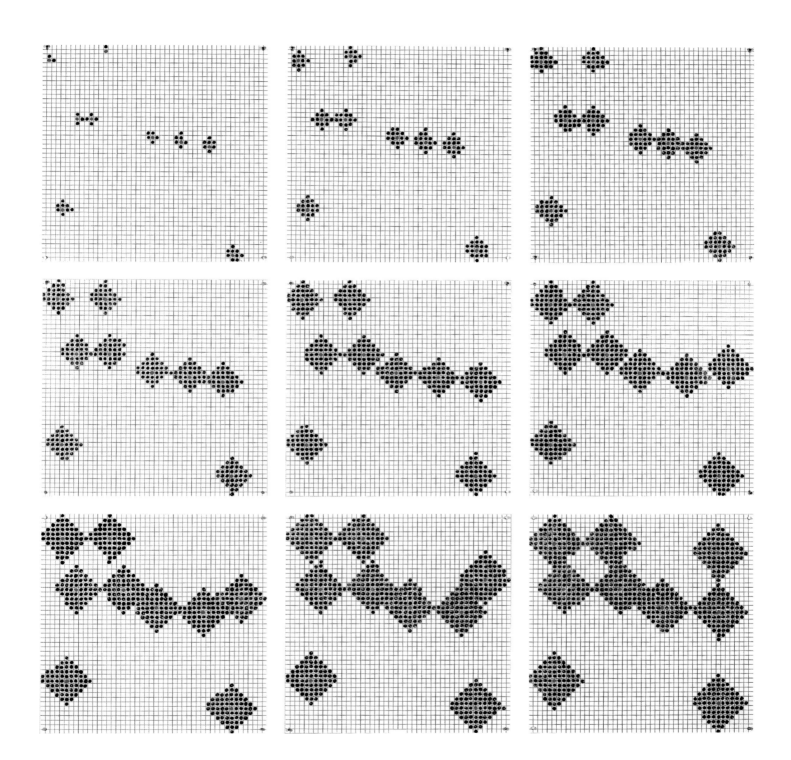

22. **Nest**, 1973
Enamel over grid silkscreened onto baked enamel on steel plates
38 x 38 inches (96.5 x 96.5 cm)

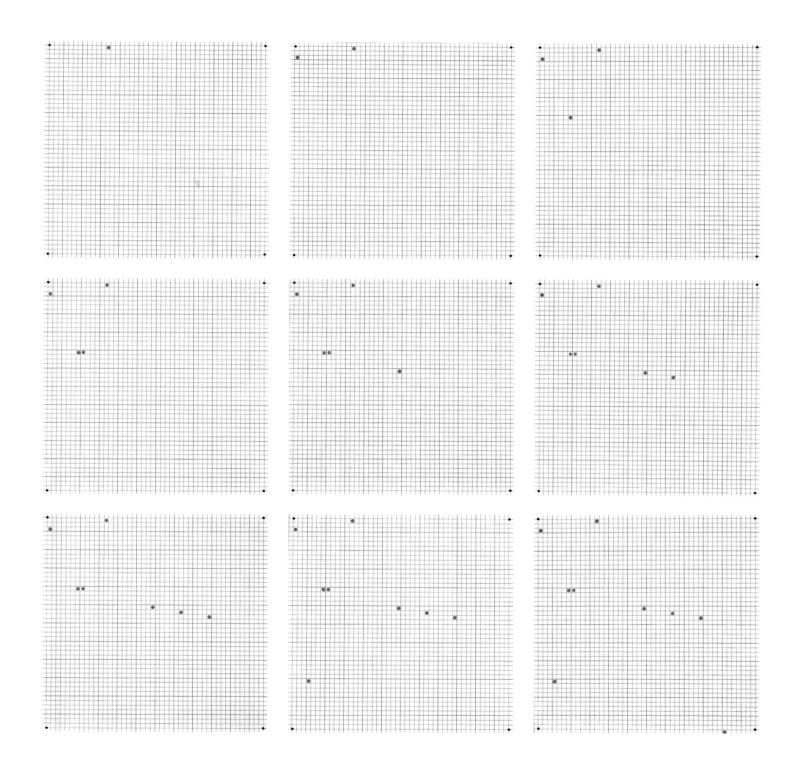

23. **Nine Points**, 1972
Enamel over grid silkscreened onto baked enamel on steel plates
38 x 38 inches (96.5 x 96.5 cm)

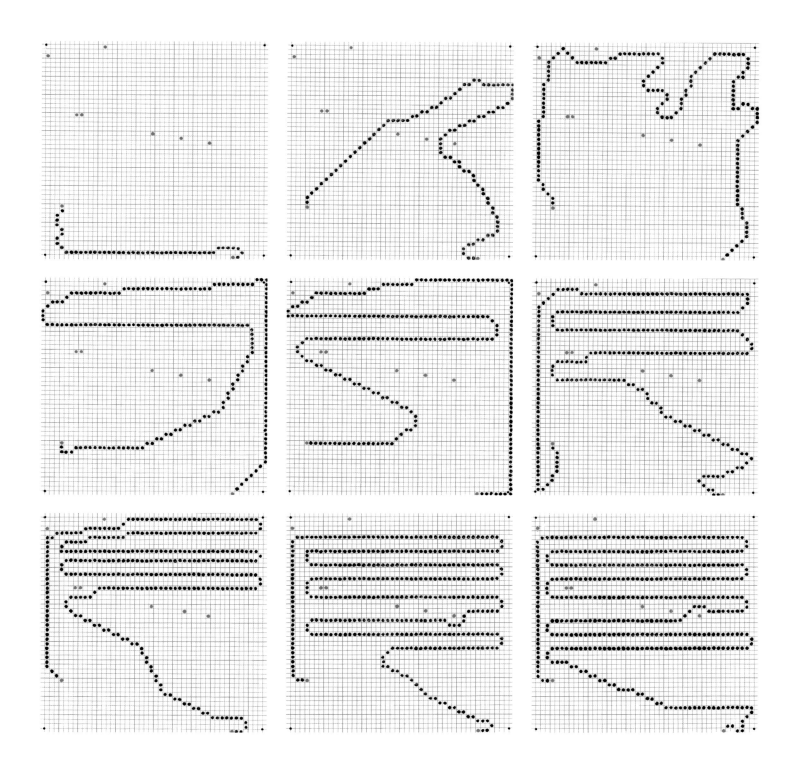

24. **1', 9' Line (Connecting Two Points)**, 1973
Enamel over grid silkscreened onto baked enamel on steel plates
38 x 38 inches (96.5 x 96.5 cm)

25. **1 Dot, 2 Dots**, 1973
Enamel over grid silkscreened onto baked enamel on steel plates
38 x 38 inches (96.5 x 96.5 cm)

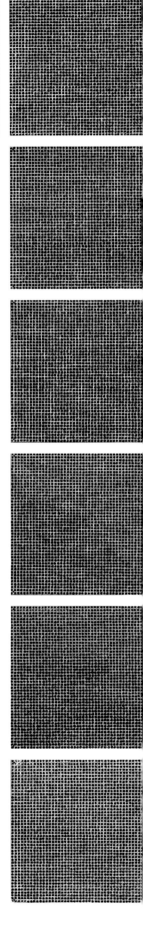

26. **Squaring: 2; 4; 16; 256; 65,536**, 1973–74
Enamel over grid silkscreened onto baked enamel on steel plates
77 x 116 inches (195.6 x 294.6 cm)

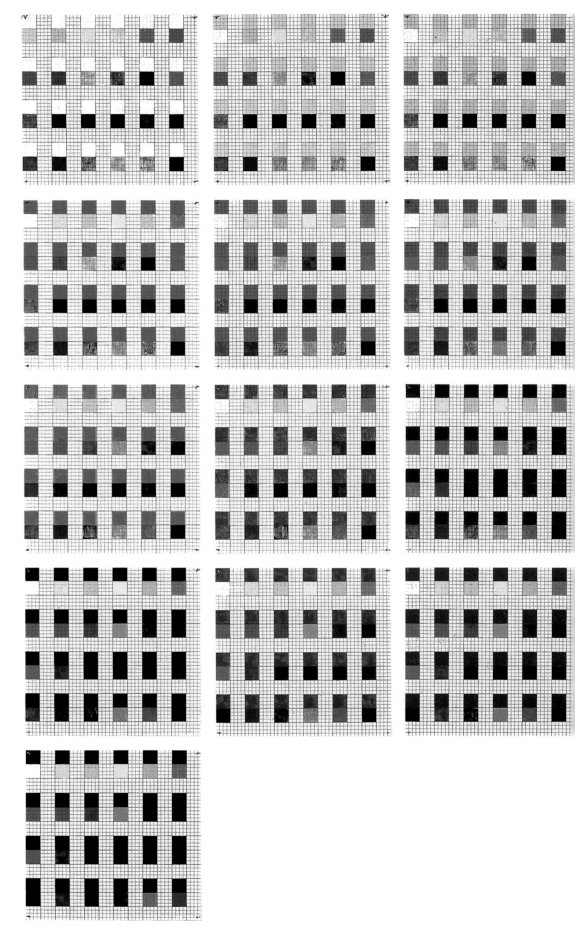

27. **Color Index I**, 1974
Enamel over grid silkscreened onto baked enamel on steel plates
64 x 77 inches (162.6 x 195.6 cm)

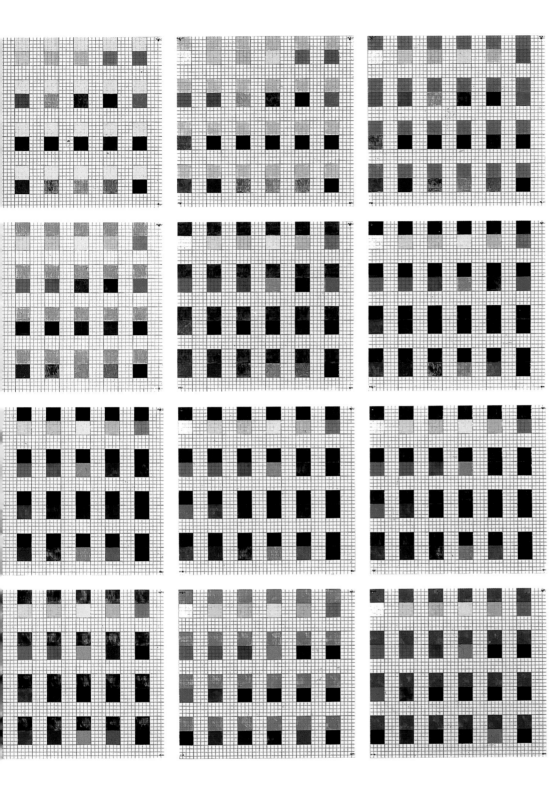

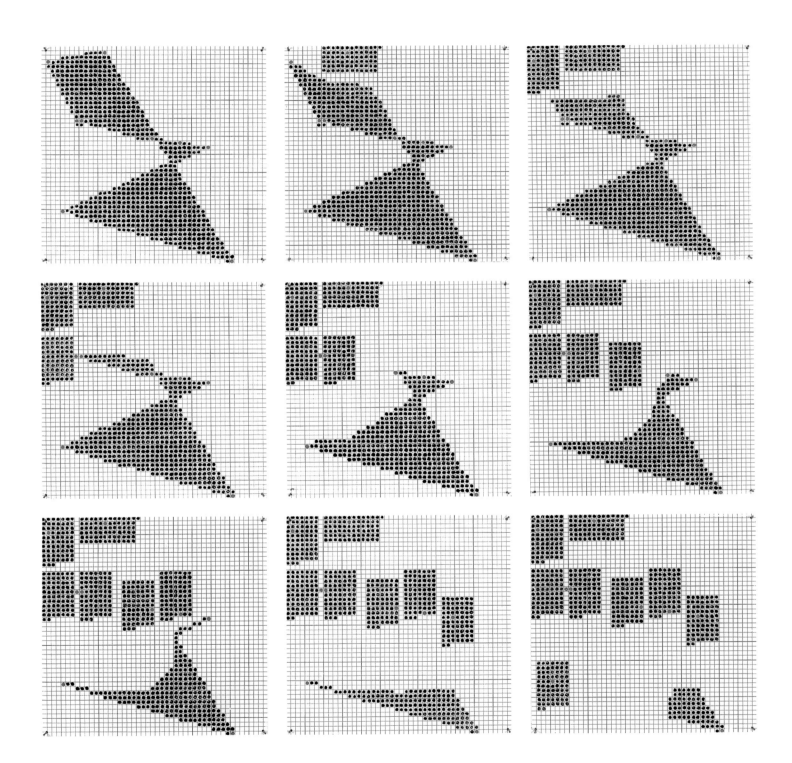

28. **Continental Drift**, 1974
Enamel over grid silkscreened onto baked enamel on steel plates
38 x 38 inches (96.5 x 96.5 cm)

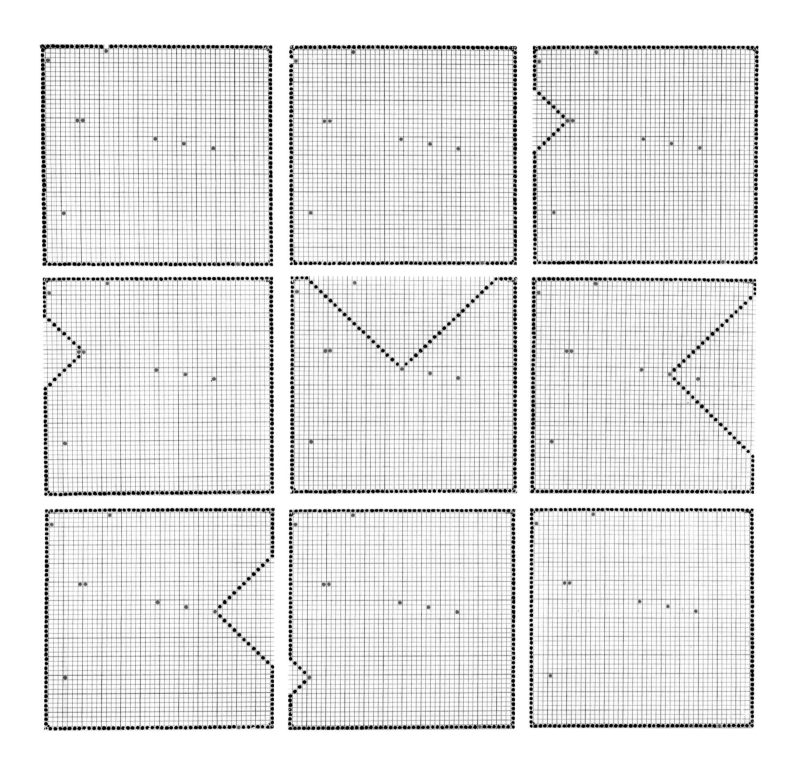

29. **Edge Lift**, 1974
Enamel over grid silkscreened onto baked enamel on steel plates
38 x 38 inches (96.5 x 96.5 cm)

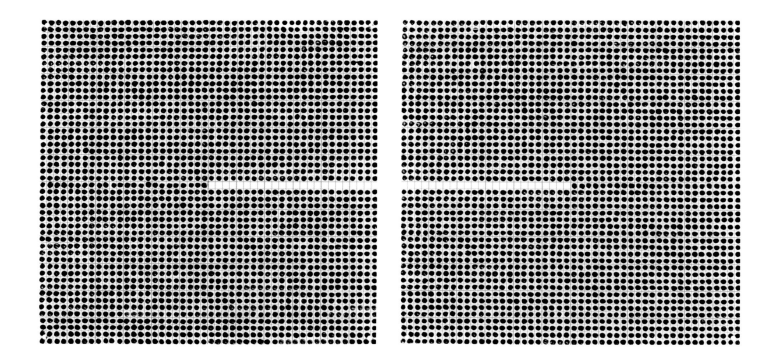

30. **One-Foot Line**, 1974
Enamel over grid silkscreened onto baked enamel on steel plates
12 x 25 inches (30.5 x 63.5 cm)

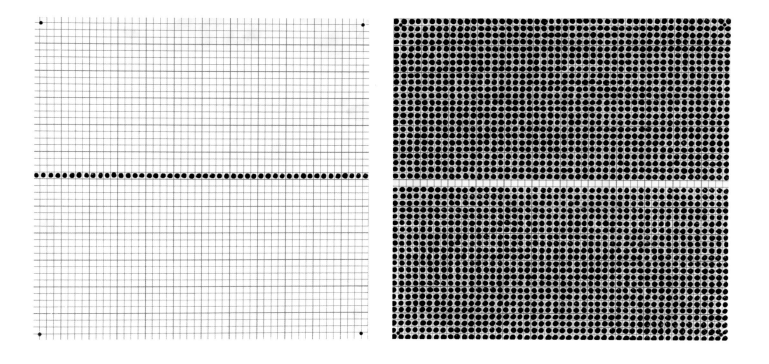

31. **Repoussé**, 1974
Enamel over grid silkscreened onto baked enamel on steel plates
12 x 25 inches (30.5 x 63.5 cm)

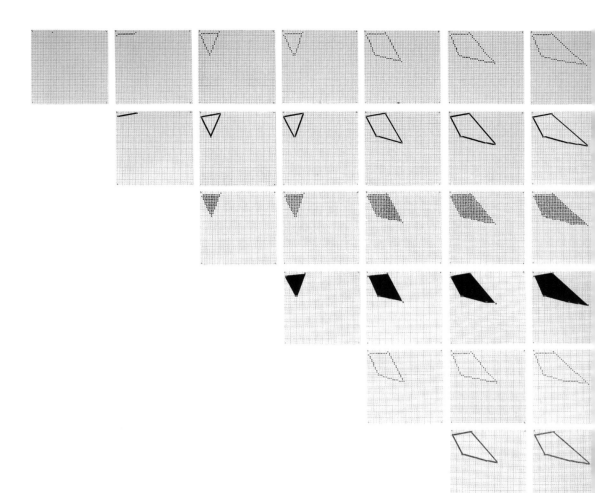

32. **Drawing and Painting**, 1974
Enamel over grid silkscreened onto baked enamel on steel plates
155 x 155 inches (393.7 x 393.7 cm)

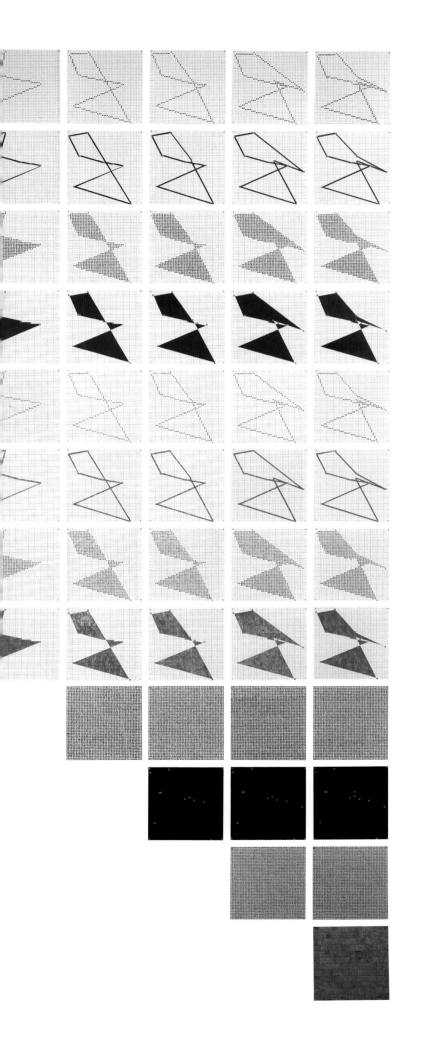

33. **Color Index II**, 1975
Enamel over grid silkscreened onto baked enamel on steel plates
25 x 168 inches (63.5 x 426.7 cm)

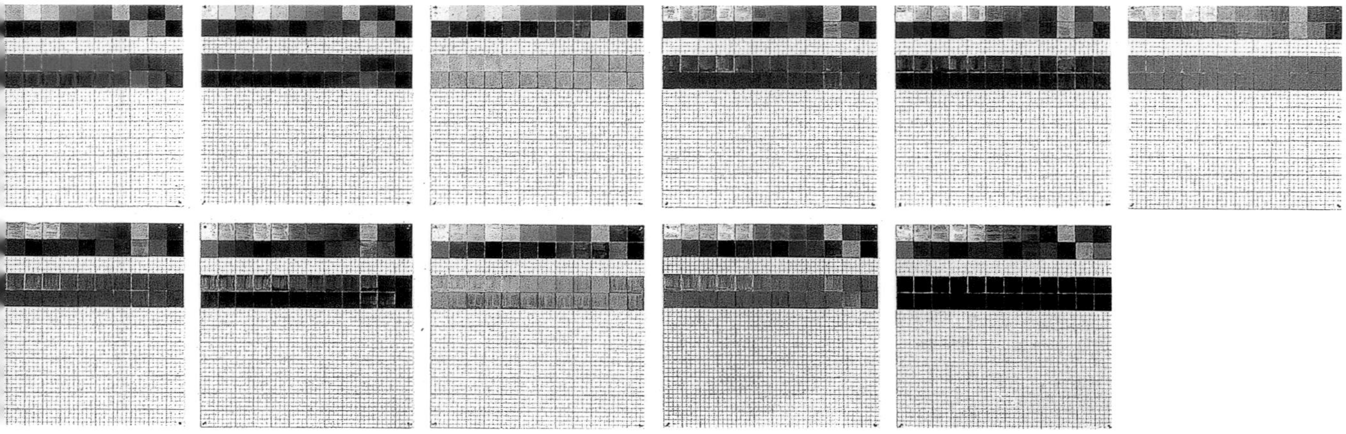

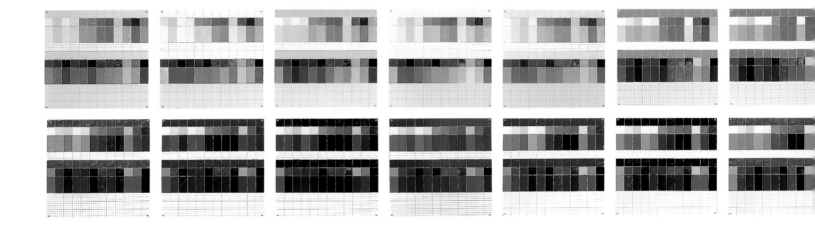

34. **Color Index III, Mixing**, 1975
Enamel over grid silkscreened onto baked enamel on steel plates
25 x 168 inches (63.5 x 426.7 cm)

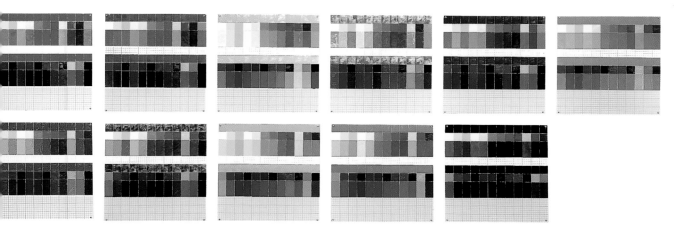

35. **Rhapsody**, 1975–76
Enamel over grid silkscreened onto baked enamel on steel plates
90 inches x 153 feet (228.6 cm x 4.66 m)
Installation views at The Museum of Modern Art, New York, 2006

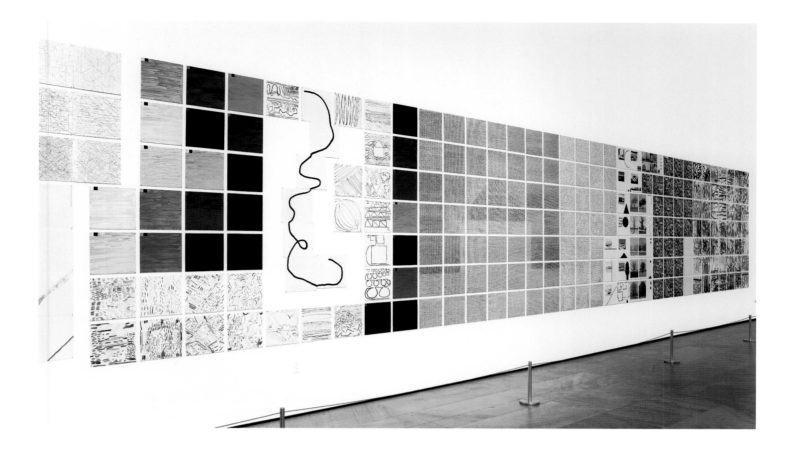

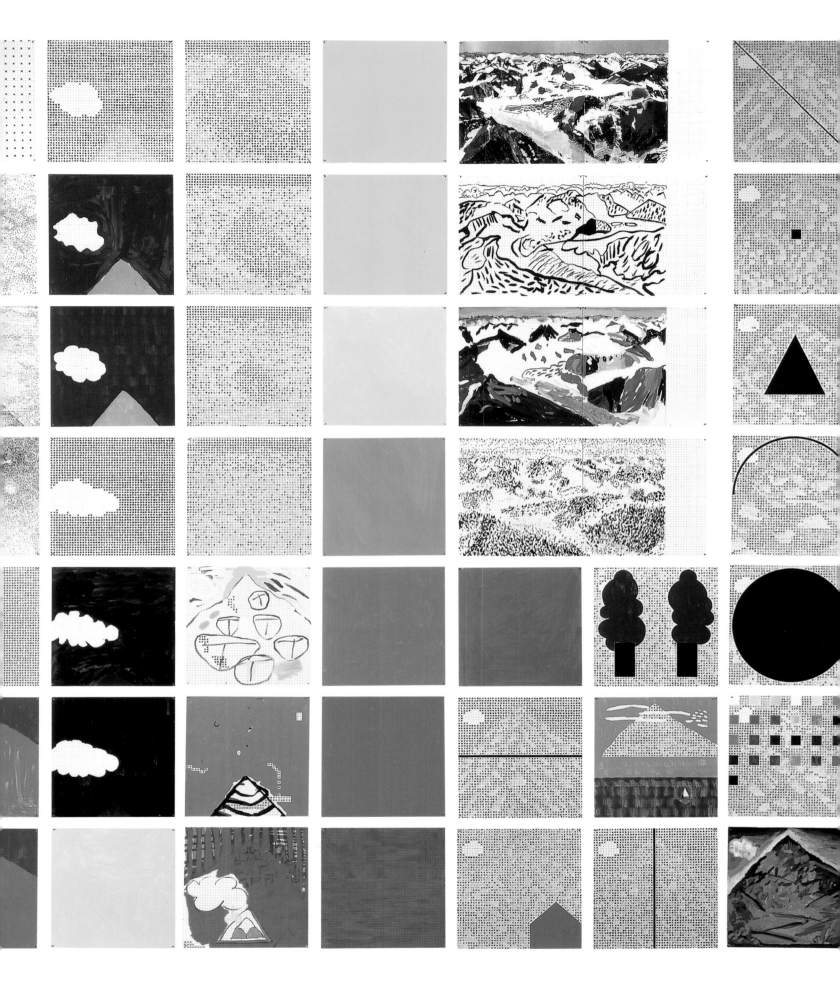

Rows 29–42, Plates 197–294

Rows 74–87, Plates 505–602

Row 4, Plate 22

Row 19, Plate 130

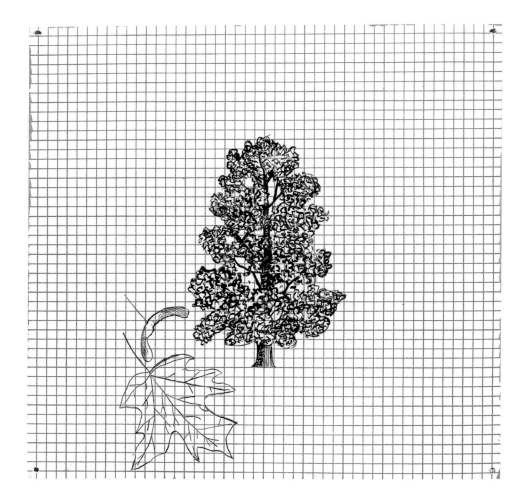

Row 23, Plate 158

Row 40, Plate 279

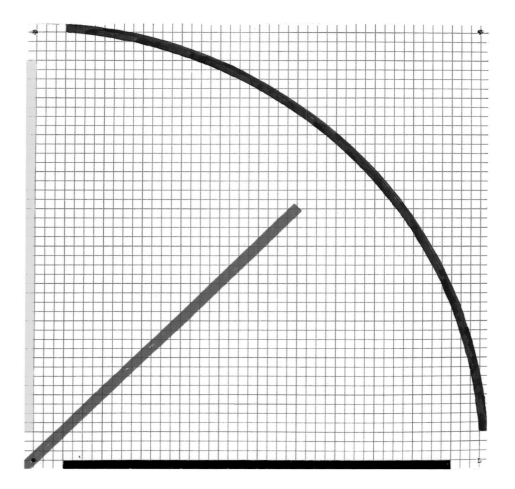

Row 47, Plate 326

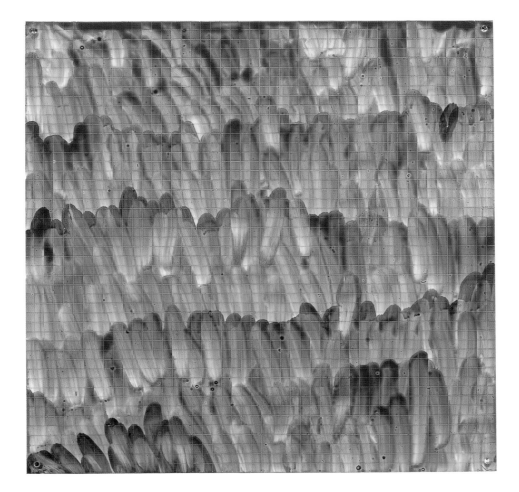

Row 128, Plate 887

Plate Captions

1. **Earth from Moon/Mars**, 1968–69, enamel over grid silkscreened onto baked enamel on steel plates, 12 x 25 inches (30.5 x 63.5 cm). Courtesy of the artist. Photo: Tom Powel

2. **Untitled (Color titles with mixing)**, 1969, crayon and pencil on graph paper, 17 x 22 inches (43.2 x 55.9 cm). Courtesy of the artist and Locks Gallery, Philadelphia. Photo: Frank E. Graham

3. **Untitled (Random sequence)**, 1969, crayon and pencil on graph paper, 17 x 22 inches (43.2 x 55.9 cm). Courtesy of the artist and Locks Gallery, Philadelphia. Photo: Frank E. Graham

4. **Untitled (Random changing spacing)**, 1969, crayon and pencil on graph paper, 17 x 22 inches (43.2 x 55.9 cm). Courtesy of the artist and Locks Gallery, Philadelphia. Photo: Frank E. Graham

5. **Untitled (Color titles with samples)**, 1969, crayon and pencil on graph paper 17 x 22 inches (43.2 x 55.9 cm). Courtesy of the artist and Locks Gallery, Philadelphia. Photo: Frank E. Graham

6. **2,304 Colors**, 1970, enamel over grid silkscreened onto baked enamel on steel plates, 12 x 38 inches (30.5 x 96.5 cm). Private collection, courtesy of Locks Gallery, Philadelphia. Photo: Courtesy of Locks Gallery, Philadelphia

7. **Lines (Set B)**, 1970, enamel over grid silkscreened onto baked enamel on steel plates, 77 x 12 inches (195.6 x 30.5 cm). Courtesy of the artist and Locks Gallery, Philadelphia. Photo: Frank E. Graham

8. **Beethoven's 13th**, c. 1970, enamel over grid silkscreened onto baked enamel on steel plates, 12 x 25 inches (30.5 x 63.5 cm). Courtesy of Paula Cooper Gallery, New York. Photo: Ellen Wilson

9. **House Piece**, 1970, enamel over grid silkscreened onto baked enamel on steel plates, 90 x 259 inches (228.6 x 657.9 cm). Private collection. Photo: Tom Powel

10. **Equivalents**, 1970, enamel over grid silkscreened onto baked enamel on steel plates, 116 x 25 inches (294.6 x 63.5 cm). Private collection. Photo: Courtesy of the artist

11. **Binary Combinations**, 1971, enamel over grid silkscreened onto baked enamel on steel plates, 64 x 88 inches (162.6 x 223.5 cm). University of California, Berkeley Art Museum, partial and promised gift of Penny Cooper and Rena Rosenwasser. Photo: Frank E. Graham

12. **Series XVIII (Grids)**, 1971, enamel over grid silkscreened onto baked enamel on steel plates, 71 x 122 inches (180.3 x 309.9 cm). Courtesy of Paula Cooper Gallery, New York. Photo: Tom Powel

13. **Series VIII (Parabolas)**, 1971, enamel over grid silkscreened onto baked enamel on steel plates, 77 x 132 inches (195.6 x 335.3 cm). Walker Art Center, Minneapolis; Gift of the T. B. Walker Foundation, 1972

14. **Series XIV (Map)**, 1971–72, enamel over grid silkscreened onto baked enamel on steel plates, 38 x 64 inches (96.5 x 162.6 cm). Collection unkown. Photo: Courtesy of the artist

15. **Count**, 1972, enamel over grid silkscreened onto baked enamel on steel plates, 38 x 38 inches (96.5 x 96.5 cm). Estate of Jack Tworkov. Photo: Frank E. Graham

16. **Four Right Angles**, 1972, enamel over grid silkscreened onto baked enamel on steel plates, 103 x 64 inches (261.6 x 162.6 cm). Courtesy of the artist and Locks Gallery, Philadelphia. Photo: Frank E. Graham

17. **Big Intersection**, 1972, enamel over grid silkscreened onto baked enamel on steel plates, 84 x 168 inches (213.4 x 426.7 cm). Private collection. Photo: Courtesy of the artist

18. **Surface Substitution on 36 Plates**, 1972, enamel over grid silkscreened onto baked enamel on steel plates, 77 x 77 inches (195.6 x 195.6 cm). Tate. Offered by HM Government in lieu of Inheritance Tax by David, Maggi, Joshua, and Daniel Gordon in memory of Max Gordon. Accepted and allocated to Tate 1992. Photo: © Tate, London 2005

19. **2001**, 1973, enamel over grid silkscreened onto baked enamel on steel plates, 38 x 38 inches (96.5 x 96.5 cm). Neuberger Museum of Art, Purchase College, State University of New York, Gift of Martin J. Sklar. Photo: Jim Frank

20. **Chicken Tracks**, 1973, enamel over grid silkscreened onto baked enamel on steel plates, 38 x 38 inches (96.5 x 96.5 cm). Collection of Sally and Wynn Kramarsky. Photo: Peter Muscato

21. **Enclosure Drift**, 1973, enamel over grid silkscreened onto baked enamel on steel plates, 51 x 51 inches (129.5 x 129.5 cm). Collection of Gilbert and Lila Silverman, Detroit, Michigan. Photo: Tim Thayer

22. **Nest**, 1973, enamel over grid silkscreened onto baked enamel on steel plates, 38 x 38 inches (96.5 x 96.5 cm). The Baltimore Museum of Art: Friends of Modern Art Fund, BMA 1985.50

23. **Nine Points**, 1972, enamel over grid silkscreened onto baked enamel on steel plates, 38 x 38 inches (96.5 x 96.5 cm). Courtesy of the artist and Locks Gallery, Philadelphia. Photo: Frank E. Graham

24. **1', 9' Line (Connecting Two Points)**, 1973, enamel over grid silkscreened onto baked enamel on steel plates 38 x 38 inches (96.5 x 96.5 cm). Courtesy of the artist and Locks Gallery, Philadelphia. Photo: Frank E. Graham

25. **1 Dot, 2 Dots**, 1973, enamel over grid silkscreened onto baked enamel on steel plates, 38 x 38 inches (96.5 x 96.5 cm). Collection of Kate Hoblitzell. Photo: Mitro Hood

26. **Squaring: 2; 4; 16; 256; 65,536**, 1973–74, enamel over grid silkscreened onto baked enamel on steel plates, 77 x 116 inches, (195.6 x 294.6 cm). Courtesy of the artist and Locks Gallery, Philadelphia. Photo: Frank E. Graham

27. **Color Index I**, 1974, enamel over grid silkscreened onto baked enamel on steel plates, 64 x 77 inches (162.6 x 195.6 cm). Herbert F. Johnson Museum of Art, Cornell University, Gift of Maria and Donald Cox, 97.035 a-y

28. **Continental Drift**, 1974, enamel over grid silkscreened onto baked enamel on steel plates, 38 x 38 inches (96.5 x 96.5 cm). Museum of Contemporary Art San Diego, Museum purchase, 1986.4.1-9. Photo: Philipp Scholz Rittermann

29. **Edge Lift**, 1974, enamel over grid silkscreened onto baked enamel on steel plates, 38 x 38 inches (96.5 x 96.5 cm). Allen Memorial Art Museum, Oberlin College, Oberlin, Ohio, Friends of Art Endowment Fund, 1977. Photo: John Seyfried

30. **One-Foot Line**, 1974, enamel over grid silkscreened onto baked enamel on steel plates, 12 x 25 inches (30.5 x 63.5 cm). The Parrish Art Museum, Southampton, New York, Gift of Paul F. Walter, 1982.10.9. Photo: Gary Mamay

31. **Repoussé**, 1974, enamel over grid silkscreened onto baked enamel on steel plates, 12 x 25 inches (30.5 x 63.5 cm). Collection of James F. Duffy, Jr. Photo: Tim Thayer

32. **Drawing and Painting**, 1974, enamel over grid silkscreened onto baked enamel on steel plates, 155 x 155 inches (393.7 x 393.7 cm). Courtesy of Paula Cooper Gallery, New York. Photo: Ellen Wilson

33. **Color Index II**, 1975, enamel over grid silkscreened onto baked enamel on steel plates, 25 x 168 inches (63.5 x 426.7 cm). Maxine and Stuart Frankel Foundation for Art. Photo: Tim Thayer

34. **Color Index III, Mixing**, 1975, enamel over grid silkscreened onto baked enamel on steel plates, 25 x 168 inches (63.5 x 426.7 cm). Collection of Mr. and Mrs. William Lamont, Jr. Photo: Tom Jenkins

35. **Rhapsody**, 1975–76, enamel over grid silkscreened onto baked enamel on steel plates, 90 inches x 153 feet (228.6 cm x 4.66 m). The Museum of Modern Art, New York, Gift of Edward R. Broida, 2005. Photos of installation views, Digital Images © The Museum of Modern Art/Licensed by SCALA/Art Resource, NY; photos of details, Courtesy of the artist

Figure Captions

Figure 1. Installation view of *Primary Structures*, The Jewish Museum, New York, April 27 to June 12, 1966. Left: Donald Judd (1928–1994), *Untitled*, 1966, and *Untitled*, 1966; center: Robert Morris (born 1931), *Untitled (2 L beams)*; and right (above): Robert Grosvenor (born 1937), *Transoxiana*, 1965. Photo: © The Jewish Museum/Art Resource/NY, Art © Judd Foundation. Licensed by VAGA, New York, NY

Figure 2. Installation view of *10*, Dwan Gallery, New York, October 1966. Works, clockwise from center foreground, by Carl Andre, Jo Baer, Donald Judd, Sol LeWitt, Robert Smithson, and Robert Morris. Photo: Courtesy of Dwan Gallery Archives, photo by John D. Schiff

Figure 3. Chuck Close (born 1940), *Susan/Pastel*, 1977, pastel and pencil on watercolor-washed paper, 30 x 21¾ inches (76.2 x 55.3 cm). Courtesy of Louis K. Meisel Gallery, New York. Photo: Courtesy of Louis K. Meisel Gallery, New York

Figure 4. Joe Zucker (born 1941), *Joe's Painting #125*, 1965, acrylic on canvas, 70 x 70 inches (177.8 x 177.8 cm). Courtesy of the artist. Photo: Courtesy of the artist

Figure 5. Joe Zucker (born 1941), *The 100-Foot Wall* (detail), 1968–69, mixed media, 8 x 55 feet (243.8 x 1,676.4 cm). Collection of the artist. Photo: Courtesy of the artist

Figure 6. Joe Zucker (born 1941), *Rose Lake* (detail), 1969, acrylic, cotton, Rhoplex on canvas, 4 x 16 feet (121.9 x 487.7 cm) (three panels, left to right: 4 x 4 feet, 4 x 8 feet, 4 x 4 feet). Collection of the artist. Photo: Courtesy of the artist

Figure 7. Richard Artschwager (born 1923), *Untitled (All Over Pattern)*, 1965, acrylic on Celotex on board, 14½ x 11½ inches (36.8 x 29.2 cm). Private collection. Photo: © 2006 Richard Artschwager/Artists Rights Society (ARS), New York, Courtesy of the artist

Figure 8. Barry Le Va (born 1941), *Bearings Rolled (Six Specific Instants: No Particular Order)*, 1966–67, ink on paper, 28 x 51 inches (71.1 x 129.5 cm), each of six sheets, 14 x 17 inches (35.6 x 43.2 cm). Courtesy of Sonnabend Gallery. Photo: Courtesy of Sonnabend Gallery

Figure 9. Eadweard J. Muybridge (1830–1904), Plate 44. *Walking Taking Off Hat,* 1885, from *Animal Locomotion,* 1887, *Volume 7, Males & Females Draped & Misc. Subjects,* collotype, 8⅛ x 13½ inches (20.6 x 34.3 cm). Addison Gallery of American Art, Phillips Academy, Andover, Massachusetts, Gift of Edwin J. Beinecke Trust. Photo: © Addison Gallery of American Art, Phillips Academy, Andover, Massachusetts

Figure 10. Frank Stella (born 1936), *Fez*, 1964, fluorescent alkyd paint on canvas, 77 x 77 inches (195.6 x 195.6 cm). Albright-Knox Art Gallery, Buffalo, New York, Gift of Seymour H. Knox, Jr., 1964. Photo: © 2005 Frank Stella/Artists Rights Society (ARS), New York, Courtesy of Albright-Knox Art Gallery, Buffalo, New York

Figure 11. Robert Ryman (born 1930), *Winsor 34*, 1966, oil on linen, 63 x 63 inches (159.1 x 159.1 cm). Private collection. Photo: © Robert Ryman, Courtesy PaceWildenstein, New York

Figure 12. Eva Hesse (1936–1970), *Untitled*, 1967, black ink on graph paper, 11 x 8½ inches (27.9 x 21.6 cm). Collection of Sally and Wynn Kramarsky. Photo: © The Estate of Eva Hesse. Hauser & Wirth Zürich London; photo by Peter Muscato

Figure 13. Agnes Martin (1912–2004), *Untitled*, 1962, acrylic priming, graphite, and brass nails on canvas, 12 x 12 inches (30.5 x 30.5 cm). Museum of Contemporary Art San Diego, Museum purchase, 1976.18. Photo: © Agnes Martin, Courtesy PaceWildenstein, New York; photo by Philipp Scholz Rittermann

Figure 14. Yayoi Kusama (born 1929), *Accumulation of Nets (No. 7)*, 1962, collage of gelatin silver prints, 29 x 24½ inches (73.7 x 62.2 cm). The Museum of Modern Art, New York, NY, USA, Acquired through the generosity of Agnes Gund (286.1996). Photo: © Yayoi Kusama, Digital Image © The Museum of Modern Art/Licensed by SCALA/Art Resource, NY

Figure 15. Mel Bochner (born 1940), *24 Reading Alternatives* (detail), 1971, felt pen on 24 sheets of paper, each 17 x 14 inches (42.9 x 35.2 cm). Musée National d'Art Moderne, Centre Georges Pompidou, Paris, France. Photo: CNAC/MNAM/Dist. Réunion des Musées Nationaux/Art Resource, NY; photo by Jacqueline Hyde

Figure 16. Lawrence Weiner (born 1942), *Untitled*, 1965, watercolor, colored pencil, and pencil on graph paper, 14 x 11 inches (35.6 x 27.9 cm). The Museum of Modern Art, New York, NY, USA, Bequest of Alicia Legg (415.2002). Photo: © 2005 Lawrence Weiner/Artists Rights Society (ARS), New York, Digital Image © The Museum of Modern Art/Licensed by SCALA/Art Resource, NY

Figure 17. Carl Andre (born 1935), *Untitled*, 1960, typewriting on paper, 11 x 8½ inches (27.9 x 21.6 cm). The Museum of Modern Art, New York, NY, USA, Gift of Sarah-Ann and Werner H. Kramarsky (371.1999). Photo: © Carl Andre/Licensed by VAGA, New York, NY, Digital Image © The Museum of Modern Art/Licensed by SCALA/Art Resource, NY

Figure 18. Donald Judd (1928–1994), *Untitled*, 1965, perforated 16-gauge cold rolled steel, 8 x 120 x 66 inches (20.3 x 304.8 x 167.6 cm). Whitney Museum of American Art, New York, 50th Anniversary Gift of Toiny and Leo Castelli (79.77). Photo: Judd Art © Judd Foundation. Licensed by VAGA, New York, NY

Figure 19. Sol LeWitt (born 1928), *Wall Drawing #1, Drawing Series II 18 (A & B)*, October 1968, black pencil, each square: 48 x 48 inches (120 x 120 cm). First installation at Paula Cooper Gallery, New York. Collection of Mr. and Mrs. Donald G. Fisher, San Francisco. Photo: © 2005 Sol LeWitt/Artists Rights Society (ARS), New York, Courtesy of the artist

Figure 20. Elizabeth Murray (born 1940), *Shrinking Lines to the Right*, 1974, oil on canvas, 28 x 24 inches (71.1 x 61 cm). Collection of Jennifer Bartlett. Photo: Courtesy of Jennifer Bartlett Studio

Figure 21. Jennifer Bartlett (born 1941), *Would You Like a Coke?*, 2003, enamel over grid silkscreened onto baked enamel on steel plates, 19¾ x 19¾ inches (50 x 50 cm.) Courtesy of the artist and Locks Gallery, Philadelphia. Photo: Tom Powel

Figure 22. Jasper Johns (born 1930), *Map*, 1961, oil on canvas, 78 x 123⅛ inches (198.1 x 312.7 cm). The Museum of Modern Art, New York, NY, USA, Gift of Mr. and Mrs. Robert C. Scull (277.1963). Photo: Art © Jasper Johns/Licensed by VAGA, New York, NY, Digital Image © The Museum of Modern Art/Licensed by SCALA/Art Resource, NY

Figure 23. Roy Lichtenstein (1923–1997), *Frightened Girl*, 1964, oil and magna on canvas, 48 x 48 inches (121.9 x 135.9 cm). Private collection. Photo: © Estate of Roy Lichtenstein

Figure 24. Wallace Nutting's colorists at their workstations, Massachusetts, c. 1915. Collection of Debra and Frank DiDaniele, Jr. Photo: Wallace Nutting

Figure 25. Jennifer Bartlett (born 1941), *Intersection*, 1970, enamel over grid silkscreened onto baked enamel on steel plates, 12 x 38 inches (30.5 x 96.5 cm). Private collection. Photo: Courtesy of the artist

Figure 26. Installation view of *Jennifer Bartlett*, Reese Palley Gallery, New York, 1972. Photo: © Peter Moore

Figure 27. Installation view showing Jennifer Bartlett's *Nine Points*, 1973–74, and other Nine-Point pieces, Paula Cooper Gallery, New York, March 1974. Photo: Courtesy of the artist; © Geoffrey Clements

Figure 28. Ellsworth Kelly (born 1923), *Seine*, 1951, oil on wood, 16½ x 45¼ inches (41.9 x 114.9 cm). Collection of the artist. Photo: © Ellsworth Kelly

Bartolomé Esteban MURILLO

Publishing Director: Paul ANDRÉ
Collaborator: Valeria GUSEVA
Translator: Oleg GLEBOV
Design: Isabelle BOISJEOL
Computerisation: DES SOURIS ET DES PAGES

Printed by SAGER in La Loupe (28) for Parkstone Publishers
Copyright 2nd term 1995
ISBN 1 85995 044 2

Bartolomé Esteban
MURILLO

The Spanish Master
of the 17th Century

Texts
Ludmila KAGANÉ

**PARKSTONE
AURORA**

PARKSTONE PUBLISHERS, BOURNEMOUTH
AURORA ART PUBLISHERS, ST. PETERSBURG

Bart.^{me} Murillo seipsum depin
gens pro filiorum votis acpreci
bus explendis

MURILLO'S WORK

BARTOLOMÉ Esteban Murillo was one of the greatest European painters of the seventeenth century.[1] The leading painter in Seville during the second half of the century, at a time when the Baroque artists had accomplished their best, Murillo started where they had left off, paving the way for the emergence of a new style, the Rococo. Murillo's paintings enjoyed vast popularity in the artist's own lifetime; they were bought by collectors from his own and other countries and were admired and emulated by many artists. His fame spread early beyond the borders of Spain.

Seville, like Madrid, was a major centre of Spanish art. Its artistic traditions were centuries-old but its architecture, sculpture and painting veritably burst into bloom in the sixteenth century when, following the discovery of America by Columbus, Seville began to play an important role in the life of the nation. Its port expanded, opening wide-ranging communications with other countries, and Seville became a prosperous city that attracted foreign artists and could support local talent as well. The city was famed for its patrons of the arts, collectors and a rich art market that particularly abounded in engravings, many of which were copies of famous European paintings.

Seville's artists knew and highly valued the Venetian school of painting, with its rich variety of colours and fluency of brushwork. The new trend known as Caravaggism, with its realistic detail and sharp chiaroscuro contrasts facilitating the delineation of forms, corresponded to their own aspirations. The trend had a strong impact on the work of Diego Velázquez, Francisco de Zurbarán, Francisco Herrera the Elder and Alonso Cano. In the mid-seventeenth century Seville's painters became familiar with the works of Peter Paul Rubens and Anthony Van Dyck, the great Flemish artists who had contributed to the development of the Baroque style. Their masterpieces provided lessons in dynamic composition, impetuous brushstroke, subtle yet rich colouring and intricate colour schemes.

In the early 1600s the most prominent art workshop in Seville was that of Francisco Pacheco, who also headed the Academy that had been

Self-portrait.
1672, National Gallery, London.

established in the city in the late sixteenth century as a centre of humanistic studies. In the early seventeenth century the Seville Academy was concerned primarily with artistic theory.[2] Pacheco himself was well acquainted with works by both Spanish and foreign artists; his interests embraced the history, theory and practice of painting, and he made a thorough study of religious iconography. His book *El Arte de la Pintura* took thirty years to write. It was completed in 1638 and published in 1649 in Seville.[3] A large part of the book was devoted to description of religious subjects and to the author's own recommendations on their presentation. For these Pacheco obtained approval from the highest Church authorities and thus formally expressed the official attitude. Being an artist, however, he also vividly reflected the prevalent artistic tastes of his time in his descriptions. Pacheco's lively narratives include tiny details wholly in the spirit of seventeenth-century Spanish paintings, in which religious subjects served as a means for depicting real life. The works of Seville artists are in themselves clear evidence of their intimate acquaintance with Pacheco's book.

Pacheco was a teacher of Diego Velázquez, and his workshop was visited by Francisco de Zurbarán and Alonso Cano, Murillo's outstanding predecessors in Seville. Velázquez painted most of his scenes from everyday life in Seville; they enjoyed great success and helped establish this genre of painting. In 1623 Velázquez left for Madrid but he kept in touch with his fellow artists in Seville. Zurbarán, meanwhile, painted religious and historical subjects almost exclusively. In 1629 he was made *maestro pintor* of Seville and was commissioned to execute large series of paintings for the monasteries and churches of the city. From 1634 to 1636 Zurbarán was in Madrid, collaborating with Spain's best painters in the decoration of the new Buen Retiro Palace, but he produced his most important cycles of paintings after his return to Seville. Alonso Cano, a native of Granada, came to Seville in 1614. His talents were not confined to painting and he also worked as an architect and sculptor. In 1638 Cano moved to Madrid and in 1652 returned to Granada. He lived not far from Seville and associated with the city's painters.

An ardent admirer of Italian painting, he contributed greatly to the spread of Italian artistic influence on Seville's painters. Murillo followed in the footsteps of his predecessors, inheriting their fine artistic skills, but his work was inevitably determined by the world outlook and artistic tastes of another epoch.

Spanish painters of the early part of the seventeenth century espoused sublime heroic ideals, embodying them either in images of saints whom they invested with the features of their contemporaries, or directly in portrayals of the great men of both the past and the present. During Murillo's lifetime these ideals had no roots in the surrounding reality. Spain, so recently the mightiest of European powers, was speeding towards political and economic collapse; poverty, hunger and disease were familiar sights. Any hopes for the better could be sought only in illusions. As the trend towards idealization faded it was replaced by an interest in the everyday life of the people with their joys, sorrows and intimate personal feelings. The saints now descended to earth, coming closer to the common man. The works of Murillo reflect this period in Spanish painting better than those of any other artist. Imbued with compassion for the sufferings of the people, they brought with them an awareness of social evils. But on the whole Murillo's works betray his passionate love of life and his admiration for the beauty of man and the world around him.

Bartolomé Esteban Murillo was born at the end of 1617 and baptized on 1 January 1618. He was the fourteenth and last child in the family and when he was ten his father died, followed a few months later by his mother. The orphaned boy was brought up in the family of his sister Anna who had married a surgeon, Juan Agustin Lagares. In his paintings Murillo later reflected the middle-class environment of his early years. In 1633 his uncle placed him as an apprentice in the studio of Juan del Castillo, little known today, but a painter who, in his time, enjoyed considerable prestige. He was the teacher of Pedro de Moya, a prominent painter from Granada; and his own gifted nephew, Antonio del Castillo, came from Cordova to take lessons with him. Juan del Castillo, incidentally, also collaborated with Alonso Cano.

Murillo's education was largely shaped by the artistic atmosphere of Seville itself, with its cathedral, churches and monasteries adorned with the works of famous painters, sculptors and architects.

Little is known of his early career. Very few of his paintings from the late 1630s and early 1640s have been preserved or identified. According to old Spanish sources, in 1642 Murillo went to Madrid to see the works of its painters and the treasures of the royal art collections. There is no documentary evidence to support this view but it is possible that he did make a short visit to Madrid.

Murillo first won fame with his series of paintings for the small cloister of the San Francisco monastery, one of the oldest and most influential monasteries in Seville, for which Zurbarán had painted his celebrated cycle of scenes from the life of St. Bonaventura. In 1645 Murillo was commissioned to execute paintings depicting scenes from the lives of St. Francis and his disciples. The thirteen surviving paintings are now scattered among various collections. Murillo's Franciscan series consists of lively and highly realistic scenes of monastic life.

San Diego de Alcalá Feeding the Poor.
1645-1650, Academia San Fernando, Madrid.

They convey the problems of contemporary society at a time when crowds of hungry people roamed through Spain seeking alms. One painting is directly concerned with this subject, *St. Diego de Alcala Feeding the Poor* (1645-1650, Academia de San Fernando, Madrid). St. Diego de Alcalá, a disciple and follower of St. Francis known from thirteenth-century Christian legends, is portrayed as a real person in a contemporary setting. The saint is shown kneeling in a prayer of thanksgiving. He is surrounded by women, children and old men begging for alms. The painter is sympathetic to them, and their features are highly individualized. The painting has a dark neutral background and a sharp contrast of light and shade, while the brush-strokes are dense and vivid. In its manner of execution this work is close to the Caravaggesque style.

The Franciscan series also includes the *Angel's Kitchen* (1646, Louvre, Paris), a painting which has no parallel in world art. The artist must have possessed that special religious feeling which entirely disposes of the distinction between things earthly and heavenly in order to have united down-to-earth and lofty motifs in such a bold manner in one work. Murillo was once again inspired by the story of St. Diego de Alcalá who was said to have a vision of angels helping him in the kitchen. The painting shows a monk illumined with radiant light (his figure is also seen on the right in the background), grandees entering through the door and witnessing the miracle (these are likenesses of Murillo's patrons), and angels. Some of the angels, with their fair appearance, slender figures and graceful motion, contrast with the rough-looking monk; other angels, the *putti*, sitting among pots and pans, are indistinguishable from ordinary children playing at being cooks. Here religious fantasy blends with real life, becoming an integral part of it.

The masterpiece of the series, the *Death of St. Clare* (1645-1650, Gemäldegalerie, Dresden), vividly reflects this illusory bond of the earthly and the heavenly: the legend tells that when St. Clare, the founder of the Order of Poor Clares, was dying, one of the nuns present at her deathbed had a vision of a procession of saintly women, Christian martyrs, led by Christ and the Virgin Mary. One of the martyrs draped St. Clare's body in a rich shroud as a reward for her voluntary sufferings on earth. Murillo used an enormous canvas about five metres in length, its elongated format suggested by the layout of the cloister, and thus was able to arrange the scene of the vision on the same level as the deathbed of St. Clare. The painting consists of

9

two parts: on the left is a dark cell with monks and nuns, a picture of the austerity of earthly life; on the right is the visionary procession of fair maidens moving in a mysteriously lit space and carrying palm branches, the symbol of martyrdom. The scene in the monastery cell is painted in a chiaroscuro manner with extremely careful modelling of spaces. The vision is rendered by softer brushwork against a clearer background. The painting was the first sign of the direction in which Murillo's style was to evolve. The *Death of St. Clare* enjoyed vast popularity and other artists used it as a model. The Hermitage is very fortunate to possess a picture (No. 21) which is a reduced studio copy of this great work.

Murillo employed different techniques to depict the earthly and the heavenly images. On the whole, however, he did not make a sharp distinction between them. In paintings from his early period all characters are treated in the monumental, elevated manner typical of Spanish art in the first half of the seventeenth century. One of his main subjects was the Virgin Mary who, as the protectress of humanity, personified the ideal of spiritual and physical beauty. Murillo executed many paintings on the subject of the Immaculate Conception showing the Virgin Mary descending from heaven to earth. The doctrine of the Immaculate Conception teaches that the Virgin was conceived without sin, as was Christ. The subject reflects the vision of St. John the Evangelist as described in the Apocalypse (Revelation 12: 1): "And there appeared a great wonder in heaven, a woman clothed with the sun, and the moon under her feet, and upon her head a crown of twelve stars." The Immaculate Conception was the most popular subject in Spanish art. In the sixteenth century the Virgin was depicted standing motionless leaning on the moon, bathed in its soft glow and surrounded by numerous traditional symbolic attributes. The iconography was not firmly established, however, and continued to develop and change over time. In the second half of the seventeenth century the subject was treated more dynamically, while its symbolism became so clear that many of the earlier allegorical features were simply omitted. The religious community of Seville was at the forefront of the movement that demanded official acceptance of the dogma of the Immaculate Conception. This teaching was indeed decreed by papal bull in 1661, but only finally approved in the nineteenth century. It is, therefore, not surprising that Murillo and his studio executed about fifty works dedicated to the Holy Virgin. One of the earliest was painted for a Franciscan monastery and is known simply as the *Large Immaculate Conception* (1650-1655, Museo de Belles Artes, Seville). The magnificent figure of the Virgin floating in the air, with her dark hair, large eyes and regular features, embodies the moral purity and mature beauty of Seville's women. This splendid image, in which the Holy Virgin appears as a sort of cosmic phenomenon, fits the subject perfectly. The emblems are carried by angels who are painted with great liveliness and immediacy as if taken from actual children. The central figure is static but the swirling of the edge of her robe produces a dynamic effect of motion in the developed Baroque style. The *Esquilache Immaculate Conception* (1645-1655, Hermitage, No. 1), begun at an earlier date, lacks the maturity and originality of the compositional structure we see in the Seville painting.

Murillo's paintings of the Virgin and Child outnumber works on this subject by any other Spanish artist. Guided by Raphael's works, Murillo endowed this archetypal image of motherhood with gentleness and warmth, but also with a sense of grave responsibility (one of his earliest *Madonnas* is in the Prado, Madrid). In contrast to the abstract ideal of the great Renaissance master, however, his figures distinctly show the ethnic features of the women he saw every day. Like Ribera, Velázquez and Zurbarán, Murillo did not synthesize the ideal of beauty but looked around him for models that conformed to his conception of divine perfection.

Murillo's paintings depicting scenes from the life of Christ are also distinguished by a keen sense of reality and a profound treatment. The tendency to introduce genre motifs into religious paintings was typical of the Spanish artists, who worked mainly for the Church and rarely had a chance to paint a secular subject, though they longed to represent real life. Murillo's paintings

The Angel's Kitchen. ▲
1646, Louvre, Paris.

The Large Immaculate Conception.
1650-1655, Museo de Bellas Artes, Seville (left).

The Virgin and Child.
1650-1655, Prado, Madrid (right).

The Death of St. Clare. ▼
1645-1650, Gemäldegalerie Alte Meister, Dresden.

such as the *Adoration of the Shepherds* (1646-1650, Prado, Madrid), the *Flight into Egypt* (*c.* 1645, Palazzo Bianco, Genoa) and the *Holy Family* (1645-1650, Prado, Madrid) are essentially genre scenes in their conception. This can be seen from the Hermitage versions of the *Adoration of the Shepherds* (1646-1650, No. 2) and the *Holy Family* (*c.* 1665, No. 8), and from the Pushkin Museum's canvas *The Flight into Egypt* (1670-1675, No. 15).

Genre painting *per se* held a much more prominent place in the work of Murillo than in that of any of his predecessors. Towards the second half of the seventeenth century genre paintings came into fashion and Spanish art patrons brought them from other countries.[4] Murillo, therefore, could study the works not only of his compatriots, above all Velázquez, but also of Dutch, Flemish and Italian genre painters. The characters in Murillo's genre pictures are mostly children. The ragged boy in the Louvre canvas of 1645-1650 is depicted in a corner of a dark room illuminated by a bright beam of sunlight. His pose, attitude and facial expression seem to have been caught in passing. The complex foreshortening of the figure and the lighting effects create a remarkably dynamic surface. Like other Spanish artists, Murillo particularly enjoyed painting inanimate objects, and the jar in the foreground and the basket of apples on the floor comprise a splendid still life. Around 1650 Murillo painted his *Boys Eating Melon and Grapes* (Alte Pinakothek, Munich) in which a trivial everyday scene is also artistically innovatory, thanks to the immediacy of the artist's perception and the ease with which he deals with the complex technical problems. The folds of the ragged clothes serve as an excuse for creating an interplay of light and shade. Murillo's fascination with his model borders on the naivety of early Renaissance art. A seed has stuck to the boy's cheek, flies are moving over the melon, while the basket of grapes in the foreground forms an exquisite still life in itself. There is more atmosphere in the background of this painting than in the *Beggar Boy* (Louvre, Paris) and the entire scene is set in a evening landscape.

Close to these works are *Girl with Fruit and*

The Adoration of the Shepherds.
1646-1650, Prado, Madrid.

The Flight into Egypt.
c. 1645, Pallazo Bianco, Genoa.

The Holy Family.
1645-1650, Prado, Madrid.

Flowers (Pushkin Museum, No. 4) and *Boy with a Dog* (Hermitage, No. 3), a rare example of two companion pieces in genre painting (both 1655-1660). The paintings are similar in composition and meaning. The shyly smiling girl holds a fruit — a symbol of maturity; the boy shows the dog a basket containing a jar-a vessel associated with woman in the iconography of seventeenth-century art.[5] Both scenes are presented against landscape backgrounds. The boy stands near a half-ruined overgrown wall with a rocky landscape behind it. Murillo may have borrowed this motif from Zurbáran, one of the first Seville artists to paint landscapes with ancient ruins in the background in the later 1630s. The boy is engrossed in playing with the dog. His appearance is attractive, but without any sentimental prettiness. He has a lively, arch

interest in daily life and rendition of atmospheric perspective, this work anticipates the realistic achievements of Western European painting in the latter half of the nineteenth century. Edouard Manet saw the *Boy with a Dog* reproduced as an engraving and was so impressed with it that he produced a similar engraving (*Le Gamin*) and a similar painting (*Portrait of the Artist's Son,* private collection, Paris).

Apart from the Seville street children, around 1655-1660 Murillo began to paint religious pictures showing the Virgin Mary, Christ and St. John the Baptist in their childhood. This series included the *Infant Jesus and St. John* (1655-1660, Hermitage, No. 5) for which Murillo borrowed the iconography from Italian art. Ecclesiastical sources mention no encounters

Beggar Boy.
1645-1650,
Louvre, Paris.

Boys Eating Melon and Grapes.
c. 1650,
Alte Pinakothek, Munich.

face with wrinkles under the eyes and closely cropped hair. Though at first sight the composition seems static, it has its own dynamism created by a sudden clash of two differently directed movements: the gaze of the spectator rises from the basket in the bottom right corner to the boy's head sharply turned the other way, towards the dog. The restrained colour scheme comprises different shades of green, pale blue, grey and brown. The clothes are painted in solid colours and the texture of the heavy crude fabric is excellently rendered. This kind of painting is still close to the Caravaggesque manner. At the same time, in his landscape setting Murillo conveys the transparency of air and the misty distance, the effect enhanced by a contrast between the light and airy background and the heavy dress. In its spontaneity of vision, strong

between Jesus and St. John in their infancy: according to the Gospels, St. John first saw Christ as a grown man. However, there existed an old Florentine tradition of depicting the Infant Jesus and St. John together (St. John was particularly venerated in Florence as its patron saint), and Murillo was fascinated by that tradition. The composition of the Hermitage painting was directly borrowed from a work by Guido Reni, now known from an engraving. Since its landscape setting and still-life motif strongly resemble those of the *Girl with Fruit and Flowers,* the Hermitage canvas must also have been painted in the later 1650s. Compared with Murillo's genre pictures, the children are much more idealized. In the same period Murillo produced a number of other pictures of the Infant Jesus and St. John, including the

Infant Jesus Asleep (1660-1670, Wernher collection, Luton Hoo, Luton, Bedfordshire, England) and the *Infant St. John with the Lamb* (1655-1660, National Gallery, London).

Murillo's art tended towards a deepening of lyrical feeling, a lightening of the paint layer and an enrichment of the palette. This can be traced not only in the works just discussed but also in his treatment of the Annunciation theme, the earliest version of which (1650-1655, Prado, Madrid) is a large, elongated canvas painted in a monumental style. The Hermitage *Annunciation* (1655-1660, No. 6) shows a more intimate approach, softer contours around the figures and objects and a wider palette.

By the mid-1650s Murillo was generally recognized as one of Seville's best painters. He created two huge canvases, *St. Isidore* and *St. Leander* (both 1655, Cathedral, Seville), which were accepted by the Cathedral. In the following year, 1656, the Cathedral authorities commissioned him to paint the *Vision of St. Antony of Padua* for the baptistry. These three works displayed his mature technique and artistry and closely approached the developed Baroque style. One of Murillo's central concerns was the use of lighting. In the Vision of *St. Antony of Padua* a dark room is illuminated by light streaming not only from heaven but also through an open door. This results in an amazingly rich chiaroscuro; the shadows are no longer heavy as in his earlier works and the subdued lighting effects soften the contrasts. Most of the canvas's surface is occupied by the vision of the Infant Jesus surrounded by numerous angels; their figures seem almost ethereal, many of them are barely suggested.

In 1658 Murillo went to Madrid where he had an opportunity to study the masterpieces in the royal collections. He was immensely impressed by the works of Venetian and Flemish painters and the mature Velázquez. By that time Velázquez had created all of his most famous paintings, and Murillo could admire not only the *Surrender of Breda* (Prado, Madrid) with its panoramic

*The Vision
of St. Antony of Padua.*
1656, Cathedral, Seville.

landscape painted with astonishing freshness and airiness, or the portraits of royalty in hunting dress against simple landscape backgrounds, with their subtly rendered atmospheric effects; he could see also the *Spinners* and *Las Meninas* (both in Prado, Madrid) in which Velázquez perfectly solved the novel problem of reproducing the atmosphere in an interior. Murillo spent about a year in Madrid. Returning to Seville in a state of creative exaltation, he and other painters embarked on the organization of an Academy of Arts. It was inaugurated on 11 January 1660, and was headed by two presidents at once, Murillo and Francisco Herrera the Younger. The 1660s were Murillo's best years, when his art reached its zenith. He produced a succession of works striking for their confident solution of pictorial problems.

In 1660 he painted the *Birth of the Virgin* (Louvre, Paris) for Seville Cathedral. The scene is set in a dark room with several sources of illumination. The central part around the Virgin is highly dynamic. The small figures of the angels turn sharply and the women are shown in perspectives, whilst the effect of movement is achieved not only by the swift linear rhythm but also by the fluent brushstrokes. This soft, free brushwork brings the work close to the paintings of Rubens. The women on the right, illuminated by the glow of the fireplace, dissolve in the semi-darkness — the same effect of airiness as is seen in Velázquez's *Spinners*. Like Velázquez, Murillo shows some figures from the back, delighting in their graceful movements.

The *Rest on the Flight into Egypt* (1660-1665, Hermitage, No. 7) resembles the above work in its warm tones, its dim contours and its airy atmosphere. The lyrical mood, the intent expression of the parents gazing at the sleeping Child, the little angels looking out from behind the bush like mischievous children, the marvellously painted still life in the foreground and the landscape bathed in warm air, everything in this picture is perfection. In the early 1660s

St. Isidore.
1655, Cathedral, Seville.

St. Leander.
1655, Cathedrale, Seville.

St. John with the Lamb. ▶
1655-1660, National Gallery, London.

▼ *The Infant Christ Asleep.*
1660-1670, Wernher collection, Luton
Hoo, Luton, Bedfordshire, England.

Murillo was particularly concerned with landscape painting. The Marquis de Ayamonte y Villamanrique commissioned him to paint a series of scenes from the life of Jacob, stipulating a landscape background to every picture. Five paintings (1660-1665) have been identified: *Isaac Blessing Jacob, Jacob's Dream* (both in the Hermitage, Nos. 9 and 10), *Jacob Laying the Peeled Rods before the Flocks of Laban* (Meadows Museum, Dallas, Texas, USA), *Laban Searching for His Stolen Household Gods in Rachel's. Tent* (Cleveland Museum of Art, USA), and the *Meeting of Jacob and Rachel* (present location unknown, probably no longer extant). On the evidence of Torre Farfán, a contemporary of Murillo, in 1665, during a festival in Seville, this series decorated the façade of Villamanrique's house.

Scenes from the life of Jacob were very popular in seventeenth-century Spanish art and they were frequently depicted in engravings, paintings and tapestries. Medieval

The Birth of the Virgin. 1660, Louvre, Paris.

theological writers used to place an elaborate allegorical interpretation on the Old Testament story of Jacob: thus, Isidore of Seville (560-636) regarded Jacob and his sons as prefigurations of Gospel characters, and found in their tribulations analogies with the persecution of Christ and his disciples. On the whole, Murillo followed the traditional iconography but he was mostly interested in landscape backgrounds.

Compositionally the canvas *Isaac Blessing Jacob* is divided into two distinct parts. The scene of the blessing is set in a dark room against an almost plain background, and executed in solid painting. The left-hand part of the canvas with the landscape is in striking contrast to the interior scene and inevitably attracts most of the viewer's attention. The broad expanse of space receding into the distance is set off by a house wall shortened in perspective, by the figure of the maid walking away from the spectator, but most of all by the atmospheric effect. Esau and his dogs returning from the chase are skilfully picked out with a few swift strokes of the brush.

Jacob's Dream, the second painting of the series, includes various allegories: the stone on which Jacob is sleeping is a symbol of foundation, the ascending and descending angels symbolize active and contemplative life, an allusion to the perfection of the main character. Jacob himself, however, has but a modest place in the composition, for Murillo focuses his attention on the landscape: problems of light in a night scene required particular virtuosity of handling. Francisco Pacheco, who clearly realized this difficulty, warned painters against attempting the task. Yet Murillo succeeded in creating an impressive night scene, making the darkness deep and transparent and avoiding harsh shadows. He enlivened the landscape with the magnificent ladder of Jacob's dream and ethereal and graceful figures of angels in multicoloured garments shining in the dark.

Jacob Laying the Peeled Rods before the Flocks of Laban shows a vista of hilly terrain brightly illuminated by the morning sun. The distant planes are barely traced with the brush, the artist's attention being caught by such poetic details as a stream rushing between the rocks, a ramshackle hut on the bank and a traveller with a horse. It is significant that in all these paintings Murillo built the composition around a clearly defined centre. In *Isaac Blessing Jacob* this was the house wall, in *Jacob's Dream* — the

16

Laban Searching for His Stolen Household Gods in Rachel's Tent.
1660-1665, Museum of Art, Cleveland, USA.

ladder with the angels, and in *Jacob with Laban's Flock* — a grove of trees. Murillo did not employ this technique in *Laban Searching for His Stolen Household Gods in Rachel's Tent*: here the space is unfolded on a grand scale. The action takes place on a sultry day and people are arranged in lively groups. The excited, gesturing, vividly portrayed figures in the foreground contrast with the travellers at the side who are depicted in a more generalized manner. As noted above, one of the paintings in the series is no longer extant but the surviving four follow the diurnal time sequence: *Isaac Blessing Jacob* takes place in the early evening, *Jacob's Dream* at night, *Jacob Laying the Peeled Rods before the Flocks of Laban* in the morning, and *Laban Searching for His Stolen Household Gods in Rachel's Tent* at midday. As Murillo was always concerned with the problem of lighting, it is not surprising that he set himself a very difficult task that was extremely bold and novel for seventeenth-century painting

— to execute open-air scenes at various times of day and night. [6]

The paintings depicting Jacob's life are perceived as fascinating stories from everyday life told by a skilful narrator. The same is true of his series of works for Sta. Maria la Blanca in Seville (*c.* 1665) in which Murillo also shows himself an interesting storyteller and exhibits an even greater mastery in solving the complicated technical problem of conveying light and air both outdoors and indoors.

The central works of the series, *The Patrician's Dream* and *The Patrician and His Wife before the Pope* (both Prado, Madrid), depict episodes from an early Christian legend. The first shows the Virgin with Child who appeared before the patrician and his wife in a dream and promised the birth of a long-awaited child. In return they were to build a church on a hill near Rome where snow had fallen in August. The sleepers are shown in homely natural poses — the patrician leans on the table and his wife nestles

Jacob Laying the Peeled Rods before the Flocks of Laban.
1660-1665, Meadows Museum, Dallas, Texas, USA.

The Patrician's Dream. c. 1665, Prado, Madrid.

down on the floor near the bed. The painter does not make any distinction between vision and reality. On the contrary, the Infant Jesus is an integral part of the intimate genre scene as he gazes with curiosity at the sleeping man and wife. The dark room is illuminated by the light streaming from the vision, the rich colours of the clothes and fabrics softly glimmer in the dark, the subtle gradations of light and shade emphasize the airiness of the scene. On the left is a brighter daylight landscape.

The second painting illustrates the next episode from the legend: the patrician and his wife asking the Pope for permission to build the church. The scene is rendered in a humorous vein (one of the men present looks intently at the patrician's wife to convince himself that she really is pregnant). The illumination here is more complex: the figure of the Pope in the foreground is set against the light so that the second plane seems to be very luminous. Yet the most radiant part of the composition is the landscape with the procession towards the hill seen in the upper portion of the background. In form and colour it is painted with such freedom and boldness that it can be regarded as a direct precursor of the best achievements of French landscape artists in the nineteenth century. The link between them and Murillo was the work of Francisco Goya, who was undoubtedly well acquainted with Murillo's paintings from Sta. Maria la Blanca. During the invasion of Napoleon's army they were removed to Madrid and then brought to Paris for the planned

Napoleon Museum. Later they were brought back to Spain and in 1816 were exhibited in the Academia de San Fernando in Madrid. Several later works by Goya betray the direct influence of these canvases.

Murillo was surrounded by numerous connoisseurs of art who admired his professional skill and who saw his work as reflecting the burning issues of the day. Among his closest supporters were the above mentioned Marquis de Ayamonte y Villamanrique, who became Protector of the Seville Academy; Justino de Neve, Canon of Seville Cathedral, who helped to obtain many commissions for Murillo and who financed work on the paintings for Sta. Maria la Blanca; Miguel Manara y Vicentelo de Leca, a family friend since 1650 and the godfather of two of Murillo's sons, who commissioned the series of paintings for the church of the La Caridad hospital; and Nicolás de Omazur, an Antwerp merchant, who contributed to Murillo's early popularity outside Spain. Murillo's portraits of Justino de Neve (1665, National Gallery, London) and Nicolás de Omazur (1672, Prado, Madrid) have survived. In the full-length portrait of Justino de Neve he is shown sitting in a chair at a table against a balustrade, a column and a curtain. It is a formal, very severe portrait. The canon, deep in thought, is dressed in a black cassock and holds a prayer-book; the clock on the table symbolizes the vanity of earthly life. The *vanitas* theme is also heard in the later half-length portrait of Nicolás de Omazur. The sitter — exquisitely elegant, his

18

black clothes set off by the fine white collar and lace frills — ponders over the skull which he holds in his hands.

It was typical of Murillo's contemporaries to dwell on the fleeting nature of life, the inevitability of death and the meaning of earthly existence. The plague of 1649 killed hundreds of people daily in Seville and the city lost more than half its population. The terrible famine of 1651 claimed numerous victims. In addition to witnessing these catastrophes, the painter had his personad tragedies. Many of his children died and in 1664 he lost his wife. Murillo concentrated entirely on his work and his productivity in the 1660s was amazing. A tenderhearted, gentle person who preserved his love for life despite all misfortunes, Murillo saw his calling in bringing his belief in good to the people. Charity was a frequent subject of his works; no other artist before him was so deeply concerned with it.

In the later 1660s Murillo executed one of his major cycles of paintings for the church of the Capuchin monastery in Seville. He was especially satisfied with the canvas *The Mercy of St. Thomas of Villanueva* (1665-1670, Museo de Bellas Artes, Seville). St. Thomas of Villanueva, Archbishop of Valencia, who lived in the sixteenth century, was famous for his works of mercy. Murillo's generation treasured memories of him and the painting was a reflection of this respect. In its subject matter, the canvas recalls Murillo's earlier work, *St. Diego de Alcala Feeding the Poor* (1640s), though with the passage of two decades the artist treated the theme in a much more mature manner: he reduced the number of figures and characterized them more sharply. The old woman looks despairingly, the old man holds his head low in abject abandon, while the expression on the boy's face is too grave for a child; perhaps the most heart-rending figure is that of the man sunk on his knees who holds his hand begging for alms, probably to feed his family. In the foreground a child reaches out to a lovely young woman whose head is sadly bowed. The painting is perceived as a desperate appeal. The poverty of the figures makes a striking contrast with the splendid architecture bathed in the light of a sunny day. Never has Spanish art so clearly proclaimed the obligation to alleviate the sufferings of the people.

The motif of charity underlies the series of paintings executed by Murillo between 1666 and 1672 for the La Caridad hospital in Seville. The Hermandad de la Caridad, or Brotherhood of Charity, was founded in the late fifteenth century and its initial purpose was to bury executed prisoners and paupers who died in the streets. In the first half of the seventeenth century, the activities of the Brotherhood ceased almost entirely, but towards the middle of the century, after the plague and the famine, they were resumed and extended in scope. In 1662 Miguel Manara y Vicentelo de Leca became Head of the Brotherhood. Local tradition identified him with Juan de Tenoria, the main hero of Tirso de Molina's *The Seducer*

The Patrician and His Wife before the Pope. c. 1665, Prado, Madrid.

of Seville, whose image, in its turn, inspired Molière to write his *Don Juan*. As a matter of fact, Miguel Manara was not the prototype of Juan de Tenoria, but the tradition was not altogether without foundation as he had written an epitaph for his tombstone in which he repented of his youthful sins. In maturity Manara gave up his sinful life and married a young woman he adored. But in 1661 his wife died and, shocked by her untimely death, in the following year Manara joined the Brotherhood of Charity. The reorganization of the La Caridad hospital and the building of a church for it became his main concern. Manara personally worked out a programme for the decoration of the church and commissioned the best Seville artists to participate in it. These were the architect Bernardo Simon de Pineda, the sculptor Pedro Roldán and the painters Juan de Valdés Leal and Murillo (who also joined the Brotherhood of Charity after the death of his wife).

The sculpture, *The Entombment* — he centrepiece of the church's retable — symbolizes the chief preoccupation of the Brotherhood, that is, the burial of the dead. Valdés Leal executed two pictures on the *vanitas* subject, the *Hieroglyphs of Death* and *Salvation*, yet Murillo's paintings held pride of place in the decoration of the church. Six of them were allegories on the six works of mercy mentioned in the Gospel (Matthew 25 : 35, 36): *Miracle of the Loaves and Fishes* ("I was an hungred, and ye gave me meat"); *Moses Striking the Rock* ("I was thirsty, and ye gave me drink"); *Return of the Prodigal Son* ("I was naked, and ye clothed me"); *Abraham and the Three Angels* ("I was a stranger, and ye took me in"); *Christ Healing the Paralytic* ("I was sick, and ye visited me"); and the *Liberation of St. Peter* ("I was in prison, and ye came unto me"). The first two paintings are still in the hospital church of La Caridad in Seville; the third is in the National Gallery of Art, Washington; the fourth is in the National Gallery of Canada,

Portrait of Nicolás de Omazur.
1672, Prado, Madrid.

Ottawa; the fifth is in the National Gallery, London; and the sixth is in the Hermitage, Leningrad (No. 12). Murillo also painted two altarpieces, *St. John of God and the Angel* and *St. Elizabeth of Hungary Healing the Sick*, both now restored to their original places in the hospital church. It is not known, however, whether three more paintings that were once also in the church formed part of the original commission or were added later. [7]

In his paintings for the hospital church Murillo continued to develop the theme of contrast between the beauty of the surrounding world and the dismal fate of the poor. Thus in the foreground of *Christ Healing the Paralytic* Christ and his disciples face a feeble, pitiful old man in a scene set against the splendid architecture of the sunlit courtyard filled with the figures of crippled and maimed people. *St. Elizabeth of Hungary Healing the Sick* emphasizes the contrast between a magnificent interior and the unwashed, destitute lepers attended by the noble ladies.

The two vast central canvases placed in the vaults of the church — the *Miracle of the Loaves and Fishes* and *Moses Striking the Rock* — are perceived as a veritable paean to the people. In these multifigured scenes, at once spontaneous and epic, Murillo not only shows the crowd but also picks out vivid and attractive characters in it. These works reveal the life-asserting spirit of Murillo's art with the utmost power.

The theme of human beauty is a constant one running through Murillo's entire work, culminating in his *Inmaculadas*, paintings on the subject of the Immaculate Conception. Murillo created a new iconography, starting to depict the Purissima as a very young girl. One of the best early versions executed between 1656 and 1660 is the *Escorial Immaculate Conception* (Prado, Madrid). In his later works on the subject Murillo sought to enhance the effect of grace and elegance while reducing the number of

Miracle of the Loaves and Fishes. ▲
1670, Hospital of La Caridad, Seville.

The Mercy of St. Thomas of Villanueva.
1665-1670, Museo de Bellas Artes, Seville (left).

Portrait of Justino de Neve.
1665, National Gallery, London (right).

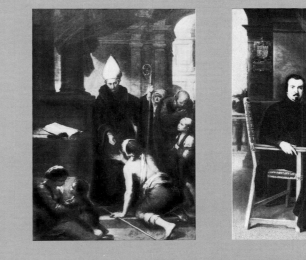

Moses Striking the Rock. ▼
1670, Hospital of La Caridad, Seville.

emblems: thus in one of the latest versions, the *Soult Immaculate Conception* of *c.* 1678, which the artist painted for the hospital of Los Venerables Sacerdotes (now in the Prado, Madrid), the angels carry no symbolic emblems at all.

The *Walpole Immaculate Conception,* painted around 1680 (Hermitage, No. 18), is one of the masterpieces of Murillo's late period. Its iconography is unusual: the composition, the general type of the Virgin and her dress are similar to those in the artist's other versions of the subject, but the angels carry no emblems and the gesture of Mary's arm raised heavenward is not repeated in any of them. Some experts, therefore, suggest that the subject

is enveloped in air and can hardly be perceived as a symbol. Experts agree that the Hermitage painting is one of the best among the numerous *Inmaculadas* created by Murillo or his studio. The idea is expressed not by symbols or emblems but by the image of the Virgin herself — the lovely inspired girl, her ethereal figure enveloped in a radiant white dress and a clear blue mantle, seems to be taking her farewell of Heaven while descending to an earth swallowed up in dark shadow. The thin, transparent paint layer, the lightly traced outlines of the figures, the rich range of delicate, almost translucent tints and the exquisite garland of angels, all anticipate the advent of a new style, Rococo.

Murillo's activity was wholly associated with

St. Elisabeth of Hungary Healing the Sick. 1670-1672, Hospital of La Caridad, Seville.

The Immaculate Conception. c. 1678, Prado, Madrid.

depicted is that of the Assumption. One can hardly agree with this suggestion, however. In the late period of his career Murillo treated his subjects quite freely. The emblems were so generally known that the painter may not have thought them obligatory. As to the gesture of Mary's upraised arm, it has analogies in works by other Spanish painters. Madrid artists nearly always depicted the Purissima with a similarly raised arm. A drawing (private collection, England) executed by Murillo about 1660, i.e. soon after his Madrid journey, shows the Virgin of the Immaculate Conception with one arm uplifted. In the Hermitage painting this gesture is somewhat modified, apparently in a search for greater expressiveness. The unusual gesture adds special charm to the image of Mary. The only symbolic attribute in this painting is a sphere with a barely discernible crescent, but it

Seville. He was born and spent most of his life there, creating numerous cycles of paintings for the cathedral, monasteries, churches, hospitals and palaces of his native city. Murillo was the most prolific of seventeenth-century Spanish painters, the number of works he executed being unsurpassed by any other Spanish master. The artist even died in the midst of his work: it is recorded that he fell off the scaffolding while painting murals for the church of the Capuchin monastery at Cadiz, near Seville, and died on 3 April 1682.

Immediately after Murillo's death the merchant Nicolás de Omazur sent the painter's self-portrait (1672, National Gallery, London) to his own home city of Antwerp to be engraved. By this time the artist's fame had spread far beyond Spain. Joachim von Sandrart, a German artist living in Rome and author of the lives of painters, wrote of him in a book published in 1683 (J. Sandrart, *Academia nobilissimae artis pictoriae,* Nuremberg). Dutch and Flemish patrons of the arts residing in Seville eagerly bought Murillo's works. Art lovers in Britain and Germany collected Murillo's paintings from the early eighteenth century and by the middle of the century he was the best-known Spanish artist in France.[8]

Murillo's paintings first found their way to Russia in the eighteenth century, soon after the foundation of the Hermitage, and in the nineteenth century the Hermitage collection of the artist's works was significantly enriched. The Russian public greatly appreciated Murillo's art. The outstanding public figure and writer Alexander Herzen considered the works of Murillo, along with those of Raphael, to represent the pinnacle of artistic perfection. In 1840, after a visit to the Hermitage, he mentioned among its best pictures the *Death of the Inquisitor Pedro de Arbués* (1664, No. 11), then called *The Holy Martyr.*[9] Later, while living abroad, Herzen continued to single out Murillo from other painters. Thus, having visited the Manchester exhibition in 1857, he wrote: "As always, it was Murillo who carried away the palm."[10] Herzen particularly noted in Murillo's art his deep sense of "life's catastrophes". It was Murillo's paintings that suggested to Herzen the idea that "the more does the artist take to heart the sorrows and problems of his time, the stronger the expression they will find under his brush".[11] Vasily Botkin, a writer, art historian and one of the subtlest Russian connoisseurs of painting, was delighted with Murillo's canvases, which he saw when visiting Spain in 1845. His admiration for the Spanish master was boundless and he wrote: "If you have any love of painting, if any picture has even once in your life touched your heart and given you one of those moments which are forever stamped on our memory and reveal to us the meaning of art better than all the books on aesthetics taken together, then go to Seville, go to see the great Murillo.

"...I cannot restrain myself from telling you of the new, the hitherto unexperienced delight which this genius has made me feel. Do not think that having studied the masters of the

Abraham and the Three Angels.
1667, National Gallery, Ottawa.

Return of the Prodigal Son.
1668, National Gallery of Art, Washington.

Christ Healing the Paralytic.
1668, National Gallery, London.

23

Italian and Flemish schools, knowing Raphael, Veronese and Rubens, you have experienced all the magic of the painter's brush; if you do not know Murillo, if you do not know him here in Seville — believe me, a whole world of inexpressible charm still remains closed to you. There is nothing that is beyond his powers: the hidden, mystic depths of the human soul, common daily life and all natural filth — he presents everything with amazing truth and reality. In Murillo's paintings, the force and airiness of colouring, impregnated with African sun, are fused with the tenderness and delicacy of the Flemish school."[12]

Vissarion Belinsky, a famous Russian literary critic, thus responded to Botkin's *Letters from Spain*: "I was especially interested in the particulars concerning Murillo... A view on the nation's paintings, so original, so unlike the most well-known schools..."[13]

Murillo's art was amazingly suited to nineteenth-century aesthetic tastes. It was oriented towards life; his characters did not overwhelm the viewer, they were on his own scale; his paintings reflected a multitude of real-life situations. The Hermitage collection served as a source of inspiration for several generations of Russian artists. To painters Murillo's work was a real revelation. They found in it those things which they themselves sought above all else: freshness of vision, an ability to record an immediate impression, beauty of colour scheme and virtuoso freedom of brushwork.

In the early twentieth century, with the development of Impressionism and Postimpressionism, Murillo's glory faded. However, Alexander Benois, a prominent Russian artist and historian, and Keeper of the Hermitage Picture Gallery, wrote: "Murillo, the one-time favourite of the crowd and the aesthetes, has lost some of his popularity now, mostly because the entire psychology typical of the seventeenth century is alien to our age. We demand from the 'old men' either staggering emotions, simple sincerity or what is the main concern of modern painting — a successful solution to purely colouristic problems. Murillo is too gentle, too delicate for us... Still, the modern attitude to Murillo is unjust. He is simply a magnificent, first-class master and an absolutely unique master... But

Murillo is not just a master, a virtuoso, a magician who created his paintings in a flight of inspiration (this technical facility of Murillo's is simply astonishing), he is also a charming, if not bewitching, poet."[14]

Alonso Cano. *The Immaculate Conception.* 1650-1652, Museo Vittoria, Valencia.

NOTES

1. For a complete monograph *see* Angulo 1981.

2. Brown 1978.

3. F. Pacheco. *El Arte de la pintura, su antigüedad y grandezas*, Madrid, 1649 (in this book we refer to the 1866 edition), 2 vol.

4. D. T. Kinkead. *An Analysis of Sevilian Painting Collections of the Mid-Seventeenth Century: the Importance of Secular Subject Matter, and Hispanism as Humanism*, Madrid, 1982.

5. J. Brown, "Murillo, pintor de temas erótiquas. Una faceta inadvertida de su obra", *Goya*, 1982, Nos. 169-171, p. 35-43.

6. In the 1660s, Claude Lorrain solved a similar problem in his paintings *Morning, Noon, Evenings* and *Night* which included biblical scenes. At one time it was thought that the French artist created a *Times of Day* series but M. Röthlisberger convincingly proved that the paintings were executed as companion pieces, and it was, perhaps, in the process of work that Claude Lorrain conceived the idea of depicting the times of day. (See M. Röthlisberger, *Tout l'œuvre peint de Claude Lorrain*, Paris, 1977, p. 116, No. 224). If this was the case, Murillo was more consistent and purposeful in setting himself this task.

7. All the paintings of the La Caridad hospital church were taken to the Alcázar during the French occupation. Afterwards they became the property of Marshal Soult and only a few of them found their way back. For details, *see* the notes on the *Liberation of St. Peter* (Hermitage), No. 12.

8. E Harris, "Murillo en Inglaterra", *Goya*, 1982, Nos. 169-171, p. 7-17; Braham 1981, p. 10-11; Ressort 1983, p. 52-53.

9. Letter to T. A. Astrakhova, dated 24 August 1840, in: *A. I. Herzen, Collected Works*, 30 vols, Moscow, 1955, vol. 22, p. 88, 327, note (in Russian).

10. Letter to N. P. Ogariov and N. A. Tuchkova-Ogariova, 4 September (23 August) 1857, Manchester, in: *A. I. Herzen, op. cit.*, vol. 26, p. 118 (The Manchester exhibition was held from 2 to 5 September 1857.)

11. Letter to M. P. Botkin, 5 March (21 February) 1859, Fullem, in: *A. I. Herzen, op. cit.*, p. 241.

12. V. P. Botkin, *Letters from Spain*, St. Petersburg, 1857, p. 149 (in Russian).

13. Letter to V. P. Botkin, [2-6] December 1847, in: *V. G. Belinski, Complete Works,* 13 vol., Moscow, 1956, vol. 12, p. 453 (in Russian).

14. Benois 1910, p. 136, 137.

Murillo, studio copy. *The Immaculate Conception.*
National Gallery, Melbourne.

The Annunciation.
1650-1655, Prado, Madrid.

The History of the
COLLECTIONS

THE history of the Hermitage collection of Murillo's works reflects Russia's artistic taste in the eighteenth and nineteenth centuries; it is linked to the activities of famous connoisseurs and to the destinies of the great European collections. The first painting by Murillo to enter the Hermitage, *The Rest on the Flight into Egypt,* was acquired for it by Denis Diderot, who did much for the newly established museum. The sculptor Etienne Maurice Falconet, a friend of Diderot's, came to St. Petersburg in the autumn of 1766 to work on the equestrian statue of Peter the Great; he corresponded with Diderot and their letters have survived to the present time. In May 1768 Diderot wrote to Falconet: "Gaignat has died. This man was mad about paintings and he owned a collection of books of all descriptions... You undoubtedly know Gaignat's collection of paintings and his library... I have written to General Betskoi. Tell him, please, that we must not miss the opportunity if we do not want crowds of foreign competitors set against us."[1]

Diderot started negotiations for the purchase of the collection of Jean de Gaignat, former secretary to Louis XV, well before the auction, turning for help primarily to his old acquaintance in Paris, I. Betskoi, a Russian nobleman and art connoisseur. The auction was held in December 1768 [2] and in March 1769 Diderot wrote to Falconet that no expense had been spared in acquiring the paintings. In April Diderot confirmed the news: "I purchased for Her Imperial Majesty at the Gaignat auction five paintings that are among the best in France — one by Murillo, three by Gerard Dout and one by Van Loo."[3] In a letter dated 11 July of the same year Diderot excitedly reported to Falconet: "As I write this letter they are opening the boxes containing that excellent Murillo of Gaignat's with three very valuable works by Gerard Dou and a splendid piece by Jean Baptiste Van Loo."[4] On 15 November 1769 Diderot wrote to Falconet: "I believe you are satisfied with what I have sent with my own hands from the Gaignat auction."[5] It can be presumed therefore that the paintings had reached St. Petersburg by this time. The Murillo discussed in the letters, *The Rest on the Flight into Egypt* (No. 7), brought forth the admiring

Rest on the Flight into Egypt.
1660-1665, The Hermitage.
Oil on canvas. 136.5 x 179.5 cm.

response from Falconet: "We must talk of Murillo on our knees; those of us who dare to look at him any other way are faithless and lawless men."[6]

Three years later the Hermitage acquired several more paintings by Murillo from France, this time from the collection of Etienne François de Choiseul et Amboise, a former minister of Louis XV, which was auctioned in April 1772.[7] N. Khotinsky, the Russian *chargé d'affaires* in France, reported to the Vice-Chancellor A. Golitsyn: "The fervour with which anybody at all was buying cannot be expressed and has no precedent. Some paintings were sold at three times the price paid by the Duc de Choiseul though everybody knew that he himself had paid over the odds."[8] Prince D. Golitsyn, who was charged with buying paintings from this collection, selected eleven canvases including two companion pieces by Murillo, *Boy with a Dog* and *Girl with Fruit and Flowers* (Nos. 3 and 4).

Only a small group of connoisseurs collected Spanish paintings in the eighteenth century. The Duc de Choiseul's wife came from the Crozat family. The sale of the Crozat collection after the death of Louis Antoine Crozat, Baron de Thiers, gave rise to bitter rivalry on the French art market. The Russian buyers, with Treasury funds at their disposal, managed to pay for the entire collection. Diderot again acted as intermediary, the preliminary negotiations continuing for about two years, starting in 1770. On 27 April 1772 Diderot wrote to Falconet that he was busy with the acquisition of the Crozat gallery.[9] He asked François Tronchin, a connoisseur and the owner of a large collection of paintings, to compile the list of the works in the Crozat collection. This manuscript catalogue has proved to be of great value since it can be compared with an earlier catalogue of the collection and thus yield information on later acquisitions. Murillo's painting *The Holy Family* (No. 8) found its way to the Hermitage as part of the Crozat collection, and according to Pierre Mariette[10] this painting had been the property of the Duc de Tallard before it was bought by Crozat.

In 1779 the Hermitage received several more canvases by Murillo as part of the collection acquired from Robert Walpole, Earl of Orford,

First Minister to George I and George II of England and one of the most famous English art collectors in the first half of the eighteenth century. The collection consisted of 198 paintings, mostly by Italian, Spanish, Flemish and French masters, which had decorated the ancestral home of the Walpole family, Houghton Hall, since the 1720s. The owner's son, the well-known writer Horace Walpole, compiled the first catalogue of the collection which was published in 1747.[11] When Horace's son decided to sell the gallery the news produced a sensation in England. On 4 December 1778 A. Moussine-Pushkin, the Russian ambassador to Britain, reported to Catherine II that "having examined in detail the paintings of the Earl of Orford together with Cipriani I may, as a faithful slave of Your Imperial Majesty, submit that they deserve to constitute a part of the very best gallery in Europe; not only amateurs but even connoisseurs have long held such an opinion in view of the many rare, capital and first-class works by the most illustrious masters.

"I have the honour to provide a circumstantial description of the damage to a few works. Two or three canvases are so threadbare that they need new supports which can be readily made either here or in Russia, according to Your Majesty's wishes, while the other paintings, namely those listed in the special appendix, are as fresh and perfectly intact as if they had been painted recently.

"All this evidence was supplied to me solely by the truthful and equally experienced Cipriani, who diligently spent the necessary time and effort for precise examination of this collection."

The ambassador then reported the arrangements for payment, and that the Earl of Orford had agreed to "... make the paintings available for despatch by sea this very summer...

"The packing of the above by skilled workmen and artisans will require my immediate presence there, Your Most Gracious Majesty, at least during the first preparations and at the time of final shipping from Lynn, which will be in no other manner but by a Navy frigate, not only because of the present war circumstances but also because many of these paintings cannot be conveniently accommodated in the merchantmen owing to their size.

"I most humbly submit to Your Imperial Majesty

Boy with a dog.
1655-1660, the Hermitage.
Oil on canvas, 70 x 60 cm.

Girl with Fruit and Flowers.
1655-1660, the Pushkin Museum of Fine Arts,
Moscow. Oil on canvas, 76 x 61 cm.

The Holy Family.
c. 1665, the Hermitage.
Oil on panel, 23.8 x 18 cm.

that most of the local nobility generally exhibit dissatisfaction and vexation about the release of these paintings from this state and there are various plans afoot for holding them here; no little assistance in countering such presumptuous designs is provided by the ardent wish of the Earl of Orford to add his paintings to the gallery of Your Imperial Majesty, rather than to sell them even to Parliament itself or, even less, to break up the collection by selling works to private individuals." [12] Catherine II eagerly awaited the arrival of that ship from England, mentioning the purchase of the Walpole gallery several times in her letters to the French enlightener Melchior Grimm. In a letter dated 6 May 1779 she complained that the gallery had not yet been purchased, but almost a year later, on 1 March 1780, she wrote that by the winter the collection was in her gallery. [13] The subsequent fate of the collection is recorded in the memoirs of the English artist Robert Ker Porter, who lived in Russia from 1805 to 1807: "The pictures were not unpacked during her life (Catherine's II), but were taken out and arranged under the auspices of her successor. Since that time the whole of the saloons in which they hung have undergone a thorough repair and decoration; and I am sorry to say that the pictures have also past under this cruel purgatory. The works may be improved, but the paintings bear manifest proofs of the reverse. The practice, common in almost all countries, of periodically cleaning and varnishing the works of ancient and great masters, is ten thousand times more destructive of their durability and value than the hand of time. I am the more surprised by the fate of these, because they are under the inspection of men of judgement and experience; but Custom is an imperious dictator..." Porter later noted once more that "most of the original works have been subjected to the destructive process of cleaning and varnishing." [14]

The Walpole collection included five paintings by Murillo: the *Assumption* (now known as the *Walpole Immaculate Conception),* the *Adoration of the Shepherds* (held to be a pendant to the former), the *Crucifixion* (all in the Hermitage, Nos. 18, 2, and 16), the *Flight into Egypt* (Pushkin Museum of Fine Arts, No. 15), and the *Virgin and Child on Black Marble* (whereabouts

The Walpole Immaculate Conception
c. 1680, the Hermitage.
Oil on canvas, 195 x 145 cm.

The Adoration of the Shepherds.
1646-1650, the Hermitage.
Oil on canvas, 197 x 147 cm.

unknown) that was given to Robert Walpole by
Sir Benjamin Keene, the English ambassador in
Madrid.

After the Walpole collection no significant works
by Murillo were acquired in the remainder of the
eighteenth century. The collection of Count de
Baudouin, purchased in 1781, brought in *Mother
with a Sleeping Child* (Hermitage),[15] now
attributed to Martinez del Mazo. In 1792, soon
after the death of Prince Grigory Potemkin-
Tavrichesky, his collection, which included
Murillo's *St. John with the Lamb* (No. 28)[16], was
bought by the Hermitage. The picture was then
regarded as an original, but was later revealed to
be a copy of the similarly entitled work in the
National Gallery, London.

Long before 1792 the Hermitage owned another
painting on a similar subject, *St. John in the
Wilderness*. It was mentioned in the catalogue of
1774 and had thus been received before this.[17] It
is not in the Hermitage now and we do not know

The Crucifixion.
c. 1675, the Hermitage.
Oil on canvas, 98 x 60.2 cm.

The Flight into Egypt.
1670-1675, the Pushkin Museum of Fine Arts, Moscow.
Oil on canvas, 101 x 62 cm.

when it disappeared, nor is any reproduction of it
extant. The *Virgin and Child on Black Marble*
was transferred from the Hermitage to Gatchina
Palace in 1799 and was lost, apparently, during
the Second World War. *Girl with Fruit and
Flowers* and the *Flight into Egypt* were
transferred to the Pushkin Museum of Fine Arts
in Moscow in 1930.

The fact of Murillo's popularity in eighteenth-
century Russia is evidenced by the publications
about the private collections of Count A. Stroganov, Prince A. Beloselsky and Count A. Bezbo-
rodko in which his works are mentioned.[18] The
1793 catalogue of the Stroganov collection refers
to *Christ as the Good Shepherd, St. John the
Baptist,* and the *Teacher.*[19] The first two paintings were, apparently, copies and their present
location is unknown, the *Teacher* is in the
Hermitage but is now attributed to an unknown
eighteenth-century artist. As for Murillo's paintings known to have been in other Russian

collections, they were not named in the literature; it seems most likely that they were copies and it is unclear what happened to them. Collectors began to exhibit particular interest in Spain in the early nineteenth century. Its art treasures became famous through the multivolume book *Travels in Spain* by A. Ponz[20] and the *Historical Dictionary of the Most Celebrated Spanish Masters of Art* by J. A. Cean Bermudez.[21] One of the first of the foreign art dealers to appear in Spain was the Frenchman J.-B. Le Brun, who purchased numerous paintings by Spanish and other European masters in 1807-1808 and published engravings from them in 1809.[22] The paintings were sold in Paris and one of them was bought by Prince Nikolai Yusupov.

Nikolai Yusupov (1750-1831), who put together the best private art collection in Russia in the early nineteenth century, had travelled all over Europe. From 1776 to 1791 he lived in Holland, England and France and in the first year of his travels he had visited Seville and Madrid. Yusupov was enchanted by Spain; later he even commissioned the German painter Heinrich Füger to execute his portrait in Spanish costume (Hermitage). After his return to Russia Yusupov was appointed Head of the Imperial Theatres, the Imperial Glass and Porcelain Factories, the Tapestry Manufactory and the Hermitage. He began to build up a collection of his own in the eighteenth century, by the end of which he owned many paintings, including works by Velázquez and José de Ribera. In 1802 Yusupov again went abroad and lived in France until 1810. On his return he settled in Moscow, keeping his collection in his town mansion and at his Archangelskoye estate near Moscow. His son and heir, B. Yusupov, brought most of the paintings to St. Petersburg to his newly built palace on the Moika Embankment in 1833-1834. The first catalogue of the Yusupov collection came out in 1839 and the collection was later described in several other publications.[23] The catalogue included two paintings by Murillo —the *Virgin and Child* and the *Infant St. John with the Lamb.* The catalogue published in 1920 did not include the *Virgin and Child,* apparently, its attribution to Murillo had been refuted. The *Infant St. John with the Lamb* (No. 27) was

Murillo, 18th century copy.
St. John with the Lamb.
The Hermitage.
Oil on canvas, 173 x 119 cm.

Unknown artist. 17th century.
Teacher.
The Hermitage (Inv. No. 5349).

transferred to the Pushkin Museum of Fine Arts in Moscow in 1924. Angulo noted in 1981 that the painting from the Yusupov collection was similar to an engraving published by Le Brun.[24] Since Nikolai Yusupov was in Paris at the time of Le Brun's sale in 1809 there are reasons to think that he purchased the painting in order to expand the Spanish part of his collection. This painting is now regarded as a free copy, executed by Murillo's studio, from the canvas now in the Prado, Madrid.

The English artist G. A. Wallis came to Spain at approximately the same time as Le Brun. He was sent there by the English art dealer W. Buchanan. Wallis witnessed the dramatic events that shook the country at this time and also affected the fate of the Spanish art treasures: the invasion of Spain by Napoleon's army in 1808, the popular uprising against the French and the establishment of a new government were accompanied by disorder, desolation and impoverishment. Napoleon and his generals looted churches, monasteries and palaces, taking the best works by Spanish painters as 'gifts' or, more directly, as items of war booty. Meanwhile the provisional administration in Spain needed money to wage war. Property confiscated from the royal palaces and from those among the nobility who supported the French invaders was sold at knockdown prices. Collectors and art dealers hastened to make use of the favourable circumstances. In 1824 Buchanan published his *Memoirs of Painting, with a Chronological History of the Importations of Pictures by the Great Masters into England since the French Revolution* (London) which graphically describe the events in Spain at that time,[25] quoting from letters written by Wallis which give an excellent reflection of the turmoil in the art trade.

Juan Bautista Martinez del Mazo. 17th century.
Mother with a Sleeping Child.
The Hermitage (Inv. No. 8761).

On 5 August 1808 Wallis wrote to Buchanan: "The times have been so dangerous to personal safety that I expected every minute to be destroyed."[26] On 25 September 1808 he urgently asked for money to be sent to him: "... You must be well convinced, that the present moment is still more favourable, and will continue to be so for two or three months, on account of the great expenses of the present war; besides which the government will sell all the property of the noblemen who have taken the French party..." Wallis concluded the letter with the following words: "Indeed, nothing is understood here at present but the *peso duro* (cash)."[27]

Art collectors were primarily searching for masterpieces of the Italian, Flemish and French schools, but at the same time they began to have a better appreciation of Spanish painting. The letter quoted above contains the following words: "Of the Spanish school we have no idea whatever in England. If they could see the two or three best Murillos of the St. Iago family, and some of the fine pictures of Velázquez, Alonso Cano, Pereda, Zurbarán, Caregni, or del Greco, really first-rate men, whose works are quite unknown out of Spain, some estimate of the high excellence of this school might then be formed. This school is rich beyond idea, and its painters are all great colourists; some of their colossal works are surprising. If you had time and could bear the horrors of travelling in Spain it would be worth while to visit this country."[28]

The mention of Murillo's canvases owned by the Santiago family is particularly interesting as it refers to the paintings with the scenes of Jacob's life now in the Hermitage. These paintings had attracted particular attention from experts on Spanish art from the very moment of their creation. They have been identified as the series of paintings mentioned in 1724 by Antonio Palomino, who reported that Murillo had executed five paintings with landscape backgrounds commissioned by the Marquis de Ayamonte y Villamanrique, who had taken them from Seville to Madrid. According to Palomino, the paintings depicted scenes from David's life and in his days they were in the palace of the Marquis de Santiago in Madrid.[29] It seems most likely that Palomino was mistaken in mentioning the name of David since half a century later, in 1787, the English poet and art connoisseur R. Cumberland wrote that "the scenes from Jacob's life" could be seen in the Santiago palace.[30] As for the scenes from David's life, they were never mentioned again in connection with Murillo, either before or after Palomino's book. Cumberland admired the paintings from Jacob's life, regarding then as the best of Murillo's works. As noted above, Wallis also described them as examples of the best in Spanish painting. Whilst Wallis was in Madrid the paintings from the Santiago palace were put on sale and, according to him, the price was "outrageous".[31] It was then that the series was split up. Wallis managed to purchase one painting, *Laban Searching for His Stolen Household Gods in Rachel's Tent* (now in the Museum of Art, Cleveland).[32] *Jacob Laying the Peeled Rods before the Flocks of Laban* passed from one private collection to another until it was acquired comparatively recently by the Meadows Museum in Dallas.[33] The *Meeting of Jacob and Rachel* was auctioned in London in 1817 and nothing is known of it since then. The last two paintings, *Isaac Blessing Jacob* and *Jacob's Dream* (Nos. 9 and 10) found their way to the Hermitage. A catalogue of the Grosvenor House collection published in 1820 informed the readers that the pictures from the Santiago palace had been seized by the French general Sebastiani as war booty.[34] Since we know that at least one of the pictures was acquired by Wallis for Buchanan, this information is clearly wrong.

Isaac Blessing Jacob.
1660-1665, the Hermitage.
Oil on canvas, 245 x 357.5 cm.

Other paintings, however, may indeed have been seized by Sebastiani. *Isaac Blessing Jacob* and *Jacob's Dream* were sent to the Hermitage from Paris in 1811 through the Russian embassy. It is unknown who put the paintings on sale, but the intermediary was Dominique Vivant Denon, General Director of the French museums, who was deeply involved in art-collecting during the Napoleonic period. He was vividly described by C. Ceram in the book *Gods, Tombs, Scholars,* in a passage which characterizes not only the person of Vivant Denon but the historic period in general: "Under Louis XV he was the curator of the collection of antiquities and known as a favourite of Mme de Pompadour. As secretary at the embassy in St. Petersburg he enjoyed the favour of Catherine II. A society man, a ladies' man, a dilettante in all the fine arts, always sarcastic and witty, he managed to be friends with everybody. Whilst in the diplomatic service in Switzerland he often visited Voltaire and executed the famous *Breakfast at Ferney.* Another drawing, in the style of Rembrandt, the *Shepherds' Prayer,* helped him to become a member of the Académie. News of the outbreak of the Great French Revolution reached him in Florence, where he was enjoying the artistic atmosphere of the Tuscan salons. Denon hastened to Paris. He, *gentilhomme ordinaire,* a recent envoy, rich and independent, now found his name on the list of emigrés and learned that his estates had been seized by the state and his assets confiscated. Impoverished, lonely, betrayed by many friends, he led a miserable existence in squalid rooms trying to get money by selling drawings, wandering in the markets and watching the heads of many of his former friends rolling in the Place de Grève, until he found an unexpected patron, the great revolutionary painter Jacques-Louis David. He was given the opportunity to make engravings of David's sketches for costumes, those same designs that were to revolutionize fashion itself. In this way he won the favour of the 'Incorruptible'; soon after he had left the dirt of Montmartre for parquet floors he made use of his diplomatic talent and received back from Robespierre his estates when his name was stricken from the list of emigrés. He made the acquaintance of the beautiful Joséphine de Beauharnais and was presented to Napoleon who liked him and took him on the Egyptian campaign. After his return from the country on the Nile, well-experienced, recognized and generally respected, he was appointed General Director of all museums. Following in the footsteps of Napoleon, the victor on battlefields throughout Europe, he 'managed' the acquisition of artistic trophies (calling it 'collecting') and thus founded one of the greatest collections in France."[35]

Vivant Denon, who had seen the first acquisitions made for the Hermitage and was thus the best possible expert for evaluating the paintings that were then being launched from Spain onto the art markets of Europe, may have helped General Sebastiani to sell the famous paintings by Murillo to Russia. The Hermitage archives contain no more than a brief record of their addition to the catalogue: "Two paintings of the (Spanish) school by the artist Murillo sent from Paris by the Russian embassy in 1811 that were not included in the catalogue owing to their being mended."[36] This report, dated 1 December 1814, deals mainly with the paintings purchased from Wilhelm Coesvelt, which constituted the bulk of the gallery of Spanish painting in the Hermitage, the first of its kind in any European country.

Little has been published about Coesvelt's collection. In his book on the history of Spanish painting outside Spain published in 1958, Gaya Nuño had good reason to deplore the fact that no data on the formation of Coesvelt's collection was available, apart from a few lines in the prefaces to the Hermitage catalogues.[37] Gaya Nuño learned from the prefaces to the catalogues of 1863 and 1909 that a total of sixty-seven

Jacob's Dream.
1660-1665, the Hermitage.
Oil on canvas, 246 x 360 cm (Inv. No. 344).

paintings had been acquired from Coesvelt, though only fifty-three of them were exhibited. He drew the erroneous conclusion that only fifty-three works were of Spanish origin and that the other paintings belonged to foreign schools. In fact, all the paintings were Spanish and their total number was larger. Since the Coesvelt collection was of primary significance for the Hermitage its story deserves to be told in detail. Buchanan writes: "Mr Coesvelt, a gentleman who had been for some time in Madrid on matters of a mercantile nature, and was connected with the banking house of Messrs. Hopes of Amsterdam. All pictures therefore that Mr. Wallis purchased came to be on a joint account of Mr Coesvelt and Mr Buchanan, owing to the facilities which he could render in furnishing money on bills drawn in England, while Mr Coesvelt, on his part, had the advantage of the knowledge and judgment of Mr Wallis as an artist, in making a selection of objects of art."[38]

The artist Wallis was, thus, a permanent advisor to Coesvelt, being an ardent admirer and a fine connoisseur of Spanish art. It is unknown when the two met but on 25 September 1808 Wallis reported from Madrid on his financial dealings with Coesvelt. By November 1809, when Wallis sent a number of paintings to England, Coesvelt owned a collection about which Buchanan wrote: "At the period that Mr. Wallis purchased these pictures, a number of fine pictures were also purchased for Mr. Coesvelt, on his private account. That gentleman had not to contend with the disadvantages which Mr. Wallis had so long laboured under, in consequence of the failure of so many houses in Spain, and he therefore had it in his power to profit by the favourable opportunities that presented themselves. He availed himself of these and formed a fine collection, which he afterwards sold to the Emperor of Russia."[39]

Alexander I stayed in Holland in June-July 1814, and on 24 October 1814 the Hermitage curator

Franz Labensky wrote that "sixty-two gilt picture frames were taken from the six crates brought in after the latest campaign, plus six small cartoons depicting the arrangement on the walls of the paintings of the Spanish school bought by His Majesty from Mr Coesvelt".[40] A later document specified that the paintings had been bought "... in Amsterdam from the banker Goesfeld for 100,000 Dutch guilders".[41] On 1 December 1814 Labensky sent another report: "Last November the Hermitage received sixty-seven paintings of the Spanish school from Holland, that had been purchased by His Imperial Majesty during the latest campaign from Mr Coesvelt in Amsterdam... We beg permission to enter all the abovementioned paintings in the General Catalogue of the Hermitage. The enclosed register includes the names of the artists and the subjects of the paintings."[42] This register contains the names of almost all well-known Spanish artists of the sixteenth and seventeenth centuries.

Then came further deliveries. According to the Hermitage records, the "paintings of the Spanish school brought from Holland in March 1815 in addition to the collection sent before that..."[43] were added to the register in July 1815. This register indicates seven new paintings. The last such report was made by Labensky in November 1815: "On 19 November four crates brought by Captain Fox from England on board his ship that had sunk in the Gulf of Vyborg were delivered to the Hermitage; on being opened the crates were found to contain ten paintings which had been considerably damaged so that all of them, including the two painted on panel, are in an extremely poor state and require an extraordinary amount of restoration."[44] The total number of paintings purchased from Coesvelt was eighty-four; sixty-seven of these were received in November 1814 from Amsterdam, seven in March 1815, also from Amsterdam, the ten remaining, as we have seen, only reached St. Petersburg in November 1815 from England. Coesvelt selected Murillo's *St. Joseph Conducting the Infant Christ* to be a personal gift to Alexander I (No. 14).[45] The collection also included Murillo's splendid *Annunciation* (No. 6). In 1814 the Hermitage received the *Infant Christ Asleep* (No. 22), ascribed to Francisco Antolinez, and the *Death of St. Clare*

(No. 21), attributed to Pedro Atanasio Bocanegra, which were later identified as studio copies of works by Murillo. These four canvases were on the first list dated November 1814 and the second batch of paintings delivered in March 1815 included the *Hilly Landscape* ascribed to Murillo that was later transferred to the Imperial Palace at Tsarskoye Selo.[46]

Murillo, studio copy.
The Infant Christ Asleep.
The Hermitage.
Oil on canvas, 57.9 x 73.6 cm.

Murillo, studio copy.
The Death of St. Clare.
The Hermitage.
Oil on canvas, 118 x 161.5 cm.

The history of the *Archangel Raphael and Bishop Domonte* (No. 19) was also linked to the events of the Napoleonic period. It was first in the Malmaison Gallery of Joséphine de Beauharnais and, according to the gallery catalogue, was acquired in 1811. When Joséphine died in 1814 her collection was inherited by her son Eugène and her daughter

Hortense[47] and the former received the *Archangel Raphael and Bishop Domonte*. Eugène de Beauharnais (1781-1824) was married in 1806 to Amalia Augusta, daughter of Maximilian Joseph, King of Bavaria. In 1814 he settled in Bavaria where from 1817 he owned the margravate of Leuchtenberg and bore the title of Duke. In 1824 his son Maximilian Eugène (1817-1852) inherited the title of Duke of Leuchtenberg and in 1839 he married the Grand Duchess Maria Nikolayevna, daughter of the Russian Emperor Nicholas I. The Leuchtenberg Gallery remained in Munich until after 1851 when it was brought to St. Petersburg.[48] After Maximilian's death the gallery became the property of his son Nikolai. In early 1917 some paintings from the Leuchtenberg Gallery, among them Murillo's *Archangel Raphael and Bishop Domonte*, found their way to the Rumiantsev Museum in Moscow. In 1924 the canvas was transferred to the Pushkin Museum of Fine Arts together with the entire Picture Gallery of the Rumiantsev Museum.[49]

Research has revealed that the painting was commissioned by Bishop Francisco Domonte for the church of the La Merced convent in Seville. It was seen in place by A. Ponz and J. Cean Bermudez in the eighteenth century, but when in 1810 the French army occupied Seville it was taken to the Alcázar with numerous other paintings.[50] Apparently, it was later seized by one of the French commanders who sold or presented it to Joséphine de Beauharnais.

Dmitry Tatishchev, Russian envoy to a number of European countries at different times, also collected Spanish works of art in the 1810s. He thus told the story of his collection in the manuscript catalogue compiled in 1843: "During my long stay abroad that lasted more than thirty-six years, between 1805 and 1841, I was in places where political events strongly affected the fortunes of many noble houses, for instance, in Naples, in Sicily and other parts of Italy, as well as in Spain, including Madrid, where I arrived in 1814 several weeks after the return of King Ferdinand VII. The French invasion here resulted in the downfall of various noble and rich houses which were forced by circumstances to sell their property so that many things, particularly rare paintings, were sold for a song,

The Annunciation.
1655-1660, the Hermitage.
Oil on canvas, 142 x 107.5 cm.

St. Joseph Conducting the Infant Christ.
c. 1670, the Hermitage.
Oil on canvas, 73 x 52 cm.

while they would never have been offered for sale at any other time... For these reasons I managed to acquire a fairly large collection of paintings..."[51] Apart from paintings, Tatishchev owned sculptures and works of applied art of antique and contemporary European origin. The list of his collection appended to his will consisted of 137 pages. Tatishchev confessed that "these works have already become known to European artists and art patrons who highly praised them."[52]

The catalogue listed 186 paintings by European masters including twenty-one Spanish names. However, the last figure is not exact since some of the canvases by unknown artists may also be of Spanish origin.[53] In accordance with Tatishchev's will his entire collection was donated to the Hermitage in 1846, where the curators reconsidered many of the attributions of the works. These were then classified as first class, second class and "unfit to be in the Imperial Gallery".[54] Sixty canvases were later transferred to various institutions in Moscow and some paintings were hung in the palaces in and around St. Petersburg.

Among the Spanish paintings, Murillo's *Infant Christ Playing with a Crown of Thorns* (now known as the *Infant Christ Pricked by a Crown of Thorns*, No. 20) was considered first class. Another Murillo, *Women Behind Bars* (No. 26), was assigned to the second class. The catalogue of the Tatishchev collection also listed as Murillos the following

The Archangel Raphael and Bishop Domonte . 1680-1681, Pushkin Museum of Fine Arts. Oil on canvas, 211 x 150 cm.

Murillo Circle. *Women Behind Bars.* The Hermitage. Oil on canvas, 41 x 58.6 cm.

canvases: the *Flight into Egypt* (this attribution was later refuted), the *Annunciation,* which was found to bear the signature of José Antolinez; a *Profile of a Chief's Head;* a *Child's Head;* another *Flight into Egypt;* the *Rest on the Flight into Egypt;* and a *Praying Angel.* Only two of these, the *Infant Christ Pricked by a Crown of Thorns* and *Women Behind Bars,* now remain in the Hermitage collection: the attribution of the first work to Murillo is not absolutely certain while the second is assigned to Murillo's circle. The other paintings either changed their attribution or were transferred to other museums; in some cases the painter could not be identified.

From the later 1810s Paris was one of the main centres for dealings in Spanish paintings. Here, in 1819, Prince V. Trubetskoi bought for the Hermitage Murillo's *Joseph with the Infant Jesus* (known now as *St. Joseph Holding the Infant Christ in His Arms,* No. 13).[55] It was transferred to the Pushkin Museum of Fine Arts in 1930. Around the same time the Hermitage acquired another painting on the same subject which was later transferred to Gatchina Palace.[56]

The Spanish Gallery became a prominent section of the Hermitage and its high artistic quality made the curators particularly careful in their selection of new acquisitions. A good opportunity presented itself in 1830 when the Russian government was offered the chance to buy the collection of

Manuel Godoy, Prince of the Peace, who had been Prime Minister to King Charles IV and effective ruler of Spain from 1792 to 1808. Godoy owned one of the best collections of paintings in Europe, a fact that was well known to art lovers. The General Director of the Spanish Mint Pedro Gonzales de Sepulveda wrote of his two visits to Godoy's gallery in November 1800 and April 1807.[57] He was impressed with the abundance of excellent canvases by Italian, Flemish and Spanish artists. On his first visit he singled out among the best Spanish works

the second consisted of good pictures, and the third was of average-quality canvases. On the whole, Quilliet praised the collection very highly, stating that it surpassed any collection owned by the nobility in other countries.

Three months after the inventory had been completed the country was shaken by events that were to have a tragic impact on the fate of its art treasures. After the popular uprising in Aranjuez in March 1808 Godoy was forced to flee from Spain. The country was invaded by French troops and the war of independence began. From

Murillo (?).
The Infant Christ Pricked by a Crown of Thorns.
The Hermitage.
Oil on canvas, 57 x 43cm.

Jose Antolinez.
The Annunciation.
The Hermitage.
(Inv. No. 6830)

St Jerome Listening to the Sounds of the Heavenly Trumpet by Jusepe de Ribera, *Venus with a Mirror* by Velázquez, *Life Is a Dream* by Antonio de Pereda, and the *Maja Nude* by Goya; on the second visit he noted the paintings by Juan de Juanez, Louis de Morales, Francisco Ribalta, Alonso Cano, and Bartolomé Murillo.

In January 1808 the French connoisseur F. Quilliet compiled a full inventory of the paintings in Godoy's collection, which listed 972 works.[58] Quilliet evaluated the pictures and put them in three classes: the first included masterpieces,

1808 to 1813 the Spanish throne was occupied by Joseph Bonaparte, who decreed that an art museum be opened in Godoy's former residence. Paintings from secularised monasteries and nationalized palaces of the royal family and the aristocracy were brought here, but many of them were sold or stolen in the period between 1808 and 1810. In August 1813 the San Fernando Academy set up a commission to make an inventory of the former Godoy gallery. This inventory now listed 381 paintings, a considerably smaller number than was noted in

1808. In January 1814 the legal bodies that implemented the nationalization of Godoy's assets compiled yet another inventory which was to be the last. In the short period between August 1813 and January 1814 the number of paintings again decreased sharply and the inventory listed only 197 paintings, many of which were transferred to the San Fernando Academy. It is unclear how exact were the inventories of 1813 and 1814 in describing the Godoy gallery since they may have included paintings from other collections. Thus, the catalogue compiled by Quilliet in January 1808 is the most complete and reliable document.

In emigration Godoy created a new collection. King Charles IV paid him an annuity and his circumstances were quite comfortable. In 1812 he bought the Villa Mattei, one of the many attractions for travellers in Rome. The author Stendhal visited it in 1817 and 1828 and the librarian from Versailles, M. Valeri, saw it between 1826 and 1828. They both noted the classical sculptures (which did not feature in Godoy's collection in Madrid).[59] In February 1826 the English painter David Wilkie visited the Villa Mattei. He wrote in his diary: "Before leaving Rome, saw the collection of the Spanish Prince of the Peace. The Murillo is in admirable condition; but, in subject and colour, I think Signor Cammuccini overrates it... The Spagnoletto rich, but disgusting. One of the finest pictures there is a Velázquez —a martyr in a red dress — the tone and execution most superb. Saw the Prince himself —somewhat of a rough character."[60] Wilkie also remarked elsewhere: "The finest Murillo in Rome he (Signor Cammuccini) says, is in the collection of the Prince of the Peace, where are also Rubens and a Spagnoletto of first-rate quality."[61]

Death of the Inquisitor Pedro de Arbués.
1664, the Hermitage.
Oil on canvas, 293.5 x 206.2 cm.

This Vincenzo Cammuccini who accompanied Wilkie was a fashionable painter in Rome and Godoy, among others, commissioned a picture from him. Wilkie, who was a collector, a skilful copyist and restorer, and was also involved in art dealing, apparently assisted Godoy in the acquisition of paintings for his second collection. But Godoy had to sell this collection when he decided to move to Paris in the late 1820s, by which time his collection included 297 works. In 1829 he engaged the services of the French dealer Friedlein, but the planned auction never took place and Godoy's second collection acquired in emigration was never catalogued.[62] Subsequent sales of paintings were kept secret, they were not reported in the press and their circumstances still remain a mystery to art historians.[63] Some light is shed on these sales by the records of acquisitions for the Hermitage preserved in the Hermitage archives and in the Central State Archives in St. Petersburg. Negotiations for the purchase of paintings from Godoy's collection for the Hermitage were opened in the summer of 1830. On 20 May 1830 Count Pozzo di Borgo, the Russian ambassador in Paris, wrote to the Vice-Chancellor K. Nesselrode that the Spanish ambassador in France, Count Ofalia, had conveyed to him the wish of the Prince of the Peace to sell paintings to the Russian government. An inventory was enclosed but unfortunately it has not been found in the archives (it was apparently handwritten). Pozzo di Borgo estimated the Godoy collection as being "among the best existing ones and containing works by the greatest masters of the Italian and Spanish schools."[64] Nesselrode passed on the proposal and the inventory to the Imperial Court Minister P. Volkonsky. The Emperor Nicholas I selected

273 paintings from the inventory and the Ministry of Finance directly issued a bill of exchange in the name of Pozzo di Borgo. [65]

The ambassador, however, did not dare to accept responsibility for such an expensive deal. He asked for consultations with experts and, specifically, with Prince G. Gagarin who was at the time in Rome since he was under the impression that the collection was there. [66] Volkonsky advised Gagarin to consult other art connoisseurs if necessary — it was repeatedly emphasized that only original paintings were to be bought. [67] As became clear later, Godoy's collection was not only in Rome since parts of it were kept in London and Paris. [68] Pozzo di Borgo requested that "for making this purchase one of the Hermitage officials be sent to Paris in order to examine the paintings personally and to make the soundest selection of those that can be acquired for the Hermitage." [69] The request was not granted. One of the letters has such a note in the margin: "Who is to be sent to Paris? It is not worthwhile." [70]

Pozzo di Borgo insisted: "The presence of a man who knows the Imperial Gallery well is, in my opinion, necessary since he would see what should be chosen from this collection." [71] The answer was again negative. No expert from the Hermitage was sent to Paris. Volkonsky wrote to Nesselrode: "I have asked His Majesty the Emperor for a permission: who will be ordered to go to Paris to inspect the paintings of the Prince of the Peace and to select those that may be acquired for the Hermitage? But His Imperial Majesty deigned me with the answer that no official should be sent to Paris for this purpose." [72] Nesselrode then wondered whether the "Emperor wished the paintings to be bought at all?" [73] But there was no question of refraining

St. Joseph Holding the Infant Christ in His Arms
c. 1670, Pushkin Museum of Fine Arts.
Oil on panel, 70 x 51 cm.

from the purchase. Volkonsky repeated once again that... "the ambassador Count Pozzo di Borgo knows closely many good artists in Paris, such as Messrs. Gerard, Fonchagne and others, whom he may entrust with the examination of these pictures to assess their quality." [74]

Pozzo di Borgo asked Baron von Stenben, a painter living in Paris, to evaluate the paintings with respect to their quality and state of preservation. The list of paintings selected by him was sent to Russia. [75] This is the most complete list of Godoy's collection put together in emigration. It included a total of 158 works.

Four of them were assigned to the first class, twenty-one to the second class, twenty-one to the third class, and 112 to the fourth class. The names of the artists and paintings were given only for the first three classes while works in the fourth class were noted only by their inventory numbers. The collection included works by the Italian painters Bonifazio, Caravaggio, Annibale Carracci, Domenichino, Garofalo, Giordano, Giorgione, Giulio Romano, Guercino, Lorenzo Lotto, Maturano, Perino del Vaga, Pontormo, Pordenone, Raphael, Reni, Sassoferrato, Spada, Titian, Vanni and Veronese. Among painters of other schools were Lairesse, Poussin, Rubens and Eeckhout.

The best piece in the collection was held to be Murillo's *Death of the Inquisitor Pedro de Arbués* (No. 11). Four other Spanish paintings were also on the list: St. *Lawrence, tale Patron Saint of Valencia,* attributed to Murillo, and the *Deposition, St. Jerome* and *Portrait of Virgil* by Ribera. The inventory compiled by Baron von Stenben was not the final choice. The sale was completed by the Louvre's agent Lafontaine, whose part in the acquisition was noted in early February 1831 by Pozzo di Borgo. [76]

The Hermitage archives contain an interesting

report which Labensky sent to Volkonsky after he had received the official list of paintings selected for acquisition. It runs as follows: "Having considered the inventory of thirty-three paintings selected from the collection of the Prince of the Peace and proposed for acquisition by the Imperial Hermitage, I have the honour to inform You that some of them, underlined with red ink in the inventory, are, in my opinion, quite extraneous because the Hermitage Gallery already has works by these artists and even more so because the above paintings are by second- and third-class masters and date from the mid-seventeenth century and later. The paintings by artists of this time do not possess the qualities of genuine examples of the fine arts that distinguish the works of 15th- and 16th-century masters, for which reason connoisseurs and famous galleries avoid expanding their collections with works of the third and other grades.

"In addition, I believe it necessary to note that the valuations for all paintings in general are too high but it should be borne in mind that the proper price for the first-class masters cannot be determined at all since it depends more on the desire of the buyer and, particularly, on the state of preservation of the paintings which, firstly, should not be worn and, secondly, should not have been retouched by the brush of an inexperienced artist." [77]

One cannot fail to notice in this report the displeasure of the curator who was well qualified to select the paintings for acquisition himself. Despite his remarks, however, Lafontaine's selection remained unchanged. In May 1831 the Emperor approved the payment. [78] In the same month Nesselrode returned the receipt for 567, 935 francs signed by the Prince of the Peace. [79]

In the summer of 1831 preparations for transporting the paintings to Russia were underway. The insurance estimates were made by the banker F. Gontar who was put in charge of transportation. He reported to Nesselrode that on 10 August 1831 the French ship *Virgin* took on board nine crates at Rouen and Le Havre. The paintings arrived in St. Petersburg[80] on 18 November 1831. Labensky reported on 28 November: "On 22 November I received 9 crates from the St. Petersburg customs house... containing 33 paintings in gilt frames from the gallery of the Prince of the Peace for the Hermitage. The said paintings are installed in the Hermitage room of the Spanish school." [81] Apart from the *Portrait of Virgil* by Ribera, all the paintings by Spanish artists from the initial list compiled by von Stenben were brought to the Hermitage. [82] As mentioned above, the most valuable piece among the works sold by Godoy was the canvas by Murillo that was put down as the *Martyre de St. Pierre d'Albens* in von Stenben's inventory. Von Stenben did not know the proper name of the saint and thus made an error. Later the painting was variously referred to as the *Martyre de St. Pierre,* [83] *St. Peter the Dominican* and *St. Peter of Verona* [84] and finally Curtis called it the *Death of the Inquisitor Pedro de Arbués.* [85] The English artist Wilkie apparently had this painting in mind when he wrote that the best work by Murillo in Rome belonged to the Prince of the Peace. Though Wilkie did not name the painting, he visited the Villa Mattei in 1826 and Godoy's complete collection was offered for sale to the Hermitage in 1830; it is unlikely that the collection changed substantially during this short period.

The *Death of the Inquisitor Pedro de Arbués* was executed by Murillo for the beatification of Arbués held on 17 September 1664. It was commissioned for the San Pablo monastery in Seville. According to some unverified sources, Manuel Godoy took this painting from the inquisition tribunal of Seville in 1804, replacing it with a copy by Joaquin Cortés. No canvas with such name, however, appeared in the inventory compiled by Quilliet in 1808, but even if Godoy had had it in his Madrid gallery he would have lost it along with the rest of his collection. We do not know yet how Godoy managed to obtain this masterpiece in Rome.

Another painting in Godoy's collection sold to the Hermitage was attributed to Murillo. In Stenben's inventory it was called *St. Laurent, protecteur de Valence, attribué à Murillo.* [86] Apparently, the attribution to Murillo was questioned even then. It is highly probable that Wilkie had meant precisely this canvas when he mentioned a martyr in a red dress by Velázquez in Godoy's Roman collection since it shows a martyr in a red tunic with a millstone around his neck and a cross in his hand (note that though there are three saints in the painting it was referred to as *St. Laurent* from the central character at the time of its acquisition). Later the attribution and the name of the painting changed several times; it was ascribed to Herrera the Younger, Francisco Ribalta, Juán Rizi[87] and referred to as *St. Florian, St. Florian, St. Dominic and St. Peter the Dominican* and *St. Quirinus, St. Dominic and St. Raymond of Penafort.* Now it is known as *St. Vicente, St. Vicente Ferrer and St. Raymond of Peñafort* and attributed to the school of Francisco Ribalta.[88] This canvas was not part of Godoy's Madrid collection and its provenance before it came to the Gallery of the Prince of the Peace is not established.

Meanwhile, the Spanish collection in the Hermitage lacked works by Velázquez. In 1833 Franz Labensky requested Alexander Gessler, the Russian consul in Cadiz, that he look for Velázquez paintings on sale in Spain.[89] In June of that year Gessler wrote: "He is one of those artists whose works are more than rare now. However, after conducting a search I managed to find some that deserve being sent to St. Petersburg."[90] The negotiations for their purchase continued for a year, during which period Gessler found a number of other canvases that were on sale. Finally, on 4 July 1834 the Court administration sent to Labensky "an inventory of paintings purchased according to the Imperial decree by our Consul-General in Cadiz, Gessler, at the expense of the administration."[91] (It is sometimes mentioned in the literature that the paintings were acquired from the "Gessler collection" but this expression is inaccurate since the consul bought them under special assignment for the Imperial Court.)

The paintings were delivered from Cadiz in two batches in 1834 and 1835, both of which included works by Murillo.[92] The first contained the *Adoration of the Shepherds* (No. 2) and *St. Antony,* the second included the *Virgin Bringing the Infant Jesus to the Temple* (now known as the *Presentation in the Temple,* No. 23), *John the Baptist Sleeping in a Landscape* (now known as the *Infant Christ Asleep,* No. 22) and the *Virgin in the Clouds Holding the Infant Jesus in Her Lap.* The *Adoration of the Shepherds* was first regarded as a study for a similarly named painting in the Wallace collection in London;

Francisco Ribalta, school.
St. Vincente, St. Vincente Ferrer and St. Raymond of Peñafort. The Hermitage (Inv. No. 374).

Murillo, follower.
The Infant Christ Asleep.
The Hermitage (Inv. No. 8836).

doubts were then voiced about its being an original and it is now considered to be a studio copy.[93] Soon after its acquisition the *Presentation in the Temple* was classified as a work by Murillo's studio but it is now defined as being from Murillo's circle.[94] The *St. Antony* was transferred to the palace at Tsarskoye Selo (and it has since disappeared). The *Infant Christ Asleep* was first transferred to the Tauride Palace in St. Petersburg and then to Gatchina Palace, but in 1933 it was returned to the Hermitage. The first name given to it was wrong as the legend on the Child's cane, *EGO DERMIS ET COR MEUM VIGILAT* (*I sleep and my heart keeps watch*), indicates that the Child is Christ. The painting is not of the highest artistic quality and seems to have been executed by a follower of Murillo. It has an original composition, however, since nothing like it is known among Murillo's works.[95] The *Virgin in the Clouds* was sold in

Murillo circle. *Presentation in the Temple.*
The Hermitage (Inv. No. 380).
Oil on canvas, 105.5 x 174.5 cm.

1854 and it is not known what happened to it after this.[96]

At the same time that Gessler was assigned his task, negotiations were under way in St. Petersburg for the purchase of the collection of the Spanish envoy in Russia, Juan Miguel de Paez de la Cadena (1766-1840), who was in Russia from 1825 to 1835. Paez de la Cadena took part in the life of St. Petersburg society and counted among his acquaintances Alexander Pushkin. In 1830 the famous Russian poet sent him New Year greetings and in 1832 was so impressed with Cadena's story of Napoleon's 18th Brumaire that he wrote it down.[97] A short time before leaving St. Petersburg Paez de la

Murillo, studio copy.
Boy with a Wreath of Oak Leaves. ▶
Monplaisir Palace, Petrodvorets.
Oil on canvas, 51.5 x 38 cm.

Murillo, studio copy.
The Adoration of the Shepherds. ▼
The Hermitage, St. Petersburg.
Oil on canvas, 43 x 60 cm.

Murillo (?).
A Flock of Sheep in a Landscape. ▶
The Hermitage (Inv. No. 9322).

Unknown artist. 17th century.
Boy Looking for Fleas on a Dog. ▶
The Hermitage (Inv. No. 333).

Cadeña decided to sell his collection. Labensky received the following communication on 11 September 1834 from the Court administration: "If the Vice-Chancellor notifies of the purchase of paintings from the Spanish Envoy, they should be taken in according to the inventory and placed in the Spanish Room of the Hermitage..."[98] The paintings were received on 1 October 1834 and in December they were included in the Hermitage catalogue.[99] The collection consisted of paintings from the Italian, Dutch, German and Spanish schools. The total number of canvases was fifty-one, twenty-four of them Spanish. The inventory listed six paintings by Murillo — a *Portrait of the Artist's Brother, Two Boys With a Dog in a Landscape*, a *Landscape with a Building on a Hill*, a *Boy with His Head Decorated with Oak Leaves* (now referred to as the *Boy with a Wreath of Oak Leaves*, No. 25), a *Flock of Sheep in a Landscape* and a *Boy Looking for Fleas on a Dog*. The first three paintings were sold in 1854.[100] The *Boy with a Wreath of Oak Leaves* was transferred to Peterhof Palace where it still is today. It is likely to be a studio copy of part of Murillo's canvas, *Two Boys Playing Dice*, in the Kunstakademie, Vienna.[101] The *Flock of Sheep*[102] was transferred to Gatchina Palace but was later returned to the Hermitage: it is now attributed to an unknown seventeenth-century artist but Murillo's name has not been ruled out. The *Boy Looking for Fleas on a Dog* was ascribed to Pedro Nuñez de Villavicencio but its Spanish origin is now refuted.[103]

One of the most important works acquired by the Hermitage in 1842 was the *Immaculate Conception* (No. 1) by Murillo, known in the literature under the names of its former owners Braschi and Esquilache. The Marquis de Esquilache, First Minister to the Spanish King Charles III, was forced to escape from Spain to his homeland in Sicily after the "Esquilache" rebellion of 1766 caused by a wave of popular dissatisfaction with his policies. Later he was reprieved but he did not return to Spain as he was appointed envoy to Venice, where he died in 1785. Murillo's painting was apparently brought by Esquilache from Spain to Sicily. After his death it became the property of Cardinal Gregorio whose mother in turn presented it to Pope Pius VI (Giovanni Angelo Braschi, 1717-

1799). The painting was then inherited by the Pope's nephew, the Duke of Braschi, and it was seen in his collection by David Wilkie, who wrote in his diary: "I accompanied Mr Weston to the Braschi palazzo to see *Antinous* and the *Assumption of the Virgin* by Murillo. It is not the first class, though the picture is original... Signor Cammuccini says that it is a well-known picture brought over from Sicily but it is overpainted."[104] The canvas was brought to St. Petersburg on 23 June 1842. It was not, however, immediately delivered to the Hermitage because according to

restoration work that continued until 1941. During the Second World War it was rolled up and taken out of Leningrad for safe-keeping. It was unrolled only for the exhibition Murillo and Seventeenth-Century Andalusian Artists in the Hermitage Collection held in 1984. We may now concur with Wilkie's opinion that the painting is indeed close to early original works by Murillo. The last significant acquisitions of Murillo's canvases by the Hermitage were made in 1852. They were associated with the notorious name of Marshal Nicolas Soult (1769-1851) who was

◀ *The Vision of St. Antony of Padua.*
1660-1680, Hermitage.
Oil on canvas, 250 x 167 cm.

The Esquilache Immaculate Conception.
1645-1655, Hermitage (Inv. No. 7146).
Oil on canvas, 235 x 196 cm.

the despatches the ship (the Danish vessel *Edouard —L.K.*) had had an accident at sea. The crates were delivered and opened as late as August and the painting was included in the Hermitage catalogue in November 1842 (Cat. 1797-1850).[105] The condition of the canvas deteriorated after travel and much restoration work was done on it. Not surprisingly, some art historians later raised doubts about the picture being an original Murillo. It was not available for examination for a long time since it was taken to Moscow in 1914 at the outbreak of the First World War and after its return was removed for

"one of the worst plunderers of Spain".[106] Soult's troops entered Seville in February 1810. He threatened the religious fraternities and church authorities with death unless they gave him their best paintings. Gaya Nuño wrote that when Marshal Soult, on his return from Spain, "went through Madrid on 2 March 1813, he was followed by a caravan of carts packed with paintings seized primarily in Andalusia".[107] It is understandable then that the auction of Soult's collection announced after his death and held in Paris in 1852 attracted great attention.
In March 1852 the auction catalogue of Soult's

collection was submitted to Fiodor Bruni, Head of the Hermitage at the time. It was suggested that he "make a note of the best paintings and those whose acquisition would be advisable to improve the Hermitage collection".[108] Bruni wrote in reply: "Since I have not any personal knowledge of the above mentioned paintings I cannot make any selection of them but I should add that the collection of Marshal Soult has for a long time enjoyed European fame and general recognition."[109] A decision was taken to send Bruni to Paris to inspect the collection. By April he was already sending reports from Paris. First of all, he selected the *Immaculate Conception* and the *Birth of the Virgin*[110] but it later transpired that France had put forward a claim to both works. Bruni reported that "no competition was feasible here". Of the *Immaculate Conception*, however, he wrote that "this painting is almost identical to the *Assumption of the Virgin* that is now in the drawing room of Her Majesty the Empress, in composition, as well as in its brushwork and its colours."[111] Bruni did not mention the *Birth of the Virgin* in his subsequent correspondence. (Both paintings were acquired for the Louvre and the *Birth* is still exhibited there while the *Immaculate Conception* was returned to Spain in 1940 and is now in the Prado in Madrid.)

Despite his first failure, Bruni managed to buy some first-class works at the auction. He wrote: "There were only four excellent paintings out of the entire gallery... those that all the journals were talking so much about. The first and most significant, the *Conception of the Virgin*, was acquired by France. The remaining three were purchased by me, namely, two Murillos, *St. Peter in Prison* and the *Infant Jesus and St. John*, and *Christ Carrying the Cross* by Sebastiano del Piombo."[112]

Bruni also took interest in some other auctions in Paris. A French art dealer, N. Moreaux, assisted him in acquiring Murillo's *Infant Christ Appearing to St. Antony in the Wilderness* (known now as the *Vision of St. Antony of Padua*, No. 17) at the auction of the Laneuville collection. Bruni wrote that this beautiful painting had been brought to Paris from Spain by a French general after the latest Spanish campaign.[113] Angulo suggested that the painting was among those included in the posthumous inventory of Murillo's possessions; in 1842 it appeared in Paris at the sale of the collection of the Marquis de Farbain Jeanson, and in 1849 it was acquired by Laneuville.[114]

The acquisitions made by Bruni were extremely valuable. The *Liberation of St. Peter* (No. 12) is one of the best-known paintings by Murillo. It had formed part of the ensemble at the La Caridad hospital in Seville. In 1800 when the Spanish King Charles IV decided to establish a museum in Madrid he asked the hospital authorities for eleven paintings by Murillo; they were to be replaced with copies, work on which was begun immediately, continuing until the

The Liberation of St. Peter.
c. 1667, Hermitage.
Oil on canvas, 238 x 260 cm.

French invasion. In 1810 all the best paintings from Seville's churches and monasteries were carried to the Alcazar where a total of 999 canvases were held. The inventory of the repository started with Murillo's masterpieces from the La Caridad hospital as the best among the chosen treasures. The *Liberation of St. Peter* became the property of Marshal Soult. Thus, Bruni was able to acquire a Spanish masterpiece for the Hermitage.

The second painting from the Soult collection, the *Infant Jesus and St. John* (No. 5), was soon classified by the Hermitage experts as a copy and it is entered as such in all catalogues. This opinion is erroneous, however. There are good grounds to think that the Hermitage painting is that which was in the royal palace in Madrid at the end of the eighteenth century and an engraving of which was executed by Manuel Carmona in 1799. The canvas was included in the inventories of the Madrid palace in 1772 and 1794 but it then disappeared, apparently during the French occupation. It is not suprising, therefore, that it may have become the property of Marshal Soult.

With these acquisitions by Bruni the Murillo collection in the Hermitage was complete. With a few exceptions the museum included all the works by the Seville master which had found their way to Russia.

The Hermitage started the classification and study of its collection in the eighteenth century. The results of the first decade of collecting were summarized in the catalogue[115] published by E. Munich in 1774. It was very brief and contained only the names of the artists and their works but it gives an idea of the initial composition of the Hermitage's painting collection. At the same time Munich was compiling a detailed catalogue[116] in three volumes that has been preserved in manuscript form (first two volumes 1773-1783; third volume 1785). In 1797 a group of authors headed by Labensky began work on a new catalogue in manuscript form[117] that contained entries on all acquisitions. This catalogue was continued until 1850 and provides interesting information on the provenance of the works and their transferrals from the Hermitage to other locations.

The first published descriptions of the Hermitage collections were short; one of the most significant was a section in the book by J. Georgi devoted to the sights of St. Petersburg.[118] In 1828 J. Schnitzler published a small book on the Hermitage[119] in which the gallery of Spanish painting was described as "a major attraction of the museum".[120] However, it mentioned only the works considered by the author to be the most remarkable. The first fairly complete description of the Picture Gallery was given in the book *Livret...* prepared by Labensky with the assistance of A. Planat[121] and published in 1838. It was of great importance for its time since it acquainted art lovers with one of the most significant collections of paintings in Europe, in particular with Spanish paintings (it should be recalled that Louis Philippe's Spanish gallery in the Louvre was opened as late as 1838). But even the *Livret* did not cover all the works kept in the Hermitage. For instance, the catalogue of 1797-1850 included thirty-two canvases by Murillo while the *Livret* mentioned only the nineteen paintings considered to be the best.

Six years later, in 1844, L. Viardot published the book *Museums of Germany and Russia*[122] in which he made use of the *Livret*. Viardot acknowledged the high value of the Hermitage's Spanish collection but on the whole he was critical of it, doubting some attributions and expressing dissatisfaction with the quality of many works. His opinions were not wholly groundless but the French art historian was unjustified in his view of the works by Murillo, who was superbly represented in the museum. The information provided in the *Livret* was also borrowed by W. Stirling in his major treatise on Spanish art (1848).[123]

The painting collections were re-examined and redistributed in the 1850s in connection with the opening of the New Hermitage. Some of the canvases were sold[124] and many were transferred to the Imperial palaces around St. Petersburg. The new *Inventory of Paintings and Plafonds...,* the compilation of which was begun in 1859, included the works that remained in the Hermitage as well as those kept elsewhere.[125] A. Somov also published a description[126] of the Picture Gallery with the newly changed composition in 1859. Preparatory work on the new catalogue was started in the early 1860s and it was published by B. Koehne[127] in 1863. The preface to the catalogue said: "The Hermitage Picture Gallery was carefully inspected in 1861 and 1862 by the well-known connoisseur of paintings Professor Waagen, Director of the Picture Gallery at the Berlin Museum. Professor Waagen presented many invaluable data both on the provenance of the pictures and on their exact attribution and, in general, his profound knowledge greatly contributed to the compilation of the present catalogue."[128] At the same time Waagen wrote his own book on the Hermitage in which he gave his own opinions on each painting.[129] In his turn, he paid tribute to B. Koehne: "I have long collected information myself but my knowledge was enriched thanks to the preface by Baron von Koehne in the catalogue that has just been published. Koehne carefully examined the archives."[130] The catalogue prepared by Koehne included entries for twenty-four paintings by Murillo and artists of his circle and the attributions of some works were changed. Waagen was a prominent art expert of his time, an extremely erudite scholar, but he was limited by the level of the art criticism of his day. Waagen boldly altered the attributions of the paintings, not always correctly as was seen later. This was especially true in the case of Spanish painting, since the Spanish school in general was much less well-known than other schools at the time. It was Waagen who originated many controversial points that have continued to be discussed in the literature. A catalogue of the paintings by Velázquez and Murillo prepared by Ch. Curtis[131] came out in 1883. It is rich in valuable data that are still of great importance, noting almost all paintings from the Hermitage and presenting new findings on their provenance. E. Brunningk and A. Somov made use of this work in a new edition of the Hermitage catalogue[132] published in 1889. At the turn of the century there was an active policy of reattribution of the Hermitage paintings, in which leading Spanish art historians took an interest: A. Beruete came to St. Petersburg in 1904 and E. Tormo y Monso in 1912. They made some suggestions on the attribution of Murillo's paintings both in the literature and in private communications.[133] E. Liphart took their views into account when he prepared a new edition of the catalogue of Italian and Spanish painting[134] published in 1912. The German art historians A. Mayer, V. von Loga and C. Justi made a significant contribution to the study of the Spanish paintings in the Hermitage.[135]

A special place in the popular literature on the

The Infant Jesus and St. John.
1655-1660, Hermitage.
Oil on canvas, 124 x 115 cm.

Picture Gallery of the Hermitage is held by the guidebook written by Alexander Benois, a connoisseur of painting whose expert opinions are of interest even today.[136]

After the October Revolution of 1917 the composition of the Hermitage collection changed considerably. Nationalized private collections were transferred to the Hermitage along with works from the Imperial palaces around St. Petersburg, while part of the Hermitage holdings was moved to the Pushkin Museum of Fine Arts, established in 1924 in Moscow. Catalogues of the Pushkin Museum were published in 1948, 1957 and 1961 and the sections on Spanish art in them were prepared by K. Malitskaya.[137] The new composition of the Hermitage collection was reflected in the catalogue of 1958 prepared by V. Levinson-Lessing and a group of co-authors (a second revised and enlarged edition appeared in 1976)[138]. The compiler of the section on Spanish art, I. Levina, added new information to the catalogue but she did not include some paintings by artists from Murillo's circle owing to difficulties in their attribution. Murillo's paintings in the Hermitage were also discussed in popular booklets by J. Schmidt and I. Levina.[139]

For a long time art historians paid little attention to Murillo. While art historical knowledge increased greatly and multi-volume treatises were published on the leading Spanish masters, Murillo was still largely ignored by scholars. The situation changed in the 1960s when the prominent Spanish art historian D. Angulo became interested in the work of the master.[140] Other historians from various countries who contributed to Murillo studies from the 1960s to 1980s included J. Gaya Nuño, J. Brown, C. Ressort, W. Stechow, M. Haraszti-Takács, A. Braham and W. Jordan.[141] Angulo published his fundamental three-volume monograph[142] on

Murillo in 1981. The monograph summarized the new discoveries made by the author and other historians. The tercentenary of Murillo's death was widely commemorated in 1982; special exhibitions were held in Spain, Britain and France and a Murillo issue of the journal *Goya* included articles by many authors.[143] An exhibition,[144] Murillo and Seventeenth-Century Andalusian Artists in the Hermitage Collection, opened in Leningrad in 1984. The catalogue of this exhibition contains updated information on the paintings and their acquisition based on recent advances in the state of our knowledge and examination of the Hermitage archives.

The exhibition took a long time to prepare. Most of the paintings that were not on permanent display had first to undergo restoration. The cleaning revealed the high artistic quality of some works that had not been appreciated before. All canvases were subjected to X-ray examination, the results of which were published by L. Viazmenskaya,[145] showing interesting features common to many paintings by Murillo and artists of his circle. The character of the underpainting and the brushwork made it possible to classify the canvases that were unquestioningly original into two groups. The most characteristic features of the first group are a certain structural rigidity of the underpainting, the small and not always clearly discernible brushstrokes, the use of impasto and the lighter local tones (the *Adoration of the Shepherds*, *Boy with a Dog*, the *Annunciation* and the *Rest on the Flight into Egypt*). In the second group, experts noted a qualitative change in the brushstrokes from soft, relatively short to expressive pastose strokes whose length and shape varies widely (the *Holy Family*, *Isaac Blessing Jacob*, *Jacob's Dream*, the *Death of the Inquisitor Pedro de Arbués*, the *Liberation of St. Peter*, *St. Joseph Conducting the Infant Christ* and the *Vision of St. Antony of Padua*). The paintings of the first and second groups date from the 1640s-1650s and the 1660s-1670s, respectively. In the analysis of works of doubtful origin a comparison of the X-ray results was made. The X-photographs of the *Esquilache Immaculate Conception* and *the Infant Jesus and St. John* were similar to those of Murillo's early works. The X-photograph of the *Infant Christ Pricked by a Crown of Thorns* is also relatively

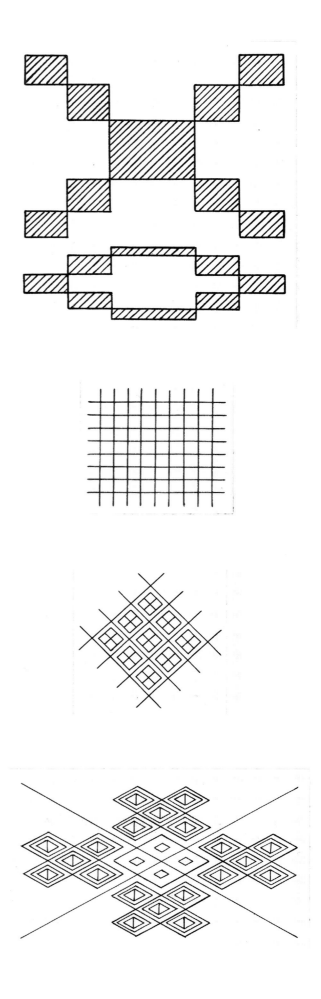

Murillo, studio copy.
The Infant St. John with the Lamb.
The Pushkin Museum of Fine Arts, Moscow.
Oil on canvas, 96 x 78 cm.

similar to those of the early works, although its technique is not as bold as in the authenticated pictures by Murillo, hence its attribution to the master in this book is questioned. The X-photographs of the *Adoration of the Shepherds* and the *Infant Christ Asleep* suggest that these works are by Murillo's studio since they exhibit some features typical of Murillo's style and some that are different. In its execution, *Women Behind Bars* differs from studio pictures, although the canvas is the same as that used for the *Infant Christ Pricked by a Crown of Thorns* and the *Infant Christ Asleep.* The X-photograph of *St. John with the Lamb* has nothing in common with those of autograph works.

Some of the X-photographs revealed alterations made by the artist himself in the process of work on the canvases (the *Rest on the Flight into Egypt. St. Joseph Conducting the Infant Christ.* the *Vision of St. Antony of Padua*). The X-rays also made it possible to determine the type of canvas Murillo used: mostly linen of the simple canvas weave but sometimes linen of the more intricate damask weave.

In the collection of paintings in the Hermitage linked with the name of Murillo fifteen originals are now identified; two more are of doubtful origin, three are studio copies, one is an eighteenth-century copy and three are by artists from Murillo's circle. It is the largest collection in the Russia and most works in this book come from here. In addition, the paintings discussed include four originals and one studio work that belong to the Pushkin Museum in Moscow and a studio copy that is on show in the Monplaisir palace at Petrodvorets near St. Petersburg. The Russian-owned works by Murillo and the artists of his circle constitute the largest collection of its kind outside Spain. It covers all the periods of Murillo's career and includes some of his famous masterpieces.

NOTES

1. Sbornik 1876, p. 258. For general information on the history of the Hermitage collection see Levinson-Lessing 1985.

2. Rémy 1768.

3. Sbornik 1876, p. 259.

4. *Ibid.*

5. *Ibid.*

6. *Ibid.*

7. J. F. Boileau, *Catalogue des Tableaux qui composent le Cabinet de Monseigneur le Duc de Choiseul, dont la vente se fera Lundi 6 Avril 1772.*

8. Sbornik 1876, p. 402.

9. *Ibid.*, p. 275. The collection was founded by Pierre Crozat and inherited in 1740 by Louis François Crozat. In 1750 it became the property of Louis Antoine Crozat, Baron de Thiers, who made a number of new acquisitions. When the Baron de Thiers died in 1770 his heirs sold the paintings to Catherine II through Denis Diderot. An inventory of the Crozat collection compiled by François Tronchin is in the Geneva archives: *Catalogue des Tableaux qui composent la Collection du Baron de Thiers acquis par Sa Majesté Imperiale tel que je l'ai dressé avec mon jugement sur chaque tableau. Envoyé à S.M.I.* The Crozat collection is discussed in Stuffmann 1968, p. 5-144.

10. Mariette 1857-1858, 4, p. 24. The Duc de Tallard, governor of Burgundy, who lived in Besançon, owned seven paintings by Murillo. They were sold at the posthumous sale of his property (see Ressort 1983, p. 52, 53).

11. "Aedes Walpolianae 1747. The Walpole collection is discussed in Braham 1981, p. 10, 11.

12. Sbornik 1876, p. 395-399.

13. *Sbornik Imperatorskogo Russkogo Istoricheskogo obshchestva* [Collection of the Imperial Russian Historical Society], St. Petersburg, 1878, vol. 24, p. 126, 135, 139.

14. R. K. Porter, *Travelling Sketches in Russia and Sweden During the Years 1805, 1806, 1807, 1808,* London, 1809, vol. 1, p. 41, 42, 44. In his guidebook to St. Petersburg of 1794, I. Georgi mentioned the paintings from the Walpole collection, but he had probably not seen them himself, having rather made use of the inventory obtained from the curator of the Hermitage gallery, Martinelli (see I. G. Georgi, *Opisaniye Rossiyskogo Imperatorskogo stolichnogo goroda Sankt-Peterburga i dostoprimechatelnostey v okrestnostiakh onogo* [The Description of the Russian Imperial Capital City of St. Petersburg and Its Suburbs], St. Petersburg, 1794, p. 450, 472).
The painter and restorer Cipriani, who had helped Moussine-Pushkin in the acquisition of the Walpole collection in England, advised him to reline the canvases and this was done for many works, including all the Spanish ones. As follows from the memoirs of Robert Ker Porter, the canvases were relined in Russia. Since lead white was used in the restoration the X-ray examination of the Walpole paintings produces practically no results.

15. The origin of this painting was unknown until recently. It was recorded as being by Murillo in the third volume of the manuscript catalogue compiled by E. Munich (Cat. 1785), then it was transferred to the palace at Tsarskoye Selo, and later returned to the Hermitage. During this time the name of the painter was dropped and it was entered in the last Hermitage inventory as a work by an unknown seventeenth-century artist. In the catalogue of 1785 the painting was listed among the works purchased in 1781 from the Comte de Baudouin in Paris, and it was in fact found in the list of this collection kept in the Hermitage archives (see *Description des Tableaux du Cabinet de Mr. le Comte de Baudouin, Brigadier des Armées du Roy, Capitaine Bataillon des Gardes Françoises). 1780.* — The Hermitage archives, inv. 6, file No. 1485; Cat. 1785, No. 2598; Kagané 1987, p. 266. The painting is now attributed to Juan Bautista Martinez del Mazo, an assistant of Velázquez, by analogy with his canvas *The Artist's Family* (Kunsthistorisches Museum, Vienna).

16. Esipov 1891, p. 39, No. 3. The provenance of the painting was unclear for a long time. According to the inscription on the engraving executed by G. Skorodumov in 1785, the painting belonged to Prince Grigory Potemkin, but the date of its entry into the Hermitage was not established. Its origin was first mentioned in the catalogue of 1889 compiled by E. Brünningk and A. Somov (Cat. 1889), who suggested that, since the painting is not noted in the *Livret* (Labensky 1838), it was probably acquired by the Hermitage after 1838. In the catalogue of 1901 A. Somov indicated that the painting was in the Winter Palace in 1797. Subsequent catalogues put the date of acquisition as being before 1797. In his preface to the catalogue of 1976 V. Levinson-Lessing noted that Potemkin's collection was acquired for the Hermitage in 1792, soon after his death. The inventory of this collection included Murillo's *St. John with the Lamb.*

17. Cat 1774, No. 46.

18. Murillo's paintings in private Russian collections during the eighteenth century are mentioned in H. Reimers, *St. Petersburg am Ende seines ersten Jahrhunderts,* St. Petersburg, 1805, p. 352, 354, 367.

19. *Catalogue raisonné des tableaux qui composent la collection du comte A. de Stroganoff à Saint-Pétersbourg, 1793,* No. 21, 22, 25.

20. Ponz 1772-1704.

21. Ceán Bermudez 1800.

22. J. Le Brun, *Recueil de Gravures au trait à l'eau-forte et ombrées, d'après un choix de tableaux de toutes les écoles, recueillis dans un voyage fait en Espagne, au midi de la France et en Italie, dans les années 1807 et 1808,* Paris, 1809.

23. Cat. 1839; A. Prakhov, "Proiskhozhdeniye khudozhest-vennykh sokrovishch kniazey Yusupovykh" [Provenance of the Yusupovs' Art Treasures], *Khudozhestvennye sokrovish-cha Rossii, 1906;* Cat. 1920; S. Ernst, *Gosudarstvenny muzeiny fond. Yusupovskaya galereya* [The state Museum Reserve. The Yusupov Gallery], Leningrad, 1924.

24. Angulo 1981, 2, p. 514, No. 2212.

25. Buchanan 1824.

26. *Ibid.*, 2, p. 219.

27. *Ibid*, 2, p. 229.

28. *Ibid*.

29. A. Palomino, *El Museo Pictórico y Escalá Óptica. III. El Parnaso Español pintoresco laureado*, Madrid, 1724 (ed. 1796, p. 627).

30. Cumberland 1787, p. 101, 102, 124, 125.

31. Buchanan 1824, 2, p. 219.

32. Stechow 1966, p. 367-376.

33. Jordan 1968, p. 288-294; W. B. Jordan, "Murillo's *Jacob Laying the Peeled Rods before the Flocks of Laban*", *Art News*, 1968, Summer, p. 31, 68, 69.

34. J. Young, *Catalogue of the Pictures at Grosvenor House*, London, 1820, p. 24.

35. C. W. Ceram, *Götter, Gräber and Gelehrte. Roman der Archäologie*, Hamburg, 1955.

36. The Hermitage archives, inv. 2, file 19, 1814.

37. Gaya Nuño 1958, p. 20.

38. Buchanan 1824, 2, p. 231.

39. *Ibid., p.* 235.

40. Report by F. Labensky to the Court administration, 24 October 1814. The Hermitage archives, inv. 2, file 17, 1814.

41. Order from the Court administration to F. Labensky, 31 July 1815. *Ibid.,* file 4, 1815.

42. Report by F. Labensky to the Court administration, 1 December 1814. *Ibid.,* file 19, 1814.

43. Order from the Court administration to F. Labensky, 31 July 1815. *Ibid.,* file 4,1815.

44. Report by F. Labensky to the Court administration, 23 November 1815. *Ibid.,* file 17, 1815. The archive documents do not include a list of the paintings in the third batch. Their names were determined from the manuscript catalogue of 1797-1850 where the works were entered after restoration.

45. According to F. Labensky, the painting was presented to Alexander I (Labensky 1838, p. 408).

46. The present whereabouts are unknown.

47. *Catalogue des tableaux de Sa Majesté l'Impératrice Joséphine dans la Galerie et appartements de son palais de Malmaison*, Paris, 1811; Lescure 1867, p. 270-285; Grandjean 1964.

48. In 1850 a catalogue and a collection of engravings of the Leuchtenberg Gallery were published in Germany. See: [Muxel], *Verzeichnis der Bilder-Galerie Seiner königlichen Hoheit des Prinzen Eugen Herzogs von Leuchtenberg in Munchen, Augsburg, 1850*; G. N. Muxel, *Gemälde Sammlung in München Seiner Königlichen Hoheit des Augusto Herzogs von Leuchtenberg und Santa Cruz Fürsten von Eichstädt... Im Umrissen auf Kupfer mit deutschen und französischen Texte herausgegeben von G. N. Muxel Inspector*, Munich (s.a).

49. The first mention of this painting in Russia appeared in the catalogue of the 1861 exhibition (see 1861 St. Petersburg, cat., p. 25, No. 114). Waagen wrote about it in 1864 (Waagen 1864, p. 370), and it has since been repeatedly discussed in the literature (see the note on the painting, Cat. Nos 67,68).

50. The origin of the painting was established by Curtis (Curtis 1883, p. 265, No. 385).

51. Last will and testament of Dmitry Pavlovich Tatishchev. The Hermitage archives, inv. 2, file 81. 1846, p. 2.

52. *Ibid.,* p. 3.

53. In the introduction to his catalogue Tatishchev mentioned that he had acquired the paintings himself. It is not known on what grounds Gaya Nuño claimed that Tatishchev had received the paintings as a gift from the Spanish king Ferdinand VII (Gaya Nuño 1958, p. 20).

54. The Hermitage archives, inv. 2, file 74, 1846, p. 208-212.

55. In the introduction to the catalogue of 1892 A. Somov wrote that "in 1819 the Emperor charged the general-adjutant, Prince Trubetskoi, with the purchase of paintings in foreign lands on occasion" and that the latter had brought several canvases from France and Italy, including, *St. Joseph with the Infant Saviour* (Cat. 1892, p. X. 164. No. 365).

56. The origin and location of the painting is unknown. The manuscript catalogue of 1797-1850 records that it was transferred to Gatchina Palace.

57. For the most complete study of the collections belonging to Manuel Godoy, see Rose Wagner 1983. The visits to Godoy's gallery by González de Sepúlveda are described in E. Pardo Canalis, "Una visita a la Galeria del Principe de la Paz", Goya, 1979, No. 148-150, p. 300 ff. and J. Rose Wagner, "La segunda visita de Gonzalez de Sepúlveda a la colección de Manuel Godoy", AEA, 1987, No. 238, p. 137-152.

58. The inventory compiled by Quilliet was published in the article: J. Pérez de Guzmán, "Las colecciones del Principe de la Paz", *La España Moderna*, 1900, vol. 140, August, p. 95 ff. A more complete and precise text is given in Rose Wagner, 1983.

59. Stendhal, *Rome, Naples and Florence in 1817*, Paris, 1956, p. 78. Stendhal, *Promenades dans Rome*, vol. 2, 1883, p. 119, 120. M. Valery (Antoine Claude Pasquen), *Voyages historiques et littéraires en Italie, pendant les années 1826, 1827 et 1828*, Brussels, 1836, p. 426.

60. A. Canningham. *The Life of Sir David Wilkie, vol. 2*, London, 1843, p. 257, 258.

61. *Ibid, p.* 253.

62. On the negotiations with Friedlein, see P. La Croix, "Note sur Godoy et Friedlein", *Boletin de l'Alliance des Arts*, No. 24 (10 June 1845), p. 374; Levinson-Lessing 1985, p. 143, 149.

63. Gaya Nuño 1958, p. 25; Rose Wagner 1983, p. 727 ff.

64. Copie d'une dépêche de l'ambassadeur comte Pozzo di Borgo au vice-chancelier, en date de Paris du 20 mai /4 juin 1830. Central state Historical Archives, fund 472, inv. 12, file No. 817, p. 2.

65. Letter to Warsaw from K. Nesselrode to Prince P. Volkonsky, 10 July 1830. *Ibid.,* p. 1. Letter from Prince P.

Volkonsky to K. Nesselrode, 15 June 1830. *Ibid.*, p. 3, 5, 9. The letters of credit were accepted in Paris by the office of the banker Rothschild.

66. Copie d'une dépêche au comte Pozzo di Borgo en date de Varsovie du 19 juin/1 juillet 1830. *Ibid.*, p. 5.

67. Copie d'une dépêche au prince Gagarin de Varsovie en date du 20 juin/2 juillet 1830. *Ibid.*, p. 8.

68. Letter of 2/14 August 1830 from Count Pozzo di Borgo in Paris to Prince P Volkonsky. *Ibid.*, p. 10.

69. Letter of 28 November 1830 from Count K. Nesselrode to Prince P. Volkonsky. *Ibid.*, p. 16, 17.

70. *Ibid.*

71. Letter of 29 October/10 November 1830 from Count Pozzo di Borgo to Vice-Chancellor K. Nesselrode. *Ibid.*, p. 19.

72. Letter of 29 November 1830 from Prince P. Volkonsky to Count K. Nesselrode. *Ibid.*, p. 22

73. Letter of 14 December 1830 from Count K. Nesselrode to Prince P. Volkonsky. *Ibid.*, p. 23.

74. Letter of 15 December 1830 from K. Naryshkin to Count K. Nesselrode. *Ibid.*, p. 24.

75. Note des tableaux extraits de la Galerie du Prince de la Paix à la suite de l'examen qui en a été fait par le Baron de Stenben, peintre de la Cour Imperiale de Russie. *Ibid.*, p. 20, 21.

76. Letter from Count Pozzo di Borgo to K. Nesselrode, 28 January/9 February 1831. *Ibid.*, p. 26. The total number of paintings belonging to Godoy, as noted later by Lafontaine, was 296 (*ibid.*, p. 271) which is one less than the number given earlier in the documents published by La Croix.

77. Report by F. Labensky to the Oberhofmarschall K. Naryshkin. The Hermitage archives, inv. 2, file 10, 1831, p. 1.

78. Central state Historical Archives, fund 472, inv. 12, file 817, p. 49.

79. *Ibid.*, p. 51.

80. *Ibid*, p. 78, 86

81. The Hermitage archives, inv. 2, file 10, 1831, p. 10.

82. Some documents in the Central state Historical Archives can provide interesting information about the art dealer Lafontaine, who selected thirty-three paintings from the list compiled by von Stenben. He had to wait for two years for appreciation of his services. He wrote in one of his letters that he made the acquaintance of Labensky's brother in Paris (where he was second secretary at the Russian embassy). The latter advised Lafontaine to offer eight paintings to the Hermitage but this offer was refused. Lafontaine appealed to Pozzo di Borgo but without success. In a letter to P. Volkonsky he complained about the impolite attitude of the ambassador and asked it to be remembered that he had kept secret the negotiations about the sale of the paintings from Godoy's gallery and that nobody in London had seen them. Volkonsky asked Pozzo di Borgo what kind of gift would be due to Lafontaine and the ambassador suggested a snuff-box for two or three thousand roubles — an equivalent to one once given by Alexander I for the appraisal of the Malmaison Gallery. A report sent to Volkonsky says: "I have the honour of presenting thereby the manufactured gold snuff-box decorated with diamonds and a mosaic landscape, evaluated at two thousand five hundred roubles as a gift graciously bestowed on the Royal French painter Lafontaine in recognition of his efforts in the selection of the paintings purchased from the Prince of the Peace for the Imperial Court." On 8 September 1833 Lafontaine sent a letter of thanks for the snuff-box (Central State Historical Archives, fund 472, inv. 12, file 817, p. 103-118).

83. The Hermitage archives, inv. 2, file 10, 1831 p. 6.

84. Cat. 1797-1850, No. 4538; Viardot 1844, p. 465.

85. Curtis 1883, p. 224, No. 380

86. Rose Wagner (1983, p. 723, note 20) assumes that Wilkie regarded this painting as being the best in Godoy's collection but this assumption is groundless.

87. L. Viardot (1844, p. 464) ascribed the painting to Herrera the Younger. G. Waagen (1864, p. 111) questioned the attribution to Murillo. A question mark was put after Murillo's name in the catalogue of 1863. Liphart noted in the catalogue of 1912 that W. von Loga attributed the painting to a Madrid artist but did not give his name. During his visit to the Hermitage E. Tormo ascribed the painting to Francisco Ribalta and it was entered thus in the catalogue of 1912. A tentative attribution to Juan Rizi was suggested in the catalogue of 1958. In the catalogue of 1976 it was entered as by Ribalta (?). D. Angulo (1981, 2, p. 533, No. 2401) believes that it can be attributed to an artist from the circle of Ribalta.

88. F. Labensky assumed that the painting shows St. Peter the Dominican, St. Dominic and St. Florian. He made the following comment on the original name of the canvas: "It is a double error. The patron saint of Valencia is not St. Lawrence but St. Vicente Ferrer, and the latter was not a martyr. We presume that the painter portrayed St. Florian, the Roman legionnaire sentenced to drowning with a millstone round his neck" (Labensky 1838, p. 409). W. Stirling (1848, 3, p. 1434) suggested that St. Dominic and St. Peter the Dominican are portrayed alongside St. Florian. G. Waagen (1864, p. 111) believed that the principal character in the painting is St. Quirinus, rather than St. Florian. Ch. Curtis (1883, p. 265) called the painting *St. Quirinus, St. Dominic and St. Raymond of Penafort*. E. Liphart entered it as *Three Saints* in the catalogue of 1912, noting that St. Vicente is at the centre, St. Vicente Ferrer with a key in his hand, on the right, and St. Raymond of Penafort, on the left, "with the index finger of his right hand raised as if preaching". In the catalogues of 1958 and 1976 the painting is named *Three Saints* without comments on who is depicted. The catalogue of 1912 gave the most correct comment but it confused the iconographic descriptions of St. Vicente Ferrer and St. Raymond of Penafort.

89. V. Antonov examined documents in the Central State Historical Archives on the acquisition of the paintings by A. Gessler and published them in Antonov 1982, p. 287-302. See also Levinson-Lessing 1985, p. 150, 288, note 192.

90. Letter from A. Gessler to the Imperial Court Minister P. Volkonsky. The Hermitage archives, inv. 2, file 26, 1833.

91. *Ibid.*, file 24, 1834.

92. The manuscript catalogue of 1797-1850 (vol. 3, p. 206) contains the following record: "All these paintings from 4708 to 4718, a total of 11, were delivered to the Hermitage in

accordance with the order of the Court administration of 25 May 1835, No. 3007, and were entered in the catalogue according to the instruction of the above administration of 7 September 1835. No. 5869."

93. See the commentary to the *Adoration of the Shepherds* (No. 2).

94 See the commentary to the *Presentation in the Temple* (No. 23).

95. *The Infant Christ Asleep.* Oil on canvas. 60.1 x 51 cm. The Hermitage. Inv. No. 8836. There is an engraving by Giacomo Francia de Bologna dated 1657 that depicts the sleeping Infant Christ and bears the same inscription (see Angulo 1981, 1, p. 422).

96. The sale of paintings from the Hermitage is discussed in N. Wrangel, "Iskusstvo i Gosudar Nikolai Pavlovich" [Art and the Tsar Nikolai Pavlovich], *Starye gody,* 1913, July-September, p. 53, 163 (see p. 142 for the note on this painting).

97. L. A. Chereisky, *Pushkin i ego okruzheniye* [Pushkin and His Milieu], Leningrad, 1976, p. 304.

98. On the receipt of pictures from cavalier Paez de la Cadena for the Imperial Hermitage see The Hermitage archives, inv. 2, file 31, 1834, p. 1.

99. *Ibid.,* p. 3.

I00. Wrangel, *op. cit.*, p. 78, 122.

101. See the commentary to the *Boy with a Wreath of Oak Leaves* (Petrodvorets, Monplaisir Palace, Cat. No. 74).

102. Oil on canvas. 25 x 42.5 cm. The Hermitage. Inv. No. 9322.

103. Catalogue of 1912 notes that the attribution to Murillo was rejected and the name of Pedro Nunez de Villavicencio was suggested by E. Tormo and V. von Loga (Cat. 1912, p. 245, 246, No. 376). D. Angulo believes that the painter was not Spanish (Angulo 1981, 2, p. 539, No. 2473).

104. Canningham 1848. 2, p. 248, 257. The provenance of the painting was traced by Ch. Curtis (1883, p. 134). Prior to its acquisition by the Hermitage it was known as the *Assumption of the Virgin,* as were many other paintings by Murillo on the subject of the Immaculate Conception.

105. On two ancient bowls... and four pictures sent to the Hermitage from abroad see The Hermitage archives, inv. 2, file 17, 1842, p. 8.

106. N. Soult is discussed in Gaya Nuño 1958, p. 17, 18.

107. *Ibid.*, p. 18.

108. Letter from P. Volkonsky to the head of the 2nd Department of the Hermitage F. Bruni. The Hermitage archives, inv. 2, file 47, 1852, p. 1.

109. Letter from F. Bruni to the Imperial Court Minister P. Volkonsky, 18 March 1852. *Ibid,* p. 2.

110. Letter from F. Bruni to the Imperial Court Minister P. Volkonsky, 10 April 1852. *Ibid.,* p. 9.

111. Letter of 19 April/7 May 1852 from F. Bruni. *Ibid.,* p. 15.

112. *Ibid., p.* 16.

113. *Ibid., p.* 17.

114.. Angulo 1981, 2, No. 281.

115. Cat. 1774. This catalogue was published in only sixty copies but it has been reprinted in the following books : J. Bernoulli, *Reisen durch Brandenburg, Pommern, Curland, Russland und Polen in den Jahren 1777 und 1778,* vol. 4, Leipzig, 1780, p. 165-277 ; *Revue Universelle des Arts,* 1861, vol. 13, p. 164-179, 244-258; vol. 14, p. 212-225; vol. 15, p. 47-53, 116-119.

116. Cat. 1773-1783, Cat. 1785.

117. Cat. 1797-1850.

118. G. Georgi, *op. cit.,* see note 14.

119. Schnitzler 1828. 120 *Ibid.*, p. 110.

121. Labensky 1838. 122 Viardot 1844.

123. Stirling 1848.

124. See note 96.

125. Inventory 1859. 126 Somov 1859.

127. Cat. 1863.

128. *Ibid.*, p. 19, 20.

129. Waagen 1864.

130. *Ibid.*, p. 17.

132. Curtis 1883. 132 Cat. 1889.

133. A. Beruete published a paper on the Hermitage paintings (Beruete 1904). In 1912 E. Tormo delivered a series of lectures in Madrid on works of art in Central and Eastern Europe; this remained unpublished but is known to Spanish art historians thanks to Gaya Nuño's book (Gaya Nuño 1958, p. 10, 11).

134. Cat. 1912.

135. The main works of Justi, Mayer and von Loga are : Justi 1892 ; Mayer 1913 ; Loga 1923.

136. Benois 1910.

137. Cat. 1948. Cat. 1957 ; Cat. 1961. K. Malitskaya also published a book in which a separate section is devoted to Murillo's work (see Malitskaya 1947).

138. Cat. 1958 ; Cat. 1976.

139. Schmidt 1926 ; Levina 1969.

140. Angulo 1961 ; Angulo 1964 ; Angulo 1966, p. 147 ; Angulo 1974.

141. Braham 1965, p. 445 ; Stechow 1966, p. 167 ; Jordan 1968 ; Brown 1970, p. 265-277 ; Brown 1976 ; Brown 1978 ; Gaya Nuño 1978 ; Haraszti-Takács 1977 ; Haraszti-Takács 1978 ; Haraszti-Takács 1982 ; Ressort 1983.

142. Angulo 1981.

143. Goya 1982, Nos. 169-171.

144. 1984 Leningrad, Hermitage (cat. compiled by L. Kagané). Kagané also published a paper on the history of the Murillo collection in the Hermitage (Kagané 1987, Collection of Spanish Painting).

145. Viazmenskaya 1987.

THE COLLECTIONS
of the Russian Museums

The Esquilache Immaculate Conception.
The Hermitage, St.Petersburg.

1. THE ESQUILACHE IMMACULATE CONCEPTION

1645-1655.
Oil on canvas. 235 x 196 cm.
The Hermitage, St. Petersburg. Inv. No. 7146.

The doctrine of the Immaculate Conception teaches that the Virgin Mary was conceived without original sin, as was Christ. It became particularly widespread in the sixteenth century. The Dominicans in Italy, however, regarded it as a heresy. The Spanish Church which took an active part in the ensuing theological strife persistently asked the Pope to give official approval of the doctrine. Spaniards were enthusiastic about the papal edicts of 1617 and 1622 which ordered removal of any mention of original sin in liturgies in honour of the Virgin. In the mid-seventeenth century the theological controversy was resumed because the Dominicans prohibited the depiction of the Immaculate Conception in some places, claiming that the concept was heretical, and attempted to win the support of the Inquisition. The Spanish Parliament protested sharply and the knightly orders threatened to start fighting in earnest. As a result, in 1661 Pope Alexander VII issued a bull proclaiming the Immaculate Conception of the Virgin Mary. The dogma of the Immaculate Conception was finally sanctioned as late as 1854 (Tormo 1914, p. 108ff, 176ff; *The Dogma of the Immaculate Conception,* Ed. by E. D. O'Connor, C.S.C., University of Notre Dame, 1958, pp. 32, 490ff). The iconography of this subject in painting was not firmly established, being based on the following passage from the Apocalypse: "And there appeared a great wonder in heaven; a woman clothed with the sun, and the moon under her feet, and upon her head a crown of twelve stars" (Revelation 12: 1). The earliest works always included the moon and the sun rays and sometimes they depicted God the Father and the Holy Spirit. The Virgin was accompanied by angels carrying her symbols —an olive and a palm branches, roses, irises, a mirror and a lily. In the background there were a portal and Solomon's throne at the top of the ladder (E. Mâle, *L'Art religieux de la fin du Moyen Age,* 2nd ed, 1922, p. 210ff.; K. Künstle, *Ikonographie der christlichen Kunst,* vol. 1, 1928, p. 646-658; E. Mâle, *L'Art religieux après le Concile de Trente,* Paris, 1932, p. 40-48).
The first *Inmaculadas* appeared in Spain in the sixteenth century and became particularly popular in Seville in the early seventeenth century. Francisco Pacheco suggested his iconography for the subject in his book *Art of Painting (El Arte de la Pintura).* In his own words, he was guided by the vision of Doña Beatrice de Silva, a Portuguese lady who had founded the Immaculate Conception convent in Toledo in the sixteenth century. According to Pacheco (Pacheco 1866, 2, p. 188-192), the representation "must correspond, most of all... to the revelation of the Evangelist approved by the Catholic Church and the authority of the saints... In this purest sacrament the Virgin is to be painted in the flowering of her age, at twelve or thirteen, as fair as possible, with beautiful and serious eyes, a perfectly shaped mouth and nose, and with rosy cheeks and wonderful loose golden hair. The humans have two kinds of beauty —of the body and the soul and both were incomparable in the Virgin." Pacheco continues: "She is to be painted wearing a white robe and a blue cloak as She appreared to Dona Beatrice de Silva. She is lit by the sun and... crowned with stars... Her feet resting upon the moon which, however, is a light and transparent sphere over the landscape (I have received permission for this image): it is better illuminated in its upper part and seen as a crescent with its horns pointing downwards." The latter feature is full of significance for Pacheco. He quotes the words of the famous Seville theologian Father Luis de Alcazar: "Painters should place the moon with the spherical side upwards at the feet of the Lady. But it is clear to the learned mathematicians that if the sun and the moon meet both horns must be seen so that the Lady cannot be on the convexity." Therefore, as Pacheco explains the Lady should be placed on the external surface of the sphere but illuminated by the sunlight reflected from the moon. And he continues: "At the top of the painting either God the Father or the Holy Spirit are usually depicted, or both, with the words... *Tota pulchra est anima mea.* The attributes of the earth are to be shown on the ground, while those of heaven, if any, should be placed among the clouds. The picture is to be embellished with full length seraphs and angels holding some of the attributes... Yet the painters have the right to improve on everything I have talked about." The last remark indicates that the subject could be interpreted quite freely and, indeed, while generally following Pacheco's instructions, the Seville painters did not feel restricted by them. In the second half of the

Above and following pages:
The Esquilache Immaculate Conception. Details.
The Hermitage, St. Petersburg.

seventeenth century they refrained from depicting a landscape at the bottom of the picture and omitted many other attributes as well. Evidence of this is Murillo's *Walpole Immaculate Conception.*

The painting entered the Hermitage as an original by Murillo and most experts always regarded it as an authentic work by the master. But as early as the late nineteenth century Justi (1892) suggested that it was produced by the artist's studio and this opinion was supported by Mayer (1923). Angulo (1981) classified it as an original, albeit with a reservation that he had never seen it and made such a conclusion on the basis of a photograph. He did not rule out the possibility that the work is a good studio copy. The picture was not included in the Hermitage catalogue of 1958 and in the catalogue of l976 there is a question mark beside Murillo's name. Most judgements about it were made on the strength of photographs In 1930 the picture was in the restoration workshop and from 1941 to 1981 it was stored in a roll. It was unrolled only for the exhibition Murillo and Seventeenth-Century Andalusian Artists in the Hermitage Collection (Leningrad, 1984). The quality of painting, the originality of the composition, the lively treatment of the detail and, finally, X-ray examination confirm the attribution to Murillo.

The angels at the bottom left of the picture are similar to the *putti* in the *Angel's Kitchen* (1646, Louvre, Paris). They lack any special idealization and their gestures are businesslike. One of the angels at the top right recalls the Infant Christ in the *Virgin and Child* (1650-1655, Prado. Madrid). The angel with roses shown in profile at the bottom left is highly characteristic of Murillo: precisely the same curving contour tracing the leg and the body can be seen in a number of his early works, for example, *San Pedro Nolasco before the Virgin of Mercy* (1645-1650, Museo de Bellas Artes, Seville). The arrangement of the angels in the upper part of the Hermitage painting is also similar to that in *San Pedro Nolasco*. The Hermitage canvas also bears some affinities to the so-called *Large Immaculate Conception* (1650-1655) from the Seville museum: in both cases the Virgin has arms folded before her, and her head is turned to the left; one foot is on the moon with horns directed downwards and the other foot is on a cloud; the clouds in both paintings are almost identical in shape, and the angels looking out from behind the cloud are similar.

The angels at the bottom right in the Hermitage canvas deserve particular mention. One of them is screened by a cloud so that only the bottom part of the figure is seen and such a facetious feature was never repeated in the versions of this work produced in Murillo's studio.

Various dates have been suggested for this painting. Mayer (1913) assigned it to 1660-1670, Gaya Nuño (1978) placed it at *c.* 1670 and Angulo (1981, 2) between 1665 and 1675. In the Hermitage catalogue of 1976 it is dated to the 1660s. Art historians thus agree that the painting could not have been executed before the 1660s. However,

this can hardly be accepted. The technique is close to that of Murillo's early works. The paints are applied in dense and impasted strokes, the outlines of the bodies and objects are very distinct, and the halo around Virgin's head is of a saturated ochreous colour which is close in tonality to Murillo's works of the 1640s. X-ray examination has revealed short precise brushstrokes similar to those in Murillo's works of the 1650s, such as *Boy with a Dog* and the *Annunciation* (both in the Hermitage; Viazmenskaya 1987).

The painting bears an iconographic affinity to works by Murillo's forerunners. The subject is treated in approximately the same way as in Alonso Cano's *Immaculate Conception* of 1642-1645 (it was in the San Isidoro church in Madrid and was destroyed in 1937) and in his *Immaculate Conception* of 1650-1652 (Museo Vittona, Valencia). In both paintings the Virgin is supported by a crescent moon with horns pointing downwards, her hands are folded in a gesture of prayer, her head is turned to the left and the heads of angels are seen at her feet. Cherubs also occur in the upper left corner. Some of the angels depicted full-length in the upper right and lower left corners carry the attributes of the Virgin: lilies, roses and a palm branch. The angels do not look weightless and easily floating as they do in Murillo's mature and later works: they are solid and their faces have a portrait quality — and this is how Murillo painted angels in his early period. It should be particularly emphasized that from the latter half of the 1650s Murillo used to depict the Virgin on a crescent moon with horns pointing upwards and illuminated both from below and from above. In the Hermitage painting, however, the horns are pointing downwards, a feature already noted in the literature (MacLaren-Braham 1970) though related to the conjecture that the painting was not an original. In our opinion, this feature is explained by the fact that the painting belongs to the early period of Murillo's career when he still closely followed Pacheco's instructions. On the basis of the above arguments, the canvas should be dated to 1645-1655.

Provenance: until 1785 Collection of Leopoldo Gregorio, Marquis of Esquilache, Sicily and Venice; Collection of Cardinal Gregorio, Rome; Collection of Pope Pius VI (Giovanni Angelo Braschi), Rome; 1799 Inherited by the Duke of Braschi, a nephew of Pius VI, Rome; 1842 Acquired for the Hermitage from the Duke of Braschi.

A replica is in the National Gallery, Melbourne (231 x 204 cm).

Exhibitions: 1984 Leningrad, No. 14.

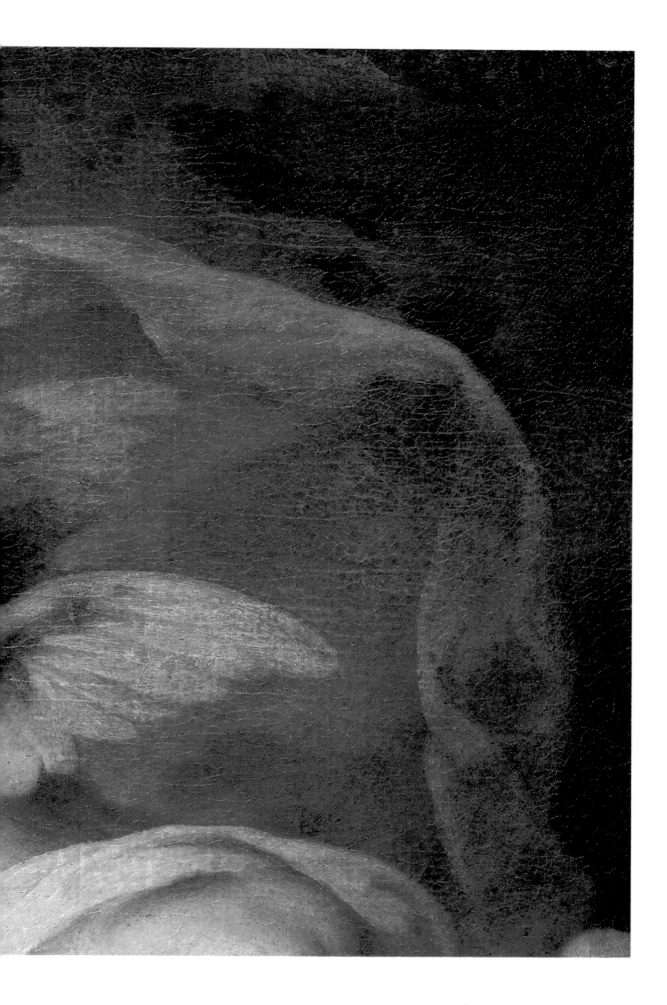

2. THE ADORATION OF THE SHEPHERDS

1646-1650.
Oil on canvas. 197 x 147 cm.
The Hermitage, St. Petersburg. Inv. No. 316.

Experts at the Hermitage restoration workshop in 1968-1969 found that the back side of the original canvas had once been coated with a dense mixture of oil, glue and chalk. The vertical seam connecting the left-hand and right-hand sides of the canvas was covered by a layer of ground chalk and glue up to 4 cm wide that concealed the negligible canvas losses along the seam. These layers had not been removed when the painting was relined some time in the past. It is, probably, precisely these layers that produced a large, sharply distinct craquelure on the painted surface that bears but a vague resemblance to the craquelures visible in other Murillo canvases. The restorers were only partially successful in reducing the relief of the craquelure and the seam. At the lower edge of the painting the threads are markedly taut owing to the fixing of the canvas to the stretcher — an indication that this edge was not cut. At the upper edge the threads are not taut suggesting that the edge probably was cut. The edges of the canvas were also removed. Numerous spots of retouching are present.

The earliest literary sources for the subject of the Adoration of the Shepherds are the Gospel according to St. Luke (2 : 15-20) and the apocrypha —the Protevangelium (Book of James) and the Pseudo-Matthew. New details were gradually added to these texts by other religious writers and a tradition of treating this subject was established in painting. The Seville artists were guided by the instructions given in Pacheco's *Art of Painting.* According to tradition, the Infant Jesus was born in a cave that was used for sheltering animals. Jesus was born at midnight and angels brought the news of this birth to the shepherds who came to adore the baby — "the purest and the fairest" as Pacheco refers to Him (Pacheco 1866, 2, p. 216-220). Pacheco wrote of two types of the representation in one, the new-born baby lies naked on the floor and the Virgin, St. Joseph and angels adore Him; in the other, the baby lies in the manger with animals around Him and shepherds watching Him. Pacheco insists that at the moment of the shepherds' coming the baby must lie wrapped in swaddling clothes in the manger strictly according to the words of St. Luke. He remarks, though, that artists preferred to paint a naked baby because "poverty is expressed better in this way" and "the naked baby is more beautiful than a swaddled one". Pacheco refers to the texts according to which three shepherds came to Jesus. As for the gifts brought by them, opinions differed. Some authorities said that the gifts were brought while others claimed that the shepherds were in a hurry, the time was late and therefore they could not bring gifts. Pacheco illustrated his instructions with a painting by Juan de Roelas who relied on a work by Bassano (this fact suggests that the Venetian painting tradition was established in Seville at that time).

Murillo follows Pacheco's guidelines in many respects. The painting is a night interior scene : the baby is in the manger, the Virgin, St. Joseph and three shepherds stand looking down on Him, the animals are at the side and the lamb brought as a gift is in the forefront. However, contrary to the insistent instructions of Pacheco, Murillo depicts a naked baby in keeping with the well-established tradition. The figures in the scene include an old woman Zelomia who, according to the apocryphal sources, came to assist the Virgin when asked by St. Joseph. All experts who wrote about this painting noted the bright glow that came from the baby in darkness. This feature could have been prompted by the following words from the Protevangelium : "And the cave suddenly was filled with a glow so bright that the eyes could not behold it and when the glow slowly subsided they saw the Infant" (1946, 47).

The painting was traditionally attributed to Murillo. It was listed as a Murillo already in the first edition of Aedes Walpolianae (1747), and this attribution was maintained in all Hermitage catalogues until 1912. Doubts about Murillo's authorship were first voiced by Mayer who did not include the painting in his catalogue (Mayer 1913). Schmidt wrote : "The *Adoration of the Shepherds* is cited here as an authentic Murillo with a reservation since the artist's authorship has been questioned in some quarters" (Schmidt 1926). The painting is noted as belonging to the school of Murillo in the Hermitage catalogue of 1958. However, Angulo (1964, 1981) and Braham (1965) insisted that the painting was an original. The Hermitage catalogue of 1976 lists it as a Murillo original.

Murillo's authorship may have been questioned owing to the painted surface. This looks unusual

The Adoration of the Shepherds. Details.
The Hermitage, St.Petersburg.

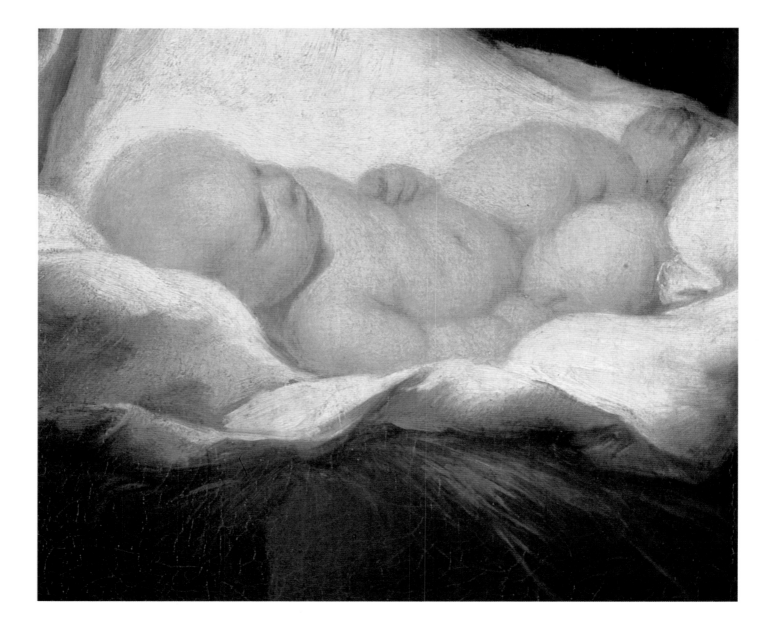

for the artist but, as is mentioned above, the craquelure that does not occur in other paintings by Murillo was caused by an old restoration. Close analogues to this painting are the *Angel's Kitchen* (1646, Louvre, Paris) and, particularly, the *Last Supper* (1650, Sta. Maria la Blanca, Seville). The gesture of the arms of the shepherd in the foreground of the *Adoration* is very similar to that of the monk standing in the right background of the *Angel's Kitchen* and to the gesture of another character that enters the door on the left. These paintings also share the sharp contrasts of light. In the character of lighting the *Adoration* is closest to the *Last Supper*; the brightly lit table in the latter produces a contrast as sharp as that of the swaddled baby in the former; the spots of light are similarly distributed on the faces in both paintings, the types of the men's faces and the gestures of the characters are also similar.

The Hermitage *Adoration* is reminiscent of the Prado *Adoration of the Shepherds* in the treatment of the subject but differs from the latter in its vertically elongated format and, hence, in composition. Both paintings are night scenes illuminated by the dazzling glow radiating from the Infant, the peasant-type faces, and the shepherd with bare feet in the foreground. The mangers with the Infant look similar, as also do the women's faces and the folds of the cloaks of St. Joseph and the young shepherd standing to the right.

All experts agreed on the date of the *Adoration*. Waagen (1864) was the first to assign it to the early period of Murillo's career. This opinion was supported by Curtis (1883). According to Angulo (1981), the painting dates from *c.* 1650. The use of chiaroscuro is typical of Murillo's early manner. It is close to the *Angel's Kitchen* and the *Last Supper* which is dated 1650. Since the Hermitage *Adoration* is close in style to the *Adoration* from the Prado which is dated to 1646-1650, it can also be assigned to the same period.

Provenance: 1779 Acquired for the Hermitage as part of the Walpole collection, Houghton Hall, England. Its pendant was thought to be the *Walpole Immaculate Conception*.

No oil copies of this work are known.

An engraving of the painting was made by V. Green (Set of Prints 1788, p. 3, XXIV)

Exhibitions: 1984 Leningrad, No. 15.

The Last Supper.
1650, Sta. Maria la Blanca, Seville.

The Adoration of the Shepherds.
Engraving by V. Green from Murillo's Painting.

68

The Adoration of the Shepherds. Detail.
The Hermitage, St. Petersburg.

3. BOY WITH A DOG

1655-1660.
Oil on canvas. 70 x 60 cm
The Hermitage, St. Petersburg. Inv. No. 386.

Boy With a Dog and its pendant, *Girl with Fruit and Flowers,* comprise the only extant pair of genre paintings by Murillo. The works are interrelated both in composition and in subject. Brown noted that Murillo's genre paintings have a concealed meaning (J. Brown, "Murillo, pintor de temas eróticos. Una faceta inadvertida de su obra", *Goya,* 1982, Nos. 169-171, p. 35-43). He compared them with the *bambocciata* genre paintings executed by the Italian, Dutch and Flemish artists living in Rome in the mid-seventeenth century; such works were very popular among the Spanish art patrons. Brown came to the conclusion that Murillo employed the same allegories in his works. Although he did not mention *Boy with a Dog* and *Girl with Fruit and Flowers,* thanks to his analysis their hidden symbolism can be easily revealed — the girl smiling shyly holds a basket with fruit a symbol of maturity while the laughing boy shows the dog a basket that contains a jar — an object associated with woman in the iconography of seventeenth-century art.

Another pair of Murillo's paintings depicting a boy and a girl were known in the eighteenth century. They belonged to the Countess de Verru, then they were sold to Paillet and later appeared at the auction of the collection of Randon de Boisset in Paris in 1777 (Curtis 1883). The paintings were identified as *A Peasant Boy Leaning on a Sill* (National Gallery, London) and *Girl Raising the Zeil* (Carras collection, London). However, Angulo (1981, 2, p. 298) voiced doubts that these works had been in the Verru collection and that they had been produced as a pair.

Boy with a Dog is traditionally regarded as Murillo's original and its attribution was never questioned. Mayer (1913) dated it to 1650-1660, Sullivan (1975-1976) placed it at *c.* 1661, Gaya Nuño (1978) at *c.* 1660 and Angulo (1981, 2) before 1660. In the Hermitage catalogues of 1958 and 1976 it is assigned to the 1650s. Its technique differs from that of Murillo's mature and later works: the outlines are not soft and the gradations of colours not sophisticated. The clothes are painted with dense flowing brushstrokes. The shirt's open collar is rendered by a long stroke of white as in *Beggar Boy* (Louvre, Paris) and *Boys*

Girl Raising the Veil.
Carras Collection. London.

A Peasant Boy Leaning on a Sill.
National Gallery. London.

Boy with a Dog.
The Hermitage, St. Petersburg.

Following pages: *Boy with a Dog.* Details.
The Hermitage, St. Petersburg.

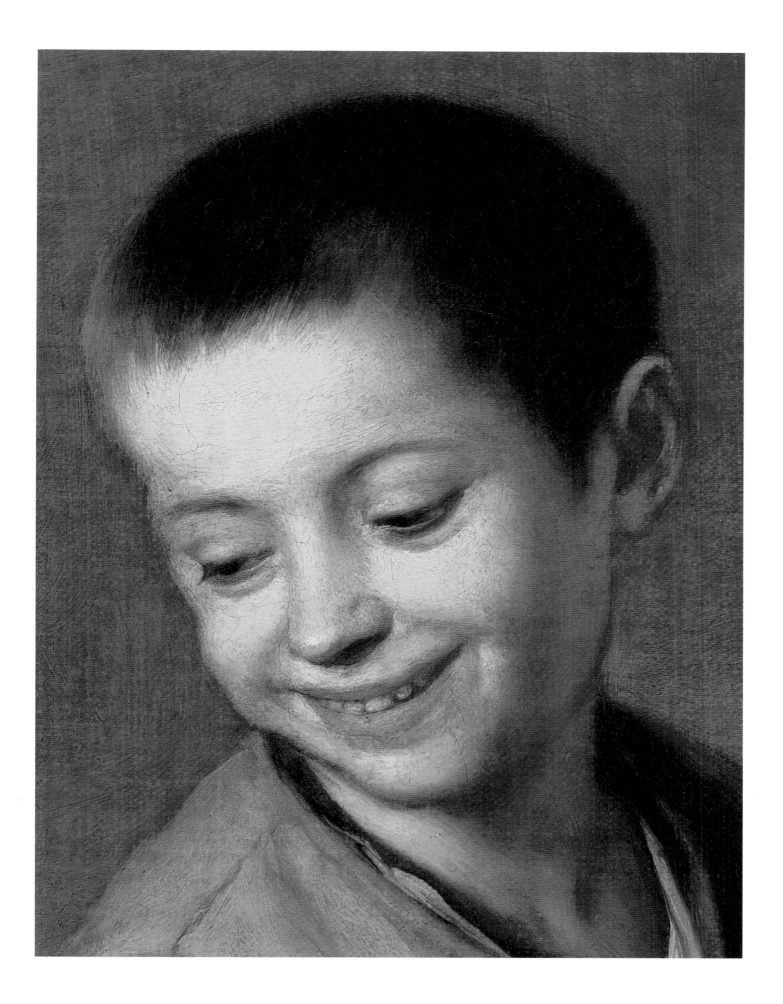

Eating Melon and Grapes (Alte Pinakothek, Munich). The outline of the jacket sleeve with a peculiar semicircular edge is also similar to that in the Louvre painting. The type of the boys in all three paintings is almost identical. Murillo is not yet seeking idealisation and endows the street urchins with lively expressive faces. The Louvre *Beggar Boy,* the earliest of Murillo's known genre paintings, is executed in the light-and-shade manner and is dated to 1645-1650. *Boys Eating Melon and Grapes* can also be assigned to *c.* 1650. Its background is also dark but the colour scheme is more complicated and varied. Seen on the right is a wall which resembles the wall in *Boy with a Dog.* The Hermitage painting was executed later than the two cited works because it has a landscape in the background. The pale blue and green background and the wall overgrown with verdure recall the background of the Hermitage *St. Lawrence* by Zurbarán. *Boy with a Dog* is, perhaps, one of Murillo's first works painted against a natural landscape in keeping with the Seville, or more specifically, Zurbarán tradition. The painting can be dated to the late 1650s.

In 1793 *Boy with a Dog* and *Girl with Fruit and Flowers* were copied by Yakov Yakimovich for a tapestry factory in St. Petersburg (Central State Historical Archives, fund 468, inv. L, part 2, file 4027, 1793, p. 132). The location of these copies is not known.

Engraved by : K. W. Weisbrod (Choiseul 1771. No. 100), G. Cardelli (dedicated to Alexander I), K. Mosolov and V. Dollet (Hermitage Gallery 1845 -1847, vol. 2 : 18).
On the basis of an engraving from this painting Edouard Manet made a similar engraving, *Le Gamin,* and a similar picture. *Portrait of the Artist's Son* (private collection, Paris).

Provenance : 1772 Acquired in Paris at the sale of the collection of Duc de Choiseul et Amboise (together with its pendant, *Girl with Fruit and Flowers,* Pushkin Museum of Fine Arts, No. 4).

Exhibitions : 1970 Osaka, vol. 4, No. 200; 1975-1976 USA-Mexico-Canada, No. 14; 1981 Madrid, p. 18, 19; 1984 Leningrad, No. 16; 1987-1988 Belgrade-Ljubljana-Zagreb. No. II.

Zurbarán. *St. Lawrence.*
1636, The Hermitage, St. Petersburg.

74

E. Manet. *Le Gamin.*
Engraving.

E. Manet. *Portrait of the Artist's Son.*
Private collection. Paris.

4. *GIRL WITH FRUIT AND FLOWERS*

1655-1660.
Oil on canvas. 76 x 61 cm.
Inv. No. 2670.
The Pushkin Museum of Fine Arts, Moscow.

See the note on *Boy With a Dog.*

Provenance: 1772 Acquired for the Hermitage by A. Golitsyn at the sale of the collection of Duc de Choiseul et Amboise in Paris (together with its pendant, *Boy with a Dog,* Hermitage); 1930 Transferred to the Pushkin Museum of Fine Arts, Moscow.

Engraved by: G. Weisbrod (Choiseul 1771, No. 101), G. Cardelli and V. Dollet (Hermitage Gallery 1845-1847, vol. 2: 22)

Exhibitions: 1984 Leningrad, No. 17.

Girl with Fruit and Flowers. Detail.
The Pushkin Museum of Fine Arts, Moscow.

Girl with Fruit and Flowers.
The Pushkin Museum of Fine Arts, Moscow

Girl with Fruit and Flowers. Detail.
The Pushkin Museum of Fine Arts, Moscow.

5. *THE INFANT JESUS AND ST. JOHN*

1655-1660.
Oil on canvas. 124 x 115 cm.
The Hermitage, St. Petersburg. Inv. No. 335.

The Gospels do not mention any meeting between Christ and St. John the Baptist in their infancy. Moreover, Fransisco Pacheco regarded such representations as a sign of simplicity and ignorance (Pacheco 1866, 2, p. 276). Nevertheless, the subject was widely used in art. This tradition goes back to fourteenth-century Florence and, according to art historians, is linked with the Renaissance world outlook and its admiration of children *(putti)* as well as with the veneration of St. John the Baptist as the patron saint of Florence (G. B. Lavin, "A Study in the Renaissance Religious Symbolism", *Art Bulletin*, 1955, June, p. 85-101). The subject of the Infant Jesus and St. John became popular thanks to an engraving by Guido Reni which was probably used by Rubens (his painting has not survived but is known from an engraving and numerous copies, one of which is in the Hermitage, Inv. No. 7359). Murillo's picture is close to them in many respects.

The painting entered the Hermitage as a Murillo original but Waagen (1864) questioned its authenticity and it was listed as a copy in the catalogue of 1863. Later, in the catalogue of 1892, Somov erroneously identified this work as a copy of the famous *Children with the Shell* in the Prado. In the catalogue of 1912 Liphart attributed it to Murillo's studio. Von Loga (1923) ascribed it without good reason to the Spanish painter Bernardo Llorente. The catalogue of 1976 lists the painting as a seventeenth-century copy of the Murillo original. The last cleaning in 1984 has shown the high quality of the painting, which again suggested that it was an original. A comparison of its radiograph with those of other works demonstrated an especially close affinity to the artist's paintings executed before 1660 (Viazmenskaya 1987).

Stylistically the picture is close to such works as *Girl with Fruit and Flowers* (Pushkin Museum, Moscow) in which the landscape and the still life are painted in a similar manner; the *Education of the Virgin Mary* (Prado, Madrid) which has a similar motif of descending angels; and the *Virgin with St. Rose of Lima* (Thyssen-Bornemisza collection, Prado, Madrid) in which the Child looks like the Infant Jesus in the Hermitage painting.

Since all the above works date from the second half of the 1650s, the Hermitage canvas may also be dated to the same period.
The Prado version, *Children with the Shell*, was produced later, in 1665-1670.

Provenance: The Royal Palace in Madrid; 1852 Acquired for the Hermitage by F. Bruni in Paris at the sale of the Marshal Soult collection.

Copies: Margrane collection, Barcelona; Church of San Anton, Seville.

*The Infant Jesus and St. John.
(Children with the Shell).
1665-1670, Prado, Madrid.*

Engraved by M. Carmona in 1799 with the inscription: *Dedicado al Lxmo. Sr. D.n Luis Maria de Borbon, Conde de Chinchon, Caballero de la Gran Cruz Real distinguida Orden Española de Carlos III. Arzobispo de Sevilla Grande de España de primera Clase. Por Don Manuel Salvador y Carmona grabador de Cámara de S. M.* (Dedicated to the gracious Signor Don Luis Maria de Bourbon, Count de Chinchon, Cavalier of the Cross of the Spanish Royal Order of Charles III, Archbishop of Seville, Spanish Grandee of the first rank. By Don Manuel Salvador y Carmona, Engraver to His Royal Majesty). There are good reasons to believe that it was the Hermitage painting which used to be in the Royal Palace in Madrid and which disappeared during the French invasion in the early nineteenth century. It completely coincides with the engraving made by Carmona. The size of the painting listed in the Inventory of the Royal Palace was 125 x 125 cm (Angulo 1981, 2, No. 217) while the size of the Hermitage painting is 124 x 115 cm, that is, the height is almost identical but the width of the Hermitage canvas is smaller since the right-hand edge has been cut. The seal of Marshal Soult has survived on the stretcher of the painting.

Exhibitions: 1984 Leningrad. No. 18.

The Infant Jesus and St. John.
The Hermitage, St. Petersburg.

Following pages :
The Infant Jesus and St. John. Details.
The Hermitage, St. Petersburg.

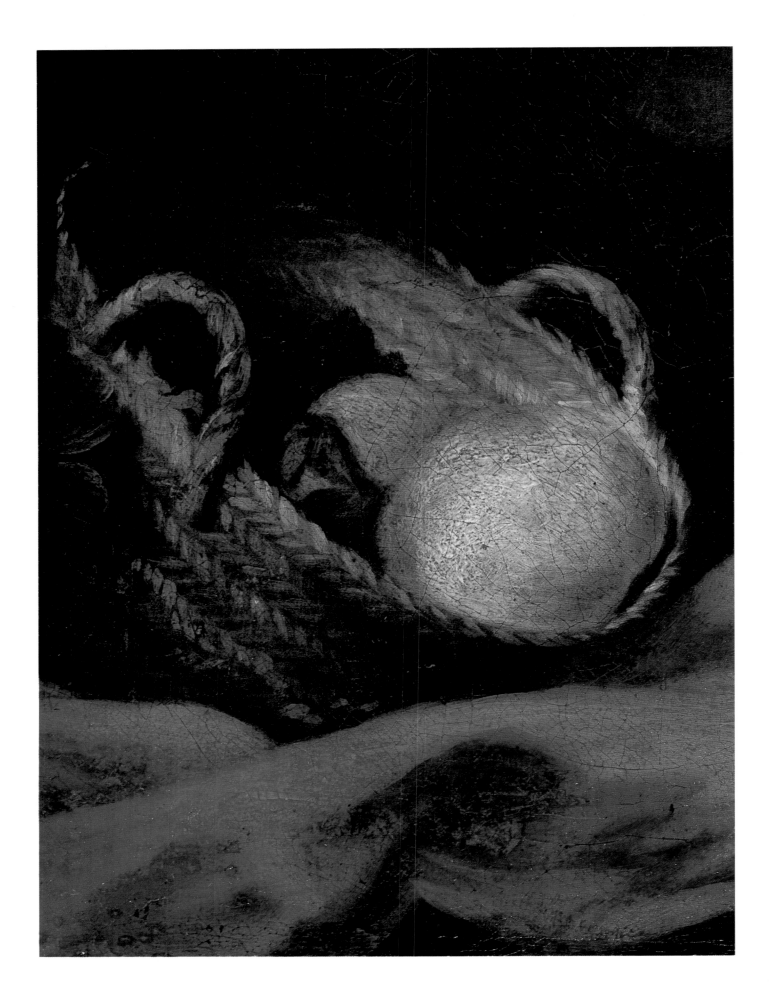

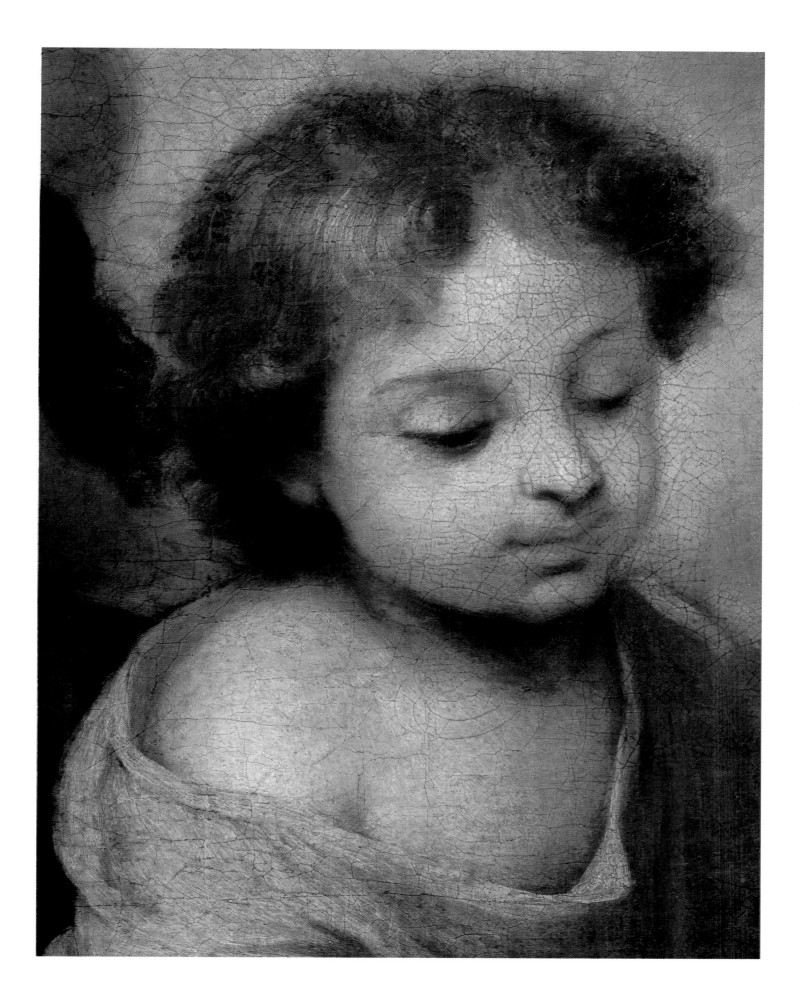

6. THE ANNUNCIATION

1655-1660
Oil on canvas. 142 x 107.5 cm.
The Hermitage, St. Petersburg. Inv. No. 346.

The main literary source for the subject of the Annunciation is the Gospel according to St. Luke (1 : 26 38). Francisco Pacheco thus describes this subject in his text, which is generally full of details: "After the return of the betrothed (Mary and Joseph — L. K.) from the temple they opened their hearts to each other on the very first night and by mutual consent gave a vow of absolute purity... They lived together in Nazareth in the house of the parents of the Virgin where she had been born and raised... Joseph plied his craft as carpenter and the Virgin... led an active and contemplative life... Four months after her betrothal the blessed time came... Archangel Gabriel came through a closed door sent by God with a message to the Holy Virgin. She was reading and meditating over Isaiah's prophesy, *Ecce Virgo Concipiet*. The angel appeared in the guise of a very handsome, light-emitting young man, modestly clothed, with a grave bearing. The conversation went on till midnight... The Virgin gave her consent, for it was precisely nine months since the moment that she gave birth to the Saviour.

"The Holy Signora was apparently kneeling before a bench or a desk with an open book on it and a table lamp aside. At nightfall she finished her work... The angel is not to be depicted descending or flying with bare feet as some painters do, he must be decently clothed and kneeling with the greatest respect before his queen and mistress and she must be modest and shy (at the age of fourteen and four months), graceful, with her hair tied down under a thin shawl, in a light blue cloak and a pink dress belted with a ribbon... The angel must have magnificent wings and simple clothes in gay, joyous tints as he was represented cleverly and successfully, decoratively and majestically by Federico Zuccaro in the *Annunciation* in Rome. In his left hand the angel may hold several lilies which are traditionally depicted since the times of the Apostles. The Virgin holds her hands down or crossed on the bosom... Above her are usually painted the Glory with the Eternal Father and many seraphs and angels, and also the Holy Ghost in the guise of a dove emitting radiant light... For greater clarity let us turn to examples. Michelangelo and Titian have left engravings on the subject. The first

The Annunciation.
The Hermitage, St. Petersburg.

depicts the Virgin standing as if she wishes to escape from the angel while the second made her coy as if she wanted to cover herself when the angel enters, and with both painters the angel is overtly naked" (Pacheco 1866, 2, p. 208-211). Murillo closely followed Pacheco's instructions and his painting can serve as an illustration to the above passage.

The attribution of the painting is traditional and never aroused any doubts. Mayer (1913, 1922) dated it to 1655-1665 and all experts later shared this opinion. Angulo (1981, 2) suggested a more precise date of *c.* 1660. Murillo started work on the subject of the Annunciation in the early 1650s. His earliest *Annunciation* is in the Prado (Inv. No. 969); it is a large, horizontally elongated canvas, the subject being treated in the grand style of Zurbarán and Ribera. A similar early variant is in the collection of Basilio Alexiades (Madrid). The Hermitage *Annunciation* was produced at a later date; the treatment of the subject is more lyrical and intimate, the number of angels is larger, the cloud with the light-emanating dove occupies a more prominent place and the outlines of the figures and objects are softened compared to the earlier versions. The paintwork is close to Murillo's canvases of the late 1650s.

Another *Annunciation* in the Prado (1655-1660, Inv. No. 970) is very similar to the Hermitage painting, although its artistic quality is inferior and it has a different colour scheme: the carmine and pink tints are replaced with sharper orange tints.

In addition to the above mentioned versions there exist other similar but later variants: in the Rijksmuseum, Amsterdam; in the Museo de Bellas Artes, Seville; in the La Caridad hospital, Seville; and in the Wallace Collection, London. In all these paintings the angel is on the right-hand side (in the Hermitage canvas, it is on the left).

The Annunciation.
1655-1660, Prado, Madrid.

Provenance: 1814 Acquired for the Hermitage from W. Coesvelt in Amsterdam.

Engraved by Huot (Hermitage Gallery 1845-1847, 2:26).

Exhibitions: 1968-1969 Belgrade, p. 29, No. 12; 1971 Tokyo Kyoto, No. 48; 1984 Leningrad, No. 19; 1985 Sapporo Fukuoka, No. 15 1988 New South Wales.

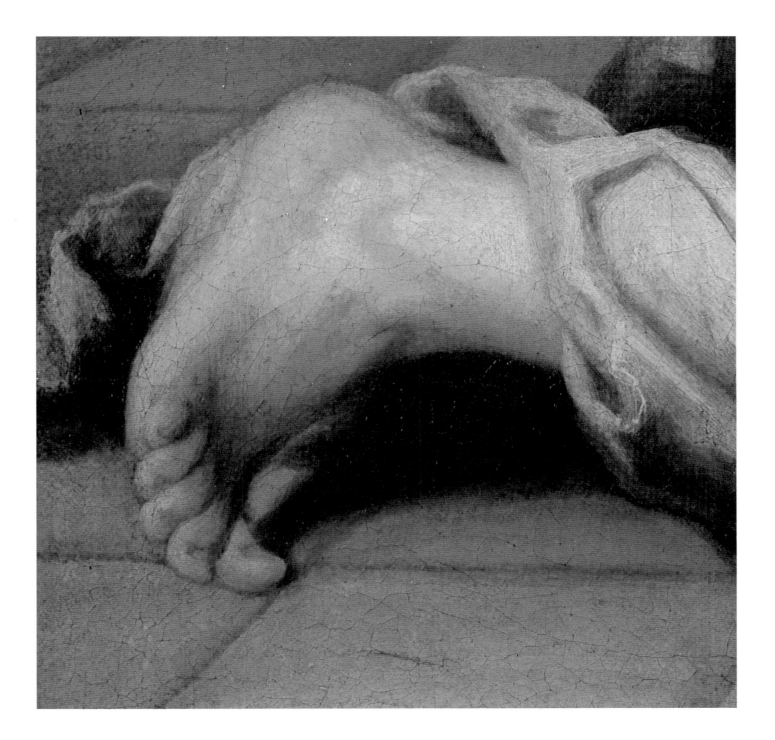

7. REST ON THE FLIGHT INTO EGYPT

1660-1665.
Oil on canvas. 136.5 x 179.5 cm.
The Hermitage, St. Petersburg. Inv. No. 340.

The subject of the *Rest on the Flight into Egypt* is closely related to that of the *Flight into Egypt*, the primary literary source for which is the New Testament (Matthew 2: 13-15). The Gospels, however, tell only about the flight of the Holy Family. The scenes of the rest on the flight are based on the apocryphal literature (Pseudo-Matthew, 13). The Seville painters who treated this subject took their guidance from Francisco Pacheco's book, *Art of Painting* (Pacheco 1866, 2, p. 235-237), in which he tells in detail how the Virgin awakened the Child at night, how the Virgin and Joseph had to hurry and could not take with them enough food and clothes, and how difficult their journey was in the wilderness. Pacheco refers to representations of the flight into Egypt by Pelegrino Tibaldi in the Escorial and by Albrecht Dürer in his engravings. He says that "if somebody wishes so he can depict this scene by the light of the moon at night... but it is difficult and therefore it is safer and more pleasant to paint it at daytime in order to avoid the rigidity of light and shade".

Murillo's heartfelt treatment of the subject echoes Pacheco's description. Such details as the sleeping Child cozily snuggling on a rock, the carefully packed belongings in the foreground and the little angels looking out from behind a bush like mischievous children, betray the artist's interest in everyday life. Iconographically the canvas is based on examples of seventeenth-century European art. Thus Angulo (1981, I, p. 420) believes that the motif of the sleeping Infant is traceable to Annibale Carracci's *Madonna with the Infant Christ and St. John the Baptist* (Hampton Court, London), an engraving from which was probably known to Murillo. Angulo also cites the *Rest on the Flight into Egypt* (early 1630s, Hermitage) by Van Dyck in which the scene includes the little playing angels. In his picture Murillo arrived at a solution consonant with those of other seventeenth-century artists, but in its originality and integrity this solution is one of the most perfect.

An earlier version is in the collection of the Count of Strafford (Barnet, Wrotham Park, 172.5 x 160 cm; Angulo 1981, 2, No. 228). It is dated to 1655-1660. The Hermitage painting is superior to this earlier version in composition, handling and colouring. X-rays reveal some changes made by Murillo during the process of work: the left wrist of the Virgin is somewhat shifted leftward and the position of the fingers is altered (Viazmenskaya 1987).

Various dates were suggested for the painting. Mayer (1913) first placed it between 1655 and 1670 but later (Mayer 1923) between 1665 and 1670. Gaya Nuño (1978) assigned it to 1668-1670. Referring to Mayer, Angulo (1981) also concludes that the painting was produced between 1665 and 1670 (although he does not give any arguments for this dating). It is therefore generally accepted that the painting was executed by Murillo in the later 1660s. However, an earlier date is not excluded. The *Rest on the Flight into Egypt* bears affinity to Murillo's *Birth of the Virgin* (Louvre, Paris). The central groups in both works are arranged along the diagonal from the lower left-hand corner to the upper right-hand corner. The little angels actively involved in the action are painted in a similar way. Both pictures are dominated by a hot brown-red tone and the paints are applied in fluid thin strokes. The landscape in the *Rest on the Flight* recalls the background in *Jacob Laying the Peeled Rods before the Flocks of Laban* (1660-1665. Meadows Museum, Dallas). At the centre of the composition, behind the Virgin, there is a cluster of bushes with a tree-trunk visible in it, and a hilly view opens to the left.

The *Birth of the Virgin* was painted in 1660, rather than 1665, as was thought earlier (D. T. Kinkead, "B. E. Murillo, New Documentation", *The Burlington Magazine*, 1979, January, p. 36, 37). The series of scenes from Jacob's life was completed by Murillo before 1665. The similarity of The *Rest on the Flight* to the above mentioned paintings suggests that the Hermitage canvas was also executed in the early, rather than late, 1660s so that the date must be 1660-1665. The X-ray examination which has revealed an underpainting similar to those occurring in Murillo's works of the early 1660s also confirms the above date (Viazmenskaya 1987).

Rest on the Flight into Egypt. Detail.
The Hermitage, St. Petersburg.

Rest on the Flight into Egypt.
The Hermitage, St. Petersburg.

Provenance: 1768 Acquired through the agency of Denis Diderot at the sale of the Jean de Gaignat collection in Paris; 1769 Entered the Hermitage.

Replicas and copies: Art Gallery, Glasgow (96.5 x 125 cm); Northbrook collection, London (137 x 166.5 cm); sale of the Loring Gallery, Madrid (138 x 183 cm); Akademie der bildenden Künste, Munich (162.3 x 188 cm); auction of the Smith collection, New York, 1910 (70.5 x 47 cm, copy of two angels); San Juan de Asanalfarache, Seville (170 x 200 cm), the composition is the same but the depiction of a woman on the left makes one think that the subject is that of the *Birth*; San Simcon, a copy by Renteyn; Juan de Soto collection, Seville (148 x 189 cm).

Engraved by J. Walker, 1789 and G. Sanders, 1805 (Hermitage Gallery 1805, p. 71, 72).

Exhibitions: 1977 Tokyo Kyoto, No. 12; 1981 Madrid, cat., p. 16, 17; 1984 Leningrad, No. 20.

A. Van Dick. *Rest on the Flight into Egypt.* Early 1630s. The Hermitage, St. Petersburg.

94

Rest on the Flight into Egypt.
1655-1660, Strafford collection.
Wrotham Park, Barnet.

◀ *Rest on the Flight into Egypt.* Details.
The Hermitage, St. Petersburg. ▼

8. *THE HOLY FAMILY*

c. 1665.
Oil on panel. 23.8 x 18 cm.
The Hermitage, St. Petersburg. Inv. No. 337.

The paint layer with the priming was transferred from the original panel to a new oakwood panel of a larger size. The edges are coated with resin and in-painted in l-cm-wide strips. Mariette (1857-1858) erroneously believed that the painting had been executed on paper glued onto a panel. European painters began to depict the everyday life of the Holy Family in the seventeenth century when the range of religious subjects in art became wider. They borrowed details from medieval legends, a source on which the following passage in Pacheco's book is based: "The Virgin, her son and her husband spent seven years in exile in Egypt... They lived among pagans, without friends and relatives, without anything but work... As the Child was growing... the Virgin was sewing a tunic of rough cloth... She clad him in it after he had been taken out of his swaddling-clothes... Their family life in Egypt in the course of seven years can be depicted by painters in a variety of ways. When I was young I decided on the following scene: in a poor house from the open door of which a part of the street is seen St. Joseph is planing a board on the carpenter's bench; a hat hangs on the wall, a saw and a compass are suspended from a rope; other tools, such as an adze, a hammer and a square, are on the floor covered with

The Holy Family.
1648-1650, National Gallery, Dublin.

The Holy Family.
c. 1650, Nooreinde Palace, The Hague.

wood shavings. The Infant Jesus, at the age of one or two, sits on the ground beside his mother, looking at the cross... The Holy Virgin dressed in a tunic and a cloak is seated on a pillow, working. Before her are a wicker basket with white cloth, scissors and thread" (Pacheco 1866, 2, p. 237).

On the whole Murillo followed Pacheco's advice but he introduced some changes which enhanced the genre character of the painting. He replaced the didactic motif of the Infant Jesus looking at the cross by the motif of the Infant held by St. Joseph reaching out for his mother.

The attribution of the painting is traditional and was never questioned. Mayer (1913) dated it to 1660-1675, Gaya Nuño (1978) c. 1665 and Angulo (1981, 2) to 1660-1665. In the Hermitage catalogue of 1958 it is assigned to 1660-1675 and in the catalogue of 1976 to 1660-1670.

The technique, fluid and flowing, with exquisite long brushstrokes, suggests a date after 1660. Some details are also close to Murillo's works of that period. The Infant strongly resembles the Child in the Hermitage *Rest on the Flight into Egypt*; the appearance of St. Joseph is also similar in both works. The sack with tools in the foreground of the *Holy Family is* placed in the bottom right-hand corner, as are the family belongings in the *Rest on the Flight into Egypt*. The architecture in the Hermitage painting differs from other versions of Murillo's *Holy Family;* the round arches and the section of the wall protruding towards the viewer

recall similar features in *Isaac Blessing Jacob* (Hermitage) dated to 1660-1665. By analogy with the above works, the *Holy Family* may be dated c. 1665. Murillo painted many works on this subject. The Hermitage picture is closely related to the versions at the National Gallery in Dublin and at the Nooreinde Palace in The Hague. There are doubts about the authenticity of a kindred version in the Ringling Museum, Sarasota (Florida, USA). Due to its small size, the Hermitage painting was often mentioned as a sketch. Munich was the first to thus classify it in the catalogue of 1773-1783. Viardot (1844) voiced the same opinion. In his latest work on Murillo, Angulo (1981, 2) also refers to the *Holy Family* as a sketch. However, back in 1838 Labensky noted that the painting looked completely finished despite its small size and could hardly be regarded as a preliminary work for a large canvas. This view can be supported by the fact that before painting this *Holy Family* Murillo had executed similar but more monumental compositions discussed above.

Provenance: The painting belonged to Duke de Tallard in Besançon. In 1756 at the posthumous auction of the Tallard assets it was sold to L. A. Crozat, Baron de Thiers (a handwritten note in the copy of the catalogue in the Institute of Arts in Paris says that the painting was purchased by Boileau who transferred it to Baron de Thiers). It was acquired for the Hermitage in 1771 together with other works from the Crozat collection (there is the Crozat stamp on the back of the panel). According to Curtis (1883), the painting entered the Hermitage later because Baron de Thiers had purchased it in 1776. Curtis, however, confused the date of the Tallard auction that had actually been held in 1756.

An engraving of the painting was made by J.-B. Tillard. One of the prints bears an inscription: X *Monsieur Crozat, Baron de Thiers. Gravé d'après le tableau original de Murillos haut de pauses 9 lignes sur 6 pouces 8 lignes de large qui est dans son cabinet* (Curtis 1883).

Exhibition: 1984 Leningrad, No. 21.

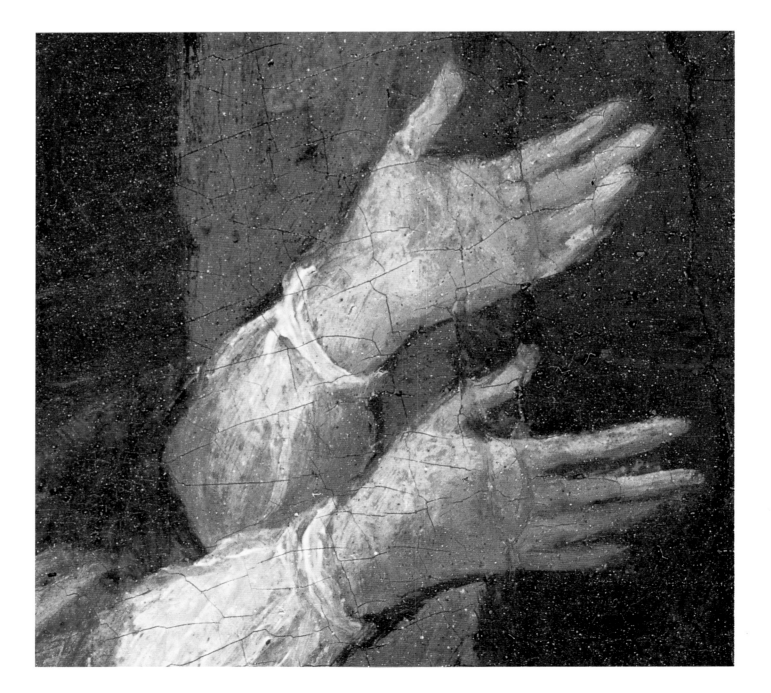

9. ISAAC BLESSING JACOB

1660-1665.
Oil on canvas. 245 x 357.5 cm.
The Hermitage, St. Petersburg. Inv. No. 332.

The subject is borrowed from the biblical story of Jacob (who also received the name of Israel). A son of Isaac and Rebecca, Jacob was much more inclined for a settled life than his elder twin brother the hunter Esau. When they were young Esau sold his birthright to Jacob for the pottage of lentils. Later Rebecca who believed that Jacob was more worthy of Isaac's inheritance obtained for him his father's blessing by guile. Jacob fled from his brother's wrath and on his journey to Harran he lay down to sleep. He dreamed of a ladder reaching up to heaven with angels going up and down. From the top God spoke to him, promising the land to Jacob's descendants, the Israelites. After experiencing a number of ordeals in exile Jacob finally returned home and was recognised as the head of the house.

The Hermitage painting is based on the Old Testament text (Genesis 27: 1 23): "...When Isaac was old, and his eyes were dim so that he could not see, he called Esau his eldest son, and said unto him, My son... behold now I am old, I know not the day of my death; now therefore take I pray thee, thy weapons... and go out to the field, and take me some venison... and bring it to me that I may eat; that my soul may bless thee before I die. And Rebekah heard when Isaac spake to Esau his son... and took goodly raiment of her eldest son Esau... and put them upon Jacob her younger son; and she put the skins of the kids of the goats upon his hands and upon the smooth of his neck; and the savoury meat and the bread, which she had prepared, into the hand of her son Jacob... He came unto his father, and said, My father: and he said... who art thou, my son? And Jacob said unto his father, I am Esau thy firstborn; I have done according as thou badest me... And Isaac said unto his son, How is it that thou hast found it so quickly my son? and he said, Because the LORD thy God brought it to me. And Isaac said unto Jacob, Come near, I pray thee, that I may feel thee, my son whether thou be my very son Esau or not. And Jacob went near unto Isaac his father; and he felt him, and said, The voice is Jacob's voice, but the hands are the hands of Esau. And he discerned him not, because his hands were hairy, as his brother Esau's hands: so he blessed him."

Medieval theological authors used to allegorize the biblical legend relating it to the events described in the New Testament. In particular, the blessing of Jacob instead of Esau was interpreted as a substitution of the New for the Old Testament (Réau 1956, 2, part 1, p. 142-155).

The English historian Harris noted that the Spanish author Isidore of Seville (560-636) saw in Jacob and his sons prefigurations of Gospel characters and found in their ordeals analogies with the persecution of Christ and his disciples (E. Harrise "Spanish Painting at the Bowes Museum", *The Burlington Magazine*, 1967, vol. 109, p. 484). Subjects from the life of Jacob were highly popular in seventeenth-century Spanish literature and art. Jordan (W. B. Jordan, "Murillo's *Jacob Laying the Peeled Rods before the Flocks of Laban*", Art News, 1968, Summer, p. 68) cites as an example, Lope de Vega's play *Jacob's Labours (Dreams That Turn Out To Be Real)* (see *Obras de Lope de Vega*, vol. 3, Madrid, 1893, p. 253-264). Angulo (1981, 2, p. 30) found the evidence that the Marquis de Sauceda in Seville owned nine tapestries with scenes from the life of Jacob. Pictures of Jacob and his sons were executed by Francisco de Zurbarán; Pedro Orrente and Francisco Antolínez created cycles of paintings devoted to Jacob. According to Stechow (1966, p. 372), Murillo's series is most closely linked to ten tapestries at the Royal Museum in Brussels which were woven in the sixteenth century from the drawings of van Orley. They include all the episodes chosen by Murillo while *Isaac Blessing Jacob* bears affinity to a drawing by van Orley. Stechow suggested that Murillo might have seen Orley's drawings or engravings from them in a book with comments on Jacob's life written by Cornelius de Lapide. But Murillo may have first of all followed the Spanish painting tradition. In the first quarter of the seventeenth century Pedro Orrente created several cycles of paintings devoted to Jacob. Murillo's canvas is strikingly similar to a version of Orrente's *Isaac Blessing Jacob* (Contini-Bonacossi collection, Florence). In both works the composition is divided into two parts, one with an interior scene and the other with a landscape; both include the figure of the maid receding into the distance, Esau with his hounds returning from the chase and the identical gesture of Rebecca taking Jacob to Isaac. There are also some differences: Orrente's painting for example features the episode of the pottage of lentils which is absent in Murillo's work. On the

Preceding pages: *The Holy Family*. Details.
The Hermitage, St. Petersburg.

Isaac Blessing Jacob. Detail.
The Hermitage, St. Petersburg.

Isaac Blessing Jacob.
The Hermitage, St. Petersburg.

whole, the paintings are similar to such an extent that we can speak of a direct continuity in the treatment of the subject.

Various dates were suggested for the painting. Justi (1892) believed that the series was created between 1645 and 1655, Mayer (1923) first assigned it to 1665-1670 and then to the 1650s, Jordan (1968) dated the series to the late 1660s, Stechow (1966) thought that it was produced after 1665. Gaya Nuño (1978) placed it at *c.* 1670 and Angulo (1981, 2), referring to the fact that the paintings with scenes from Jacob's life decorated the façade of the Seville mansion of the Marquis de Villamanrique, dated them to *c.* 1660. In the Hermitage catalogue of 1958 the painting is dated to the 1650s and in the catalogue of 1976 to 1665-1670. The arguments put forward by Angulo seem most convincing. The paintings are distinguished by a mature craftmanship and apparently for this reason most historians have assigned them to the late 1660s recently. However, in the scene of Jacob's blessing, for instance, the painting is still very dense, it lacks the lightness of a later work, the *Liberation of St. Peter* (Hermitage) produced *c.* 1667. The series of scenes from Jacob's life could have been painted by Murillo soon after his return from Madrid where he studied the works of Venetian Flemish and Dutch artists in the royal collections. Murillo was also influenced by the paintings of Madrid artists, primarily those of Velázquez with their ingeniously rendered landscape backgrounds. Even before his trip to Madrid Murillo had tried his hand at painting scenes in natural settings. Back in Madrid, he was well prepared to start a large series of paintings with landscape backgrounds.

Murillo's paintings illustrating Jacob's life were identified by some historians as the pictures of David's life described by Antonio Palomino: "One should not ignore the excellent abilities of our Murillo in the art of landscapes that occur in his historical compositions. It happened so that the Marquis de Villamanrique decided to commission a cycle of scenes from the life of David for which Murillo was to paint the figures and Iriarte to execute the landscapes (as we mentioned above, he was well versed in them). Murillo said that Ignacio (Iriarte) had first to prepare the landscapes and then he would fit in the figures. Iriarte answered that Murillo had first to paint the figures and then he would fit in the landscapes. Murillo was irritated with this argument and said: 'If you think your landscapes are needed you are mistaken,' and thus he alone executed these paintings with narrative scenes and landscapes, a creation as wonderful as other works by him; they were brought to Madrid by the above mentioned Signor marquis" (A. Palomino, *El Muses Pictórico y escala optica. Vol.* 3: *El Parnaso español pintoresco laureado.* Madrid, 1724, p. 173).

The consensus is that Palomino erroneously gave the name of David while he had in mind Jacob since a Seville author Torre Farfán wrote in 1666 that the façade of the Marquis de Villamanrique's mansion was decorated with paintings devoted to the lives of Abraham and Jacob set against landscape backgrounds (Angulo 1981, 2, p. 29). The English author Cumberland who possibly knew the oral legend about the origin of these works pointed to Palomino's error as early as the eighteenth century. He highly praised the five paintings, considering them Murillo's best: "The great historical paintings of the Life of Jacob in the possession of the Marquis de Santiago at Madrid are the finest compositions which I have seen of Murillo. If I had to be guided by the impression these fascinating depictions of nature produced on my senses and to make an immediate choice I think I would prefer these canvases before anything else: this is a miracle of art incomparable to anything, apart from Titian's *Venus.*" And he continued: "The series consists of five large compositions depicting Jacob's life at various stages of his story. These pictures were originally in the collection of the Marquis de Villamanrique who first of all wished to have scenes from David's life painted by Murillo with backgrounds executed by Iriarte... Murillo did everything himself, without Iriarte's assistance, choosing Jacob's story instead of David's" (Cumberland 1782, 2, p. 101, 124).

The series that survived until the early nineteenth century (now the location of only four canvases is known) consisted of the following paintings: *Isaac Blessing Jacob. Jacob's Dream* (both in the Hermitage). *Jacob Laying the Peeled Rods before the Flocks of Laban* (Meadows Museum, Dallas, USA) and *Laban Searching for His Stolen Household Cods in Rachel's Tent* (Cleveland Museum of Art, USA). The fifth painting, the *Meeting of Jacob and Rachel,* appeared for the last time in 1817 at the sale of the A. Delahante collection in London (Angulo 1981, 2).

The most remarkable components of the paintings depicting Jacob's life are the landscapes. As

104

Isaac Blessing Jacob. Detail.
The Hermitage, St. Petersburg.

follows from Palomino's words, when Murillo received this commission he was not as yet a recognized master of landscapes, otherwise Ignacio Iriarte would not have been invited to take part in the work. It was, perhaps, for this reason that Murillo replaced the story of David with that of Jacob because according to tradition the latter was represented in paintings against landscape backgrounds. It is difficult to say in what sequence the paintings were created, but if one considers them in the order of the events in the biblical story one can note how the artist gradually perfected the composition of landscape backgrounds. In the first scene, *Isaac Blessing Jacob.* the composition is divided into two distinct parts and, though the landscape is marvellous, the device of the wall section protruding towards the viewer looks archaic: it was typical of Spanish painting in the first half of the seventeenth century. In *Jacob's Dream* the landscape fills the entire canvas but the scene still has a pronounced centre. Here Murillo depicts a nocturnal landscape which, in Pacheco's opinion, is the most difficult task for a painter. The soft light differs markedly from the sharp chiaroscuro contrasts of the Caravaggists. Murillo may have been acquainted with night landscapes by Dutch artists, for a similar representation of the moon looking out from behind the clouds occurs in Dutch paintings. Art historians generally note that Murillo was influenced by Flemish landscape engravings with their monumental trees, gnarled tree-trunks and hilly spaces as if seen from above. In *Jacob Laying the Peeled Rods before the Flocks of Laban* the centre of the composition is also emphasized but the lit space opening in the depths of the picture looks more integral than in *Jacob's Dream.* Finally, *Laban Searching for His Stolen Household Gods in Rachel's Tent* has the most perfect landscape in the series in which the figures are freely arranged throughout the space that possesses an organic unity of its own. Perhaps Murillo did execute the paintings in the order of the events in the biblical story, gradually perfecting his workmanship.

Produced between 1660 and 1665, the series of scenes from Jacob's life was brought by its owner, the Marquis de Villamanrique, to Madrid, probably in 1677 (Angulo 1981 n 2, p. 30). In 1724 it belonged to Count de Santiago in Madrid. Stechow (1966) suggested that the family name of the count was Manrique and that the paintings had originally been commissioned for this family while Palomino confused the name of Manrique with Villa-manrique; Angulo, however, justifiably refuted this suggestion. In 1775-1676 Swiburn saw one of the paintings in the Santiago collection (H. Swiburn, *Travels through Spain in the Years 1775 and 1776,* London, 1779, p. 351). In 1787 Cumberland saw the entire series in the same collection (Cumberland 1787, 2, p. 101, 124). Buchanan's agent, G. Wallis, wrote in 1808 that the series was put up for sale (Buchanan 1824). In 1811 *Isaac Blessing Jacob* and *Jacob's Dream* were acquired for the Hermitage through the agency of Vivant-Denon, General Director of the French museums. In 1820 Young reported that the French general Sebastiani had taken from Madrid, as war booty, numerous paintings, including those from the house of the Marquis de Santiago (J. Young, *Catalogue of the Pictures at Grosvenor House.* London, 1820, p. 24). Thus arose the assumption that the Hermitage canvases had been among them.

Provenance: The painting was commissioned by the Marquis Villamanrique, protector of the Seville Academy, for his house in Seville. It was apparently brought to Madrid in 1677; from 1724 it belonged to Count de Santiago in Madrid; in 1810 it was seized by the French general Sebastiani (?). It was acquired for the Hermitage in 1811 in Paris through the agency of Dominique Vivant-Denon, General Director of the French museums (together with *Jacob's Dream* which is also in the Hermitage).

Exhibitions: 1984 Leningrad, No. 22.

Isaac Blessing Jacob. Detail. ▶
The Hermitage, St. Petersburg.

P. Orrente. *Isaac Blessing Jacob.*
Contini-Bonacossi collection. Florence.

10. JACOB'S DREAM

1660-1665.
Oil on canvas. 246 x 360 cm.
The Hermitage, St Petersburg. Inv. No. 344.

The painting reflects the words of the biblical text: "And Jacob went out from Beersheba and went toward Haran. And he lighted upon a certain place, and tarried there all night, because the sun was set; and he took of the stones of that place, and put them for his pillows, and lay down in that place to sleep. And he dreamed, and behold a ladder set up on the earth, and the top of it reached to heaven: and behold the angels of God ascending and descending on it. And, behold, the Lord stood above it, and said, I am the Lord God... the land whereon thou liest, to thee will I give it, and to thy seed..." (Genesis 28: 10-13).
In theological literature Jacob's ladder symbolized the virtues; the ascending angels were the symbol of contemplative life whereas the descending ones were an allegory of active life.

Provenance: see *Isaac Blessing Jacob.*

A studio copy of the central part of the painting is in the Duthuit collection, London.

Exhibitions: 1984 Leningrad, No. 23.

Following pages: *Jacob's Dream.*
The Hermitage, St. Petersburg.

Top and p. 112-113: *Jacob's Dream*. Details.
The Hermitage, St. Petersburg.

11. DEATH OF THE INQUISITOR PEDRO DE ARBUÉS

1664.
Oil on canvas. 293.5 x 206.2 cm.
The Hermitage, St. Petersburg. Inv No. 302.

Pedro de Arbués (1441-1485), the first inquisitor of Aragón, was selected for this post by the Spanish Grand Inquisitor Tomas de Torquemada. On 14 September 1485, the Jews Duran and Esperan murdered him at night while at prayer in the Saragossa cathedral, in revenge for the persecution of their kin. In 1664 Pedro de Arbués was beatified by the Church and in 1867 he was canonized as a saint. Mayer (1913) dated the painting to 1660-1670, Gaya Nuño (1978) to 1668-1670 and Angulo (1981, 2) to c. 1664. In the Hermitage catalogues of 1958 and 1976 it is dated to 1660-1670. Angulo put forward the most convincing arguments for his date. He refers to a literary source, the description of the celebrations in the San Pablo monastery marking the beatification of the inquisitor on 17 September 1664 which runs, among other things, as follows: "Above the curtain is a painting on canvas 4 varas (334 cm) in height and of a proportional width where, by order of the tribunal, the martyrdom of this saintly man is depicted by the famous brush of Bartolomeo Murillo..." *(Relación Sumaria de los festivos demostraciones con que... la Inquisición... Ia Beatificación del synclito Mártir Pedro de Arbués... el 17 de septiembre de 1604*, Seville, 1664).
The mentioned painting and the one in the Hermitage differ somewhat in size but apparently the latter was trimmed.
Justi (1892) paid attention to the fact that the face of Pedro de Arbués in Murillo's painting bears no resemblance to the authentic sculpture of the inquisitor in the Theo Capella, Saragossa. It has been suggested that there is a preparatory drawing for the Hermitage painting; it appeared at the exhibition French and Italian Drawings of the 16th and 17th Centuries in French Private Collections as *Death of Pedro de Arbués* (Paris, Galerie Claude Aubry, 1971, Cat. No. 75). Angulo (1981, 2) noted, however, that the man in the drawing is kneeling before a pagan deity on a pedestal. In his opinion, the similarity between the figures of the murderers in the drawing and the painting may be explained either by the fact that the draughtsman knew Murillo's painting or that the drawing and the painting were based on the same source — perhaps, an engraving printed in time for the celebration of the beatification of the

Death of the Inquisitor Pedro de Arbués.
The Hermitage, St. Petersburg.

114

inquisitor. Angulo believes that the drawing displayed at the above exhibition could not be attributed either to Murillo or any artists of his school.

When the painting was sold to the Hermitage it was erroneously named *Le Martyr de St. Pierre d'Albens par Murillo* (Central State Historical Archives, fund 472, inv. 12, file 817, p. 2). Later the name was changed to *Le Martyr de St. Pierre (ibid.,* p. 29). In the catalogue of 1797 — 1850 the painting was listed as *St. Peter the Dominican* but Labensky (1838) questioned this identification. Viardot (1844) believed that the subject of the painting was the Martyrdom of St. Peter of Verona. Curtis (1883) named it *San Pedro de Arbués.*

Death of the Inquisitor Pedro de Arbués. Detail.
The Hermitage, St. Petersburg.

Provenance: 1664 Painted for the church of the San Pablo monastery, Seville; later, in the inquisition tribunal, Seville, and in the M. Godoy collection, Rome; 1831 Acquired for the Hermitage from M. Godoy in Paris.

Copies: in the Cordoba museum (Cordoba school, was ascribed to Augustin Grands); in the Academia de Bellas Artes, Mexico (by Baltasar Echave Ibia); in a private collection, Madrid; and in the Vatican, Rome.

Engraved by M. Arteaga in the seventeenth century and I. Robillard (Hermitage Gallery 1845-1847, 1: 6).

Stirling (1848, 3) suggested that Godoy had taken the painting from the inquisition tribunal of Seville and replaced it with a copy by Joaquin Cortés. Curtis (1883) added that this happened in 1804, but Angulo (1981, 2) noted that Standish (1840) had claimed to have seen this painting in the church of San Francisco in Seville whence it had been brought to Rome and then to London where it had been bought by the Russian government. Angulo believed, however, that Standish could have made a mistake. In his monograph on Murillo, Angulo (1981, 2) identified the Hermitage painting as the one listed as *San Pedro* in the inventory of Godoy's gallery compiled by Quilliet in 1808. But the published text of this inventory (Juan Perez de Guzmán, "Los colecciones del Príncipe de la Paz", *La Espana Moderna,* 1900, August, vol. 140, Madrid) includes no painting by Murillo of this name. Rose Wagner (1983) indicated another entry in Quilliet's inventory, namely *Ecole de Murillo. Mort de St. Pascual... très bon.* But the error

in the picture's name seems strange, as is the idea that a work of such high quality could be attributed to Murillo's school. Rose Wagner believes that the canvas was among the works selected by the French from Godoy's confiscated collection to be sent to Paris in 1810 (under the title of *San Pedro).* But even in this case it is not certain that the painting belonged to Godoy and was not brought to his gallery together with numerous other works of art from one of the various churches, monasteries and palaces in Madrid. It thus cannot be firmly established that the painting was part of Godoy's collection in Madrid, since this suggestion still lacks full documentary substantiation.

It is unknown how Godoy managed to acquire this painting in emigration, but it was, apparently, this work that David Wilkie (Canningham 1848) wrote about in his diary after his visit to the Villa Mattei in Rome in 1826. On 23 February 1826 he noted: "The finest Murillo in Rome he (Signor Cammuccini — L. K.) says, is in the collection of the Prince of the Peace..." Five days later, after his visit to Godoy's gallery, Wilkie wrote: "Before leaving Rome, saw the collection of the Spanish Prince of the Peace. The Murillo is in admirable condition, but in subject and colour I think Signor Cammuccini overrates it." Wilkie did not mention the subject of the painting but four year later, in 1830, Godoy's entire collection of paintings was offered for sale to the Hermitage and its inventory started with the best work in it, *Le Martyr de St. Pierre d'Albens par Murillo.*

Exhibitions: 1984 Leningrad, No. 24.

12. THE LIBERATION OF ST. PETER

c. 1667.
Oil on canvas. 238 x 260 cm.
The Hermitage, St. Petersburg. Inv. No. 342.

According to the Gospels. St. Peter was put into prison on three separate occasions. When he was in prison for the second time he was freed by an angel. The painting depicts the scene described in the New Testament: "Now about that time Herod the king stretched forth his hands to vex certain of the church... he proceeded further to take Peter also... And when he had apprehended him, he put him in prison, and delivered him to four quaternions of soldiers to keep him; intending after Easter to bring him forth to the people... And when Herod would have brought him forth, the same night Peter was sleeping between two soldiers, bound with two chains: and the keepers before the door kept the prison. And, behold, the angel of the Lord came upon him, and the light shined in the prison: and he smote Peter on the side, and raised him up, saying, Arise up quickly. And his chains fell off from his hands. And the angel said unto him, Gird thyself, and bind on thy sandals. And so he did. And he saith unto him, Cast thy garment about thee! and follow me" (Acts 12: 1-8).

This painting by Murillo symbolizes one of the works of mercy visiting a prisoner mentioned in the Gospels (Matthew 25, 36). Its allegorical meaning is explained in the inventory of the La Caridad hospital for which it was produced (Brown 1970; see also the section *Murillo's Life and Work* in this book).

The subject of the Liberation of St. Peter was widely used by seventeenth-century European artists (Annibale Carracci, Domenichino, Lanfranco, Preti and Ribera in Italy; Pereda, Roelas and Jose Antolínez in Spain). Murillo may have known engravings from their paintings. One such engraving made in 1657 by Hendrik Bary from the painting by Gijsbert van den Kuyl is close to Murillo's work (F. W. H. Hollstein, *Dutch and Flemish Etchings. Engravings and Woodcuts.* vol. 1, Amsterdam, 1949, p. 104). Rôlthlisberger (1961) noted that the *Liberation* bears compositional affinities to the drawing by Claude Lorrain dated to 1640-1641 *(Liber Veritatis 51.* British Museum, London). This observation suggests that there was a common iconographic source of an earlier date than the engraving by Bary.

The *Liberation of St. Peter* was one of the canvases which decorated the church of the La Caridad hospital in Seville. The series was commissioned by Miguel Mañara y Vicentelo de Leca who headed the Brotherhood of Charity from 1664. According to his iconographic programme, the series had to illustrate the seven works of mercy, six of which are mentioned in the Gospel while the seventh, of a later date, the burial of the dead, was the main activity of the Brotherhood. In addition, two paintings were dedicated to the motif of *vanitas* and became known as the *Hieroglyphs of Death*. All works in the ensemble had an allegorical meaning. The sculpture, the *Entombment,* executed by Pedro Roldán on the central retable symbolized the burial of the dead. The *Hieroglyphs of Death* were created by Juan de Valdés Leal. The larger part of the ensemble was painted by Murillo who also joined the Brotherhood in 1665. He produced six pictures corresponding to the appropriate passages in the Gospel (for details, see the section *Murillo's Life and* Work) and two altarpieces. St. *John of God and the Angel* and *St. Elizabeth of Hungary Healing the Sick.*

According to old sources, Murillo finished the series for the La Caridad hospital in 1674. Brown (1978) who had examined the hospital archives found that in June of 1670 all six paintings depicting the works of mercy were already in the church. The *Liberation* was dated to 1671-1674. However, Angulo (1981, 2, p. 88) cites a document which says that it was placed in the church on 27 August 1667.

A possible preliminary study for this painting is now in the National Gallery, Prague (Stepanek 1969).

In 1800 the La Caridad hospital was ordered to transfer eleven paintings to the newly established Royal Museum in Madrid. It was decided to replace the original paintings with copies. By 1 May 1803 the Seville painter Joaquin Cortés had made three of them, including the *Liberation*. Angulo (1981, 2) believes that it is precisely this copy that is now in the Aranjuez Palace. In Tormo's opinion (E. Tormo, *Aranjuez*, Madrid, 1931, p. 31), this copy was painted by Manuel Esquivel. Other copies are in the Menendez Pidal collection (Madrid) and in Alcázar (Seville).

The Liberation of St. Peter.
The Hermitage, St. Petersburg.

Provenance: c. 1667 Painted for the La Caridad hospital, Seville; after 1810 Collection of Marshal Nicolas Soult, Paris; 1852 Acquired for the Hermitage at the sale of the Soult collection, Paris.

An engraving of the painting was published in Reveil 1828-1834, 3, p. 178 and in *L'Illustration*. 1852, 31 May.

In 1810, during the French occupation of Seville, the best paintings from the city's churches and monasteries were taken to Alcázar. Some of them, including the *Liberation*, became the property of Marshal Soult. According to Curtis (1883), in 1835 the painting was sold to the Louvre and was displayed there for several days but later it was returned to the owner.

Exhibitions: 1984 Leningrad, No. 25.

C. Lorrain.
The Liberation of St. Peter.
Drawing, 1640-1641, British Museum, London.

The Liberation of St. Peter.
c. 1667, Galerie Nationale, Prague.

The Liberation of St. Peter. Detail. ▶
The Hermitage, St. Petersburg.

The Liberation of St. Peter.
Engraving by H. Bary
from the painting by G. van den Kuyl.

13. *ST. JOSEPH HOLDING THE INFANT CHRIST IN HIS ARMS*

c. 1670.
Oil on panel. 70 x 51 cm.
The Pushkin Museum of Fine Arts, Moscow. Inv. No. 196.

The name of St. Joseph does not appear in the canonical biblical texts. His life with the Virgin Mary and Christ is described in the apocryphal literature (the main literary sources are the Protevangelium or the Book of James and the Story of Joseph the Carpenter, 4th century). One of St. Joseph's main attributes is a flowering rod (a sign from Heaven that he was chosen to be the Virgin's husband) and a lily (the symbol of chastity).

In Spain, representations of St. Joseph gained wide currency in the seventeenth century largely because of the popularization of this saint by St. Teresa. Murillo often depicted St. Joseph in scenes from the life of the Holy Family and also with the Infant Christ. His pictures on the latter subject involve four iconographic types: the full-length figures of St. Joseph and the Infant Christ, both standing; the full-length figure of St. Joseph seated, with the Infant Christ; St. Joseph conducting the Infant Christ; and the half-length figure of St. Joseph holding the Infant Christ in his arms. The Moscow painting is of the last type. Similar variants are in the Ringling Museum, Sarasota; Washington University, St. Louis; and Duke de Montpensier's collection, Seville.

All art historians agree that this painting dates from Murillo's late period. Mayer (1913) dated it to 1672-1682 and Angulo (1981) *c.* 1670.

St. Joseph Holding the Infant Christ in His Arms.
1670-1675, Washington University, Saint Louis.

St. Joseph Holding the Infant Christ in His Arms.
1670-1675, Ringling Museum, Sarasota.

Provenance: 1819 Acquired by Prince V. Trubetskoi in Paris; 1930 Transferred to the Pushkin Museum of Fine Arts, Moscow.

Engraved by J. G. de Navia.

St. Joseph Holding the Infant Christ in His Arms. Details.
Pushkin Museum of Fine Art, Moscow.

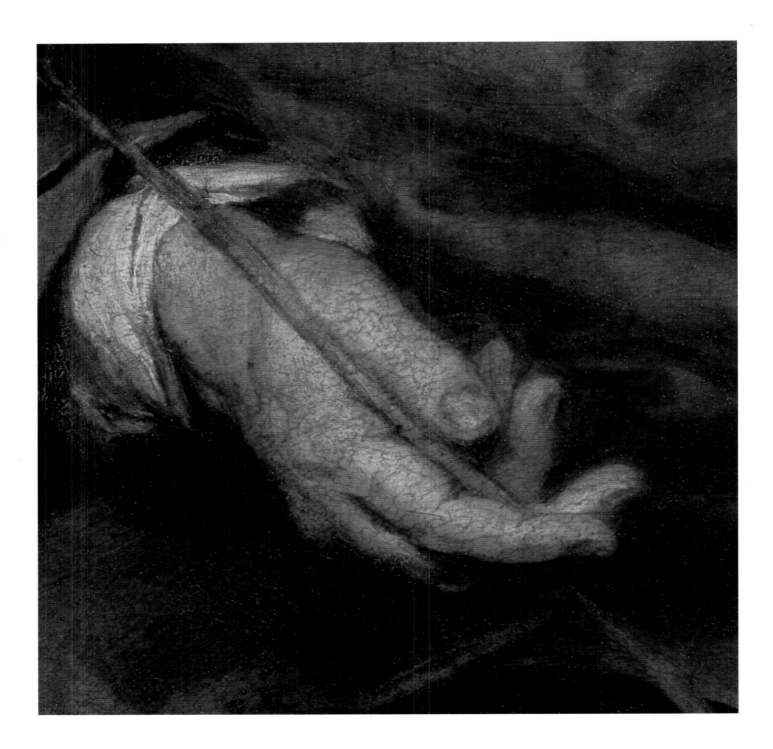

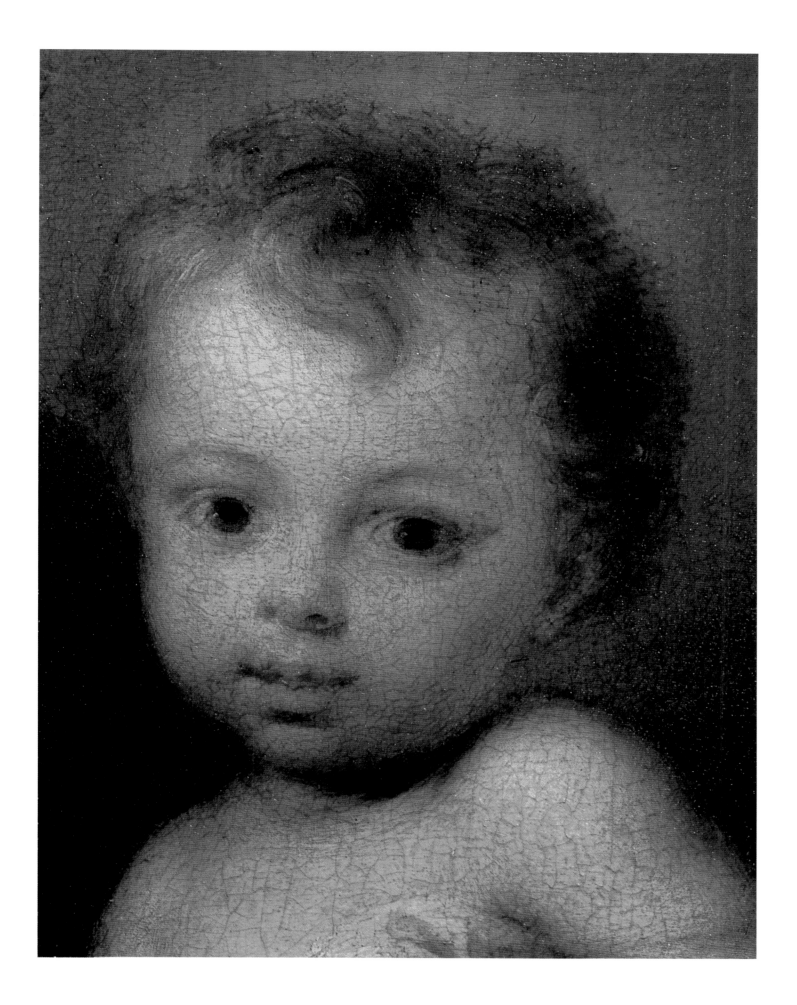

14. ST. JOSEPH CONDUCTING THE INFANT CHRIST

c. 1670.
Oil on canvas. 73 x 52 cm.
The Hermitage, St. Petersburg. Inv. No. 336.

For the subject, see the note on *St. Joseph Holding the Infant Christ in His Arms.*

The iconography of the painting could be based on the following words spoken by Christ in an apocryphal book: "Then I remembered the day when he had walked with me in Egypt and I thought about all the hardships he had had to endure because of me" *(Apocryphal Stories of Christ. III. Book of Joseph the Carpenter*, St. Petersburg. 1914, p. 52, in Russian).

The attribution of the picture to Murillo is traditional. Murillo's authorship is confirmed by the X-ray photograph which shows the changes introduced in the process of work: initially Joseph's head was more inclined to the left and the right hand of the Child was also shifted.

Mayer (1913) dated the painting around 1665-1680 whereas Gaya Nuño (1978) and Angulo (1981, 2) assigned it to *c.* 1670. The Hermitage catalogues of 1958 and 1976 place it between 1665 and 1680.

Several drawings by Murillo depicting St. Joseph conducting the Infant Christ are in the National Library (Madrid), the Louvre (Paris) and the Kunsthalle (Hamburg). According to Rohl (1961), the drawing in the National Library served as a preliminary sketch for the Hermitage painting. Angulo (1961, 1974) noted a similarity between the faces of St. Joseph in this painting and in the Louvre drawing. Brown (1976), however, rightly observed that the Kunsthalle drawing is most closely related to the Hermitage painting and probably served as a preliminary sketch for it. Brown also noted the iconographic affinity between the faces of the Infant in the Hermitage painting and in the drawing, the *Virgin and Child,* from the collection of Count de Alcubierre in Madrid. This drawing, like the Kunsthalle sketch, is dated to the 1670s. The refined transparency of the Hermitage work, typical of Murillo's late manner, permits its dating to *c.* 1670.

Angulo (1961) lists among the earliest known versions the work which appeared at the Charpentier sale in 1933 in Paris and which he assigns to *c.* 1660. This painting neither has a wall on the right nor the architecture on the far left.

A close version in point of time is in the Valdes collection (Bilbao), which has numerous buildings in the left background. The Hermitage version is one of the latest works on the subject.

St. Joseph Conducting the Infant Christ.
Drawing, Kunsthalle, Hamburg.

Provenance: 1814 Received from Amsterdam as part of the Coesvelt collection; according to Labensky (1838), it was a gift from W. Coesvelt to the Emperor Alexander I of Russia.

Copies: in the Prometey Gallery, Bologna (38.5 x 30.5 cm, signed *Escalante):* in the Descalzas convent, Lima; in the Sanchez Sanz collection, Madrid (166.5 x 101.5 cm); in the La Frage collection, New York (274 x 165 cm); and in the Thuellene collection, Paris.

Exhibitions: 1968-1969 Belgrade No. 13; 1984, Leningrad, No. 27.

128

St. Joseph Conducting the Infant Christ.
Valdes collection, Bilbao.

St. Joseph Conducting the Infant Christ.
c. 1660, Charpentier collection, Paris.

130

15. *THE FLIGHT INTO EGYPT*

1670-1675.
Oil on canvas. 101 x 62 cm.
The Pushkin Museum of Fine Arts, Moscow. Inv. No. 2671.

For the subject, see the note on the *Rest on the Flight into Egypt* (No. 7).
The attribution of the picture to Murillo is traditional. A description of the Walpole Gallery (Aedes Walpolianae 1747) related its technique to that of Van Dyck. All historians later supported this opinion. Mayer (1913) dated the work to 1675-1680 whereas Angulo (1981, 2) placed it at *c.* 1670.
A number of versions are extant. The earliest one is in the Palazzo Bianco in Genoa (*c.* 1645, 210 x 163 cm). It is a magnificent genre scene with a host of everyday details rendered in a Caravaggesque vein. The version in the Institute of Arts in Detroit (207 x 162.5 cm) was executed in approximately the same period, between 1645 and 1650. A later version is in the Museum of Fine Arts in Budapest (155.5 x 125 cm). The subject here is treated more intimately, the surrounding space is widened, the scale of the figures is reduced and there are angels in the sky. The Budapest version is dated to 1660-1670. Compositionally it is most closely related to the picture in the Pushkin Museum, but the latter has a higher artistic quality, its technique is softer and more airy while the postures and gestures of the figures are more natural. The stylistic features of the painting are typical of the artist's works of 1670 to 1675.

The Flight into Egypt.
1660-1670, Museum of Fine Arts, Budapest.

The Flight into Egypt.
1645-1650, Institute of Art, Detroit.

Provenance: 1779 Acquired for the Hermitage as part of the Walpole collection in Houghton Hall, England; 1930 Transferred to the Pushkin Museum of Fine Arts, Moscow.

Engraved by J. Spilsbery in 1788 (Set of Prints 1788, vol. 1, p. 4, XLV).

Exhibitions: 1984 Leningrad, No. 29.

The Flight into Egypt. Details.
Pushkin Museum of Fine Arts, Moscow.

16. THE CRUCIFIXION

c. 1675.
Oil on canvas. 98 x 60.2 cm.
Inscribed on top of the cross:
IESUS NAZAREN / REX / IUDEORUM.
The Hermitage, St. Petersburg. Inv. No. 345.

According to the Gospels, Jesus was crucified by order of Pilate, being accused of calling himself the King of the Jews. Various interpretations of the Crucifixion exist in world art being based on the Gospels and other religious literature. Murillo's painting follows the description in the Gospel according to St. John: "And he bearing his cross went forth into a place called the place of a skull, which is called in the Hebrew Golgotha: where they crucified him, and two others with him, on either side one, and Jesus in the midst. And Pilate wrote a title, and put it on the cross. And the writing was, *Jesus of Nazareth the King of the Jews...* Now there stood by the cross of Jesus his mother, and his mother's sister, Mary the wife of Clophas, and Mary Magdalene. When Jesus therefore saw his mother, and the disciple standing by, whom he loved, he saith unto his mother, Woman, Behold thy son! Then saith to the disciple, Behold thy mother! And from that hour that disciple took her unto his own home... Then came the soldiers... saw that he was dead already... one of the soldiers with a spear pierced his side..." (John 19: 17-19, 25-27, 32-34).

The painting shows only a part of Golgotha with the dead Christ. St. John the Divine, the Virgin and Mary Magdalene are depicted at the foot of the cross.

The painting was traditionally attributed to Murillo and no doubts were raised until recently. However, Angulo (1981, 2) suggested that the work should be attributed to Murillo's school. The *Crucifixion* entered the Hermitage together with the *Flight into Egypt* (Pushkin Museum, Moscow) which was considered its pendant. Though in the eighteenth century paintings were often paired by chance and not by the artist himself, these two pictures are similar in style and probably were executed for the same cycle at the same time. The folds of the clothes and the landscapes in both works are rendered in a similar manner. The *Crucifixion* is also close in style to Murillo's *St. Joseph Conducting the Infant Christ.* Christ's body in the Hermitage *Crucifixion* is treated similarly as in the *Crucifixion* in the Prado (1660-1667, Inv. No. 967) which is undoubtedly an original. This suggests that the Hermitage picture is also an original.

A close version, ascribed by Angulo to a pupil of Murillo, is in the Meadows Museum, Dallas. It shows the same characters but their arrangement is different: the nearest to the cross is St. John the Divine, not the Virgin; also changed are the position of Christ's figure, the pose of Mary Magdalene and the plaque with the inscription on the cross. In the painting at the Meadows Museum the drapery is less refined, the faces and figures are less expressive and the chiaroscuro contrasts are less subtle. In comparison with this work the artistic merit of the Hermitage painting is higher, though it has been considerably damaged by restorations. Having bought the painting, A. Moussine-Pushkin wrote from London in December of 1778 (Sbornik 1876) that the *Crucifixion* by Morel (Murillo) has blackened", that is, darkened. During subsequent cleaning the painted layer was heavily washed.

Viardot (1844) assigned the *Crucifixion* to Murillo's early period. Mayer (1913), on the contrary, dated it to 1675-1682 and his opinion is generally accepted in the literature. Indeed, the small scale of the figures, the soft outlines and the airy landscape background indicate that the painting is from a later period and may be dated *c.* 1675.

Provenance: 1779 Acquired as part of the Walpole collection in Houghton Hall, England (was thought to be a pendant to the *Flight into Egypt,* Pushkin Museum of Fine Arts, Cat. 55, 56).

Engraved by J. Spilsbery (Set of Prints 1788. p. 4, XLVI).

Exhibitions: 1969 Travelling. Cat. p. 5, 6, 14; 1984, Leningrad, No. 28.

Murillo, school. *The Crucifixion.*
Meadows Museum, Dallas, Texas.

The Crucifixion.
1660-1667, Prado, Madrid.

17. THE VISION OF ST. ANTONY OF PADUA

1660-1680.
Oil on canvas. 250 x 167 cm.
The Hermitage, St. Petersburg. Inv. No. 308.

St. Antony of Padua, one of the most popular Franciscan saints, was born in Lisbon in 1195 and died in 1231 in Padua where he spent the last two years of his life. Legends about him became widespread in the fourteenth century and are very similar to those about the life of St. Francis of Assisi. The appearance of the Child Christ to St. Antony of Padua was a favourite subject among Spanish, especially Seville, artists (AASS, June, vol. 2, p. 705).

The painting's attribution to Murillo is traditional and never aroused any doubts. Somov (Cat. 1892) assumed that it preceded the *Vision of St. Antony of Padua* from Seville Cathedral, created in 1656. Mayer (1913) assigned it to a later period, 1675-1680, and Angulo (1981, 2) to 1670-1680. In the Hermitage catalogue of 1958 it is dated to 1665-1670 and in the catalogue of 1976, to 1675-1680. The painting for Seville Cathedral was apparently the earliest work by Murillo on this subject. St. Antony is shown kneeling in an interior; above him is the Child standing in the clouds and surrounded by angels. Ten years later, in the series of paintings (1665-1670) for the Capuchin monastery in Seville, Murillo depicted this scene somewhat differently: the Child is represented sitting on a book before St. Antony against a landscape background (1665, Museo de Bellas Artes, Seville). In a later painting from the Kaiser-Friedrich-Museum in Berlin (destroyed in 1941-1945) and its version from the Museum des Beaux-Arts in Bordeaux, both dated *c.* 1675, Christ is embraced by the saint. In composition the Hermitage painting seems to be intermediate between the works in Seville Cathedral and the Seville museum while some features in it are close to the canvas executed for Seville Cathedral. The technique of the Hermitage work, however, is much more mature. X-ray examination shows that the composition of the painting underwent changes. The face of the Child was repainted: originally it was higher to the right. The face of St. Antony was repainted twice. Representations in the lower painted layers were executed in a different manner than the final version in which the modelling of spaces is more refined. Probably, the work was finished a long time after it had been started. According to the above considerations this painting can be dated to a wide interval of time between 1660 and 1680. Angulo (1966) suggested that it had been included in the inventory compiled after Murillo's death (1682). A similar version is in the Pages collection, Seville.

The Vision of St. Antony of Padua.
1665, Museo de Bellas Artes, Seville.

Provenance: until 1682 Murillo's studio, Seville; after 1810 Property of Marquis de Farbaine Jeanson. Paris; from 1849 Laneuville collection, Paris; 1852 Acquired for the Hermitage from the Laneuville collection.

Engraved by K. Mosolov.

Exhibitions: 1984 Leningrad, No. 26.

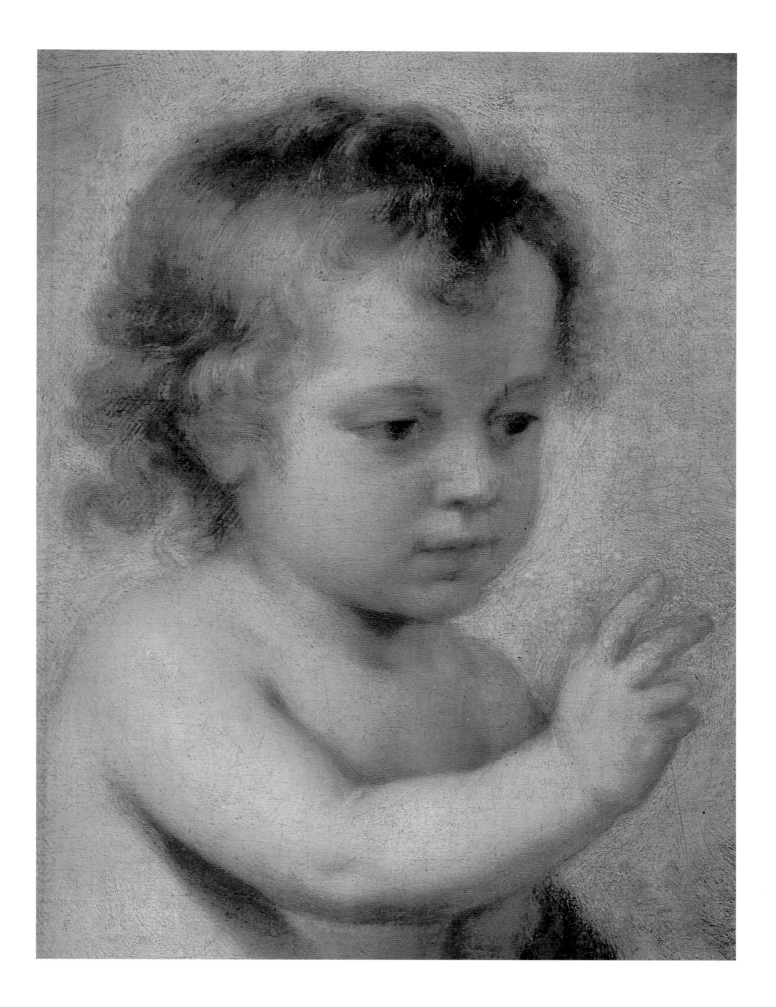

The Vision of St. Antony of Padua. Detail.
The Hermitage, St. Petersburg.

18. *THE WALPOLE IMMACULATE CONCEPTION*

c. 1680.
Oil on canvas. 195 x 145 cm.
The Hermitage, St. Petersburg. Inv. No. 387.

There was no consensus about the subject of the painting. Some identified it as the Assumption, others as the Immaculate Conception (see the note on the *Esquilache Immaculate Conception*).

In the iconography of the Assumption the Virgin appears as an ideally beautiful woman; in the fifteenth century she was sometimes represented standing on the moon. The treatment of this subject largely influenced the iconography of the Immaculate Conception. For instance, in his *Immaculate Conception* Guido Reni separated its upper part with the *Assumption* from its lower portion depicting apostles around an empty sarcophagus (H. Hibbard, "Guido Reni's Painting of the Immaculate Conception", *Bulletin of the Metropolitan Museum of Art.* 1969, Summer, vol. 28, p. 1930).

It is not surprising, therefore, that the paintings on the subjects of the Immaculate Conception and the Assumption were later confused. The extent of such confusion is demonstrated by Viardot who writes: "the Assumptions the most current name of which in Spain is the Immaculate Conception..." (L. Viardot. *Notice sur les principaux peintres de l'Espagne.* Paris, 1839, p. 41). Moreover, in the Protestant countries the subject of the Immaculate Conception was not generally recognised and frequently the names of such paintings were deliberately changed.

Curtis (1883) who distinguished between the Assumption and the Immaculate Conception nevertheless retained the title of the *Assumption* for this painting, reasoning that the angels in it do not carry the emblems of the Purissima. The Spanish art historians Beruete (1904) and Tormo (1914) clarified the matter when they visited the Hermitage in the early twentieth century and agreed that the subject of the painting was the Immaculate Conception. Beruete specially noted that the painting is erroneously listed in the Hermitage catalogues as *The Assumption.* Subsequently both names were applied to this painting by different writers. Gaya Nuño (1978) and Angulo (1981, 1) refer to it as the *Asunción* (Assumption). Angulo puts forward the following explanation: "Perhaps, since the Virgin depicted is

The Walpole Immaculate Conception.
The Hermitage, St. Petersburg.

of a very young age the painting was regarded... as the *Immaculate Conception* by Tormo (1914), Mac-Laren (1952)... and Elisalde (1955). The absence of the moon is not decisive here because the Madrid artist Antolínez who painted the Immaculate Conception usually omitted it, but the angels carry no symbols of Eternal Glory while, on the other hand, the ascending motion is very strongly expressed." Moreover, Angulo believed that the gesture of Mary's arms is typical of the Asunción subject.

In the Hermitage catalogues of 1958 and 1976 the painting is listed as the *Assumption.*

Let us first consider the passage from Francisco Pacheco's book which is devoted to the subject of the Assumption. After noting that the Virgin died at the "age of 72 minus 24 days", the author writes: "When the time of her miraculous death drew nearer, the Lord extended new mercies to Madonna: her glorious transition to the other world was witnessed by the apostles and disciples miraculously sent for her consolation and for blessing her... She died not of some sickness, she never had had such... but from the passionate desire to meet her son... There is no doubt that on the third day she was resurrected and ascended in flesh and in spirit to Heaven... This event is celebrated as Asunción, the Assumption of the Virgin, and not as Ascención (the Ascension) as of Christ... One should not depict the Virgin surrounded by angels that look as if they assist in lifting her body... one should understand that she was accompanied by the Holy Ghost... It is reasonable to paint her as very beautiful, at an age much younger than she really was because the virginity preserves the external beauty and freshness... moreover, the Virgin suffered from no sickness or distress that could have reduced her beauty and thus she must be painted as if she were thirty years old..." (Pacheco 1866, 2. p. 262-267). In seventeenth-century Spanish painting the subject of the Assumption was usually depicted as a two-partite scene with apostles at an empty coffin below and the ascending Virgin above. The Virgin's arms could be folded or outstretched. In fact, there are two paintings on the subject which are attributed to Murillo or to his circle: in the *Assumption* at the Ringling Museum (Sarasota) the Virgin is shown with outstretched arms, while in the *Assumption* from the Wallace collection (London) her arms are folded. Therefore, the Virgin's outstretched arms in the Hermitage

painting cannot serve as an absolute proof of the subject being the Assumption. The absence of the emblems of the Purissima cannot be regarded as a weighty argument either. The Hermitage painting dates from the late period of Murillo's career when the artist sought new approaches to the subject. The symbols were so generally known that Murillo employed them quite freely. In *c.* 1678 he painted the *Soult Immaculate Conception* for the hospital of Los Venerables Sacerdotes in Seville (now in the Prado, Madrid). Except for the moon, Murillo omitted all other attributes of the Purissima in this painting. Incidentally, even in one of his earliest *Inmaculadas,* the so-called *Large Immaculate Conception* of 1650-1655 for the Franciscan monastery (now in the Museo de Bellas Artes, Seville) there are no emblems in the angels' hands. The Hermitage picture has almost the same composition as the *Soult Immaculate Conception:* only the gesture of the Virgin's arms and the moon are repeated in a modified form.

Art historians usually note the absence of the moon in the Hermitage *Immaculate Conception,* but it is not the case. The cloud under the Virgin's knee envelopes a sphere with a hardly discernible crescent in its upper part. In the above mentioned *Large Immaculate Conception* the sphere with a crescent is painted in a similar fashion, but in this early work Murillo designated the sphere quite distinctly.

The gesture of the Virgin's arms in the Hermitage painting makes her image more dynamic and enhances the effect of ascent, although similar effects are present in many other *Inmaculadas* conveying the hovering in the air. On the other hand, some of the angels in the Hermitage painting evoke the sensation of descent rather than ascent. Other Spanish artists also depicted the Holy Virgin with outstretched arms, for instance, Francisco de Zurbarán in his *Immaculate Conception* of 1661 (Museum of Fine Arts, Budapest). Madrid painters almost always represented the Virgin with one arm raised. Angulo (1981, 1) discussed a drawing by Murillo in a private English collection (it is sketched on the back side of a letter by Zurbarán, which permits its dating to *c.* 1660). It is a sketch of the *Immaculate Conception* with the figure of the Virgin poised to soar upwards with an arm uplifted in the spirit of Madrid painters. A natural assumption is that Murillo modified and developed this motif in the painting under discussion. Tormo (1914), who was fascinated by the Hermitage

150

The Escorial Immaculate Conception.
1656-1660, Prado, Madrid.

The Immaculate Conception.
c. 1668, Museo de Bellas Artes, Seville.

Zurbarán. *The Immaculate Conception.*
1661, Museum of Fine Arts, Budapest.

painting, calling it "my Immaculate Conception", was of the opinion that this gesture was the artist's most fortunate discovery. Tormo regarded the gesture not as a sign of going up to Heaven but as a sign of taking leave, of moving away. Indeed, the iconography of this painting is very unusual, even unique for Murillo's work but this does not give reason, for considering it an *Assumption*. It is difficult to believe that in a painting on the subject of the Assumption the artist would have employed the image, the composition and the colour scheme typical of the *Inmaculadas*. The young age of the Virgin is a weighty argument in favour of the *Immaculate Conception*. Before us is *la niña,* a girl. It was precisely in this way that Pacheco advised the artists to paint the Virgin, "in the flowering of her age at twelve or thirteen, as a lovely girl", while in the pictures of the Assumption he recommended to depict her at the age of thirty. None of the Spanish artists followed Pacheco's instructions so closely as Murillo.

Representations of the Virgin Mary as a girl appeared in Murillo's paintings on the subject of the Immaculate Conception from the 1650s. One of the earliest is the *Escorial Immaculate Conception* (Prado, Madrid), dated to 1656-1660. A decade later Murillo repeated a similar image in the *Immaculate Conception* commissioned for the Capuchin monastery in Seville (*c.* 1668, now in the Museo de Bellas Artes, Seville). In the opinion of Tormo (1914) and Malitskaya (1947). the same model posed for the Hermitage painting and the one in the Seville museum (according to a legend it was Murillo's daughter). Angulo believed that in both Hermitage paintings *(Esquilache* and *Walpole)* Murillo used the same model but one can hardly agree with this view (Angulo 1981, 2). The faces of the models are very similar typologically, as is often the case with Murillo, but the Virgin in the *Esquilache Immaculate Conception* looks older.

The attribution of the Hermitage painting is traditional and was never doubted. Mayer (1913) assigned it to 1670-1680 and this date is universally accepted in the literature, including the Hermitage catalogues of 1958 and 1976. As noted above, in composition the painting is most similar to the *Soult Immaculate Conception* commissioned for the Seville hospital of Los Venerables Sacerdotes. Between 1676 and 1678 Murillo created a picture cycle for this hospital. The virtuoso compositional and colour scheme of the Hermitage work indicates that it was painted not before this time and should be dated *c.* 1680.

Mayer (1934) believed that the drawing in the Kunsthalle (Hamburg) was a preliminary study for the painting. Angulo (1981, 2) did not agree with this and, indeed, neither the face of the Virgin nor the gesture of her arms are similar in the painting in the drawing. Angulo voiced the opinion that the pose of the Virgin Mary was influenced by the *Assumption* by Rubens (versions of it are in the Kunsthistorisches Museum, Vienna, in the Musée Royaux des Beaux-Arts, Brussels, and in the Gallery, Liechtenstein).

Provenance: 1779 Acquired as part of the Walpole collection in Houghton Hall, England (upon its entry into the Hermitage was considered a pendant to the *Adoration of the Shepherds*).

Engraved by V. Green. 1776, an unknown engraver in the *Hermitage Gallery* by F. Labensky (vol. 3, unpublished), Huot (Hermitage Gallery 1845-1847. 2:20), and H. Struck, 1884.

Exhibitions: 1984 Leningrad, No. 30.

19. *THE ARCHANGEL RAPHAEL AND BISHOP DOMONTE*

1680-1681.
Oil on canvas. 211 x 150 cm.
The Pushkin Museum of Fine Arts, Moscow. Inv. No. 253.

According to the biblical and apocryphal texts, the Archangel Raphael was the protector of pilgrims and other travellers; he possessed the power to cure the sick and exorcise the evil spirits causing sickness. He helped Tobias to expel the evil spirit from the maiden Tobias was to marry, and to restore the eyesight of Tobit, Tobias' father (Book of Tobias 5, 4, ff. and the apocryphal book of Enoch).

Francisco Domonte (died 1681 or 1684), a native of Seville, entered the La Merced monastery in 1633. Later he served as the chief vicar in Peru and donated a large capital to the La Merced Calzada. In 1680 Domonte was made Bishop of Archon and obtained the post of *auxiliar* in Seville (Angulo, 1981, 2).

The painting was commissioned for the monastery by Domonte. There is a surviving entry in its inventory for 1732 which says: "El San Rafael con el retrato del Illustrissimo Señor don Fr. Domonte es de don Bartolome Morillo el mas cierto imitador de la naturaleza quien no tubo competidor en su siglo en lo movido y cargado" (St. Raphael with the portrait of the Illustrious Señor don Fr. Domonte by don Bartolome Murillo. the most accurate imitator of nature with whom nobody in his century could compete in the rendition of movement and airiness) (Quoted after: Angulo 1981, 2).

The dating of the painting is problematic. Waagen (1864) assigned it to the "second period" of Murillo's career, that is, approximately, 1660s-1670s. Malitskaya (1847) dated it *c.* 1680 arguing that Domonte was consecrated as a bishop in 1680 and died in 1681. Angulo (1981, 2) put forward the same arguments but noted that on the grounds of style the work should be placed within an earlier period.

Malitskaya suggested that the panting may have been based on the study *The Archangel Raphael* (oil on canvas, 30.5 x 22 cm; Boehler collection, Lucerne; later at a sale in Madrid). In this study, though, the archangel is depicted with a fish and. in all likelihood, it was originally intended for a representation of Tobias and the angel. Angulo dates the study *c.* 1670. Murillo paid special attention to representations of angels, one of the earliest among which dates from 1650-1655 (de Rozier collection, Madrid). In the 1660s Murillo produced a series of drawings with angels (Louvre, Paris; Brown 1976, p. 121-126; Ressort 1983, p. 40-45, Nos 63-71). Between 1665 and 1668 Murillo painted the *Guardian Angel* for the church of the Capuchin monastery in Seville (now in Seville Cathedral). The Moscow painting is close to it in style.

It cannot be ruled out that the *Archangel Raphael and Bishop Domonte* was painted in the latter half of the 1660s and the bishop's mitre and crosier were added later after Domonte had been made bishop. No reliable evidence is available, however, for dating the painting to the 1660s and therefore it must be dated to the period after 1680, that is, after Domonte had been consecrated.

Following pages:
The Archangel Raphael and Bishop Domonte. Details.
The Pushkin Museum of Fine Arts, Moscow.

Provenance: Church of the La Merced Calzada monastery, Seville; 1810 Alcázar, Seville; after 1811 Malmaison Gallery of Josephine Beauharnais, Paris; 1814 Inherited by Eugene Beauharnais (from 1817 Duke of Leuchtenberg), transferred to Munich; from 1824 Property of Maximilian, Duke of Leuchtenberg; after 1851 Transferred to St. Petersburg with other paintings from the Leuchtenberg Gallery; from 1852 Property of Nikolai Maximilianovich, Duke of Leuchtenberg; from 1890 Property of Georgi Nikolayevich. Duke of Leuchtenberg; 1917 Entered the Rumiantsev Museum, Moscow; Since 1924 Pushkin Museum of Fine Arts, Moscow.

Engraved by G. Muxel (*Gemälde Sammlung in München Seiner Königlichen Hoheit des Augusto Herrings von Leuchtenberg und Santa Cruz Fürsten von Eichstädt...*).

Exhibitions: 1861 St. Petersburg, No. 114; 1886 St. Petersburg, No. 88.

156

20. *THE INFANT CHRIST PRICKED BY CROWN OF THORNS*

Murillo (?).
Oil on canvas. 57 x 43 cm.
The Hermitage, St. Petersburg. Inv. No. 339.

The subject of the Infant Christ pricked by a crown of thorns—a symbol of his future sufferings—was very popular among seventeenth-century Seville artists. It was repeatedly interpreted by Francisco de Zurbarán and the painters of Murillo's circle. Quite often such works were paired with representations of the young Virgin engaged in needlework.

The painting entered the Hermitage as an original by Murillo but Waagen (1864) soon raised doubts about it. In the catalogue of 1863 it was listed as a work ascribed to Murillo while in the catalogue of 1892 it was attributed to Murillo with a query. Liphart (Cat. 1912) registered it as an original, noting that there were some doubts on this matter. The Hermitage catalogues of 1958 and 1976 present it as a work by an unknown seventeenth-century Spanish artist. Angulo (1981, 2) believes the panting to have been executed by Murillo's studio.

A close version which belongs to the Prado, Madrid (Inv. No. 1318, kept at the War Ministry) is identical in composition but the technique is different, as are the face of the Child and the drawing of the chair. It also has cherubs in the background around Christ's head that are absent in the Hermitage painting. The Prado version had been attributed to Murillo (Angulo 1981, 2, No. 1327) but in the latest inventory of the museum it is listed as a painting by Pedro Nuñez de Villavicencio ("El Prado disperse", *Boletín del Muses del Prado,* 1981, No. 5. May-August, p. 136, No. 1318). The Hermitage work was painted by another artist. A similar face of the Child occurs in the *Infant Jesus and St. John* (Hermitage. Leningrad); these works are also close in style as follows from a comparison of their X-ray photographs: the brushstrokes and the chiaroscuro handling of the underpainting in both cases exhibit almost no differences (Viazmenskaya 1987). The *Infant Christ Pricked by a Crown of Thorns* is somewhat inferior to the *Infant Jesus and St. John* in execution but one cannot rule out the possibility that the former work is an original by Murillo.

In addition to the Prado version, there are other variants of a lower quality in the Sedelmeyer collection (Paris), the Torrontegi collection (Bilbao), the Medin collection (Seville) and the Meña collection (Madrid).

P. Nuñez de Villavicencio.
The Infant Christ Pricked by a Crown of Thorns.
Prado, Madrid.

Provenance: 1846 Entered the Hermitage as part of the D. Tatishchev Bequest.

Exhibitions: 1984 Leningrad, No. 31.

160

21. *THE DEATH OF ST. CLARE*

Murillo, studio copy.
Oil on canvas. 118 x 161.5 cm.
The Hermitage, St. Petersburg. Inv. No. 1459.

The painting was cut off on the right. The stretcher is of an old origin with mitred middle pieces obviously made after the painting had been cut.

The legend tells that St. Clare of Assisi was a disciple of St. Francis and the founder of the Order of Poor Clares. She was presumably born in 1193 and was ordained as a nun by St. Francis in 1212. She lived in a convent exemplifying the Franciscan idea of poverty and died in 1253. She was canonized in 1255. Sister Benvenuta who was among the nuns present at Clare's death had a vision of a procession of saintly maidens in white robes with palm branches in their hands, led by Christ and the Virgin Mary, one of the maidens laying on the body of St. Clare a rich coverlet (AASS. Augusti, p. 739-763). The subject of the Death of St. Clare was treated by Italian and German painters. In Spain, apart from Murillo, Juan de Valdés Leal executed in 1652 a *Death of St. Clare* for the Convent of Poor Clares in Carmona. His work reflects the influence of Murillo. Angulo (1981, 1, p. 261; 2, p. 13), who studied the iconography of the subject in detail, referred to the chronicles which mention four monks at St. Clare's deathbed. In Murillo's painting, however, there are only three monks. In Angulo's opinion, the monk kneeling on the left is a portrait of one of the donors.

The *Death of St. Clare* was painted for the small cloister of the St. Francis convent in Seville as part of the series created between 1644 and 1646. The Hermitage painting was acquired as a work by Pedro Atanasio Bocanegra. It was Viardot (1844) who identified it as a copy of Murillo's work. Later it was described in the literature as a Bocanegra (Cat. 1863), as a copy of Murillo's work (Curtis 1883. Cat. 1901) and even as being by both Murillo and Bocanegra (Blanc 1869). Liphart (Cat. 1912) did not include the painting in the Hermitage catalogue apparently because of the difficulties with its attribution. It was also not included in the catalogue of 1958 while in the catalogue of 1976 it appeared under the name of Bocanegra with a query. Angulo (1981) suggested that the copy was made by an eighteenth-century artist. In the catalogue of the exhibition Murillo and Seventeenth-Century Andalusian Artists in the Hermitage Collection (1984) it was noted as a copy by Bocanegra but Perez Sanchez believed (oral statement) that it was executed in Murillo's studio in view of its high quality and closeness to the artist's works.

Provenance: 1814 Bought from W. Coesvelt in Amsterdam.
Exhibitions: 1984 Leningrad, No. 32.

22. *THE INFANT CHRIST ASLEEP*

Murillo, studio copy.
Oil on canvas. 57.9 x 73.6 cm.
The Hermitage, St. Petersburg. Inv. No. 293.

Representations of the Infant Christ asleep appeared in fifteenth-century Italian art, becoming especially popular among the Bologna painters in the seventeenth century. The subject was an allegory on the death of Christ. Murillo treated this subject both with symbolic emblems (the skull and cross) and without them.

Upon its entry into the Hermitage the painting was attributed to the Seville artist Francisco Antolinez but later it was erroneously ascribed to Jose Antolinez under whose name it was listed in the catalogue of 1863. Curtis (1883) was the first to note that the painting was a copy of Murillo's work from the Grosvenor Gallery of the Duke of Westminster in London (now it is in the Wernher collection, Luton Hoo, Luton. Bedfordshire, England). The painting was included in the catalogue of 1912 as a copy of Murillo's work and it was omitted in the Hermitage catalogues of 1958 and 1976.

The copy is of a very high quality with subtle light-and-shade effects and a harmonious colour scheme. As the X-ray photograph shows, its technique is close to that of works by Murillo's studio, in particular, the *Infant Christ Pricked by a Crown of Thorns* (Hermitage). It cannot be ruled out that the copy was actually made by Francisco Antolinez (c. 1644, Seville before 1700, Madrid), a pupil of Murillo. The canvas was acquired in Spain in the early nineteenth century and the attribution was apparently traditional.

Angulo (1981, 1, p. 421) suggested that such works were intended for tombstones or funerary urns.

The original painting was executed c. 1660 and the copy could have been made shortly afterwards.

Provenance: 1814 Bought from W. Coesvelt in Amsterdam.

Other such copies are in a private collection (Barcelona) and in the collection of Almazan Gomez Moreno (Madrid). Some copies were mentioned in the literature (Angulo 1981, 2, p. 193).

Exhibitions: 1984 Leningrad, No. 33.

The Death of St. Clare.
The Hermitage, St. Petersburg.

139

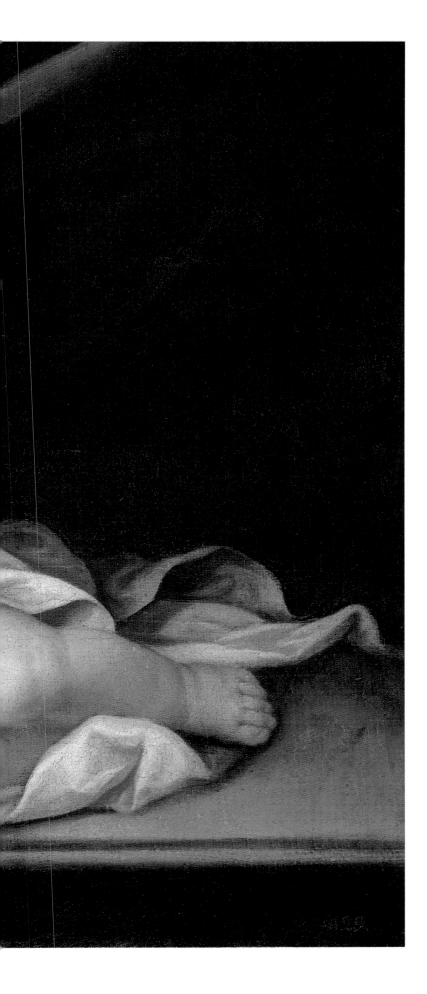

The Infant Christ Asleep.
The Hermitage, St. Petersburg.

23. *PRESENTATION IN THE TEMPLE*

Murillo, circle.
Oil on canvas. 105.5 x 174.5 cm..
The Hermitage, St. Petersburg. Inv. No. 380.

According to the Gospels, on the fortieth day after his birth Christ was brought to the Temple to be 'consecrated to the Lord', where he was recognized as the Messiah by a devout old man, Simeon (Luke 2 : 22-40).

The painting entered the Hermitage as an original by Murillo but later Waagen (1864) questioned his authorship. In the catalogue of 1863 it was listed as a work by Murillo's school and in the catalogue of 1912 as a copy of Murillo's painting (without reference to the original). It was not included in the Hermitage catalogues of 1958 and 1976. Angulo (1974) pointed to a similar composition in the Domínguez collection (Seville) which he thought to be by a pupil of Murillo. In the same article Angulo mentioned a drawing, possibly by Murillo, that appeared at a sale in Paris. The two works mentioned above are similar to the Hermitage canvas in composition but not identical. The quality of the Hermitage painting does not allow us to ascribe it either to Murillo or his studio.

Murillo, circle. *Presentation in the Temple.*
A. Dominguez collection, Seville.

Provenance: 1834 Acquired with other pictures for the Hermitage by A. Gessler, the Russian Consul-General in Cadiz; Since 1835 The Hermitage.

Exhibitions: 1984 Leningrad, No. 36.

168

24. *THE ADORATION OF THE SHEPHERDS*

Murillo, studio copy.
Oil on canvas. 43 x 60 cm.
The Hermitage, St. Petersburg. Inv. No. 341.

For the subject, see the note on the *Adoration of the Shepherds* (Hermitage, Inv. No. 316).

The painting was acquired by the Hermitage as an original by Murillo. Labensky (1838) regarded it as a "finished sketch". Curtis (1838) identified it as a sketch for the painting from the Wallace collection in London, which is signed and dated a. 1665 (145.5 x 217 cm). Later Liphart (Cat. 1912) reported that V. von Loga doubted that the work was an original. It was not included in the Hermitage catalogues of 1958 and 1976. Angulo (1981, 2) noted the high quality of the painting and suggested that it was a studio copy. The results of X-ray examination also indicate that the work is by Murillo's studio.

The Adoration of the Shepherds.
c. 1665, Walles collection, London.

Provenance: 1834 Acquired with other pictures by A. Gessler, the Russian Consul-General in Cadiz.

Exhibitions: 1984 Leningrad, No. 35.

169

The Adoration of the Shepherds.
The Hermitage, St. Petersburg.

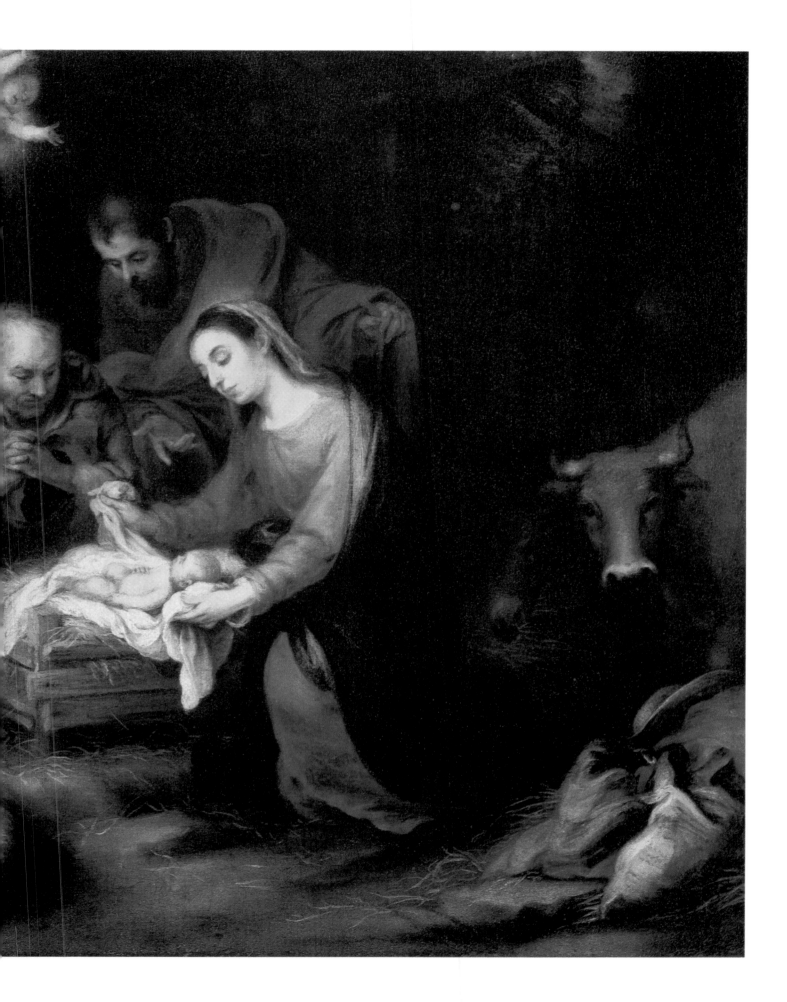

25. *BOY WITH A WREATH OF OAK LEAVES*

Murillo, studio copy.
Oil on canvas. 51.5 x 38 cm.
Monplaisir Palace, Petrodvorets.

According to the seventeenth-century tradition the oak leaves on the Child's head symbolized his moral and physical strength (J. Chevalier, A. Gheebrant, *Dictionnaire des Symboles*. Paris, 1973, p. 348).

Upon its entry into the Hermitage the painting was considered a Murillo. In the catalogue of 1863 it was included as belonging to the "school of Murillo" and in the catalogue of 1892 as a free copy of Murillo's *Two Boys Playing Dice* from the Kunstakademie in Vienna. Goldovsky and Znamenov (1981) erroneously identified the painting as a work of an unknown eighteenth-century Flemish artist.

Provenance: 1834 Acquired by the Hermitage as part of the collection of the Spanish envoy M. Paez de la Cadena; 1925 transferred to Petrodvorets.

26. *WOMEN BEHIND BARS*

Murillo, circle.
Oil on canvas. 41 x 58.6 cm.
The Hermitage, St. Petersburg. Inv. No. 338.

Following pages: *Women Behind Bars*. The Hermitage, St. Petersburg.

Upon its entry into the Hermitage the painting was entitled *Two Female Heads Behind Bars*. Waagen (1864) suggested that it portrays a Seville procuress Selestina and her daughter. Mayer (1913) called the painting *Selestina and Her Daughter in Gaol*. The Hermitage catalogue of 1958 contains a note that the painting depicts characters from the novel *Selestina or Tragicomedy of Callisto and Melitea* by Hernando de Rojas. However, Angulo (1981, 2) sees no grounds for such a view while the bars, in his opinion, do not imply that the women are in prison: these could be the bars in the window of their own house. Since the title *Selestina and Her Daughter* is not traditional but was given arbitrarily and without argumentation it should be rejected.

The painting entered the Hermitage as Murillo's original but soon this attribution was doubted. Viardot (1860) thought that the picture was a study by Velázquez. Mayer (1913) suggested that it was painted by a seventeenth-century Madrid artist. In the old Hermitage catalogues, however, it was listed as Murillo's original and in the catalogue of 1912 as a work by Murillo's school. The catalogue of 1976 describes it as a work by an unknown seventeenth-century Spanish artist. Angulo (1981, 2) believes that it could have been created by a pupil of Murillo and thus may be attributed to Murillo's school.

The subject of the painting is close to Murillo's range of motifs; there is a similar work by him *Women from Callega* at the Window in the National Gallery of Art, Washington. In colour and texture, a similar curtain occurs in the *Infant Christ Asleep* (Hermitage): the weave of the canvas is the same as in the *Infant Christ Asleep* and the *Infant Christ Pricked by a Crown of Thorns* (Hermitage). However, the radiograph shows a significant difference from the style of Murillo and his studio in the brushwork and the distribution of light and shade. Thus one can draw the conclusion that the author is a Seville artist who worked about the same time as Murillo but who was not his pupil.

Provenance: 1846 Received by the Hermitage as part of the Tatishchev Bequest.

Exhibitions: 1984 Leningrad, No. 37.

Women from Gallega at the Window.
National Gallery, of Art Washington.

177

27. THE INFANT ST. JOHN WITH THE LAMB

Murillo, studio copy.
Oil on canvas. 96 x 78 cm.
Fragments of the inscription on the band: *ECCE AGNUS DEI.*
The Pushkin Museum of Fine Arts, Moscow. Inv. No. 1501.

According to Christian tradition, St. John the Baptist was the last of the prophets and the forerunner of Christ who prophesied the coming of the Messiah. The Gospels only briefly mention that as a child he lived in the desert (Luke 1: 80). But it is also said there that St. John first saw Christ as a grown man (John 1: 29, 36). However, even in works depicting St. John as an infant, seventeenth-century artists used the Latin inscription *ECCE AGNUS DEI,* that is, the words St. John uttered when meeting Christ. Francisco Pacheco's instructions are of interest in this respect: "His attributes... /include/ ... the lamb meaning Christ whom St. John the Baptist called God's lamb though he saw him as a grown man. The second attribute is the cross: some believe that it should not be painted... They say that St. John carried it on his staff only after the death of the Saviour... But it should be borne in mind that, apart from the old tradition of representation, it is important that St. John was a prophet... and just as it is not reproachable to paint the Infant Christ embracing the cross, sleeping on it, or playing with it in His Mother's arms, it is admissible and legitimate to place Him in the representations of His forerunner, St. John, at any age" (Pacheco 1866, 2, p. 272. 273).

In the Yusupov collection the painting was regarded as a Murillo original. In the Pushkin Museum (Cat. 1957) it was ascribed to Murillo's school. Angulo (1981. 2) considered it a free studio copy from the work in the Prado (1670-1680; 121 x 99 cm. Inv. No. 963).

The Infant St. John with the Lamb.
1670-1680, Prado, Madrid.

The Infant St. John with the Lamb.
Engraving by J.-B. Lebrun from Murillo's painting.

Provenance: 1808 Property of J.-B. Le Brun, Paris; from 1810 N. Yusupov collection, Moscow; from 1834 B. Yusupov collection, St. Petersburg; since 1924 Pushkin Museum of Fine Arts, Moscow (transferred from the State Museum Reserve).

Engraved by J.-B. Le Brun *(Recueil de gravures... d'après un choix de tableaux... recueillies dans un voyage fait en Espagne 1807 et 1808,* Paris, 1809. No. 336).

28. ST. JOHN WITH THE LAMB

Murillo, 18th-century copy.
Oil on canvas. 173 x 119 cm.
Inscribed on the band below: *ECCE AGNUS DEI*.
The Hermitage, St. Petersburg. Inv. No. 290.

For the subject, see the note on the *Infant St. John With the Lamb* (Pushkin Museum, Inv. No. 1501). The painting was received as a work by Murillo and was considered an original until Waagen (1864) identified it as a copy of a picture (164.5 x 106 cm) from the National Gallery in London. Mayer (1913) believed that the Hermitage copy was made by Miguel de Tobar, probably because a similar copy by this painter is in the San Isidoro church in Seville. Thanks to its high quality the Hermitage copy always attracted the attention of art historians. Schmidt (1926) suggested that it was Murillo's own replica. It was listed as an original in the catalogue of 1958 but again as a copy in the catalogue of 1976. Angulo (1981, 2) also regarded it as a copy. X-ray examination confirms this opinion.

Viazmenskaya (1987) drew the conclusion that in the underpainting the face, arms and legs of St. John are modelled schematically. Meanwhile the X-ray examination of the Hermitage paintings by Murillo demonstrates that one of the most typical features of his creative method was the detailed modelling of eyes, lips and spaces of the face. The radiograph of the present picture clearly shows that the brushstrokes are applied in the same direction and have approximately the same length. This style differs sharply from Murillo's free and dynamic manner.

The original is dated to 1655-1660 (MacLaren-Braham 1970).

Judging by the free pastose brushwork, the copy was executed in the eighteenth century.

There was a pendant to *St. John with the Lamb* entitled *Christ as the Good Shepherd* (both paintings were in the same collection until 1840: now the latter is in the G. Lane collection, Peterborough, England).

Other similar copies are in the Lovelace collection, England; in two private collections, Madrid; in the G. Stirling-Maxwell collection, Glasgow; at a Sotheby auction in London (1.11.1961); in the San Isidoro church, Seville; in a private collection, Stadhampton; and in a private collection (Sofia). The Hermitage piece was repeatedly copied in St. Petersburg in the nineteenth century.

Provenance: 1792 Received by the Hermitage as part of the G. Potemkin collection.

Christ as the Good Shepherd.
G. Lane Collection, Peterborough. England.

Engraved by G. Skorodumov in 1785 (with the inscription *Ex tabulae picta Murillo quae est in Museo Serenissimum Principiis Gregory Alexandrinis Potemkin*) and by I. Robillard (Hermitage Gallery 1845-1847, 2: 17).

According to the inscription on the engraving by Skorodumov, in 1785 the painting was in the G. Potemkin collection. For a long time its subsequent history remained unclear. Its provenance was first mentioned in the catalogue of 1889 though it was said there that the painting had apparently been acquired by the Hermitage after 1838 since it had not been included by Labensky in his *Livret* (1838). Somov (Cat. 1901) found out that in 1797 the work was among the paintings of the Winter Palace. The subsequent Hermitage catalogues noted the time of its entry: prior to 1797. Comparatively recently the name of the painting was found in the inventory of the Potemkin Gallery (Kagané 1987) sold to the Hermitage in 1792 by Potemkin's heirs (Esipov 1891).

Exhibitions: 1984 Leningrad, No. 34.

BIBLIOGRAPHY

MANUSCRIPT CATALOGUES AND INVENTORIES

Cat. 1773-1783 — Cat. 1785
E. Münich, *Catalogue raisonné des tableaux qui se trouvent dans les Galeries et Cabinets du Palais Imperial à Saint-Pétersbourg.* St. Petersburg, 1773-1783, vols. 1-2; 1785, vol. 3 (Hermitage Archives, fund 1, inv. VI-a. No. 85).

Cat. 1797-1850
Catalogue of the Hermitage Paintings Compiled by Order of Paul I by Academy Artists Akimov, Gordeyev, Ugriumov and Kozlovsky with the Participation of the Hermitage Curator F. I. Labensky, in 1797. Begun 1797, last entries 1850 (Hermitage Archives, fund 1, inv. VI, No. 87).

Inv. 1859
Inventory of the Paintings and Plafonds in the 2nd Department of the Imperial Hermitage. Begun 1859. last entries 1929 (kept in the Department of Western European Art).

CATALOGUES

Cat. 1774
[E. Münich] *Catalogue des tableaux qui se trouvent dans les Galeries et Dans les Cabinets du Palais Imperial de Saint-Pétersbourg,* St. Petersburg, 1774.

Cat. 1839
Musée du prince Yousoupoff: contenant les tableaux marbres, ivoires et porcelaines qui se trouvent dans l'Hôtel de son excellence à Saint-Pétersbourg. St. Petersburg, 1839.

Cat. 1850
[G. N. Muxel] *Verzeichniss der Bilder Galerie Seiner Königlichen Hoheit des Prinzen Eugen Herzogs von Leuchtenberg in München.* Augsburg, 1850.

Cat. 1863-1916
[B. de Koehne] *Ermitage Imperial. Catalogue de la Galerie de tableaux.* St. Petersburg, 1863 (the inventory numbers in this catalogue are repeated in all editions up to 1916).

Cat. 1889
[E. Brünningk, A. Somov] *The Imperial Hermitage. Catalogue of the Picture Gallery. 1 Italian and Spanish Painting.* St. Petersburg, 1889 (in Russian). Reprint: [E. Brünningk, A. Somoff] *Ermitage Imperial Catalogue de la Galerie des tableaux.* 3rd ed. 1. *Les écoles d'Italie et d'Espagne.* St. Petersburg. 1891.

Cat. 1892
[A. Somov] *The Imperial Hermitage. Catalogue of the Picture Gallery. 1. Italian and Spanish Painting.* St. Petersburg, 1892 (in Russian). French editions published in 1899 and 1909.

Cat. 1901
[A. Somov] *The Imperial Hermitage. Catalogue of the Picture Gallery. 1. Italian and Spanish Painting.* St. Petersburg, 1901 (in Russian).

Cat. 1909
A. Somoff, *Ermitage Impérial. Catalogue de la Galerie des tableaux. Les écoles d'Italie et d Espagne.* St. Petersburg, 1909.

Cat. 1912
[E. K. Liphart] *The Imperial Hermitage. Catalogue of the Picture Gallery. 1. Italian and Spanish Painting.* St. Petersburg, 1912 (in Russian).

Cat. 1916
[A. Somov] *The Imperial Hermitage. A Concise Catalogue of the Picture Gallery,* Petrograd, 1916 (in Russian).

Cat. 1920
The State Museum Reserve. Catalogue of the Art Works of the Former Yusupov Gallery, Petrograd, 1920 (in Russian).

Cat. 1948, Cat . 1957, Cat. 1961
The Pushkin Museum of Fine Arts. Catalogue of the Picture Gallery. Compiled by K. Malitskaya and V. Shileiko. Edited by Prof. B. Vipper, Moscow, 1948 (reprinted in 1957 and 1961) (in Russian).

Cat. 1958
[V. Levinson-Lessing and a group of authors from the Hermitage Department of Western European Art] *The State Hermitage. Department of Western European Art. Catalogue of Paintings,* vols. 1, 2. Introduced by V. Levinson-Lessing, Leningrad-Moscow, 1958 (in Russian).

Cat. 1976
The State Hermitage. Western European Painting. Catalogue. 1. Italy, Spain, France, Switzerland. Introduced by V. Levinson-Lessing (2nd edition, revised and enlarged). Leningrad, 1976 (in Russian).

Cat. 1986
The Pushkin Museum of Fine Arts. Catalogue of the Picture Gallery. Introduced by I. Kuznetsova Moscow, 1986 (in Russian).

REFERENCES

Aedes Walpolianae 1747
Aedes Walpolianae or a Descriprion of the Collection of Pictures at Houghton Hall in Norfolk, the Seat of the Right Honourable Sir Robert Walpole, Earl of Orford. Londres, 1747 *(Ibid., 1750, 1767).*

Alfonso 1886
L. Alfonso, *Murillo, el hombre, el artista, las obras,* Barcelona, 1886.

Angulo 1961.
D. Angulo Iñiguez, *Miscelánea Murillesca,* AEA, 1961, No. 133, p. 1-24.

Angulo 1964
D. Angulo Iñiguez, *Murillo: El retrato de Nicolás de Omazur adquirido por el Museo del Prado. Varios bocetos. «La Adoración» de Leningrado.* AEA, 1964, No. 148, p. 269-280.

Angulo 1966
D. Angulo Iñiguez, "Bartolomé Murillo. Inventario de sus bienes." *Boletín Academia Historia, 1966.*

Angulo 1971
D. Angulo Iñiguez, "Pintura del siglo XVII", in: *Ars Hispaniae,* Madrid, 1971, v. 15.

Angulo 1974.
D. Angulo Iñiguez, *Algunos dibujos de Murillo,* AEA, 1974, No 186, p. 97-108.

Angulo 1981
D. Angulo Iñiguez, *Murillo,* Madrid, 1981, 3 vols.

Antonov 1982
V. Antonov, *La Adquisición de Gessler para el Ermitage.* AEA, 1982, No 219.

Bazin 1958
G. Bazin, *Musée de l'Ermitage: les grands maîtres de la peinture.* Paris, 1958 (German edition: 1960).

Bénézit 1976
E. Bénézit, *Dictionnaire critique et documentaire des peintres, sculpteurs, dessinateurs et graveurs,* Paris, 1976, 10 vols.

Benois 1910
A. *Benois: Guidebook to the Picture Galery of the Imperial Hermitage,* St. Petersburg, 1910 (in Russian).

Benois 1912
A. Benois, *The History of Painting of All Times and Nations. 4. Spanish Painting from the 16th to 18th Centuries,* Petrograd, 1912 (in Russian).

Beroquí 1932
P. Beroquí, "El Museo del Prado. Apuntes para su história", *BSEE* 1932, v. 40.

Beruete 1904
A. Beruete y Moret, "Museo del Ermitage. Escuela española". *La Lectura.* 1904. No. 41, May.

Blanc 1869
Ch. Blanc, W. Bürger, P. Mantz, L. Viardot, P. Lefort, *Histoire des Peintres de toutes les écoles. Ecole Espagnole.* Paris, 1869.

Braham 1965
A. Braham, "The Early Style of Murillo", *The Burlington Magazine.* 1965, v. 107.

Braham 1981
A. Braham, *The National Gallery. El Greco to Goya. The Taste for Spanish Paintings in Britain and Ireland.* London, 1981.

Brown 1970
J. Brown, "Hieroglyphs of Death and Salvation: The Decoration of the Church of the Hermandad de la Caridad. Seville", *The Art Bulletin.* 1970, v. 52.

Brown 1976
J. Brown, *Murillo and His Drawings.* Princeton, 1976.

Brown 1978
J. Brown, *Images and Ideas in Seventeenth-Century Spanish Painting.* Princeton. 1978.

BSEE
Boletín de la Sociedad Española de Excurciones.

Buchanan 1824
W. Buchanan, *Memoirs of Painting, with a Chronological History of the Importation of Pictures by the Great Masters into England since the French Revolution.* London, 1824, 2 vols.

Calvo Seraller 1981
F. Calvo Seraller, "Tesoros del Ermitage. Museo del Prado, Madrid", *El Pais.* 1981, 2 May.

Camón Aznar 1983
J. Camón Aznar, *La Pintura española del siglo XVII. Summa Artis. Historia general del Arte,* 3 ed., Madrid, 1983, v. 25.

Canningham 1848
A. Canningham, *The Life of Sir David Wilkie.* London, 1848, 2 vols.

Ceán Bermudez 1800
J. A. Ceán Bermudez, *Diccionario histórico de los más ilustres profesores de las Bellas Artes en España.* Madrid, 1800, 6 vols.

Choiseul 1771
Recueil d estampes gravées d'après les tableaux du Cabinet de Monseigneur le Duc de Choiseul, par les soins de S-r Basan, MDCCLXXI. A Paris.

Choiseul 1772
Catalogue des tableaux... de Monseigneur le Duc de Choiseul... en son hôtel, rue de Richelieu. 1772, Paris, April 6-10.

Clément de Ris 1879
L. Clément de Ris, *Musée Impérial de l'Ermitage à Saint-Pétersbourg.* GBA, 1879, April.

Cumberland 1782
R. Cumberland, *Anecdotes of Eminent Painters in Spain During the 16th and 17th Centuries.* London, 1782, 2 vols. *(ibid., 1787).*

Curtis 1883
Ch. Curtis, *Velázquez and Murillo.* London, 1883.

Dalton 1869
H. Dalton, *Murillo und seine Gemälde in der Kaiser Ermitage zu St. Petersburg.* St. Petersburg, 1869.

Descargues 1961
P. Descargues, *Le Musée de l'Ermitage.* Paris, 1961.

Essipov 1891
G. Esipov, "Inventories of the Houses and Movable Property of Prince Potemkin-Tavrichesky, Purchased from His Heirs by the Empress Catherine II", *Readings* at *the Imperial Society of Russian History and Antiquities at Moscow University.* 1891, book 4 (in Russian).

Gaya Nuño 1958
J. A. Gaya Nuño, *La Pintura española fuera de España. Historia y Catálogo,* Madrid, 1958.

Gaya Nuño 1978
J. A. Gaya Nuño, *L'Opera completa di Murillo.* Milan 1978 *(ibid., 1980).*

Gelder 1967
J. G. van Gelder, "Murillos Heilige Familie uit de verz. Bourke", *Bulletin Rijksmuseum.* 1967.

Gestoso y Pérez 1889
J. Gestoso y Pérez, *Sevilla monumental y artistica.* Séville, 1889-1902, 3 vols.

Goldovski, Znamenov 1981.
G. Goldovsky, V. Znamenov, *Monplaisir Palace in the Louer Park of Petrodvorets.* Leningrad, 1981 (in Russian).

Gómez Imaz 1896
M. Gómez Imaz, *Inventario de los cuadros sustraídos por el Gobierno intruso en Sevilla el ano 1810.* Seville, 1896 (see.: I. H. Lipschutz, *Spanish Painting and the French Romantics.* Harvard/Cambridge, 1972).

Grandjean 1964
S. Grandjean, *Inventaire après décès de l'Impératrice Joséphine à Malmaison.* Paris, 1964.

Haraszti-Takács 1977
M. Haraszti-Takács, *Murillo.* Budapest, 1977 *(ibid., Berlin, 1978).*

Haraszti-Takács 1978
M. Haraszti-Takács, *Deux peintres espagnols ayant servi de modèles à Manet. Acta Historiae Artium Academiae Scientiarum Hungaricae.* Budapest, 1978, v. 24, f. 1-4.

Haraszti-Takács 1982
M. Haraszti-Takács, "Œuvres de Murillo dans les collections hongroises", *Bulletin du Musée Hongrois des Beaux-Arts.* 1982, N° 58-59.

Hermitage 1978
The Hermitage Western European Painting of the Thirteenth to Eighteenth Centuries. Introduced by E. Kozhina, Leningrad, 1978.

Hermitage Gallery 1805
The Hermitage Gallery: Line Engravings, St. Petersburg. vol. 1, 1805 (in Russian and French).

Hermitage Gallery 1845-1847
The Imperial Hermitage Gallery: Lithographs by French Artists. St. Petersburg, 1845, vol. 1; 1847, vol. 2 (in Russian and French).

Hernández Díaz 1933
J. Hernández Díaz, *Murillo,* in: *Thieme-Becker Lexikon.* 1933, v. 22, p. 202.

Jordan 1968
W. Jordan, "A Museum of Spanish Painting in Texas", *The Art Journal.* 27, 1968, Spring.

Justi 1892
C. Justi. *Murillo.* Leipzig, 1892 *(ibid., 1904).*

Kagané 1977.
L. Kagané, *Spanish Painting of the 16th-18th Centuries in the Hermitage. Guidebook.* Leningrad, 1977 (in Russian).

Kagané 1987
L. Kagané, "Murillo's Paintings in the Hermitage. The History of the Collection", *Muzei 7. Art Collections of the USSR.* Moscow, 1987, p. 263-279 (in Russian).

Kagané 1987, Collection of Spanish Painting
L. Kagané, "The Collection of Spanish Painting in the Hermitage during the 18th Century", *Western European Art of the 18th Century. Publications and Studies.* Leningrad, 1987, p. 12-27 (in Russian).

Kagané 1988
L. Kagané, *Murillo.* Leningrad, 1988.

Konradi 1917
V. Konradi. *Among the Hermitage Painting.* Petrograd, 1917 (in Russian).

Labensky 1838
[F. I. Labensky], *Livret de la Galerie Impériale de l'Ermitage de Saint-Pétersbourg.* St. Petersburg, 1838.

Lafond 1930
P. Lafond, *Murillo.* Paris, 1930.

Lefort 1892
P. Lefort, *Murillo et ses élèves. Catalogue raisonné de ses principaux ouvrages.* Paris, 1892.

Leningrad, Hermitage 1964
The Hermitage. Painting. 17th and 18th Centuries. Introduction and notes by V. Levinson-Lessing and staff members of the Hermitage, Prague-Leningrad, 1964 (English edition 1965-1967; Spanish edition 1969).

Levina 1969
I Levina, *Murillo's Paintings in the Hermitage.* Leningrad, 1969 (in Russian).

Levinson-Lessing 1985
V Levinson-Lessing. *The History of the Hermitage Picture Gallery (1764-1917).* Leningrad, 1985 (in Russian).

Lescure 1867
M. de Lescure, *Malmaison.* Paris, 1867.

Liphart 1910
E. Liphart, "The Imperial Hermitage. New Acquisitions and Rehangings", *Starye Gody.* 1910, January (in Russian).

Loga 1923
V von Loga, *Die Malerei in Spanien von XIV. bis XVIII. Jahrhundert,* Berlin, 1923.

Mac Laren-Braham 1970
N. Mac Laren, *The Spanish School. National Gallery Catalogues.* London, 1952 (2nd ed, Allan Braham, 1970).

Malitskaya 1947
K. Malitskaya, *Spanish Painting. 16th and 17th Centuries.* Moscow, 1947 (in Russian).

Malitskaya 1957
K. Malitskaya, "A Little-Known Painting by Murillo", *Iskusstvo.* 1957, No 6 (in Russian).

Mariette 1857-1858
P. J. Mariette, *Abecedario.* Paris, 1857-1858, ó vols.

Mayer 1913
A. L Mayer, *Murillo. Des Meisters Gemälde* [Klassiker der Kunst], Stuttgart/Berlin, 1913.

Mayer 1922
A. L. Mayer, *Geschichte der Spanischen Malerei.* Leipzig, 1922.

Mayer 1923
A. L. Mayer, *Murillo.* Berlin. 1923.

Mayer 1934
A. L. Mayer, "Anotaciones al arte y a las obras de Murillo", *Revista Española de Excursiones.* 1934.

Mercey 1852
F. B. Mercey, "La collection du Maréchal Soult", *Revue des Deux Mondes.* 1852 (idem., *Etudes sur les Beaux-Arts.* 1855, vol. 2, p. 246-275).

Mihan 1944
G. Mihan, "Masterpieces Collected for the Hermitage by Catherine II and Her Successors", *Apollo.* April 1944.

Mireur 1911-1912
Mireur, *Dictionnaire des ventes d'art.* Paris, 1911-1912. vol. 5.

Montoto 1923
S. Montoto, *Murillo.* Seville, 1923.

Muñoz 1942
A. Muñoz, *Murillo.* Rome, 1942.

Neustroyev 1904
A Neustroyev, "The Duke of Leuchtenherg Collection of Paintings", in Treasures of Art of Russia, 1904, No 2-4 (in Russian).

Ortiz de Zuñiga 1677
D. Ortiz de Zuñiga, *Anales eclesiásticos y seculares de la más noble y muy leal ciudad de Sevilla... desde el año de 1246 hasta el de 1671....* Seville 1677 (reprint: *Ilustrados y corregidos por D. A. M. Espinosa y Carcel.* Madrid. 1975-1976, 5 vols.).

Pacheco 1866
F. Pacheco, *El Arte de la Pintura. su atigüedad y grandezas.* Madrid, 1866, 2 vols.

Palomo 1682
Palomo, *Noticia historica de la Santa Casa de la Caridad.* Seville, 1682.

Pemán 1961
C. Pemán, "Acerca de los llamados almuerzos velazqueños", AEA, 1961, No 136.

Perez Delgado 1972
R. Perez Delgado, *Bartolomé Estebán Murillo.* Madrid, 1972.

Ponz 1772-1794
A. Ponz, *Viaje de España. en que se da noticia de las cosas apreciables y dignos de saberse que hay en ella.* Madrid, 1772-1794, 9 vols. (ibid.. 1947).

Putevoditel 1981
Pushkin Museum of Fine Arts. Guidebook to the Picture Callery. Edited by T. Sedova, Moscow, 1981 (in Russian).

Réau 1956
L. Réaut, *Iconographie de l'art chrétien.* Paris, 1955-1959, 3 vols.

Rémy 1756
Rémy & Glomy, *Catalogue raisonné de tableaux. sculptures... qui composent le cabinet de fèu M. Le duc de Tallard.* Paris, 1756.

Rémy 1768
P. Rémy, *Catalogue raisonné des tableaux. groupes et figures de bronze qui composent le cahinet de feu monsieur Gaignat ancien secrétaire du roi et receveur des consignations.* Paris, 1768.

Ressort 1983
Cl. Ressort, *Murillo dans les musées français.* Paris, 1983.

Reveil 1828-1834
[Reveil] *Musée de Peinture et de Sculpture... dessinée et gravée à l'eau-forte par Reveil avec des notices par Duchêsne.* Paris, 1828-1834, 16 vols. (ibid.. 1872, 10 vols.).

Rohl 1961
L. Rohl, *Lettras y Colores.* Mexico, 1961.

Rose Wagner 1983
Rose Wagner, *Manuel Godoy. patrón de los artes y colecciones,* 2 vols., 1983, Madrid.

Röthlisberger 1961
M. Röthlisberger, *Claude Lorrain,* London, 1961, 2 vols.

Saltillo 1933
Marqués de Saltillo, *Mr. Frédéric Quilliet comisario de Bellas Artes del Gobierno intruso 1809-1814,* Madrid, 1933.

Sbornik 1876
Collection of the Imperial Russian Historical Society, St. Petersburg, vol. 17, 1876 (in Russian).

Schmidt 1926
J. Schmidt, *Murillo*, Leningrad, 1916 (in Russian).

Schnitzler 1828
J. H. Schnitzler, *Notice sur les principaux tableaux du Musée Impérial de l'Ermitage à Saint-Pétersbourg*, St. Petersburg, 1828.

Set of Prints 1788
Set of Prints Engraved after the Most Capital Paintings in the Collection of Her Majesty, the Empress of Russia, Lately in the Possession of the Earl of Orford at Houghton in Norfolk, London, 1788.

Somov 1859
A. Somov, *Paintings in the Imperial Hermitage*. St. Petersburg, 1859 (in Russian).

Soult 1852
Catalogue raisonné des tableaux de la Galerie de feu M. le Maréchal-Général Soult, duc de Dalmatie, dont la vente aura lieu à Paris dans l'ancienne Galerie Lebrun les mercredi 19, ven. 21 et .sa. 22 mai 1852...

Standish 1840
F. H. Standish, *Seville and Its Vicinity*, London, 1840.

Stechow 1966
W. Stechow, "B. E. Murillo. *Laban Searching for His Stolen Household Gods in Rachel's Tent*" *The Bulletin of the Cleveland Muveum*, vol. 53, 1966.

Stepanek 1969
P Stepanek, "La pintura española en la Galería Nacional de Praga", *Ibero-americana pragencia*, 3, 1969.

Stirling 1848
W. Stirling-Maxwell, *Annals of the Artists of Spain*, London, 1848, 3 vols.

Stromer 1879
T. Stromer, *Murillo. Leben und Werke*, Berlin, 1879.

Stuffmann 1968
M. Stuffmann "Les Tableaux de la collection de Pierre Crozat. Historique et destinée d'un ensemble célèbre, établis en partant d'un inventaire après décès inédit (1740)", GBA, 1968, vol. 72, p. 5-44.

Sullivan 1975-1976
E. Sullivan, "B. E. Murillo. *Boy uith a Dog*". *Master Paintings from the Hermitage and the State Russian Museum, Leningrad*, New York, 1975-1976.

Tormo 1914
E. Tormo, "La Inmaculada y el arte español" BSEE, 1914, p. 108 ff., 176 ff.

Tubino, 1864
F. M. Tubino, *Murillo, su época, su vida, sus cuadros*, Seville, 1864.

Viardot 1844
L. Viardot, *Les musées d'Allemagne et de Russie*, Paris, 1844.

Viardot 1860
L. Viardot, *Les musées d'Angleterre, de Belgique, de Hollande et de Russie*, Paris, 1860.

Viazmenskaya 1987
L. Viazmenskaya, "Technical and Technological Analysis of Murillo's Paintings from the Collection of the Hermitage", *Reports of the State Hermitage*, issue 52, 1987, p. 51-57 (in Russian).

Waagen 1864
G. F. Waagen, *Die Gemäldesammlung in der Kaiserlichen Ermitage zu St. Petersburg nebst Bemerkungen über andere dortige Kunstsammlungen*, Munich, 1864.

Weiner 1923
P. P. Weiner, *Les chefs-d'œuvre de la Galerie de Tableaux de l'Ermitage à Petrograd*. Munich, 1923.

Wrangell 1909
N. Wrangell, *Les chefs-d'œuvre de la Galerie de Tableaux de l'Ermitage Imperial à St. Pétersbourg*, Munich, 1909.

Zervos 1932
C. Zervos. "A propos de Manet", *Cahiers d'Art*, Nos 8-10, 1932.

LA
Legenda Aurea (Jacque de Voragine le Bien heureux, *La Légende dorée*, Paris, 1913).

EXHIBITIONS

1861 St. Petersburg
Index of the Collection of Paintings and Rare Art Works Belonging to Members of the Imperial Family and Private Individuals in St. Petersburg (Exhibition of 1861), St. Petersburg, 1861.

1886 St. Petersburg
Catalogue of the Picture Gallery of His Imperial Majesty Duke N. M. Leuchtenberg Exhibited in the Rooms of the Imperial Academy of Arts, St. Petersburg, 1886.

1968-1969 Belgrade
Western European Paintings (16th-18th Centuries) from the Collection of the State Hermitage. The Narodny Museum, Belgrade, November 1968-January 1969 (in Serbian).

1969 Travelling
[A. Kostenevich] *Western European Art. 15th-19th Centuries*. Travelling exhibition of works from the Hermitage collections. Leningrad, 1969.

1970 Osaka
Discovery of Harmony. Expo '70. Comprehensive Catalogue, Osaka, 1970, 5 vols.

1971 Tokyo-Kyoto
One Hundred Masterpieces from USSR Museums. Tokyo and Kyoto, 1971.

1975-1976 USA-Mexico-Canada
Master Paintings from the Hermitage and Russian Museum, Leningrad, 1975-1976.

1977 Tokyo-Kyoto
Master Paintings from the Hermitage Museum, Leningrad. The National Museum of Western Art, Tokyo, 10 September-23 October 1977; The Kyoto Municipal Museum of Art, Kyoto, 4 November-11 December 1977.

1981 Madrid
Tesoros del Ermitage. Museo del Prado, Madrid, April-July 1981.

1984 Leningrad
L. Kagané *Murillo and Seventeenth-Century Andalusian Artists in the Hermitage Collection. Exhibition Catalogue*. Leningrad, 1984.

1985 Sapporo-Fukuoka
Paintings by Western European Masters from the Hermitage Collection. 13 July-22 August 1985. Hokkaido Museum of Modern Art, Sapporo, 1985 (in Japanese).

1987 Delhi
Masterpieces of Western European Art from the Hermitage, Leningrad. Exhibition Catalogue. Leningrad, 1987.

1987-1988 Belgrade-Ljubljana-Zagreb
Hermitage Masterpieces. Paintings and Drawings. 15th-18th Centuries. Belgrade-Ljubljana-Zagreb 1987-1988 (in Serbian).

1988 New South Wales-Victoria
Masterpieces of Western European Art from the Hermitage. 15th-20th Centuries, Leningrad. 10 March-1 May 1988. Art Gallery of New South Wales, 13 May-3 July 1988, National Gallery of Victoria.

BIOGRAPHICAL OUTLINE

The Archangel Raphael.
c. 1670, Whereabouts unknown
(formely in the Boehler collection, Lucerne).

December 1617
Birth of Bartolomé Esteban Murillo.

1 January 1618
Baptized in the parish church of Sta. Maria Magdalena.

1627
Death of Murillo's father.

1628
Death of Murillo's mother. The boy became a ward of his sister Anna's husband, Juan Agustin Lagares, a surgeon.

1633
Supposedly intended to travel to the West Indies (Columbia). Apprenticed to Juan del Castillo (1584-1640), a relative on his mother's side. In his shop Murillo met Alonso Cano (1601-1667).

1642-1645
May have travelled to Madrid, but there is no documentary evidence.

26 February 1645
Began work on a series of paintings for the Franciscan monastery in Seville. Married Beatriz de Cabrera y Sotomayor y Villalobos.

24 March 1646
Baptism of Murillo's first daughter, Maria (died 1650).

9 May 1646
Took Manuel de Campos as an apprentice.

1646
The *Angel's Kitchen* (Louvre, Paris), the first of the known dated paintings.

1650
The *Last Supper* (Sta. Maria la Blanca, Seville).

7 April 1650
Baptism of his fourth child, with Miguel Mañara as godfather.

28 July 1651
Invited to Marchena by the Duke of Arcos.

20 September 1651
Baptism of Murillo's son, with Miguel Mañara as godfather.

1652
An *Immaculate Conception* with a portrait of Juan de Quirós (Archiepiscopal palace, Seville).

8 February 1655
Baptism of Murillo's daughter Francisca Maria (who joined the convent de la Madre de Dios in 1668).

1655
St. Leander and *St. Isidore* (Cathedral, Seville).

1656
The Vision of St. Antony of Padua (Cathedral, Seville).

1658
Journey to Madrid.

1660
The Academy of Arts founded in Seville, with Murillo and Francisco Herrera the Younger as Presidents. The *Birth of the Virgin* (Louvre, Paris).

22 October 1661
Birth of Gaspar Esteban, Murillo's eighth child (a future priest).

1 January 1664
Burial of Murillo's wife.

30 August 1664
Commissioned to paint the main retable for the monastery of St. Augustin.

1664
Death of the Inquisitor Pedro de Arbués (Hermitage, St. Petesburg), commissioned for the monastery of San Pablo in Seville.

1660-1665
Paintings for the church of Sta. Maria la Blanca in Seville.

1665
Portrait of Justino de Neve (National Gallery, London). Joined the Hermandad de la Caridad or Brotherhood of Charity.

1665-1670
Picture cycle for the Capuchin monastery in Seville.

1666-1672
Picture cycle for the La Caridad hospital.

1671
Paintings for the Capella del Sagrario for the feast of the canonization of San Fernando.

1672
St. Elizabeth of Hungary Healing the Sick and *St. John of God and the Angel* for the Hospital of La Caridad. *Portrait of Nicolás de Omazur* (Prado, Madrid).

1680
Portrait of Canon Miranda (Duchess of Alba collection, Madrid).

1681
The *Mystical Marriage of St. Catherine* (Capuchin monastery, Cadiz).

3 April 1682
Death of Murillo.

P. Nuñez de Villavicencio.
Maria as a Girl at Needlework.
Prado, Madrid.

CONTENTS

The Infant Jesus and St. John.
Engraving by M. Carmona
from Murillo's painting.

Guido Reni.
The Infant Jesus and St. John.
Engraving.